The Sermon
on the
Mount
—— and ——
Human
Flourishing

The Sermon
on the
Mount
and
Human
Flourishing

A THEOLOGICAL COMMENTARY

Jonathan T. Pennington

Baker Academic

a division of Baker Publishing Group
Grand Rapids, Michigan

Published by Baker Academic
a division of Baker Publishing Group
PO Box 6287, Grand Rapids, MI 49516-6287
www.bakeracademic.com

Paperback edition published 2018
ISBN 978-1-5409-6064-1

Printed in the United States of America

The Library of Congress has cataloged the hardcover edition as follows:
Names: Pennington, Jonathan T., author.
Title: The Sermon on the Mount and human flourishing : a theological commentary / Jonathan T.
    Pennington.
Description: Grand Rapids : Baker Academic, 2017. | Includes bibliographical references and index.
Identifiers: LCCN 2017001691 | ISBN 9780801049637 (cloth)
Subjects: LCSH: Sermon on the mount—Criticism, interpretation, etc.
Classification: LCC BT380.3 .P46 2017 | DDC 226.9/06—dc23
LC record available at https://lccn.loc.gov/2017001691

In keeping with biblical principles of creation stewardship, Baker Publishing Group advocates the responsible use of our natural resources. As a member of the Green Press Initiative, our company uses recycled paper when possible. The text paper of this book is composed in part of post-consumer waste.

22 23 24   7 6 5 4

.

*The labors behind this book are dedicated
to the David and Christa Arney family
of Northwest Oklahoma,
salt-of-the-earth and light-of-the-world people
in whom I have witnessed Christ-centered
and kingdom-oriented suffering,
wholeness, and flourishing.*

For where your treasure is there also will be your heart.

Matthew 6:21

No one is able to serve two lords, for the one he will hate and the other he will love, or he will be devoted to the one and think little of the other. You are not able to serve money and God.

Matthew 6:24

The kingdom of heaven is like a merchant in search of fine pearls, who, on finding one pearl of great value, went and sold all that he had and bought it.

Matthew 13:45 (ESV)

He went away sorrowful, for he had great possessions.

Matthew 19:22 (ESV)

Contents

PART 3: THEOLOGICAL REFLECTION

Acknowledgments

This book has been a long time in the making, both in thought and in writing. As a student and scholar of the Gospel according to Matthew for nearly fifteen years, it was inevitable that I was drawn into the beautiful but nearly inescapable vortex that is the Sermon on the Mount.

The idea behind providing a commentary on the Sermon that also sets it into its historical, conceptual, and theological contexts came directly from many years of teaching on the Sermon. This teaching occurred in various classes at my own institution as well as while a visiting professor at Reformed Theological Seminary–Orlando, Southeastern Baptist Theological Seminary, and to eager missionaries enrolled in my classes in Australia and New Zealand. Just as important, I have also taught on the Sermon in assorted church settings across the United States and other countries. As I circled toward my own understanding of the Sermon it became increasingly clear to me that I needed to articulate in writing what I was learning, at the very least for my own clarity of understanding.

My original editor at Baker Academic, James Ernest, likewise thought it would be good for me to put all this in writing, and he exercised incredible patience and kindness as I labored to do so. Unfortunately, my protracted labors meant that by the time of the completion of the manuscript James was no longer at Baker. Nonetheless, under the excellent leadership of Jim Kinney, the folks at Baker Academic, including my adept new editor, Bryan Dyer, continued to work with me. Brian Bolger and his team have also provided excellent editorial help that has improved the clarity of the prose at many points. This is now my third book with Baker Academic (with another project in the works), and I have never regretted a moment of this enriching relationship.

Over the multiyear germination of this book several students have served me in collecting articles and books and in helping with transliteration and proofing. These include Choongjae Lee, Brian Renshaw, Brian Davidson, Stuart Langley, Daniel Morrison, Trey Moss, and Stephen Mitchell. Nathan Ridlehover also deserves special mention for reading each chapter and interacting in detail. Other friends and colleagues have graciously given of their time to read all or a portion of the manuscript and provide feedback, including Doug Blount, Leroy Huizenga, Ben Askins, Michael Spalione, Garrett Walden, and Garrick Bailey. The SBTS Library staff, especially Kevin Hall and Matt Miller, have always been willing to track down books and articles and deliver them to me with a cheerful spirit. The indexes were done graciously and efficiently by Philip Chia, Choongjae Lee, Matt McMains, and Andres Vera.

As I complete this book, I sense both satisfaction at its completion and regret at its weaknesses. In the latter category I experience some compunction that I was not able to more fully engage with premodern interpretation in the commentary proper, despite my great desire to do so. Also, while I have attempted something more than a historical and literary reading, I am conscious that limitations of time, space, and expertise have kept me from the greater engagement with dogmatic and constructive theology that a more thoroughgoing theological reading would require.

Abbreviations

General

BCE	before the Common Era
ca.	*circa*, about, approximately
CE	Common Era
chap(s).	chapter(s)
ed.	editor (pl. eds.), edition, edited by
e.g.	*exempli gratia*, for example
esp.	especially
fut.	future
Gk.	Greek
Heb.	Hebrew
ibid.	*ibidem*, in the same source
p(p).	page(s)
pt.	part
repr.	reprint
rev.	revised
s.v.	*sub verbo*, under the word
v(v).	verse(s)
vol(s).	volume(s)
vs.	versus

Divisions of the Canon

NT	New Testament
OT	Old Testament

Ancient Texts, Text Types, and Versions

LXX	Septuagint

Modern Versions

ESV	English Standard Version
NIV	New International Version
NRSV	New Revised Standard Version

Hebrew Bible / Old Testament

Gen.	Genesis
Exod.	Exodus
Lev.	Leviticus
Num.	Numbers
Deut.	Deuteronomy
Josh.	Joshua
Judg.	Judges
Ruth	Ruth
1–2 Sam.	1–2 Samuel
1–2 Kings	1–2 Kings
1–2 Chron.	1–2 Chronicles
Ezra	Ezra
Neh.	Nehemiah
Esther	Esther
Job	Job
Ps./Pss.	Psalms
Prov.	Proverbs
Eccles.	Ecclesiastes
Song	Song of Songs
Isa.	Isaiah
Jer.	Jeremiah
Lam.	Lamentations
Ezek.	Ezekiel

Dan.   Daniel
Hos.   Hosea
Joel   Joel
Amos   Amos
Obad.   Obadiah
Jon.   Jonah
Mic.   Micah
Nah.   Nahum
Hab.   Habakkuk
Zeph.   Zephaniah
Hag.   Haggai
Zech.   Zechariah
Mal.   Malachi

New Testament

Matt.   Matthew
Mark   Mark
Luke   Luke
John   John
Acts   Acts
Rom.   Romans
1–2 Cor. 1–2 Corinthians
Gal.   Galatians
Eph.   Ephesians
Phil.   Philippians
Col.   Colossians
1–2 Thess. 1–2 Thessalonians
1–2 Tim. 1–2 Timothy
Titus   Titus
Philem.   Philemon
Heb.   Hebrews
James   James
1–2 Pet. 1–2 Peter

1–3 John 1–3 John
Jude   Jude
Rev.   Revelation

Apocrypha and Septuagint

4 Macc.   4 Maccabees
Sir.   Sirach
Wis.   Wisdom of Solomon

Old Testament Pseudepigrapha

T. 12 Patr.   Testaments of the Twelve
              Patriarchs
T. Iss.   Testament of Issachar
T. Levi   Testament of Levi
T. Reu.   Testament of Reuben
T. Sim.   Testament of Simeon

Dead Sea Scrolls

1QS   Rule of the Community
4Q525/
   4QBeat Beatitudes

Mishnah and Talmud

b.   Babylonian Talmud
m.   Mishnah

Apostolic Fathers

Barn.   Barnabas
2 Clem.   2 Clement
Did.   Didache

Secondary Sources

ACCS   Ancient Christian Commentary on Scripture
BDAG   Bauer, Walter, Frederick W. Danker, William F. Arndt, and F. Wilbur
          Gingrich. Greek-English Lexicon of the New Testament and Other
          Early Christian Literature. 3rd ed. Chicago: University of Chicago Press,
          2000
BECNT   Baker Exegetical Commentary on the New Testament
CBQ   Catholic Biblical Quarterly
ConC   Concordia Commentary
DJG   Dictionary of Jesus and the Gospels. Edited by Joel B. Green and
          Scot McKnight. Downers Grove, IL: InterVarsity, 1992

DNTB	*Dictionary of New Testament Background.* Edited by Craig A. Evans and Stanley E. Porter. Downers Grove, IL: InterVarsity, 2000
DTIB	*Dictionary of Theological Interpretation of the Bible.* Edited by Kevin J. Vanhoozer, Craig G. Bartholomew, Daniel J. Treier, and N. T. Wright. Grand Rapids: Baker Academic, 2005
EDNT	*Exegetical Dictionary of the New Testament.* Edited by Horst Balz and Gerhard Schneider. ET. 3 vols. Grand Rapids: Eerdmans, 1990–93
EMSDS	Evangelical Missiological Society Dissertation Series
ExpTim	*Expository Times*
FC	Fathers of the Church
HTR	*Harvard Theological Review*
IBC	Interpretation: A Bible Commentary for Teaching and Preaching
ICC	International Critical Commentary
Int	*Interpretation*
JBL	*Journal of Biblical Literature*
JETS	*Journal of the Evangelical Theological Society*
JSJSup	Journal for the Study of Judaism Supplement Series
JSNT	*Journal for the Study of the New Testament*
JSNTSup	Journal for the Study of the New Testament Supplement Series
LCL	Loeb Classical Library
NICNT	New International Commentary on the New Testament
NIDNTT	*New International Dictionary of New Testament Theology.* Edited by Colin Brown. 4 vols. Grand Rapids: Zondervan, 1975–85
NIDOTTE	*New International Dictionary of Old Testament Theology and Exegesis.* Edited by Willem A. VanGemeren. 5 vols. Grand Rapids: Zondervan, 1997
NIGTC	New International Greek Testament Commentary
NIVAC	NIV Application Commentary
NovT	*Novum Testamentum*
PNTC	Pillar New Testament Commentary
SBLDS	Society of Biblical Literature Dissertation Series
SHBC	Smyth & Helwys Bible Commentary
SNTSMS	Society for New Testament Studies Monograph Series
TDNT	*Theological Dictionary of the New Testament.* Edited by G. Kittel and G. Friedrich. Translated by G. W. Bromiley. 10 vols. Grand Rapids, 1964–76
TLNT	*Theological Lexicon of the New Testament.* C. Spicq. Translated and edited by J. D. Ernest. 3 vols. Peabody, MA: Hendrickson, 1994
WBC	Word Biblical Commentary
WUNT	Wissenschaftliche Untersuchungen zum Neuen Testament
ZECNT	Zondervan Exegetical Commentary on the New Testament

Translation of the Sermon on the Mount

^{5:1}*When he saw the crowds he ascended the mountain. And when he sat down his disciples came to him.* ²*And he opened his mouth and taught them, saying:*

³Flourishing are the poor in spirit because the kingdom of heaven is theirs.

⁴Flourishing are the mourners because they will be comforted.

⁵Flourishing are the humble because they will inherit the world.

⁶Flourishing are the ones hungering and thirsting for righteousness because they will be satisfied.

⁷Flourishing are the merciful because they will be given mercy.

⁸Flourishing are the pure in heart because they will see God.

⁹Flourishing are the peacemakers because they will be called the children of God.

¹⁰Flourishing are the ones persecuted on account of righteousness because the kingdom of heaven is theirs.

¹¹Flourishing are you whenever people revile and slander and speak all kinds of evil things against you on account of me.

¹²Rejoice and be glad because your reward is great in heaven. In this same way people slandered the prophets who came before you.

¹³You are the salt of the earth. But if this salt ceases to be salty, with what will it be made salty again? This salt is good for nothing except being thrown away, where it will be trampled by people. ¹⁴You are the light of the world. A city that is built upon a mountain cannot be hidden. ¹⁵Neither do people light a lamp and then put it under a basket. Rather, they put it on a lampstand and then it gives light to everyone in the house. ¹⁶In this way let your light shine in the presence

of everyone such that they see your good works and glorify your Father who is in heaven.

[17]Do not think that I have come to abolish the Law or the Prophets. I have not come to abolish but to fulfill. [18]Truly I say to you that until heaven and earth pass away not an iota or one pen stroke of the Law will pass away, until all is accomplished. [19]Whoever, therefore, lessens one of the least of the commandments and teaches others in this way, that person will be called least in the kingdom of heaven. But whoever does these commandments and teaches others will be called great in the kingdom of heaven.

[20]For I tell you that if your righteousness does not surpass that of the scribes and Pharisees then you will never enter into the kingdom of heaven.

[21]You have heard that it was said to the people long ago, "You shall not murder, and whoever commits murder will be liable to judgment." [22]And I say that everyone who is angry with his brother or sister will be liable to judgment. And whoever says to his brother or sister, "You moron!" will be liable to the court. And whoever says, "You fool!" will be liable to the fiery hell.

[23]Therefore if when you are offering your gift at the altar you remember that your brother or sister has some issue with you, [24]leave your gift there before the altar and go and first be reconciled to your brother or sister and then go and offer your gift.

[25]Quickly make things right with your adversary, even as you are on the way to court, lest your adversary hand you over to the judge and the judge hand you over to the guard and you are thrown in prison. [26]Truly I say to you that you will certainly not get out of there until you have paid back the last cent.

[27]You have heard that it was said, "Do not commit adultery." [28]And I say to you that everyone who looks at another man's wife with lustful intent has already committed adultery with her in his heart. [29]But if your right eye creates a stumbling block for you, then pluck it out and cast it away from you. For it is far better if you lose part of yourself rather than your whole body be cast into hell. [30]And if your right hand creates a stumbling block for you, cut it off and cast it away from you. For it is far better if you lose part of yourself rather than your whole body go into hell.

[31]It was said, "Whoever sends his wife away must give her a certificate of divorce." [32]And I say to you that everyone who divorces his wife except on account of sexual immorality makes her commit adultery, while everyone who marries such a divorced woman commits adultery.

³³*You have heard that it was said to the people long ago, "You shall not break your vow, but instead, fulfill whatever vow you have made to the Lord." ³⁴And I say to you, do not make vows at all, neither by heaven, which is the throne of God, ³⁵nor by earth, which is the footstool of his feet, neither by Jerusalem, which is the city of the great king. ³⁶Neither should you make a vow by your head, because you are not able to make even one of your hairs white or black. ³⁷But instead let your word be "Yes" or "No." Anything that goes beyond this is from the evil one.*

³⁸*You have heard that it was said, "An eye for an eye and a tooth for a tooth." ³⁹And I say to you that you should not resist an evildoer, but if someone slaps you on the right cheek, turn and offer the other cheek as well. ⁴⁰And if someone sues you and desires to take your coat, give him your shirt as well. ⁴¹And if someone forces you to go one mile, go two miles with him. ⁴²Give to anyone who asks you and do not turn away from anyone who wants to borrow from you.*

⁴³*You have heard that it was said, "Love your neighbor and hate your enemy." ⁴⁴And I say to you, love your enemy and pray for those who persecute you ⁴⁵in order that you may be the children of your Father in heaven, who shines the sun on both evil and good people and brings rain to both the righteous and unrighteous. ⁴⁶For if you only love the ones who love you, what reward will you have? Do not even tax collectors do that? ⁴⁷And if you only love your brothers and sisters, how are you doing more righteousness? Do not even gentiles do that?*

⁴⁸*Therefore, you shall be whole as your heavenly Father is whole.*

⁶:¹*Be careful that you don't perform this righteousness for the purpose of being seen by others. For if this is the case you will have no reward with your Father who is in heaven.*

²*Therefore, when you are giving to help the needy, do not sound a trumpet before you, as the hypocrites do in the synagogues and in the streets so that they might receive glory from others. Assuredly I tell you that this is their only reward. ³But when you are giving to help the needy do not let your left hand know what your right hand is doing, ⁴such that your giving to the needy is done in secret. And your Father who sees what happens in secret will reward you.*

⁵*And when you pray do not be like the hypocrites because they love to pray standing in the synagogues and at the corners of the main streets so that they might be seen by others. Assuredly I tell you that this is their only reward. ⁶When you pray go into your private room, shut*

the door, and pray to your Father who is in the secret place. And your Father who sees what happens in secret will reward you.

[7]In your praying do not babble on like the gentiles, for they reason that with their many words they will be heard. [8]Do not be like them, for your Father knows what you need before you ask him.

    [9]Therefore, you shall pray in this way:

Our Father who is in heaven,
    Let your name be sanctified,
    [10]Let your kingdom come,
    Let your will be done,
    As these are in heaven, let them be also on the earth.
    [11]Give to us our daily bread
    [12]And forgive us our trespasses as we also forgive those who trespass against us.
    [13]Do not lead us into temptation, but deliver us from the evil one.

[14]For if you forgive others their trespasses against you, your heavenly Father will forgive you. [15]But if you do not forgive others, your heavenly Father will not forgive you.

[16]And when you fast, do not be like the hypocrites who look gloomy, for they disfigure their faces so that they might be seen by others to be fasting. Assuredly I tell you that this is their only reward. [17]When you fast anoint your head with oil and wash your face [18]so that it doesn't look like you are fasting to others, but it is apparent to your Father who is in the secret place. And your Father who sees in the secret place will reward you.

[19]Do not lay up for yourselves treasures on the earth, where moth and rust disfigure and where thieves can break in and steal. [20]Rather, lay up treasures for yourselves in heaven where moth and rust cannot disfigure and where thieves cannot break in and steal. [21]For where your treasure is there also will be your heart.

[22]The eye is the lamp of the body. Therefore, if your eye is whole and generous then your whole body will be enlightened. [23]But if your eye is evil and greedy then your whole body will be darkened. Thus, if the light that is in you is darkness, what darkness that is! [24]No one is able to serve two lords, for the one he will hate and the other he will love, or he will be devoted to the one and think little of the other. You are not able to serve money and God.

[25]On account of this I say to you: Do not be anxious about the things of your life, what you will eat or what you will drink, nor about your

body, how you will clothe yourselves, for is not life more than food and the body more than clothing?

²⁶Consider the birds of the air, that they do not sow seeds, nor harvest crops, nor gather it into barns, and yet your Father in heaven feeds them. Are you not much more valuable than they? ²⁷Who among you is able to add even an hour to his life by being anxious?

²⁸And why are you anxious about clothing? Consider the flowers of the field, how they grow; they do not work or spin thread for cloth. ²⁹Yet I tell you that not even Solomon in all his glory was clothed like one of these. ³⁰But if God in this way clothes the grass of the fields, which is here today but tomorrow will be thrown into the fire, how much more will he clothe you, people of little faith?

³¹Therefore, do not be anxious, saying—"What will we eat?" or "What will we drink?" or "What will we wear?"—³²for the gentiles seek after all these things and your heavenly Father knows that you need all these things. ³³Instead, seek first the kingdom and the Father's righteousness, and all these things will be given to you.

³⁴Therefore, do not be anxious about tomorrow for tomorrow will be anxious for itself. Each day has enough of its own trouble.

⁷:¹Do not judge unfairly, lest you be judged the same way. ²For by the kind of judgment with which you judge others, you will be judged; and with whatever measure you measure to others, it will also be measured to you.

³Why do you see the speck in your brother or sister's eye but in regard to the plank of wood in your own eye you pay no attention? ⁴How can you say to your brother or sister, "Let me remove that speck from your eye." Look! There is a plank of wood in your own eye! ⁵You hypocrite! First remove the plank from your own eye and then you can see clearly to remove the speck from your brother or sister's eye.

⁶Do not give sacred things to dogs or throw pearls in front of pigs. If you do, the pigs will trample them with their feet and the dogs may turn and tear you apart.

⁷Ask and it will be given to you. Seek and you will find. Knock and the door will be opened to you. ⁸For everyone who asks receives, and everyone who seeks finds, and to everyone who knocks the door is opened. ⁹There is not a person among you, is there, who when his son asks him for bread, will give him a stone? ¹⁰Or if he asks for a fish, he won't give him a serpent, will he? ¹¹If you, therefore, who are evil know to give good gifts to your children, how much more will your Father who is in heaven give good gifts to those who ask him? ¹²Therefore, in everything, whatever you would want others to do to you or for you, in this same way treat them, for this is the Law and the Prophets.

¹³*Enter through the narrow gate, for the gate is wide and the road that leads to destruction is easy, and the ones entering through that gate are many.* ¹⁴*But how narrow the gate is and how difficult the road is that leads to life, and the ones who find it are few!*

¹⁵*Watch out for false prophets, who will come to you clothed like sheep but on the inside are ravenous wolves.* ¹⁶*You will recognize them by their fruit. Grapes are not harvested from thornbushes, nor are figs from thistles, are they?* ¹⁷*In the same way, every healthy tree produces good fruit, but every decayed tree produces bad fruit.* ¹⁸*A healthy tree is not able to produce bad fruit, nor is a decayed tree able to produce good fruit.* ¹⁹*Every tree that does not produce good fruit is cut down and thrown into the fire.* ²⁰*Thus, you will recognize them by their fruit.*

²¹*Not everyone who says to me, "Lord, Lord," will enter into the kingdom of heaven, but only the one who does the will of my Father who is in heaven.* ²²*Many people will say to me on that day, "Lord, Lord, in your name we prophesied, and in your name we cast out demons, and in your name we produced many miracles, didn't we?"* ²³*And then I will pronounce to them, "I have never known you! Depart from me, you who work lawlessness."*

²⁴*Therefore, anyone who listens to my words and practices them can be compared to a wise person who built his house on rock.* ²⁵*The rain fell, and the rivers rose, and the winds blew and beat against that house. And yet it did not collapse because it had been founded upon rock.* ²⁶*But anyone who listens to my words and does not practice them can be compared to a foolish person who built his house on sand.* ²⁷*The rain fell, and the rivers rose, and the winds blew and beat against that house, and it did collapse, and it was a massive crash.*

²⁸*And when Jesus had finished saying these words the crowd was astonished at his teaching,* ²⁹*for he was teaching them with such authority, not as their scribes taught.* ⁸ᐟ¹*And when he came down from the mountain great crowds followed him.*

Introduction

An Overall Reading Strategy for the Sermon

This book is a historical, literary, and theological exposition of the Sermon on the Mount (Matt. 5–7). More specifically, I am providing a reading of the Sermon that situates it in the dual context of Jewish wisdom literature and the Greco-Roman virtue tradition, both of which are concerned with the great theological and existential question of human flourishing.

Many readers of this book will initially be interested only in the commentary on the Sermon on the Mount. This can be found in part 2, chapters 6–11. I hope that those expositional chapters will indeed serve as a help in interpreting the plain sense of the text of the Sermon and as a reference work to which readers can return.

However, I believe one's reading of the Sermon (and of this book) will be impoverished if only those commentary sections are digested. This is because in the opening chapters of part 1 I lay out what I believe is the foundation for a good reading of the Sermon. The first five chapters are the guiding sketch by which the mosaic artist knows how to place each tessera to form the desired portrait the Sermon is painting. Or to change the metaphor, these initial chapters provide the map orientation for the complicated but scenic journey of ascending the mountain that is Matt. 5–7. To continue the analogy, the last chapter of this book, chapter 12 (part 3), then, will bring us safely back down from the Sermon's mountain to the broad and spacious place of how the Sermon fits into the grand view of God's redemptive work with a theological reflection on the topic of the book's title, human flourishing.

All this to say, whether you are a pastor, scholar, student, or generalist, my point in writing this book is to provide not merely an expositional commentary but also an overall reading strategy and integrated theological interpretation of the Sermon. This book contains commentary with a different purpose: to provide an exposition of the message of the text as we have it in Matt. 5–7, sensitive to its historical setting, literary form, and theological point.

Before setting off on the journey, it will be beneficial to pause and take stock of how we got to this point and what the next leg of the trip should look like. We will do so by briefly considering several different readings of the Sermon throughout history.

Readings of the Sermon in History

The Sermon on the Mount as Litmus Test

Nearly every book on the Sermon begins with some discussion of the history of the interpretation of the Sermon. For some readers, the idea of studying the history of interpretation before looking at the Sermon itself may evoke the sentiments of Mark Twain: "The researches of many commentators have already thrown much darkness on this subject, and it is probable that, if they continue, we shall soon know nothing at all about it."

Nevertheless, starting with the history of interpretation is indeed a worth-while enterprise because understanding others' thoughts before focusing on our own is an essential ingredient in the growth in knowledge and wisdom. As Hans-Georg Gadamer rightly states, "The recognition of the possibility that the other might be right is the heart of hermeneutics."[1]

Moreover, the study of the history of interpretation of the Sermon is not merely perfunctory nor the pickup game on the esoteric mental playground of the biblical scholar or historian. Quite the contrary, a discussion of how the Sermon has been read and applied over time is a fascinating and imme-diate window on many relevant theological issues. Because the Sermon has been the most commented upon portion of Scripture throughout the church's history and because the Sermon contains so many weighty issues, it is both easy and informative to examine how the many different traditions of Chris-tianity have read it.

Without exception, one's reading of the Sermon says much about one's understanding of Jesus and Christian theology. Indeed, in my years of studying

1. See Jean Grondin, *Introduction to Philosophical Hermeneutics* (New Haven: Yale University Press, 1994), 124. Originally from Gadamer's Heidelberg Colloquium on July 9, 1989.

the Sermon and its reception I have come to see that the Sermon serves as a great *litmus test* for any reader's broader theological commitments and understanding. The Sermon, standing as it does as the first teaching of the new-covenant documents, likewise reveals much about how one understands several issues of theology and Christian practice. Views on a wide range of issues are revealed in one's reaction to the Sermon, including the role of the law in the new covenant, what role virtue plays in one's ethical system (if any), the importance of acts of piety in the Christian life, the relationship between faith and works, one's eschatological orientation or lack thereof, the function of suffering in the Christian life, and the idea of God as Father, to name a few.

Because the Sermon has been so beloved and well used throughout church history, the different ways of reading the Sermon are legion.[2] The researcher knows he or she is in deep water when discovering that there is not only an unmanageable amount of secondary material on the Sermon but also a cottage industry of tertiary work that organizes and summarizes the secondary literature. That is, there is a felt need not only for scholarship on the Sermon but also scholarship on the works of various scholars/theologians on the Sermon. In fact, these taxonomical surveys of the history of the interpretation of the Sermon are of great value and well worth reading.[3] Shorter versions can be found in most commentaries on the Sermon as well.[4] I will offer a very brief summary here for the purpose of getting to my own suggested overall reading of the Sermon.

In his interesting book from 1960, *Understanding the Sermon on the Mount*, Harvey K. MacArthur discusses twelve of the attempted answers to the question of how to apply and understand the Sermon, and he quips that these might be called "Versions and Evasions of the Sermon on the Mount." Ironically in light of how influential the Sermon has been throughout church

2. See further, H. K. McArthur, *Understanding the Sermon on the Mount* (New York: Harper & Brothers, 1960), 11. From the earliest days of the church, the Sermon has been the most commented upon and exposited portion of the Bible. In the indices to the fathers of the first three centuries one will find Matt. 5 is quoted far more frequently than any other, and chaps. 5–7 are quoted far more frequently than any other three consecutive chapters. The same trend continues in the modern period, with countless commentaries and sermons not only on Matthew but also specifically on the Sermon.

3. Jeffrey P. Greenman, Timothy Larsen, and Stephen R. Spencer, eds., *The Sermon on the Mount through the Centuries: From the Early Church to John Paul II* (Grand Rapids: Brazos, 2007). One of the beefiest is Clarence Bauman, *The Sermon on the Mount: The Modern Quest for Its Meaning* (Macon, GA: Mercer University Press, 1991), in which he gives a detailed discussion of nineteen major interpretive views just spanning the period from Leo Tolstoy (late nineteenth century) to the 1970s.

4. See esp. Ulrich Luz, *Matthew 1–7: A Commentary*, rev. ed., trans. James E. Crouch, Hermeneia (Minneapolis: Fortress, 2007), 177–81.

history, many today could be rightly charged with neglecting and avoiding the Sermon. As Glen Stassen and David Gushee argue in their book, *Kingdom Ethics*, Christians often evade Jesus, especially what he says in the Sermon. The result is not good: "This evasion of the concrete teachings of Jesus has seriously malformed Christian moral practices, moral beliefs and moral witness. Jesus taught that the test of our discipleship is whether we act on his teachings, whether we 'put into practice' his words. This is what it means to 'build our house on rock' (Mt. 7:24)."[5]

Part of the reason there are so many interpretations (or evasions) of the Sermon is that the Sermon itself *creates* problems for serious readers. There is the simple problem of its incredibly high demands and the apparent impossibility of doing what it says fully and consistently. Related to this is the question of legalism: If one were to take the Sermon seriously as the entrance requirements for the kingdom of heaven, then is this not a kind of anti-gospel legalism, and is this not exactly what Paul labors so greatly against in his epistles? How does obeying Jesus's teachings in the Sermon fit into the Pauline doctrine of justification by faith? Related to this, what does "righteousness" mean in the Sermon as compared to Paul's usage in his writings? Another problem the Sermon raises is how we are to understand these teachings from the new Moses (Jesus) in relation to what the old Moses said in the Torah/the Law, given on that other mountain much earlier. This is an important question to ask regarding the relationship of the new covenant to the old in general, but it is made very pointed by the content of the Sermon itself, which explicitly says that Jesus has not come to abolish the Law (5:17), yet he clearly reinterprets it in significant ways.

So the point is again that a careful reading of the Sermon creates theological, pastoral, and practical problems. It is to these problems that the various interpretations speak, and to these we can now turn in brief.

Readings from the Patristic and Medieval Periods

We must begin by noting that broadly speaking, in the patristic period, both in the East and West, the Sermon was *not* perceived as problematic. Quite the contrary, the Sermon was seen as paradigmatic and foundational to understanding Christianity itself, coming as it does as the first teaching in the First Gospel, in the fourfold Gospel book that served as the primary locus of understanding of the faith.[6] Representative of this dominant view is

5. Glen H. Stassen and David P. Gushee, *Kingdom Ethics: Following Jesus in Contemporary Context* (Downers Grove, IL: IVP Academic, 2003), 11.

6. For a number of arguments supporting the central role that the Gospels played in the earliest church, see Jonathan T. Pennington, *Reading the Gospels Wisely: A Narrative and Theological*

John Chrysostom, who saw the Sermon as completely in accord with Paul's teachings and as providing the vision for the *politeia* or kingdom community that Christ is establishing in and through his people.[7] Similarly, the great and influential Augustine wrote an entire commentary on the Sermon, seeing it as "the perfect measure of the Christian life."[8] Obviously the later Protestant wrestling with how Jesus's teaching might fit into (a Lutheran reading of) Paul had not yet been perceived as problematic. In general, the patristic interpretation of the Sermon can be summarized as a natural and comfortably consistent reading flowing out of the hellenized Jewish setting in which the Sermon was produced, one that focuses especially on the Sermon as casting a foundational vision for the virtuous Christian life.

As Christianity developed and became the official religion of a widespread area, a common reading strategy emerged and was practiced in many monastic traditions, especially in the West. This interpretation of the Sermon came from and perpetuated the widespread notion that there are two kinds of Christians—the monks and priests who have a special religious calling, and the average lay Christian people who make up the masses of baptized but otherwise minimally Christian churchgoers. In this understanding, the teachings of Jesus are divided up into "precepts" and "counsels," with the precepts being necessary for all people for salvation, while obedience to the counsels is necessary if one wants to achieve perfection and the higher calling. It is not difficult to see how this relates to the dominant Catholic tradition in the West, with its developing priestly class. This formalized distinction between the universal commandments applicable to all people (*praecepta*) and the *consilia evangelica*, which are relevant only to the clergy and certain spiritually qualified people, still exists in the Roman Catholic tradition.[9] The most extreme form of this is found in the vigorous monastic reformer Rupert of Deutz, who argued that salvation by grace is for the laity and secular clergy

---

Introduction (Grand Rapids: Baker Academic, 2012), 229–58. One strong example of this view is Cyril of Alexandria, who argues that the Gospels are the most central part of Scripture because the Son speaks in an unmediated fashion. See chap. 4 of Matthew R. Crawford, *Cyril of Alexandria's Trinitarian Theology of Scripture* (Oxford: Oxford University Press, 2014).

7. See Margaret Mitchell, "John Chrysostom," in Greenman, Larsen, and Spencer, *Sermon on the Mount through the Centuries*, 19–42.

8. Augustine, *The Lord's Sermon on the Mount* 1.1.1, trans. John J. Epson (London: Longman and Green, 1948). Augustine's reading of the Sermon will be influential throughout this book (even if not often quoted explicitly) because of the virtue ethic and human flourishing approach that he models.

9. This does not appear to be Augustine's position, nor even that of Thomas Aquinas, who remains a moderate Augustinian. Cf. Aquinas, *Summa theologiae* I-II, questions 107–8, where he says that the Sermon is the *nova lex* for all Christians, in both its precepts and counsels, and he quotes Augustine to this effect.

while salvation through the works of the Sermon is for the zealous monks.[10] While certainly not all theologians of Roman Catholic tradition would draw the lines the same way as Rupert, the basic view of two levels of Christians can still be found pervasively in this tradition.

Readings from the Reformation Period

In contrast to the Catholic idea of two levels of Christians, the Protestant Reformers emphasized the opposite—the priesthood of *all* believers and justification by faith for *all*.[11] And for Martin Luther the Sermon on the Mount was likewise the perfect battlefield for defining his understanding of the gospel over against his Roman contemporaries. For Luther, the Sermon does not present special teachings that some special people can obtain, but quite the opposite: it is the impossibly high demands of the Sermon that are meant to make all people aware of their sin and poverty before God and thereby turn to Christ in faith. Like the old-covenant law, the Sermon is a preparation for the gospel, the prime example of Luther's ubiquitous law-gospel hermeneutical paradigm.[12] Dale Allison calls this reading of the Sermon "The Impossible Ideal" view.[13] The standard of the Sermon is set so high that it casts us back upon grace. Understandably, this reading of the Sermon does not result in a positive, constructive use for the Sermon, as it is viewed primarily in negative terms. Intended or not, this view, which stands in stark contrast to the Roman Catholic monastic interpretation, contributes to the neglect, evasion, or at least confusion regarding the Sermon in much of the Protestant tradition.[14]

10. Benedict Viviano, "The Sermon on the Mount in Recent Study," in *Matthew and His World: The Gospel of the Open Jewish Christians; Studies in Biblical Theology* (Fribourg: Academic Press; Göttingen: Vandenhoeck & Ruprecht, 2007), 53. See especially Brigitta Stoll's major work, *De Virtute in virtutem: Zur Auslegungs- und Wirkungsgeschichte der Bergpredigt in Kommentaren, Predigten und hagiographischer Literatur von der Merowingerzeit bis um 1200* (Tübingen: J. C. B. Mohr, 1988).

11. Related, as Servais Pinckaers observes, was the shift in the late medieval period from understanding ethics as about human flourishing to ethics as about law-abidingness (via the Manualists) that shaped Luther's reaction. See Pinckaers, *Morality: The Catholic View*, trans. Michael Sherwin (South Bend, IN: St. Augustine's Press, 2001–3), 32–41.

12. As is typical with influential thinkers, Luther himself was a bit more nuanced on the positive use of the Sermon than the Lutheranism that followed him, though his bombastic and prophetic rhetoric on law versus gospel set the trajectory for this contrastive view of the Sermon. See Joel D. Biermann, *A Case for Character: Towards a Lutheran Virtue Ethics* (Minneapolis: Fortress, 2014); and the discussion in chap. 12 below.

13. Dale C. Allison, *The Sermon on the Mount: Inspiring the Moral Imagination* (New York: Crossroad, 1999), 5.

14. One reading that relates to the Lutheran view, though its origins may not be directly from it, is that of classical dispensationalism, a primarily American, fundamentalist form of Christianity that had a widespread influence in the late nineteenth and early twentieth centuries. For

By way of comparison, we may note a couple of Protestant views contemporary with Luther that take a different tack. One is that of the Reformed or Calvinist tradition. The varied interpretations of the Sermon again provide great insight into an important difference between the Lutheran and Reformed traditions here, with the latter's emphasis on the "third use of the Law." That is, the Reformed tradition does not emphasize such a great law-gospel contrast but rather teaches that there is a productive use of law/covenantal instructions understood in the context of grace. This allows for a slightly different reading of the Sermon than Luther's. In Calvin's reading of the Sermon we see Jesus rescuing the law of God from the Pharisees, who emphasized its external acts instead of its heart. The Sermon is the compendium of the doctrine of Christ, the new-covenant law. Unlike Luther's negative reading, for Calvin the Sermon can be fulfilled by Christians not in the flesh but by the grace given through the Holy Spirit, through dependence on God alone. We are weak, but God grants us what we need to obey him.[15]

In their interpretation of the Sermon, both Luther and Calvin were interacting with and reacting to the other major early Protestant reading, that of the Anabaptists. By way of contrast to both the Roman Catholic tradition and the Lutheran and Reformed traditions, the Anabaptists (whence come the Amish and Mennonite traditions), emphasized the radical, literal reading of the Sermon. Key to the theological and practical outworking of this branch of Christianity is indeed an application of the Sermon with no exceptions. Thus, the Anabaptist tradition has typically advocated the rejection of oaths of any kind, encouraged the nonviolence of turning the other cheek, and applied other literalistic readings of the Sermon.[16]

Luther himself, as well as those in his tradition, was very aware of this Anabaptist reading and found it not only mistaken but even dangerous to

---

classical dispensationalists, the Sermon is not applicable to Christians today because it comes from a pre-Christian "dispensation," during the period of the law (from Sinai to Calvary), not from the period of grace (Calvary to the parousia). Therefore, the kingdom of heaven that Jesus is speaking about in the Sermon was the offer of a millennial kingdom to Jews. As a result, its teachings do not apply to Christians at all, even as an impossibly high ideal.

15. I am in debt to Charles Quarles's helpful, brief summary of Calvin in his *Sermon on the Mount: Restoring Christ's Message to the Modern Church* (Nashville: B&H, 2011), 8. See also Scott Spencer, "John Calvin," in Greenman, Larsen, and Spencer, *Sermon on the Mount through the Centuries*, 129–52.

16. A helpful and insightful understanding of this way of reading the Sermon can be found in Stanley Hauerwas's essay on John Howard Yoder and Dietrich Bonhoeffer in Greenman, Larsen, and Spencer, *Sermon on the Mount through the Centuries*, 207–22. As an important aside, note that the Lutheran Bonhoeffer, as part of his emphasis on the "visible" church as opposed to an "inward" or pietistic view of Christianity, came to reject the private-public distinction that had developed in Lutheranism.

society. As a result, Luther provided another important way of reading the Sermon in addition to his "Impossible Ideal" reading. This may be called the doctrine of the Two Kingdoms. Luther was concerned about a renunciation of society and withdrawal from the world, something he saw in both the Anabaptist tradition and monastic Roman Catholicism. His Two Kingdoms view sought to circumvent this while also recognizing how the Sermon applied to everyone. A distinction is made between the spiritual/private realm and the civil/public realm.[17] The Sermon speaks to the former, to individual morality; it does not prescribe public policy. One implication is that a Christian may do something as a member of society or officer of the public that one would not be allowed as an individual (e.g., capital punishment). That is, as a Christian one must not retaliate, but as a lawyer or prince or householder one can and indeed must uphold justice and order.[18] As pragmatically helpful as this view is in many ways, in effect Luther ended up with yet another version of the counsels-versus-precepts bifurcation, splitting not some people into each category but each person into both. Instead of the dualism of two kinds of people, the result is a two-realms dualism, splitting one's attitudes from one's actions.[19] This goes against the whole-person focus that we will see appear as the dominant theme in the Sermon.

The Roman Catholic tradition, by way of contrast, has tended to interpret the Sermon in terms of virtue formation (for some or for all), with numerous manifestations depending on the assorted branches within the Roman Catholic Church and their various theological and cultural influences. A Thomistic reading, which emphasizes a Christian understanding of virtue ethics and development, probably remains the most influential way to read the Sermon, tied closely as it always is to Catholic moral theology.

Readings from the Modern Period

With all the countless ways the modern period has affected and shaped our present understanding of Christianity, contemporary Christians have also wrestled with the radical nature of the Sermon's teachings. As a result, we

17. A recent attempt at revising this Two Kingdoms view from within a more Reformed perspective can be found in David VanDrunen, *Living in God's Two Kingdoms: A Biblical Vision for Christianity and Culture* (Wheaton: Crossway, 2010), though it is debated whether this is truly a Reformed view or not, especially in relation to Abraham Kuyper. See, e.g., John M. Frame, *The Escondido Theology: A Reformed Response to Two Kingdom Theology* (Lakeland, FL: Whitefield Media Productions, 2011).

18. For a deeper understanding of this influential understanding, see Susan Schreiner, "Martin Luther," in Greenman, Larsen, and Spencer, *Sermon on the Mount through the Centuries*, 109–28.

19. Stassen and Gushee, *Kingdom Ethics*, 130.

have a panoply of modern readings of the Sermon. These include what might be termed the "existential" reading, which focuses on one's inner intentions. As Dale Allison describes this view, the Sermon doesn't prescribe laws but "speaks instead to the individual about attitudes and internal dispositions."[20] It is about what we should *be*, not what we should do. One helpful version of this is that of Søren Kierkegaard, who emphasized a way of reading Scripture that caused an awakening or existential crisis / honesty about one's self before God.[21] Other modern readers, often moving away from traditional Christian views, have argued that the Sermon is the entirety of the gospel message. That is, rather than the traditional emphasis on sin and atonement, redemption, and supernatural new birth, the Sermon provides a vision for better humans and a better human society, with Jesus as the great misunderstood philosopher. This is the enduring value of the Sermon for many. Somewhere in between these readings are assorted ways in which readers have sought to take seriously the Sermon but modified its tone in a variety of ways—noting the hyperbolic nature of Jesus's commands that need to be toned down in real life or seeing Jesus as teaching general moral principles through specific illustrations that are not to be taken literally or absolutely.[22]

Another reading from within the Dutch Reformed tradition is that of Herman Ridderbos. It is worth reviewing here not because it has been particularly influential but because it is insightful and shows the complexity of issues at hand, which many of the other views do not take into account. We may term this way of interpreting the Sermon the "fulfillment-complexity" reading. In Ridderbos's essay "The Significance of the Sermon on the Mount," he presents a sophisticated reading of the Sermon that involves a few steps of thought.[23]

First, Ridderbos points out the central importance of Matt. 5:17, where Jesus states that he came to "fulfill" the law. He understands this to mean that Jesus fulfills the law by his teaching; that is, he demonstrates the true content and purpose of the law. Next we must recognize that God's law (in

20. Allison, *The Sermon on the Mount*, 6.

21. Søren Kierkegaard, *For Self-Examination: Judge for Yourselves*, ed. and trans. Howard V. Hong and Edna H. Hong, Kierkegaard's Writings 21 (Princeton: Princeton University Press, 1991). Kierkegaard's favorite section of Scripture was the book of James, which is organically related and conceptually similar to the Sermon, calling us to look into the mirror of God's revelation and not forget it when we walk away. See Richard Bauckham, *James* (New York: Routledge, 1999), 1–10. See also David Crump, *Encountering Jesus, Encountering Scripture: Reading the Bible Critically in Faith* (Grand Rapids: Eerdmans, 2015).

22. See Charles Talbert's helpful summary of MacArthur in *Reading the Sermon on the Mount: Character Formation and Decision Making in Matthew 5–7* (Grand Rapids: Baker Academic, 2006), 29, 45.

23. Herman Ridderbos, *When the Time Had Fully Come: Studies in New Testament Theology* (Eugene, OR: Wipf & Stock, 2001), 26–43.

the Old and New Testaments) is not just meant to be external, but that God has always also been concerned with the inner disposition, with the heart. Thus far Ridderbos is clearly following Calvin's lead. He goes on to note that we must also observe that the law is very complex, that righteousness calls for different applications of the law at different times. For example, we can consider the love of a father for his child. This love will be expressed differently at different times according to the need, sometimes firm, sometimes gracious. From an external perspective it may look inconsistent, but it is in fact all from the same love.

From this Ridderbos observes that Jesus did not exclude or overturn this many-sided character of the law. In his own life he modeled this true application of the law in different circumstances—sometimes not resisting evil (e.g., in his own crucifixion) while at other times violently resisting it, as seen in his conflicts with the Pharisees and scribes. He is both a lion and a lamb, and both spring from the same root, the Law and the Prophets, from the necessity of the one law looking different in different circumstances. Therefore, Ridderbos argues, we must not limit the extent of the validity of the Sermon in any way. The significance of the Sermon lies in the fact that the will of God, as it is revealed in his law, strives to be fulfilled in the full, rich sense that Jesus gave that word. "On the other hand, we should not give a priori and unrestricted validity to all the *concrete commandments* of Jesus, as if he meant to express the entire volume of the law in a few concise commandments."[24] For example, the commandment not to swear is addressed against Pharisaical casuistry of his day but is not intended to overturn all pious oaths as are found in the Old Testament; all of Jesus's teachings must be understood truly and correctly as in full accordance with the Law and the Prophets because of Matt. 5:17. Ridderbos concludes by observing that only such an interpretation can rightly keep together the teachings of the kingdom and real life. Otherwise, these two are wrongly separated. In many ways Ridderbos's reading is a typical Reformed approach with a more robust sense of the need to contextualize ethics in an ongoing way. He does not use the language of "virtue" (nor its robust tradition of reflection), but there is some overlap.

Non-Western and Non-Caucasian Readings

We should note that all of the readings above come from the European tradition of Christianity. This is understandable because of my own situatedness as an author as well as the massive influence that Christianity had

24. Ridderbos, *When the Time Had Fully Come*, 39.

on the West for nearly two thousand years. However, as the center of global Christianity continues to shift both south and east, we will be wise to hear from perspectives beyond those that are Western and Caucasian.

It is often not easy in the Anglophone world to get access to non-Western views, however, because there are still relatively few works written in English that reflect a more global perspective. Moreover, getting a full sense of non-Western perspectives on the Sermon proves difficult because our access to them typically only comes from Western-produced and Western-influenced modern commentaries.[25] Thus, in a variation on the Heisenberg uncertainty principle, the very access that we have to these perspectives skews and changes them because the access point is usually only given through scholars who have been trained in the West (or under Western influence) writing in a very Western form and style. Nonetheless, we are beginning to make progress in hearing other voices. What follows are a few comments I have gleaned from various sources.

In a fascinating essay John Y. H. Yieh offers an analysis of how three different twentieth-century Chinese Christians read and appropriated the Sermon on the Mount.[26] Yieh thoughtfully sets each of these interpreters into their social context and shows that, while there are differences in their readings (based mostly on their different theological convictions), what is consistent among their readings of the Sermon is that "they treat the Sermon on the Mount first and foremost as a morality text and take it for granted that character formation of the reader is the very final goal of their biblical interpretation."[27] Yieh points out that this focus on character formation is typical of the Chinese intellectual tradition, especially in the educational program of Confucianism.

From a South Korean perspective, the Sermon on the Mount is mostly read in the churches with a focus on the "blessings" of the Beatitudes. Specifically, with the massive growth of the church in South Korea has come a heavy influence of the health and wealth gospel. In this context the Sermon is read with a skewed emphasis on getting blessings from God: the "Eight Blessing" program

25. Some recent attempts at bringing a more global perspective on the Bible to the West, albeit in a modern, Western commentary genre: Daniel Patte, ed., *Global Bible Commentary* (Nashville: Abingdon, 2004); Brian K. Blount, ed., *True to Our Native Land: An African American New Testament Commentary* (Minneapolis: Fortress, 2007); Tokunboh Adeyemo, ed., *Africa Bible Commentary: A One-Volume Commentary Written by 70 African Scholars* (Grand Rapids: Zondervan, 2010); Brian Wintle, ed., *South Asia Bible Commentary: A One-Volume Commentary on the Whole Bible* (Grand Rapids: Zondervan, 2015).

26. John Y. H. Yieh, "Reading the Sermon on the Mount in China: A Hermeneutical Inquiry into Its History of Reception," in *Reading Christian Scriptures in China*, ed. Chlöe Starr (London: T&T Clark, 2008): 143–62.

27. Ibid., 157.

based on the Beatitudes read in a materialistic way. At the same time, due to the influence of the West on Korean churches and theology, there is a strong ethical and at times even Lutheran impossible-ideal reading.[28]

Moving farther south in Asia, it is difficult to quantify how distinct the readings of the Sermon are today. In the new *Southeast Asia Bible Commentary*, the notes on Matt. 5–7 are almost entirely typical commentary-style interpretations peppered with a few references to South Asian figures and ideas, including Gandhi, fatalism, and practices in Asian religions.[29] Much more penetrating in insight is a brief essay by R. S. Sugirtharajah on the reappropriation of the Sermon by two influential Indian thinkers, Raja Rammohun Roy and Mahatma Gandhi.[30] Sugirtharajah notes that the Sermon was very influential for both of these Hindu thinkers as they sought to understand true religion in the midst of colonial Christian influence and missions activity. They both found in the Sermon the ingredients of true religion, which was not about doctrines and beliefs but about ethical practices of truth and nonviolence. Neither had any interest in the historical Jesus or much else of the Bible (even the rest of Matthew), but instead they integrated their piecemeal reading of the Sermon into a broader view of ethics rooted in the Hindi Scriptures. In this way they could dialogue with (and even try to persuade) both British colonials and Indian Christians using this mutually cherished Sermon.

The *Africa Bible Commentary* is similar in form to the *South Asia Commentary* and likewise provides Western-style commentary. It does highlight several ways in which African peoples see different emphases in the Sermon. For example, the Beatitudes are more properly understood (at least by the particular commentator) as being macaristic statements about the state of happiness rather than divine blessings (see chap. 2 in this book). The idea of being a peacemaker (Matt. 5:9) plays a much larger and more tangible role in many countries that have been plagued by genocide and other forms of violence. Also, discussion of money and wealth (6:19–34) takes on a different sense in postcolonial nations that are influenced by Western consumption habits while lacking many of the natural resources and infrastructure of Western capitalism. Teachings on wealth and subsistence living sound very different to the African ear than to the Westerner today, probably much closer to how these teachings would have been understood in first-century Galilee.

28. This information comes to me from the analysis of the use of the Sermon in South Korean churches by my PhD student Choongjae Lee, a native Korean who has been educated both in South Korea and in the United States.

29. Wintle, *South Asia Bible Commentary*, 1230–37.

30. R. S. Sugirtharajah, "Matthew 5–7: The Sermon on the Mount and India," in Patte, *Global Bible Commentary*, 361–66.

Within the West another voice to be heard is that of the African American community. The edited volume *True to Our Native Land* provides an African American commentary on the New Testament.[31] The comments on the Sermon again reveal many similarities to other commentaries, yet certain emphases are distinct. For example, in the discussion of the first Beatitude there is a much more nuanced and sensitive discussion of what it means to experience poverty than is typical in modern commentaries. It is not just a matter of money or powerlessness. "Poverty was a social category and not just an economic one."[32] Matthew 5:21–48 is likewise understood from a different perspective, as being instructions about how to overcome violence and evil not with retaliation but with repentance, reconciliation, and generosity.[33] In discussing the petitions of the Lord's Prayer, the commentator notes that readers should be reminded that we need to assist God in creating a good society, not letting evil continue by sitting back and doing nothing, an important way in which the African American community has led the charge.[34] Taken together, these non-Western and non-Caucasian voices remind us that all readings of the Sermon (including those in the West) are contextualized readings, interpretations that are inevitably situated in particular cultures and times and worldviews. This review of how the Sermon has been read is brief and cannot explore the many nuances that comprise the ways Christians have wrestled with and applied the Sermon. I have painted here only with the broadest brush, though I trust the general contours can be identified. From the bird's-eye perspective, the most important observation is that each of these views offers insight into the complexity of the Sermon. We cannot simply identify one of these readings as right and the others as all wrong. Each has a contribution to make to our understanding.

There are multiple ways we can and should approach the Sermon and, therefore, multiple beneficial readings to be offered. This is not to say, however, that each reading is equally beneficial or insightful. Some are indeed better than others. I will offer in this book my own reading, which I obviously believe has

31. Blount, *True to Our Native Land.*

32. Michael Joseph Brown, "Matthew," in Blount, *True to Our Native Land*, 91.

33. Brown's comments on the Sermon are excellent and insightful overall, yet I am also perplexed by a passing comment that the reference to disciples having their own houses with prayer rooms reflects the "middle class attitude" of Matthew's Gospel, which may account for "its historic lack of popularity among African Americans" (ibid., 93). My lack of understanding of what Brown might mean is likely a function of my own lack of cultural contextualization.

34. It is not an accident that Bonhoeffer's own conversion via reading the Sermon on the Mount and his decision to fight anti-Semitism in Germany was a direct result of his witnessing the racial tensions and work of African Americans for civil rights in New York in 1930–31. See Charles Marsh, *Strange Glory: A Life of Dietrich Bonhoeffer* (New York: Random House, 2014).

something to offer beyond—and sometimes in stark contrast to—what has already been said. Nonetheless, the best readings of the Sermon will remain sensitive to the voices and perspectives of others.

An Overall Reading Strategy for the Sermon: Human Flourishing

Fundamentally, this entire book seeks to provide the answer to the question that has just been raised from our survey of the history of interpretation: *What is the Sermon really saying theologically and practically?* Acknowledging that there is much benefit in multiple ways of reading the Sermon, I want to suggest that there is a general reading strategy for the Sermon that both makes sense of its many parts *and* accomplishes the highest goal of reading, to be of benefit to the reader.

Because the entirety of this book is an incarnational unfolding of what I think this best-practices reading strategy is and because the point of the current chapter is introductory, I will only offer a sketch of what this overall reading is. Chapters 1–5 will unpack and articulate this vision with argumentation and clarification, and chapter 12 will round out the discussion more fully. Sandwiched in the middle in chapters 6–11 is the exposition of the text that will also point to the same questions.

The argument of this book is that the Sermon is Christianity's answer to the greatest metaphysical question that humanity has always faced—*How can we experience true human flourishing?* What is happiness, blessedness, *šālôm*, and how does one obtain and sustain it? The Sermon is not the only place in the New Testament or whole Bible that addresses this fundamental question. I would suggest that this question is at the core of the entire message of Scripture. But the Sermon is at the epicenter and, simultaneously, the forefront of Holy Scripture's answer.

Some readings of the Sermon in Christian history have touched on this in part, but none has provided an integrated reading of the parts and the whole of the Sermon from this perspective. The overall reading strategy I am suggesting, then, is twofold: (1) providing a thematic way to understand the Sermon as one integrated message, and (2) providing a vision for the whole purpose of reading the Sermon.

In the first instance, the argument of this book will be that the Sermon's answer to the human-flourishing question is that true human flourishing is only available through communion with the Father God through his revealed Son, Jesus, as we are empowered by the Holy Spirit. This flourishing is only experienced through faithful, heart-deep, whole-person discipleship, following

Jesus's teachings and life, which situate the disciple into God's community or kingdom. This flourishing will only be experienced fully in the eschaton, when God finally establishes his reign upon the earth. As followers of Jesus journey through their lives, they will experience suffering in this world, which in God's providence is in fact a means to true flourishing even now.

In short, Jesus provides in the Sermon a *Christocentric, flourishing-oriented, kingdom-awaiting, eschatological wisdom exhortation.* My aim in this book is not to force a virtue or human-flourishing reading onto the Sermon but instead to show that understanding these themes—particularly flourishing through wholeness—makes the most sense of the theology of the Sermon and gives us clear footholds to ascend its heights.

It is important to note that this dual emphasis on human flourishing/wisdom and God's coming kingdom is not merely coincidental. Rather, in accord with both the Jewish and Greco-Roman traditions (and more broadly in the ancient world), a king was understood to be the "living law," the leading sage/philosopher who rules and rules righteously *precisely because he* (or she in the case of a great queen) *is the epitome of wisdom and virtue.* Within the Jewish tradition one can immediately think of David and the original "son of David," Solomon, who are depicted as great kings (though ultimately flawed) precisely because they ruled and reigned with such *wisdom.* The Greek (and broader ancient) tradition is even more explicit along the lines of this necessity for a good king. "One role of the ideal king in antiquity is to embody the law internally and to produce good legislation that transforms the people and leads them in obedience to the law."[35] The ideal king is the virtuous one who himself imitates the gods, becoming an animate or living law, which then produces harmony for his subjects.[36]

My point is that these themes of virtue leading to human flourishing and the kingdom of God are mutually informing and deeply related. In the Sermon we meet a person who is simultaneously the fulfillment and incarnation of both; he is the complete and virtuous human and the true king. Thus, a human flourishing reading of the Sermon (which itself is indisputably about the kingdom) is not a foreign interpolation but in fact makes sense in the ancient world.

In the second case, and organically related to the first, I am suggesting that the best overall approach to the purpose of reading the Sermon is aretegenic and *pros ōphelimon.* By "aretegenic" I mean "for the purpose of forming character or virtue (*aretē*)."[37] The reason teachers teach and preachers preach and

---

35. Josh Jipp, *Christ Is King: Paul's Royal Ideology* (Minneapolis: Fortress, 2015), 45.
36. Ibid., 50–51.
37. Readers familiar with my *Reading the Gospels Wisely* may recall that I argue that a key aspect of the overall purpose of the Gospels is aretelogical, which I defined as "for the purpose

philosophers philosophize is so that their hearers will grow in understanding, affection, and orientation, and thereby change for the betterment of themselves and those around them. Thus, our reading of the Sermon, which is clearly focused on providing a vision for a way of being in the world, should naturally and rightly be focused on reading for the purpose of being transformed. All other readings, as beneficial as they can be—historical, literary, dogmatic, political, postcolonial, grammatical, linguistic, text-critical—are at best steps toward the highest form of reading, reading for personal transformation.[38]

By *pros ōphelimon* I mean a reading strategy that focuses on what is most useful or *beneficial*. This Greek phrase comes by way of the excellent work of Margaret Mitchell on the practice of scriptural interpretation in earliest Christianity.[39] Mitchell argues that in the patristic period and beyond there was an awareness that good interpretation of Holy Scripture resided in "a carefully calibrated balance among three cardinal virtues of ancient textual interpretation." These are *akribeia* ("precision," "keen attention"), a close examination of what the text says in whole and in part; *ōpheleia* (benefit), an awareness of the *benefit* for present readers; and *epieikeia* (clemency), which seeks to keep the two in balance.[40] In the following exposition of the Sermon I seek this same approach: I will wrestle with details of the text large and small but always pull back to ask the big-purpose question regarding what is the most beneficial reading.

---

of developing virtue." My suggestion here is the same, though I am changing terms to one that better fits and that I gladly acquired from Ellen Charry—"aretegenic." This word describes reading and study that generates or inculcates virtue (*aretē*) in the recipient. See Ellen T. Charry, *By the Renewing of Your Minds: The Pastoral Function of Christian Doctrine* (Oxford: Oxford University Press, 1999), 16–19.

38. Markus Bockmuehl provides a helpful sketch of the characteristics of the "ideal reader" of the New Testament, one that we can assume the NT authors expect as the model. This ideal reader has a personal stake in the truth claims of the text, has undergone a religious, moral, and intellectual conversion, takes the NT as authoritative, is ecclesially situated, and is assumed to be inspired in the sense of filled with the Spirit (Bockmuehl, *Seeing the Word: Refocusing New Testament Study* [Grand Rapids: Baker Academic, 2006], 68–74). This sketch accords well with the voice of the NT, and I think that it leads well into an understanding of reading for the purpose of personal transformation.

39. Margaret Mitchell, *Paul, the Corinthians, and the Birth of Christian Hermeneutics* (Cambridge: Cambridge University Press, 2012).

40. Ibid., 108.

PART 1

Orientation

1

The Encyclopedic Context
of the Sermon

Base Camp: Understanding the Encyclopedic Context (with Help from Umberto Eco)

Any wise mountain climber spends thoughtful time in preparation before beginning the ascent. This preparation involves many elements, including mental and physical training, analyzing the goal, collecting equipment, and finding a good guide. All of this ultimately comes together at the foot of the mountain in the base camp.

This chapter is the base camp for our ascent of the Sermon on the Mount. In this base camp I will provide a reconnaissance of the mount that lies before us and how best to approach it. This reconnaissance reveals that to reach the highest vistas of the Sermon we must become competent readers who understand the encyclopedic context in which the Sermon exists.

Everything is in a context. This sentence, this paragraph, this chapter, this book, and its title all exist in a printed context. This is literary context. There are other contexts as well. There is the original context of me sitting on my red couch early one Sunday morning, before anyone else in my house is awake, writing that sentence. There are several later contexts of me revising this paragraph, each with their own historical situatedness. There is the context of the now, a very different one: your context as a reader. Your place in time and space makes your context different from mine as the writer. My writing exists in the complex context of my whole life up to this point;

your reading does too, with your life. Today is shaped and formed by all the days that came before it, turtles stacked on top of each other from the foundation of the world until this moment. If you come back and read this paragraph again sometime in the future, while its compositional context and intent will not have changed, much else will have, resulting in a different contextual reading.

One of the most insightful thinkers who can help us understand the importance of these multiple contexts is Umberto Eco, especially in terms of his notions of the context of the cultural encyclopedia and the Model Reader. Eco, famous for his voluminous and influential output of everything from best-selling novels to technical works on translation theory, was a semiotician. Semiotics is a branch of literary and linguistic study that focuses on how signs and symbols function in human communication.[1] His academic work focuses on how language works to communicate meaning through cultural signs and phenomena.[2] This is where the idea of contexts becomes so important for reading and interpreting any text, such as the Sermon.

Eco is a heavyweight thinker who steps into the ring of a heated, long, and highly publicized fight between theorists on how to interpret literature and how meaning occurs. At the risk of oversimplification, in one corner are those who emphasize the role of the author who produced the original text. In the other corner are those who suggest that the reader plays the determinative role in meaning production. Again, with some unfortunate but necessary oversimplification, this could be called the difference between objectivism and subjectivism or modernism and postmodernism, between authorial intent and reader response, when these categories are applied to the interpretation of texts (hermeneutics).

Eco's position, which comes to greater clarity and strength over the course of his long career, is unique and provides a helpful way forward on these complicated debates. In short, Eco recognizes the complexity of the experience

1. For further study on semiotics, see Umberto Eco, *The Role of the Reader: Explorations in the Semiotics of Texts* (Bloomington: Indiana University Press, 1984); and Eco, *Semiotics and the Philosophy of Language* (Bloomington: Indiana University Press, 1984).

2. The following summary is heavily dependent on the fine work of Leroy Huizenga, *The New Isaac: Tradition and Intertextuality in the Gospel of Matthew* (Leiden: Brill, 2012), with some additional thoughts from Ross Wagner, *Reading the Sealed Book: Old Greek Isaiah and the Problem of Septuagint Hermeneutics* (Tübingen: Mohr Siebeck, 2013). Another helpful and somewhat different appropriation of Eco in biblical studies can be found in Heath Thomas, *Poetry and Theology in Lamentations: The Aesthetics of an Open Text*, Hebrew Bible Monographs (Sheffield: Sheffield Phoenix, 2013). Further exploration can also be found in Richard B. Hays, Stefan Alkier, and Leroy A. Huizenga, eds., *Reading the Bible Intertextually* (Waco: Baylor University Press, 2009), esp. chaps. 1 and 14.

of reading and how different cultural contexts and traditions affect what one discerns in a text and what resonances it evokes. Yet in contrast to much of literary theory today, Eco insists on the importance of *intention* in the creation of a text and on the historical situatedness of the author, who exists in a particular time and place. This puts Eco at odds with much of postmodern literary theory, including that of the poststructuralists and even other semioticians.[3] One cannot simply use a text to say whatever one wants—well, of course, one can do that, but this is not a good theory for literature or a good practice if one wants to *interpret* texts. One cannot ignore the author as if he or she has no role in the meaning: the "words brought by the author are a rather embarrassing bunch of material evidences [if one is trying to ignore them] that the reader cannot pass over in silence, or in noise."[4] Rather, "interpreting texts involves discerning the nature of the text, the very intent of the text, composed of words and strings of words that have conventional meanings and functions."[5]

Eco's unique contribution is that he provides a model for how this text-focused reading relates to the complexity of the enculturated nature of language and communication and the experience of readers. The key to understanding what Eco is saying here is his idea of "encyclopedic competence." Eco argues that the meaning of words and phrases should not be approached with a *dictionary* model, where understanding of the language is stored in the dictionary while knowledge of the real world—its culture, history, beliefs—is stored separately, in the *encyclopedia*. On the contrary, Eco shows that we can never "sever language from its location and function within a cultural framework." Language is a social phenomenon and thus *real*, not abstract and ideal.[6] Communication and texts come from real people in real situations, complete with cultural assumptions and evocations; communication does not exist outside of these historical realities. A dictionary approach to language relates facts in a discursive, point-to-point way; but "the idea of encyclopedia attempts to take into account a process of interpretation which takes the

---

3. As Huizenga notes, "In Eco's view, the poststructuralists are not correct, and critical deconstruction is not true; the kind of passionate play advocated by the later [Roland] Barthes and his associates ignores the real nature of cultural conventions concerning language" (*New Isaac*, 54).

4. Eco, "Interpretation and History," in *Interpretation and Overinterpretation*, ed. Stefan Collini (Cambridge: Cambridge University Press, 1992), 24, quoted in Huizenga, *New Isaac*, 55.

5. Huizenga, *New Isaac*, 55. Kevin Vanhoozer has provided much help in wrestling with the abiding role of the author and textual intent in light of deep reflections on the nature of literature and language. See Vanhoozer, *Is There a Meaning in This Text? The Bible, the Reader, and the Morality of Literary Knowledge*, 2nd ed. (Grand Rapids: Zondervan, 2009).

6. Huizenga, *New Isaac*, 26.

form of an inference."[7] Or, in the words of John Haiman, "Dictionaries relate words to other words. Encyclopedias, in more or less sharp contradistinction, relate words to extralinguistic facts,"[8] or cultural realities. By way of example, Stefan Alkier notes that in the encyclopedia of cultural understanding of the Roman Empire there would have been an entry for "love spell," even though in most modern Western cultures there would not.[9] This difference speaks to the fact that our reading entails understanding not only the words but also the cultural differences between us and the text before us.

Thus, rather than thinking about language and texts in terms of a dictionary, we must consider language and texts as products of a certain cultural phenomenon, something that can only be understood and described with a massive encyclopedic understanding. For Eco, the "encyclopedia" is the totality of the collection of all possible cultural interpretations and phenomena in which a text is created; it is the "grand universe of semiosis" or signs.[10] The encyclopedia is "the cultural framework in which the text is situated and from which the gaps of the text are filled."[11] Therefore, the encyclopedia is never finished and exists only as a regulative idea; the potential associations of meanings are endless as culture continues to develop.

But here is the key idea and what separates Eco from the poststructuralists. For poststructuralism (and much of current literary theory and discussions of intertextuality), reading is completely open as one explores the infinite process of semiosis, where meaning is never really found and certainly not in any authorial intention in the text. For Eco, by contrast, texts are particular instantiations of encyclopedic materials and thus arrest the infinite play of semiosis that one might engage in as a reader.[12] Every text is not just language but is also an actualization of some aspects of the cultural encyclopedia in which it was created. And because texts are created in real situations and have an intention, through historical, cultural, and literary analysis a good reader can actually "isolate a given portion of the social encyclopedia so far as it appears useful in order to interpret certain portions of actual discourses (and texts)."[13] Or to

7. Umberto Eco, *A Theory of Semiotics* (Bloomington: Indiana University Press, 1976), 164.

8. John Haiman, "Dictionaries and Encyclopedias," *Lingua* 50 (1980): 332. For more on the distinction between dictionary and encyclopedic contexts, see Umberto Eco, *Kant and the Platypus: Essays on Language and Cognition* (New York: Harcourt, 1997), 224–79.

9. Stefan Alkier, "New Testament Studies on the Basis of Categorical Semiotics," in Hays, Alkier, and Huizenga, *Reading the Bible Intertextually*, 235.

10. Huizenga, *New Isaac*, 26.

11. Stefan Alkier, "Intertextuality and the Semiotics of Biblical Texts," in Hays, Alkier, and Huizenga, *Reading the Bible Intertextually*, 8.

12. Huizenga, *New Isaac*, 56.

13. Ibid., 28.

say it more simply, because words come from and evoke cultural resonances (not simply denote dictionary meanings) we must interpret texts sensitive to those cultural evocations.

The Model Reader then, for Eco, is the one who sits at the juncture where the particular text connects with the cultural encyclopedia in the most coherent and economic way possible.[14] The best readings of a text will seek to approximate the position of the Model Reader through an ever-increasing competence in encyclopedic understanding (imperfect though it must be). The Model Reader is one who reads sympathetically and "with the grain" of the text.[15] Good reading involves an "interpretive cooperation" by which the reader of a text, "through successive abductive inferences, proposes topics, ways of reading, and hypotheses of coherence, on the basis of suitable encyclopedic competence."[16] The event of reading is much more complex than perceiving the words or syntax before us. Rather, "the work of reading (or hearing, for that matter) demands, in addition, the activation or anesthetizing of cultural encyclopedic knowledge, which permits that which is deciphered or heard to become a meaningful whole."[17] Texts have an intention (*intentio operis*) and a good reader will seek to understand this. The internal coherence of the text is what guides us to discern which readings are out of bounds and which are best.[18] For example, one can attempt to read Thomas á Kempis's *Imitation of Christ* as if it were written by the French novelist Céline. This game might be amusing and produce some intellectual fruit. However, while some lines of the *Imitation of Christ* can be read through this grid, the overall coherence of the text speaks against this. On the contrary, when one reads the *Imitation of Christ* according to the Christian medieval encyclopedia, each part of it appears coherent.[19]

Bringing Eco to the Sermon

There is a point to this excursus into the understanding of Umberto Eco. It is this: *Eco's model helps us see that the best readings of the Sermon will be*

---

14. Ibid., 23.

15. As noted above, Markus Bockmuehl takes this further and provides some insightful reflections on the character and profile of the implied reader of the New Testament. See Bockmuehl, *Seeing the Word: Refocusing New Testament Study* (Grand Rapids: Baker Academic, 2006), 68–74.

16. Umberto Eco, "Two Problems in Textual Interpretation," in *Reading Eco: An Anthology*, ed. Rocco Capozzi (Bloomington: Indiana University Press, 1997), 44.

17. Stefan Alkier, "New Testament Studies on the Basis of Categorical Semiotics," 235.

18. See Huizenga, *New Isaac*, 29n42.

19. Umberto Eco, "Overinterpreting Texts," in *Interpretation and Overinterpretation*, 65, discussed in Wagner, *Reading the Sealed Book*, 43.

sensitive to its encyclopedic context while seeking to approximate the experi-
ence of the Model Reader.

More specifically, I will argue that the form, material, and verbiage of the
Sermon reveal that it lies at the nexus of two seemingly opposed but provi-
dentially coordinated contexts—the Second Temple Jewish tradition and the
Greco-Roman virtue tradition. Any reading of the New Testament that is
seeking to understand it in its encyclopedic context requires attention to both
its Greek and Jewish origins.[20] As Paul Johannes Du Plessis observes, ignoring either the Greek or Jewish background of the New Testament "would be
as futile an attempt at theology as playing on a one-stringed violin is a poor
assay at music."[21]

Moreover, both of these contexts ultimately point to the same meta-idea—
human flourishing. To read the Sermon in the best and most beneficial way is
to read it as the Model Reader, aware of how these overlapping encyclopedic
contexts and their shared emphasis on human flourishing form the Sermon.

I should note as well that I am not suggesting here merely a fancier-sounding
way of doing historical and cultural backgrounds, even a discussion of the
"worldview" of first-century Christians. This kind of historical, cultural,
social-scientific, and conceptual background work is very good and beneficial
and will indeed appear throughout the following arguments. But with Eco I
am suggesting that more is needed than this, an approach that is sensitive to
how texts communicate and how language functions at the evocative or connotative level, not merely the denotative. We need an understanding of the
social and linguistic encyclopedic context in which the Sermon was uttered
so that we might hear it in a model way.[22] To these contexts (which together
make up the encyclopedic context of the New Testament) we can now turn.

---

20. While recognizing the essential importance of the canonical context and tradition of
Matthew, Huizenga likewise offers a reading of Matthew (in his case, concerning the figure of
Isaac and the Akedah) that also takes into account the broader cultural encyclopedia of Second
Temple Jewish texts beyond the Old Testament.

21. Paul Johannes Du Plessis, *Teleios: The Idea of Perfection in the New Testament* (Kampen: Kok, 1959), 35.

22. Kavin Rowe's recent and significant monograph *One True Life: The Stoics and Early
Christians as Rival Traditions* (New Haven: Yale University Press, 2016) highlights how Christianity is situated in the Greco-Roman world, which was rich in philosophical reflections about
what true life is and how to live it, by exploring the thought of Seneca, Epictetus, and Marcus
Aurelius alongside that of Paul, Luke, and Justin Martyr. Rowe's project is different from my
argument here, however, in that Rowe (following MacIntyre) emphasizes the incommensurability/
untranslatability of different traditions/ways of life, such that a simple comparison of texts
and concepts is not possible. While I acknowledge the danger of a modernist version of "encyclopedic" textual comparison (see Rowe chapter 7), there is still value in understanding the
ways in which the Greek and Jewish traditions overlap and mutually inform each other and how
Christianity offers an alternative to both, drawn from both conceptual worlds.

Context 1: The Story of Israel and Second Temple Jewish Wisdom Literature

The survey of this context must necessarily be brief and in the nature of a précis because we are addressing a topic as large as Scripture itself and involving many complex streams, rivers, and eddies. But in short, to understand the Sermon well in its encyclopedic context we must start with the most fundamental observation—namely, that the Sermon comes to us historically, literarily, and theologically in the context of Israel's story and self-understanding. Jesus, Christianity, and the New Testament documents are birthed directly out of Judaism, and so whatever else we understand about their meaning must be grounded in this reality. Any reading that ignores this is a decontextualized reading that may bear some fruit but cannot be described as sensitive to the intention of the text.

Specifically, Jesus and the authors of the New Testament see themselves as part of the grand story of God's creation and redeeming work in the world, a world that had a beginning and will have an end, or at least a renewed beginning. The foundational orientation to this story occurs in Gen. 1–11, where we learn that God, who is the sole creator of all that is, has set his especial love upon humanity as the apex of his creation. The tension of the story is that humanity fails in both its love for him and love for one another, resulting in a darkening of mind and heart and ultimately death, rather than flourishing life. God then sets in motion the mysterious, arduous, and long-term plan for the reversal of this state, beginning with Abraham and flowing through his descendants.

The theology of the Old Testament, to whatever extent we can talk in this somewhat anachronistic way, is *the biblical story* of the working out of this redemption and restoration through its many twists and turns. Consistent throughout this long story is God's trustworthy and loving character and humanity's perpetual and cyclical untrustworthiness and unloving actions. The great hope that is woven throughout the accounts of Israel's history and the prophetic writings that accompany it is that God is going to finally bring about the restoration of the Edenic state, with humanity restored, redeemed, in proper relationship to God and one another, and experiencing the flourishing life that was lost.[23] The *šālôm* or peace that was known in relationship with God at creation will come again when God restores his *šālôm* on the earth.[24] This can also be described as creation entering into

23. See Exod. 15:1–18; Isa. 51:3; 65:17–25; Ezek. 36:35.
24. Isa. 51:11; 52:7; 54:10; 55:12–13; 66:12; Ezek. 34:25; 37:26.

its final Sabbath rest.[25] This interpretation of the world and this hope for the future are the backdrop and props of the stage on which the dramatic story of Jesus, Christianity, and the New Testament writings are played out.

Even more specifically, Jesus, Christianity, and the New Testament documents come from what is called the era of Second Temple Judaism, the time between the return from exile and rededication of the temple in the sixth century BCE and its second destruction in CE 70. Even though no Jews living, worshiping, hoping, and writing during this time thought of themselves as living in "the Second Temple period," this is a helpful category for us looking back on this time period because there are certain distinctive characteristics and developments that affect the shape and content of earliest Christianity.

Many other studies have documented and pondered these effects.[26] What is particularly relevant for our understanding of the Sermon is the role of wisdom literature in the Second Temple period and how it interacts with eschatological and apocalyptic writings. We will see that this wisdom-apocalyptic thread of Jewish literature provides a particularly important encyclopedic context for understanding the Sermon. The Jewish Scriptures, understood at the broadest level, are telling this redemption story as worked out in history. Yet there is also an earthy profundity through which the Scriptures deal with real life and human experience in all its depth. That is, the Bible does not present its understanding of the world as a set of abstract ideals and universal truths but rather as life being lived out imperfectly with all its messiness, by real people stumbling through this world. As a result, much of the writings deal with nitty-gritty details of how to live life in a way that will result in peace and happiness—with instructions as diverse as how to handle money, to the approach young men should take regarding young women, to how to deal with foolish people in society. All of this and more is found in what we call the Wisdom literature of the Bible.[27]

---

25. See Gordon Wenham, *Rethinking Genesis 1–11: Gateway to the Bible* (Eugene, OR: Cascade, 2013).

26. A classic work is Martin Hengel, *Judaism and Hellenism: Studies in Their Encounter in Palestine during the Early Hellenistic Period*, trans. John Bowden (1974; repr., Minneapolis: Fortress, 1981). See also N. T. Wright, *The New Testament and the People of God* (Minneapolis: Fortress, 1992); John M. G. Barclay, *Jews in the Mediterranean Diaspora: From Alexander to Trajan (323 BCE–117 CE)* (Berkeley: University of California Press, 1999); John J. Collins, *Between Athens and Jerusalem: Jewish Identity in the Hellenistic Diaspora* (Grand Rapids: Eerdmans, 1999). Recently Robert S. Kinney has argued persuasively in *Hellenistic Dimensions of the Gospel of Matthew* (Tübingen: Mohr Siebeck, 2016) that the hellenistic aspects of Matthew's Gospel need to be recognized, not only the Jewish background.

27. While there are forms and themes of wisdom throughout various portions of the Bible (including some "wisdom psalms," such as Pss. 37, 49, and 73), the Wisdom literature is typically

The Wisdom literature consists of proverbs, memorable sayings (aphorisms), parables, stories, and ethical instruction. It also includes reflections on existence, divine justice, and life's meaning, especially in the confusing complexity of human experience when things do not work out as planned.[28] In this the Bible is consistent with the wide variety of other ancient literature that also wrestles with human wisdom and what makes for the virtuous and flourishing life.

What makes the Scriptures distinct is that the radical monotheism of the biblical understanding means that "at the center of wisdom literature was the idea that religious devotion, the fear of the Lord, preceded all knowledge, indeed was its final destination as well."[29] Moreover, the approach to ethics, or virtuous living, in the Old Testament is rooted in God's nature as the model for virtue—not humanity's ideals for virtue. This begins in the context of Adam and Eve's relationship with God. Virtue in the Bible finds its meaning in the context of this story framed through the issue of relationship between God and humanity and between one human and another. Therefore, as Jacob Neusner observes, in the Jewish Scriptures "all virtuous traits then find their place within that encompassing vision that explains who we are by telling the story of creation culminating in Adam, Eve, and Eden." The meaning of virtue is found in the context of the Torah's "story of humanity's life from creation through Sinai to redemption at the end of time, and from birth to the grave and ultimate resurrection."[30]

As this story of redemption and virtue unfolds, a series of crises occur, which begin to make clear that God's restoration to šālôm-full Edenic flourishing will only come fully at the eschaton, or the end of this age of human experience. The prophets increasingly promise and paint a picture of this coming age, accompanied usually by the exhortation to order one's life around the virtues of this final state. Increasingly this eschatological literature becomes also apocalyptic in form and worldview. This means that the vision for this future, eschatological state is given by divine revelation to a limited number, those who are faithful to God in the midst of a world ignorant of and opposed to God. This vision is *revealed* by God, hence its apocalyptic (which means "revealed") nature. An influential part of Second Temple

---

identified as Proverbs, Job, and Qoheleth/Ecclesiastes in the Hebrew Bible, plus Sirach and the Wisdom of Solomon from the Second Temple period.

28. "Wisdom Literature," in *Dictionary of Judaism in the Biblical Period*, ed. Jacob Neusner and William S. Green, vol. 2 (Peabody, MA: Hendrickson, 1999), 672.

29. Ibid., 672.

30. Jacob Neusner, "Virtue in Formative Judaism," in *The Encyclopedia of Judaism*, ed. Jacob Neusner, Alan J. Avery-Peck, and William S. Green, vol. 3 (London: Continuum, 1999), 1466.

Jewish literature manifests the form and worldview of such an apocalyptic eschatological understanding.

And here is where it gets very interesting. Much of this apocalyptic eschatological literature is deeply interwoven with wisdom themes and writings. At first glance these would seem to be opposite and unrelated topics and approaches, but further reflection reveals that this is a natural, inevitable, and important connection. Because the virtues or ethics of the Bible are tied to the story of redemption and God's relationship with humanity—with wisdom providing the practical reflections on how to experience this flourishing—it is appropriate that the literature that looks to the final time of restoration will also focus on practical virtue as well. This is in fact what we find in much of the Second Temple literature.

"Apocalyptic [literature] was essentially ethical," as R. H. Charles observed.[31] This connection between ethical wisdom literature and apocalyptic eschatology is manifested through what Grant Macaskill describes as inaugurated eschatology, "within which the revealing of wisdom to an elect group—set apart from unfaithful Israel—plays a key role."[32] There are many examples of this kind of wisdom-giving, inaugurated eschatology in Second Temple literature, including 1 Enoch, various documents from Qumran, and the New Testament itself.

Indeed, the New Testament manifests this understanding in many ways, both reinforcing Jewish morality and molding and shaping it in a distinctly eschatological and Christian way. As Dale Allison points out, belief in imminent, eschatological judgment—something Jesus emphasizes—tends to result in the reinforcement of moral traditions, but at times it also revises certain elements within a moral tradition. This is because:

> The expectation of a new world entails the end of the present world and of its conventional customs and social arrangements; and if those customs and arrangements are soon to go, one's present way of life can hardly continue as ever. One rather is strongly encouraged to become, in anticipation, less tied to the present state of the world.[33]

This is precisely what we find in the apocalyptic and eschatologically urgent perspective of the New Testament. Based on the imminent return of

31. R. H. Charles, *The Apocrypha and Pseudepigrapha of the Old Testament in English* (Oxford: Clarendon, 1913), 2:ix.

32. Grant Macaskill, *Revealed Wisdom and Inaugurated Eschatology in Ancient Judaism and Early Christianity*, JSJSup 115 (Leiden: Brill, 2007), 297.

33. Dale C. Allison Jr., "Apocalyptic Ethics and Behavior," in *The Oxford Handbook of Apocalyptic Literature*, ed. John J. Collins (Oxford: Oxford University Press, 2014), 297.

the kingdom of God, John the Baptist calls people to repentance (Matt. 3:2; Mark 1:5); Jesus enlists disciples to abandon their livelihoods and follow him (Mark 1:16–20); and the moral instruction throughout the New Testament is rife with such radical, end-of-the-age views on money, possessions, celibacy, and missional urgency (Matt. 6:24; 19:16–26; 28:18–20; Luke 12:33; 1 Cor. 7:8; 1 Tim. 3:3; 6:10; Heb. 13:5).

To reorient us to the larger point: all of this discussion is providing a key for understanding the encyclopedic context in which the Sermon sits. Understanding the story and worldview that is up and running before Jesus delivers the Sermon on the Mount gives great insight into the shape and flavor of its teachings. As we will see, the Sermon manifests a genetic relationship to the perspective of this Second Temple apocalyptic wisdom (or inaugurated, apocalyptic eschatology), providing a vision for virtue that is oriented to God's coming restorative kingdom, and is given to those who have ears to hear and build their lives wisely upon Jesus's teaching (Matt. 7:24–27). All of this talk of wisdom and virtue leads us naturally to discuss that other key encyclopedic context at work within the Sermon, the Greco-Roman virtue tradition.

Context 2: The Greco-Roman Virtue Tradition

If seeking to summarize Jewish history in a few pages is a daunting task, so too is attempting to survey the history of the Greco-Roman virtue tradition. As all ancient philosophy was primarily moral philosophy, with virtue the great thread tying it all together, to speak of the Greco-Roman virtue tradition is to evoke the entirety of the history of ancient Western philosophy. But for our discussion here, this must be only an evocation.

The goal in this section is to provide a brief overview of the issue of virtue in Greek philosophy so as to fill in the picture of this aspect of the Sermon's encyclopedic context. The reason this is important, as we will see, is that much of the language and concepts of the Sermon show evidence of a connection to and perspective overlapping with the realm of Greek moral philosophy. Jesus is more than a sage or philosopher according to Matthew's high Christology, it is true, but he's not less.[34] Indeed, in many ways Jesus is depicted like an ancient

---

34. Studies of how Matthew presents Jesus as a teacher are surprisingly not many, but one may consult John P. Meier, *The Vision of Matthew: Christ, Church, and Morality in the First Gospel* (New York: Paulist Press, 1979); Samuel Byrskog, *Jesus the Only Teacher: Didactic Authority and Transmission in Ancient Israel, Ancient Judaism, and the Matthean Community* (Stockholm: Almqvist & Wiksell, 1994); John Yueh-Han Yieh, *One Teacher: Jesus' Teaching Role in Matthew's Gospel Report* (Berlin: de Gruyter, 2004); Chris Keith, *Jesus' Literacy: Scribal Culture and the Teacher from Galilee* (London: T&T Clark, 2013) and also *Jesus against the*

philosopher or sage in the Gospels.[35] Charles Talbert surveys the different kinds
of teachers in the ancient world and asks how readers of Matthew would
perceive Jesus based on his depiction. He concludes that "for a Mediterranean
auditor of this Gospel, the closest analogy would have been a philosopher and
his disciples."[36] Similarly, even though he sees the Sermon as being somewhat
distinct from the historical Jesus and even Matthew himself, Hans Dieter Betz's
analysis of the Sermon leads him to conclude that its form and function are
closest to Hellenistic moral philosophical works in epitome form, such as that
of Epictetus and Plutarch.[37] Wayne Meeks also sets the New Testament into the
context of the ethical approaches of the ancient world, showing how Christianity
inherits much of its grammar from Israel, Greece, and Rome. This includes
Matthew, who produces a "messianic biography" for the purpose of helping
shape the morality, beliefs, and attitudes of the Christian community.[38] Thus,

---

Scribal Elite: The Origins of the Conflict (Grand Rapids: Baker, 2014). For works on Jesus as
a sage or wisdom teacher, see Ben Witherington III, *Jesus the Sage: The Pilgrimage of Wisdom*
(1994; repr., Minneapolis: Fortress, 2000); Macaskill, *Revealed Wisdom and Inaugurated Eschatology*; James D. G. Dunn, *Christology in the Making: A New Testament Inquiry into the
Origins of the Doctrine of the Incarnation* (Grand Rapids: Eerdmans, 1996); M. J. Suggs, *Wisdom, Christology, and Law in Matthew's Gospel* (Cambridge, MA: Harvard University Press,
1970); Celia Deutsch, *Hidden Wisdom and the Easy Yoke: Wisdom, Torah and Discipleship in
Matthew 11:25–30* (Sheffield: JSOT Press, 1987).

35. Yieh, *One Teacher*, provides a helpful analysis of how Matthew presents Jesus as a teacher
in comparison with contemporary Judaism (the Teacher of Righteousness from Qumran) and
Greek philosophy (Epictetus), showing both similarities and differences. See also Keith, *Jesus
against the Scribal Elite*, 15–66, and Kinney, *Hellenistic Dimensions of the Gospel of Matthew*,
especially chap. 7.

36. Talbert, citing Vernon Robbins, notes four ways in which Jesus and his followers in Matthew's Gospel would have been seen as like ancient philosophers: (1) philosophers gathered
disciples by summons; (2) a philosopher's disciples followed him; (3) the disciples are with him
and memorize his teachings; (4) the disciples receive benefit from being with the philosopher
(Talbert, *Matthew*, Paideia: Commentary on the New Testament [Grand Rapids: Baker Academic, 2010], 20–21).

37. Hans Dieter Betz, "The Sermon on the Mount (Matt. 5:3–7:27): Its Literary Genre and
Function," in *Essays on the Sermon on the Mount* (1985; Minneapolis: Fortress, 2009), 1–16.
He states most succinctly, "The literary genre of the SM [Sermon on the Mount] is that of
an epitome presenting the theology of Jesus in a systematic fashion," enabling the disciple to
become a "Jesus theologian" (15). This is a helpful insight. I disagree with Betz, however, that
the Sermon is independent of and indeed in conflict with the rest of Matthew. See the hearty
critique of Betz on this point in Graham Stanton, *A Gospel for a New People: Studies in Matthew* (Edinburgh: T&T Clark, 1992), 310–25. Robert Kinney also argues that the Sermon is an
epitome, noting the potential critiques of Betz but showing that one can adopt this interpretation
of the literary function of the Sermon without agreeing with Betz's conclusions about textual
sources. See Kinney, *Hellenistic Dimensions of the Gospel of Matthew*, 172.

38. Wayne Meeks, *The Moral World of the First Christians* (Philadelphia: Westminster, 1986).
Meeks discusses the social setting of first-century Christianity and the traditions of Greece and
Rome on the one hand and Israel on the other. His discussion of Matthew is found on pp. 136–43.

there is historical grounding in the Gospels' depiction to consider how Jesus's teaching might relate to the philosophies of the day.

Returning to our overview of Greek philosophy, we must start with the search for happiness, the great quest and focus of all ancient moral philosophy. Whether it be Stoicism, Epicureanism, Aristotelianism, or hedonism, philosophers in the Greco-Roman tradition were consciously and explicitly driven to answer the question of what makes people truly happy.[39] In this sense Greco-Roman philosophy was at once practical and moral. Notably, in contrast to today's ideas of happiness, this moral-philosophical notion of happiness does not mean merely a temporary, subjective state of mind but an overall life that is satisfied and meaningful. This is summed up often with the Greek word *eudaimonia*, best translated now with the gloss "human flourishing."[40]

In the following chapter we will explore more what this idea means and its relationship to the key biblical word *makarios*. For now the point to be made is that there is a consistent thread in the Greco-Roman tradition that rested the goal of human flourishing on the pursuit of virtue. In conscious contrast to hedonism, which suggests that mere pleasure is the only goal and the only *eudaimonia* worth having, the ancient philosophers sought to persuade their hearers that it was only through the lifelong, intentional pursuit of virtue (practiced moral character) that one could find true flourishing. The different philosophies debated a number of issues within this idea, such as what role fortune or circumstances play in our flourishing and what the role of emotions are. But they all agreed that the only hope for the flourishing that all humans long for is to pursue virtue—practiced and developed wisdom—learned over time.[41]

39. The same can be said for non-Western philosophical and religious approaches. For example, see the articles on Buddhism in Susan A. David, Ilona Boniwell, and Amanda Conley Ayers, eds., *The Oxford Handbook of Happiness* (Oxford: Oxford University Press, 2013). At the same time, Charles Taylor points out that the pursuit of happiness/human flourishing in Buddhism is substantively different from that in the Western traditions (especially Christianity) in that the conditions of bliss in Buddhism are "so 'revisionist' that it amounts to a departure from what we normally understand as human flourishing" (Taylor, *A Secular Age* [Cambridge, MA: Harvard University Press, 2007], 17). My focus is on the Greco-Roman tradition because it is more directly relevant as a historical, linguistic, and theological context for the Sermon.

40. The older English rendering of this important word as "happiness" has now been replaced in philosophical discussion with "human flourishing," dating back at least to the work of G. E. M. Anscombe in 1958. John M. Cooper notes that "human flourishing" is a better translation of Aristotle's *eudaimonia* because it reflects more fully the idea that *eudaimonia* is not a subjective mental state over a short period of time but "the possession and use of one's mature powers," during which the future looks bright and one experiences "the fulfillment of the natural capacities of the human species" (*Reason and Human Good in Aristotle* [Cambridge, MA: Harvard University Press, 1975; repr., Indianapolis: Hackett, 1986], 89n1).

41. Darrin McMahon, "The Pursuit of Happiness in History," in David, Boniwell, and Ayers, *Oxford Handbook of Happiness*, 254. See also McMahon's fuller treatment, *Happiness: A*

Consistent among these philosophers was the idea that what is truly ethical or "the good" is defined not in terms of mere actions or choices but rather in terms of the moral agent himself or herself. Ethics is about who we are as people and who we can and should become. In contrast to Kantian ethical approaches, as Daniel Harrington and James Keenan observe, a virtue-ethics approach is concerned with these three basic questions: Who are we? Who ought we to become? How do we get there?[42] The virtues (or vices) of the person are "the disposition to act in certain ways and to do so reliably—characteristically—over time."[43] Stephen Fowl describes virtues as "those habits of seeing, feeling, thinking, and acting that, when exercised in the right ways and at the right times, will enhance one's prospects of both recognizing, moving toward and attaining one's proper end."[44] The reason that ethics must focus on the agent before the action is summed up in the old adage *actio sequitur esse*, "action follows essence." What we do morally is the fruit of who we are. This is the genius of the virtue-ethics understanding, or to put it in Greco-Roman terms, philosophy.

Aristotle (382–322 BC) is not alone in this "virtue ethics" understanding of life, but his version in many ways sits at the apex of this tradition; he is certainly its most abidingly influential progenitor. Aristotle's views can be found particularly clearly in his *Nicomachean Ethics*, written as an aid to his son to spell out the steps to a good life (cf. Prov. 1–9). The "good life" (human flourishing) contains what is morally, prudentially, and intellectually good altogether. As noted above, for Aristotle it is virtue as the orientation of life that leads to *eudaimonia*.[45] This virtue is not only moral choices, as we tend to think of in ethics today, but learned practical wisdom (*phronēsis*). Practical wisdom is what enables a moral agent to figure out how to act well in any circumstance that will arise. "A man of practical wisdom is he who has the ability to deliberate . . . it is a truthful characteristic of acting rationally in matters good and bad for man."[46]

History (New York: Grove, 2006). The classic work that reintroduced discussion of virtue into moral philosophy today is Alisdair MacIntyre, *After Virtue: A Study in Moral Theory*, 3rd ed. (Notre Dame, IN: University of Notre Dame Press, 2007).

42. Daniel Harrington and James F. Keenan, *Jesus and Virtue Ethics: Building Bridges between New Testament Studies and Moral Theology* (London: Sheed & Ward, 2005), 207. Glen Stassen and David Gushee have also provided an excellent resource that builds a Christian ethical view based on a virtue reading of the Sermon—Stassen and Gushee, *Kingdom Ethics: Following Jesus in Contemporary Context* (Downers Grove, IL: IVP Academic, 2003).

43. Daniel J. Treier, *Introducing Theological Interpretation of Scripture: Recovering a Christian Practice* (Grand Rapids: Baker Academic, 2008), 92.

44. Ibid., 92, quoting Fowl in *DTIB*, 838.

45. Julia Driver, *Ethics: The Fundamentals* (Malden, MA: Blackwell, 2006), 138.

46. Aristotle, *Nicomachean Ethics*, trans. Martin Ostwald (Indianapolis: Bobbs-Merrill, 1962), 152–53, quoted in Driver, *Ethics*, 138.

Also, for Aristotle the virtuous person is the one who functions in the "mean" or balanced state, able to control and regulate his or her feelings and emotions as well as to act rightly. "Aristotle's picture, then, of the virtuous person is the person who functions harmoniously—his desires and emotions do not conflict with what he knows to be right. They go together. . . . the excellent human being is not conflicted; he does not suffer inner turmoil and the struggle between reason and passion."[47] Or as Paula Gottlieb describes it, the "good Aristotelian human being enjoys acting virtuously, his thinking and feelings are in sync."[48]

Aristotle taught that a virtuous person is the one who exhibits harmonious psychological functioning—that is, both the *desiring* and *judging* parts of the soul must be in harmony. It is less virtuous to know and do the right thing if we don't also desire it than to both desire and do the right thing.[49]

The implication as this is developed for Aristotle is that doing good by accident or intuition is not truly virtuous, but virtue comes from deliberating and learning what is good and then both desiring and acting upon it. In shooting an arrow at a target an unskilled person may occasionally get lucky and hit the bull's-eye (and a skilled person may also occasionally miss), but the goal is to learn the practical skills of archery so as to generally succeed. This is *phronēsis*, or the practical wisdom that we should pursue over time. There is both a trained vision and action. Virtue entails or necessitates an intentional wholeness of person (*teleios*). We cannot be virtuous accidentally or in part. A virtuous action is one that includes all of who we are as humans—reasoning, affections, and embodied actions—our whole person.

These ideas of the necessity of wholeness of person (*teleios*) and the end goal (*telos*) of virtue as human flourishing will prove to have profound conceptual overlap with the Sermon. But raising and discussing these ideas here is not merely conceptual. There is a strong historical-contextual reason for seeing a connection. The reason is that in the centuries leading up to Jesus's time, Second Temple Judaism had become deeply hellenized—that is, influenced by Greek ideas and culture. This hellenization or Greek (and Greco-Roman) influence ranged on the spectrum from full adoption to open rejection, but in

47. Driver, *Ethics*, 141.

48. Paula Gottlieb, "Aristotle's Ethics," in *The Oxford Handbook of the History of Ethics*, ed. Roger Crisp (Oxford: Oxford University Press, 2013), 54.

49. Driver, *Ethics*, 83–84. Plato also discussed lack of psychological harmony as an obstacle to happiness with his analogy of the human soul as a charioteer who must control two horses simultaneously. One is reason and the other is our emotions and appetites. Unless these are properly trained and brought into unity with each other, a person can never be happy. See Plato, *Phaedrus*, 246a–254e.

every case Second Temple Jewish understanding was forever changed by its interactions with Greek and Roman culture.[50] How much more is this true of the first-century sect of Judaism that would become orthodox Christianity, which, note well, presents its canonical documents not in Hebrew or Aramaic but in Greek and which defines itself as creating one new human race out of both Jew and Greek. Christianity is born within and enters into dialogue with Greco-Roman culture.[51] As Betz notes in reflecting on the similarities between hellenistic philosophy and the Sermon ("SM"): "As a matter of fact, large sections of the ancient world at the time of the SM seem to have shared many of these concepts and methods, differing only in philosophical school terminology and in the cultural and religious milieu."[52] Kinney likewise notes the similarities between the Sermon and contemporary hellenistic philosophy regarding rhetorical style, similar topics of discussion, and possibly direct influence of Plato's *Republic*.[53]

There are a number of ways in which Second Temple Judaism and Greek moral philosophy overlap, showing the great influence of these Greek notions and also providing us with insight into the context in which the Sermon was situated. Luke Timothy Johnson points out that one very viable way to be Jewish in the Second Temple period was indeed to understand one's Jewish faith in terms of moral transformation, very much along the lines of Greek moral philosophy.[54] For example, in Josephus's well-known depiction of the various first-century Jewish sects as "schools" (*haireseis*), he describes their convictions and practices in terms familiar to Greek philosophy. He also clearly shades his portrait of the Essenes in the direction

---

50. See Hengel, *Judaism and Hellenism*; Collins, *Between Athens and Jerusalem*; Luke Timothy Johnson, *Among the Gentiles: Greco-Roman Religion and Christianity* (New Haven: Yale University Press, 2009). See especially Kinney, *Hellenistic Dimensions of the Gospel of Matthew*. Kinney notes that while the Jewish background to Matthew is obviously important, Matthean scholarship in recent decades has been imbalanced in only considering this aspect of Matthew's cultural context and has not taken into consideration the deeply hellenistic nature of Second Temple Judaism. Distinguished professor David Daube argues in "Rabbinic Methods of Interpretation and Hellenistic Rhetoric" (*Hebrew Union College Annual* 22 [1949]: 239–64) that even classical rabbinic methods of interpretation can be traced to the influence of Hellenistic rhetorical techniques.

51. Recent decades of NT scholarship have produced much good scholarship on the ways in which early Christianity was interacting with its Roman imperial setting. As with all things, this can be overdone and the Roman imperial backdrop can mistakenly become the sole lens through which the NT is read. For a balanced view, see Scot McKnight and Joseph B. Modica, eds., *Jesus Is Lord, Caesar Is Not: Evaluating Empire Studies Today* (Downers Grove, IL: InterVarsity, 2013).

52. Betz, "Sermon on the Mount (Matt. 5:3–7:27)," 9.

53. Kinney, *Hellenistic Dimensions of the Gospel of Matthew*, 214–15.

54. Johnson, *Among the Gentiles*, 123–25.

of the Pythagoreans, the Pharisees in that of the Stoics, and the Sadducees in that of the Epicureans.[55] In Jewish wisdom literature there are possible connections between Qoheleth in its final form and Epicureanism. But more certainly, there is the indisputable influence of Platonism on the influential book Wisdom of Solomon. Other examples include the *Testaments of the Twelve Patriarchs*, which weaves together both wisdom and apocalyptic, treating the standard Aristotelian virtues and vices in the respective twelve "testaments," and 4 Maccabees, which functions as an encomium on the virtue of courage. Above all we have the extensive and complex writings of Philo of Alexandria, who "interprets the biblical narrative and laws in terms of Greek philosophy and, in particular, Greek moral discourse."[56] Philo is interested in presenting Judaism and its writings not as barbaric and absurd but as sophisticated moral lessons and laws that are meant to cultivate virtue and moral transformation.[57] Summing up, Johnson observes that many faithful Jews during the Second Temple period were not seeking to turn away from their ancestral religion or its practices but desired to understand and explain it in terms of virtue or moral transformation. "They sought as well to shape a character in conformity with God's will at the level of internal dispositions and of the curing of the passions, and in pursuit of this goal, they employed the language and insights of Greco-Roman philosophy."[58]

Human Flourishing and Wholeness: The Nexus of These Two Contexts in Matthew's Cultural Encyclopedia

The point of the preceding exploration is to offer insight into two of the largest and most influential aspects of the culture in which the Sermon was created, the Second Temple Jewish wisdom and the Greco-Roman virtue traditions. The Sermon was birthed from the union of two parents who had themselves already been joined together in the Second Temple period. Thorough understanding of these contexts is not required for any person desiring to pick up and read the Sermon and apply it to their lives. Yet, the best readings will come from seeing how the text of the Sermon draws from and activates these dominant parts of the cultural encyclopedia in which it was born. The best readers will seek to approximate the Model Reader, who

55. Ibid., 123.
56. Ibid., 124.
57. Ibid.
58. Ibid., 125.

perceives the aspects of his or her culture that are being activated through the words of the Sermon.

Just describing the context of the Second Temple period with its Greco-Roman flavor would be beneficial and provide insight at various points into the Sermon's workings. But what is most striking and relevant is this: *These two contexts overlap conceptually in a very significant way in that both are addressing the great topic of wholeness and human flourishing.* That is, there is a thick nexus, or band of interconnectivity, that exists between these two seemingly unrelated or even opposed aspects of early Christianity's birthplace—Second Temple Judaism and the Greco-Roman virtue tradition. But it is precisely at the nexus point that the Sermon's main thrust can be found. Namely, *the Sermon is offering Jesus's answer to the great question of human flourishing, the topic at the core of both the Jewish wisdom literature and that of the Greco-Roman virtue perspective, while presenting Jesus as the true Philosopher-King.* Understanding this will provide a powerful gestalt, or interpretive paradigm, for reading and interpreting the Sermon.

Even as the spouses in a strong marriage will have ways in which they overlap in view and other ways in which they are individuals, so too the union of these two traditions has both overlap and distinction. Both traditions share the question, How is true happiness or flourishing found? And at the basic level both will answer this question with the notion that human flourishing will only be realized through a person's virtue or wholeness, experienced both individually and communally. Both traditions emphasize that the person or the agent is the most important focus for morality and flourishing; mere circumstance or fortune is not determinative, but rather whether the agent orients his or her life virtuously. This is the ethics of virtue, focusing on the good as a way of being in the world that will result in the goal (*telos*) of flourishing and happiness.

Yet each of these contexts also provides its own genetic contribution to the child that is the Sermon. The Greco-Roman tradition provides a well-explored territory of philosophical discussion and debate about virtue, what it looks like, and how to achieve it. The back and forth sparring of the great philosophical traditions on this issue provided ample opportunity for insights to be gained. And it is of course the very language of Greek coming from this conceptual world that will form and frame early Christianity, including the final form of the Sermon. This great tradition, with its emphasis on ethics as virtue, a way of being in the world aiming at flourishing, bequeaths to all in its wake a robust vision for society's flourishing as achieved through paideia. For society to flourish, its leaders must embark on a virtue-developing program of paideia, or whole-person education. This paideia approach to education and instruction is driven by the goal of shaping people into the beautiful Ideal. The forming of individuals through a vision for flourishing and models of virtue is one of the greatest gifts of the Greco-Roman tradition to early Christianity.[59]

One of the important ways the Greco-Roman virtue tradition can be discerned in the Sermon is through Matthew's employment of several key Greek words whose evocations would be clear in first-century hellenized Judaism. Terms such as *makarios* (flourishing), *teleios* (whole, complete), *phronimos* (wise one), *mōros* (fool), *dikaiosynē* (righteousness, justice), *misthos* (reward),[60] and *ta agatha* (the good) are all important Matthean terms that cannot be fully appreciated apart from the Greco-Roman encyclopedia.[61] Additionally, the Sermon and Matthew as a whole manifest deep connections with the hellenistic tradition in the use of education vocabulary, the rhetorical forms, and even resonances of Plato and Homer.[62]

The Second Temple wisdom literature tradition, coming itself from the broader history of Israel, passes on to the Sermon this same vision for whole-person flourishing, but with some distinct characteristics. Particularly, the DNA of this tradition encodes the understanding that true flourishing can be found only in the context of "the fear of the Lord" and a covenantal relationship with the one and only creator God. The radical—at its root—theocentricity of this tradition affects and modifies its understanding of flourishing. The great human-flourishing question is answered by way of the need for covenantal relationship with the true God of the universe and the necessity of a future orientation to the coming time of restoration, in which flourishing will truly occur for those who live virtuously in alignment with God.[63] This time and space of restoration can be described as God's

59. See the helpful discussion in Jason A. Whitlark, "Cosmology and the Perfection of Humanity in Hebrews," in *Interpretation and the Claims of the Text: Resourcing New Testament Theology; Essays in Honor of Charles H. Talbert*, ed. Jason A. Whitlark, Bruce W. Longenecker, Lidija Novakovic, and Mikeal C. Parsons (Waco: Baylor University Press, 2014), 117–28.

60. On the Aristotelian backdrop to *dikaiosynē* and *misthos*, see Johan C. Thom, "Justice in the Sermon on the Mount: An Aristotelian Reading," *NovT* 51 (2009): 319–26.

61. An excellent example of recognizing the conceptual overlap of virtue ideas—along with necessary worldview differences—in the Greco-Roman tradition and early Christianity is Kyriakoula Papademetriou, "From the *Arete* of the Ancient World to the *Arete* of the New Testament: A Semantic Investigation," in *Septuagint Vocabulary: Pre-History, Usage, Reception*, ed. Jan Joosten and Eberhard Bons (Atlanta: Society of Biblical Literature, 2011), 45–63. Papademetriou points out that for Plato and Aristotle *aretē* consisted of wisdom, courage, temperance, and justice, of which wisdom (*phronēsis*) and justice/righteousness (*dikaiosynē*) were considered central and characteristic (48).

62. All of this is argued persuasively in Kinney, *Hellenistic Dimensions of the Gospel of Matthew*.

63. Charles Taylor notes in *A Secular Age* that Christianity (and God himself) is certainly positive on humans flourishing but that "Thy will be done" is not equivalent to "Let humans flourish"—loving and worshiping God is the ultimate end (17).

reign/kingdom. Holiness in this understanding is a wholeness that is aligned not only with culturally conditioned reflections on flourishing discovered in philosophical speculation but also with divine revelation and command. Additionally, the vision is more expansive than the individual person and even communal flourishing; it looks forward to an age when God spreads this flourishing to all of his creation, with *šālôm* transforming the earth that is now in full-blown rebellion against him. All of creation is looking forward to its final Sabbath rest, when *šālôm* is everywhere. Between now and then human flourishing is a possibility but never fully or completely. This theistic and eschatological flavor of the Second Temple understanding of virtue is dominant and unmistakable as coming from the Jewish side of the marriage. Indeed, in this mixed marriage of Jewish and Greco-Roman parents, the Sermon-son definitely favors his Jewish mother and is being raised in the religion of the former, not the latter.

Thus, to conclude this discussion we can arrive at an important point and depict this dual context intentionally. The point is that both of these contexts overlap in their goal of and emphasis on whole-person human flourishing, but the basic orientation of the Sermon is first and foremost that of the eschatological story of Israel, the coming of God's reign/kingdom with Jesus as the King. This redemptive-historical perspective greatly shapes and modifies the virtue vision of the Sermon relative to its otherwise similar approach in Greco-Roman philosophy.

The Sermon still lies precisely at the nexus of these two traditions, and this means that understanding something of both of them will provide great insight into how the Sermon speaks and what vision it is casting. It is best to depict this nexus-point relationship in terms of the flowing story of Israel that has an injection of the Greco-Roman tradition at the crucial point of the birth of Christianity. The intersection of the two traditions occurs at this juncture in history and produces a vision for human flourishing that uses categories and concepts from the Greco-Roman tradition, but is framed by and aiming toward the broader and deeper God-centered, eschatologically oriented Jewish tradition.

The Sermon in the Context of Moral Theories and Ethics

To conclude this base-camp orientation to the Sermon we need finally to locate the Sermon in one other context. This time we are dealing not with the contexts operative at the origin of the text but an important context throughout the history of its interpretation: the context of various moral theories.

The Sermon's content has always required the reader to wrestle with its moral and ethical claims. Indeed, the high ethical stance and focus of the Sermon has been one of the main reasons it has been such a perennial focus of interpretation not only for the church but even for those outside who are seeking to understand Christianity. There is no other place in Scripture where we find such a concentrated paraenesis, or ethical exhortation manual.

This can be seen when studying the history of interpretation of the Sermon, which we surveyed briefly in the previous chapter. This history is not only a history of doctrinal interpretation or theological application of the Sermon, but as much or even more, it is a history of moral theories derived from or placed upon the Sermon. Thus, even as the Sermon has a revealing litmus test function for different theological views, so too does it for the sundry theories of morality and ethics that philosophers and religious leaders have continually debated.

There are other surveys of the moral or ethical interpretation available, often mixed in with histories of interpretation, but Scot McKnight provides one of the most succinct and beneficial ones in his short commentary on the Sermon.[64] For his survey of the history of interpretation, rather than the typical approach of tracing readings of the Sermon through historical periods, McKnight introduces the Sermon by noting different ways it has been read ethically. With great deftness and clarity he surveys deontological, utilitarian, and virtue-ethics approaches, noting that each has some truth but none completely aligns with Jesus's teaching. McKnight offers an insightful threefold taxonomy of different moral theories, each of which finds support in Scripture:

- Ethics from Above—morality based on commands, as seen in the Law
- Ethics from Beyond—morality based on the eschaton, as seen in the Prophets
- Ethics from Below—morality based on wisdom, as seen in the Wisdom literature

64. Scot McKnight, *The Sermon on the Mount*, The Story of God Bible Commentary (Grand Rapids: Zondervan, 2013), 1–17.

McKnight notes that all of these approaches are helpful and are biblically based. Each is needed to understand the grand vision of the ethics of the Sermon.

These categories and analysis are very helpful and perceptive. He is right that most readings of the Sermon focus on only one approach—ethics from above, below, or beyond; deontological, utilitarian, or virtue ethics—and thereby ultimately misunderstand Jesus's teaching. In what follows in this book I will present an ethical way of reading that is grounded in an understanding of morality that likewise does not fit neatly into any of these categories but seeks a hybrid.

Thus, I agree with McKnight. However, I will suggest that this same data needs to be framed differently. We need to put the em-*pha*-sis on a different syl-*la*-ble, which affects how one understands the whole. Specifically, I will argue that the virtue-ethics approach is not merely one of three beneficial approaches but is the core biblical and human ideal that organizes the others. The virtue-ethics approach (McKnight's ethics from below) focuses on being a certain kind of person, on learning practical wisdom and a way of being in the world that will result in one's flourishing. This approach makes sense of why this inner-person focus is such a consistent theme throughout Scripture and why it is also found in refracted form in so much of philosophy and culture. Ethics/morality is fundamentally and ultimately about us becoming a certain kind of person.

Therefore, flattening all three categories—above, beyond, below—into a nondescript "Jesus has all three approaches" way does not take sufficient account of how the Scriptures themselves (including the Sermon) present morality, nor does it provide enough explanation for how people change and grow. McKnight is right to recognize that the Scriptures teach all three, but I would suggest more strongly that we should understand the structure of the three in a more hierarchical relationship, with virtue ethics as the foundation. Or better, it is best to see these different approaches to ethics as organically related, with the virtue-ethics approach as the core.

What makes the biblical view of ethics different from other virtue-ethics approaches outside of Scripture is that biblical virtue ethics is also "from above" (based on divine revelation) and "from beyond" (based on the hope of the coming eschaton). Thus, McKnight's threefold understanding is essential, while we also need to recognize that there is a structure to how these three aspects of the Scripture's moral teachings fit together. In the remainder of the book I will seek to show that this virtue-ethics approach—framed and modified by these other biblical categories—is the key to understanding Jesus's teaching in the Sermon.

2

Makarios

Macarisms underneath and in the Beatitudes

Introduction: A Track of Two Conceptual Rails

In the previous chapter I argued that the best reading and interpretation of the Sermon on the Mount is found through recognizing its situatedness at the crossroads of the Second Temple Jewish world and the Greco-Roman virtue tradition. In this chapter and the following one, I will argue that this understanding of the Sermon rides on a track of two conceptual rails. Attending to these two concepts demonstrates that my proposed reading of the Sermon is reasonable while providing a conceptual framework to make sense of the Sermon's message overall. Thus, these two rails constitute a track that runs both ways—coming from the past into the Sermon and running through the Sermon to an overall interpretation.

These rails are summed up in two Greek words: *makarios* and *teleios*. They are both transliterated rather than translated here because close examination reveals that there is no good, single gloss in English that communicates the complexity, beauty, and nuance of these weighty words. Even though there are many cultural-encyclopedic issues running in the background when translating a concrete word like "truck" or "banana," the complexities and nuances are orders of magnitude greater when attempting to translate large and abstract concepts such as happiness (≈ *makarios*) and wholeness (≈ *teleios*). Thus, this chapter and the next will explore the nooks and crannies of these words in their encyclopedic context in historical Greek usage, especially in hellenized Second Temple Judaism.

We will discover that these two important concepts do much to explain the Sermon. The overall thematic vision of the Sermon rests on these two pillars—the eschatological and virtue-ethics ideas of *makarios* (typically but unhelpfully translated "blessed") and *teleios* (typically but unhelpfully translated "perfect"). Both of these are central in the Jewish Scriptures and in the Greco-Roman virtue tradition, the very nexus in which the New Testament finds itself. We will begin with *makarios*.

Makarios: A Translation Dilemma

We start with *makarios* because this is how the Sermon begins. After the introductory setup of Matt. 5:1–2, where Jesus ascends to the mountainside and assumes the posture of the teacher, the Sermon proper begins with the famous Beatitudes (5:3–12), a striking series of nine statements that each begin with the Greek word *makarios* (here in the plural form, *makarioi*). These have been called the "Beatitudes" in the English tradition by way of a transliteration of the Latin translation of *makarios*—*beatus*, which means "happy, blissful, fortunate, or flourishing." A more technical literary term than "Beatitudes" is *macarism* (formed also via transliteration). A macarism is a *makarios* statement that ascribes happiness or flourishing to a particular person or state. A macarism is a pronouncement, based on observation, that a certain way of being in the world produces human flourishing and felicity. Macarisms are widespread throughout the ancient world, within Judaism and without.[1] The Sermon begins with a strong series of macarisms.

This much is clear. What is difficult, however, is how to render *makarios* into English. This is not a mere speculative exercise; it has very significant import for how the Beatitudes are interpreted overall. Unfortunately, many commentators do little exploration of this complex issue. Scot McKnight is an exception. He notes both the Jewish and Greek philosophical backgrounds of this word as well as the difficulty of translating it into English. We cannot avoid this matter, however, because as McKnight rightly observes, "on this one word the entire passage stands and from this one word the whole list hangs. Get this word right, the rest falls into place; get it wrong, and the whole thing falls apart."[2]

---

1. See Raymond Collins, "Beatitudes," in *Anchor Bible Dictionary*, ed. David Noel Freedman, 6 vols. (New York: Doubleday, 1992), 1:629–31.

2. Scot McKnight, *The Sermon on the Mount*, The Story of God Bible Commentary (Grand Rapids: Zondervan, 2013), 32.

Typical in English translations of the Bible, the Beatitudes are glossed as "Blessed are . . .": "Blessed are the poor in spirit," "Blessed are the meek," and so forth. Occasionally a translation will deviate from this tradition and use "Happy," but this is rare and somewhat risky from a publishing perspective.[3] Somewhat more frequently, Matthean commentators will explore this word more deeply and suggest something other than "Blessed," but this is also the exception more than the rule.

As noted, the difference between translating the Beatitudes as, for example, "Blessed are the poor in spirit" and "Happy/Flourishing are the poor in spirit" is significant. The first is a statement (in English) that indicates active, divine favor; the second is a macarism, a declared observation about a way of being in the world. To understand the difference between these translation choices and the ensuing confusion, we must turn back to the Hebrew Bible and its influential translation into Greek, the Septuagint (LXX).

ʾAšrê and *Makarios* in the Hebrew Bible and Septuagint[4]

The Old Testament cares about human flourishing. It communicates this in a number of ways and with a number of concepts, the largest of these is probably the idea of *šālôm*.[5] In the Hebrew Bible an important idea that along with *šālôm* communicates human flourishing is the word *ʾašrê*. This will prove to be very important as the background to the Beatitudes. The Hebrew *ʾašrê* is an abstract noun that always occurs as a construct intensive. This means that it is always followed by and connected with the *who* being described as *ʾašrê*: "*ʾašrê* is the one who . . ." Of the forty-five occurrences of *ʾašrê* in the Hebrew Bible, twenty-six are found in the Psalter, eight in Proverbs, and the other eleven are scattered throughout the rest of the canonical books.[6] The etymological

3. My brief survey of various English translations reveals that nearly all render *makarios* as "blessed," probably due to the heavy influence of the King James Version, with but a few exceptions rendering it "Happy," including the Basic Bible in English (1949, 1964), the Common English Bible, Today's English Version, and J. B. Phillips's paraphrase. N. T. Wright's translation (*The Kingdom New Testament* [New York: Harper Collins, 2012]) uses the somewhat ambiguous "Blessings on."
4. The following section is a modified version of my essay "A Biblical Theology of Human Flourishing," the website for the Institute for Faith, Work, and Economics, March 4, 2015, https://tifwe.org/resource/a-biblical-theology-of-human-flourishing-2/.
5. In addition to assorted theological dictionary entries on *šālôm*, see esp. Nicholas Wolterstorff, *Educating for Shalom: Essays on Christian Higher Education*, ed. Clarence W. Joldersma and Gloria Goris Stronks (Grand Rapids: Eerdmans, 2004). We will return to Wolterstorff and the issue of bringing *šālôm* to the earth in chap. 12.
6. There is also a related denominative verb *ʾšr*, meaning "to pronounce happy, call blessed," that occurs nine times. See Waldemar Janzen, "ʾAŠRÊ in the Old Testament," *HTR* 58, no. 2 (1965): 215.

roots of this word have been debated, but they very likely stem from Proto-Semitic and Egyptian roots meaning "prosperity, good luck, and happiness."[7] *'Ašrê* typically occurs in rather formulaic statements, following a pattern of *'ašrê* + descriptive statement + occasional reinforcement or expansion of descriptive statement.[8] Notably, this is the same form that appears in the Beatitudes.

'Ašrê is found especially in the Psalms and Proverbs. It is particularly appropriate there because it is a poetic and wisdom-related word. *'Ašrê* describes the happy state of the one who lives wisely. In this sense it is closely related to *šālôm*.

There is a twofold usage of *'ašrê* in Psalms 1 and 2 that sets the tone for its frequent usage throughout the Psalter: "Blessed/Happy/Flourishing is the man" (1:1); "Blessed/Happy/Flourishing are all who take refuge in him" (2:12b). "These statements serve as a paradigm for the usage of *'ašrê* throughout the book (23x), combining the wisdom and devotional sides of the word, namely obedience to Torah (1:1–3) and reverent worship of the Lord alone (2:10–12)."[9] In the Psalms, the truly happy one is the one whose God is Yahweh (Ps. 33:12), the one who receives from him and honors him.[10] Ellen Charry surveys several psalms to ask how they depict the asheristic life and rightly concludes that in the Psalms the specificity of the Pentateuchal legislation is nowhere in sight. Rather, it is simply summed up as Torah, and the divine commands and ordinances are now described as a "salutary way of life that is summarized as reverence, keeping the commandments, taking refuge in the Lord, being humble, walking in his way, and so on."[11]

Thus, *'ašrê* refers to true happiness and flourishing within the gracious covenant God has given. Like the prophetic literature, the Psalms offer the promise of flourishing and happiness (fertility, prosperity, security) through faithfulness to the Lord, the very things that the wicked promise apart from the Lord. There is a struggle in Israel about which way to live, and the Psalms play an important part in creating the vision of the only path to true flourishing. "Covenantal obedience is the rudder, the compass, the map, and the provision for one's voyage through life."[12]

The other place *'ašrê* regularly occurs is Proverbs, which also makes an appeal to find full human flourishing through wise living. In Proverbs the

---

7. Ibid., 216.
8. Ibid., 218.
9. Michael L. Brown, "אַשְׁרֵי," *NIDOTTE* 1:571.
10. Ibid.
11. Ellen T. Charry, *God and the Art of Happiness* (Grand Rapids: Eerdmans, 2010), 214.
12. Ibid., 215.

'ašrê one is primarily the person who finds wisdom and lives wisely (cf. Prov. 3:13a; 8:32, 34; 14:21; 29:18). This person is naturally extolled as "happy" or "flourishing." Included in this concept is the wisdom of the one who fears the Lord and is therefore blessed (Prov. 16:20; 28:14). Indeed, in Proverbs reverence for the Lord is central to understanding what it means to be wise and therefore 'ašrê. The sages explain and interpret reverence "in terms of practical wisdom that cultivates behavior and character traits that build healthy communities."[13] In this sense it is clearly asheristic; that is, Proverbs promotes a way of being in the world that will result in personal and corporate flourishing.

Rarely is 'ašrê used in the Pentateuch or prophetic literature, where *brk* is more frequent (see below). Notably, the prophetic usage of 'ašrê is almost entirely limited to Isaiah,[14] in which the word is used twice in a way similar to the Psalms: first, in Isa. 30:18 proclaiming the happy state of the person who even in the midst of suffering waits upon and trusts in the Lord; second, in Isa. 32:20 as the summary word to describe the happy state of those who will live and flourish under the coming king who will reign in righteousness (32:1–8), the very context where *šālôm* also occurs with great import.

Continuing in the tradition beyond the Hebrew Bible, we can note that in rabbinic usage 'ašrê follows the pattern of the Psalms and Proverbs, "in particular the wisdom emphasis on the truly happy state of the Torah-keeping life."[15] The idea continues to be an appeal to human flourishing through orientation to God's revelation.

When we turn to the New Testament, we see that this same idea continues with the Greek equivalent to 'ašrê, the word *makarios*. As with any Greek word in the New Testament, there is a dual context: the Greco-Roman usage of the first century and the long-standing and extremely influential Greek translation of the Hebrew Bible, the Septuagint (LXX). To understand how a Greek term or concept is used in the New Testament, one must recognize that not only the normal daily usage of the speaker is at play but also the deep and prominent influence of the Jewish heritage as manifested in the Septuagint.[16]

13. Ibid., 218.

14. The only other occurrence of 'ašrê in the prophetic literature of the Hebrew Bible is in the later eschatological passage of Dan. 12:12.

15. Brown, "אַשְׁרֵי," 572.

16. For more on the influence of the Septuagint, see Tessa Rajak, *Translation and Survival: The Greek Bible of the Ancient Jewish Diaspora* (New York: Oxford University Press, 2009), 1–23. For concise discussion of the various ways the Septuagint has influenced the New Testament, see Karen H. Jobes and Moisés Silva, *Invitation to the Septuagint* (Grand Rapids: Baker Academic, 2000), 19–26. For a more detailed treatment, see Natalio Fernández Marcos, *The Septuagint in Context: Introduction to the Greek Versions of the Bible* (Leiden: Brill, 2000), 303–62.

When one considers this dual context for the frequent occurrence of *makarios* in the New Testament, we see how the *'ašrê* (and *šālôm*) tradition of human flourishing continues. The continuation is striking in two ways. First, the translational relationship between *'ašrê* and *makarios* is quite exceptional. That is, very rarely in the Septuagint translation of the Hebrew Bible does one find a close one-to-one correspondence of terms and ideas. Typically a gloss is found that works, but quite a bit of variation naturally occurs. That is, a Hebrew word is usually rendered with a variety of Greek words across the vast expanse of time and genres that the Hebrew Bible represents; a consistent, one-to-one translation equivalent is unexpected and uncommon. Notably, however, *'ašrê* in the Septuagint is always rendered as *makarios*.[17] Apparently this is because the two terms and concepts overlap with little remainder. This striking correspondence gives us great reason to believe that the Greek Bible's *makarios* communicates the same idea of human flourishing and well-being as *'ašrê*.

The other striking thing about this relationship and the other part of the dual context of the Greek word *makarios* is the first-century Greco-Roman context. In Classical Greek, *makar* is a common word referring first to the state of the gods and secondarily to human beings who live a life of happiness like that of the gods, meaning their lives are beyond care, labor, and death. Very importantly for our understanding, *makarios* is often used as a synonym for the essential Greek philosophical term *eudaimonia* (especially important for Aristotle, as mentioned in the previous chapter), which connotes inner happiness and satisfaction, the state of the truly good life or human flourishing.[18] This corresponds precisely with what we have already seen as the usage of *'ašrê* in the Hebrew Bible. In Second Temple Jewish literature composed in Greek (including parts of the Septuagint that do not have corresponding Hebrew writings), *makarios* clearly refers to human

17. Janzen, "'AŠRÊ in the Old Testament," 216. K. C. Hanson agrees: "That *'ašrê* and μακάριος are equivalents is established by their one-to-one correspondence in the LXX's translation of the MT" ("How Honorable! How Shameful! A Cultural Analysis of Matthew's Makarisms and Reproach," *Semeia* 68 [1995]: 88). In two instances the translator of Proverbs (14:21; 16:20) uses the related adjective *makaristos* instead of *makarios*, but this in no way undermines the significance of the unusually strong correspondence between *'ašrê* and *makarios*. The conceptual overlap between these word groups is further strengthened by the way the LXX handles the verb forms. Only twice does the LXX not use *makarizein* for *'ašrê*. In Prov. 3:18 the translator uses *asphalēs*, "firm, steadfast," and in Prov. 31:28 *ploutizein*, "to flourish financially."

18. Friedrich Hauck, "μακάριος, μακαρίζω, μακαρισμός," *TDNT* 4:362–63. Ulrich Luz concurs, stating that in Koine Greek one can hardly distinguish *makarios* from *eudaimonia*, both of which mean "happy" in the fullest sense of the word (*Matthew 1–7: A Commentary*, rev. ed., trans. James E. Crouch, Hermeneia [Minneapolis: Fortress, 2007], 190).

flourishing or fullness of earthly life. One is *makarios* who has a wife (Sir. 25:8; 26:1), children (Gen. 30:13; Ps. 127:5; Sir. 25:7; 4 Macc. 16:9; 18:9), beauty (Song 6:9), earthly well-being, riches, honor, wisdom (Job 29:10, 11; cf. Isa. 32:20).[19]

All of this provides the essential background to understand the occurrences of *makarios* in the Sermon. In light of the previous discussion of the meaning of *'ašrê* and its direct translation into *makarios*, it becomes clear that something other than a pronouncement of divine blessing is at hand. Rather, continuing in the *'ašrê* wisdom tradition, Jesus begins his public ministry by painting a picture of what the state of true God-centered human flourishing looks like. He is making an appeal and casting an inspiring vision, even as the Psalms, Proverbs, and Isaiah do, for what true well-being looks like in God's coming kingdom.[20] At the same time, this is understood in the context of the Greek philosophical tradition with its appeal to flourishing and happiness. As Scot McKnight notes in his discussion of the Beatitudes, "the entire history of the philosophy of the 'good life' and the late modern theory of 'happiness' is at work when one says, 'Blessed are. . . .'"[21]

Human Flourishing as *'Ašrê / Makarios* through *Brk*

There is a specific reason that I have continued to use the transliterated *'ašrê* and *makarios* rather than translate them into English. Even though both words are regularly translated with the English gloss "bless," this is problematic because it perpetuates the confusion between *'ašrê* and another word translated as "bless," *brk*. The result is the obfuscation of the sense of human flourishing that *'ašrê* and *makarios* communicate.

We may return to the discussion of how *'ašrê* is consistently translated into Greek with *makarios*. Typically both of these words come into English as "blessed." The problem is that there is another, distinct Hebrew and Greek word pair that *also* gets regularly translated into English as "blessed" or "bless." This is the frequently occurring Hebrew word *brk/bərākâ* and its

19. Georg Bertram, "μακάριος, μακαρίζω, μακαρισμός," *TDNT* 4:364–67.

20. Proverbs 3:13 in the LXX is an example of a verse that shows that macarisms are primarily wisdom literature, used here in conjunction with two other clearly Greek wisdom terms, *sophia* and *phronēsis*: *makarios anthrōpos hos heuren sophian kai thnētos hos eiden phronēsin* (flourishing is the one who finds understanding and sees/obtains [practical] wisdom).

21. McKnight, *Sermon on the Mount*, 32. For an expansion of this view, see R. T. France, *The Gospel of Matthew*, NICNT (Grand Rapids: Eerdmans, 2007), 160–61, where he titles his discussion of the Beatitudes "The Good Life."

regular Septuagint Greek gloss, *eulogeō/eulogētos*. The result is rampant confusion between these two distinct word groups.

The Hebrew root *brk* occurs 327 times as a verb and another 71 times as a noun in the Hebrew Bible. It is spread throughout most of the Old Testament but is highly concentrated in the Pentateuch (especially Genesis and Deuteronomy, which account for 25 percent of the Old Testament occurrences)[22] and Psalms in passages that deal with the patriarchs, the divine blessings and curses on nations, the covenants, and worship of the Lord.[23] By means of *brk* God actively gives and enables his word to go forth, resulting in benefits such as fertility, authority, peace, and rest.[24] Blessings and their negative counterpart, curses, are formal pronouncements by someone in authority, either from God directly or from an authorized mediator: usually a king, priest, or clan patriarch.[25] Such blessings from God are bestowed and received in the context of relationships, the most significant of which in the Hebrew Bible is God's relationship with Abraham (wherein "bless" is frequently used). Blessing and its corresponding negative, cursing, are also connected with two symbolic mountains (Deut. 11:26–32): Mount Ebal (curses) and Mount Gerizim (blessings).[26] What makes a blessing a blessing is God's relationship with and favorable attitude toward a person or group of people; the benefit (or the "blessing") is secondary to the relationship.[27]

For our purposes, we can make a crucial observation in comparing *brk* and *'ašrê*. Like *brk*, *'ašrê* is often used with the same recipients as the word *brk*: to describe descendants, fields and flocks, and security from enemies. This helps us see the organic relationship between *brk* and *'ašrê*, namely, that "receipt of that which blessing [*brk*] has to bestow qualifies a person or group to be called *'ašrê*."[28]

But, very importantly, *this does not mean that the two words are synonymous, nor should they be glossed the same way*. That is, there is a basic and significant distinction maintained between the (verb) "blessing," which is an

22. James McKeown, "Blessings and Cursings," in *Dictionary of the Old Testament: Pentateuch*, ed. T. D. Alexander and David W. Baker (Downers Grove, IL: InterVarsity, 2003), 83.

23. The preceding data all come from Robert Gordon, "ברך," *NIDOTTE* 1:757–58.

24. McKeown, "Blessings and Cursings," 83–87.

25. Hanson, "How Honorable! How Shameful!," 85–86. The clearest example of a priestly blessing is the Aaronic blessing of Num. 6:22–27. Cf. 1QS 2:1–10, where this blessing is coupled with the Levitical curse on the wicked.

26. McKeown, "Blessings and Cursings," 85.

27. Christopher Wright Mitchell, *The Meaning of* BRK *"To Bless" in the Old Testament*, SBLDS 95 (Atlanta: Society of Biblical Literature, 1987), 165–67.

28. Janzen, "'AŠRÊ in the Old Testament," 223. Mitchell describes it this way: possession of blessing (*brk*) is the prerequisite for being *'ašrê* (*Meaning of* BRK, 103). Psalm 144:12–15 provides a good example of the two ideas overlapping.

active word and whose subject is typically God, and the state of those who receive this blessing or flourishing, described as the *'ašrê* person. The one who pronounces an asherism (or macarism), such as in Ps. 1 ("How happy is the one . . .") is not "blessing" others in the *brk* sense of initiating, effecting, or inaugurating favor. Rather, *'ašrê* is an exclamatory description of the state of happiness, privilege, or fortune that is upon someone as observed by someone else, a bystander, *not* the one providing or initiating the blessing. Asherisms/macarisms are not "words of power" or statements about God actively favoring someone; they do not occur in ritual settings, and one never prays for a macarism/asherism nor refers to oneself as *'ašrê*.[29]

Again, *'ašrê* and *brk* are not synonymous. "*'Ašrê* stresses a state of happiness, while *brk*, though not excluding such a state, in keeping with its passive participial form speaks more of being empowered or favored as the recipient of blessing from the Lord, and thus 'blessed.'"[30] God is spoken of as being *brk* but never as *'ašrê* (even as he alone is *eulogētos* in the New Testament).[31]

Proclaiming an asherism or macarism is to make a *value judgment* upon another member of the community's behavior and commitments. Asherisms "articulate the values of the community, sage, or teacher and pronounce the subject(s) 'honorable.'"[32] They have an implied hortatory function; the implication is that "if one wishes to join the ranks of the happy, one should emulate their virtuous conduct or attitudes."[33] Macarisms don't generally describe actions but rather people who are in a certain state.[34] To restate the important point, *'ašrê/makarios* is the key biblical term to describe one in a state of human flourishing, and this should not be confused with the divine action of blessing, God actively causing human flourishing. Asherisms/macarisms are wisdom literature; blessings are covenantal language. We can illustrate this important relationship between *'ašrê/makarios* and *brk/eulogētos* in this way:

29. Hanson, "How Honorable! How Shameful!," 89.

30. Gordon, "ברך," 763.

31. Only in 1 Timothy (2x) is the Greek equivalent (see below) *makarios* used for God, but this is clearly the exception, not the rule, and likely reflects later usage. *Pace* D. A. Carson ("Matthew," in *The Expositor's Bible Commentary*, rev. ed., 13 vols., ed. Tremper Longman III and David E. Garland [Grand Rapids: Zondervan, 2010], 1:161), this singular biblical occurrence does not suggest that there is no distinction between *'ašrê/makarios* and *brk/eulogētos*. The evidence is overwhelmingly in the other direction.

32. Hansen, "How Honorable! How Shameful!," 92.

33. David E. Garland, "Blessing and Woe," *DJG*, 78.

34. Ceslas Spicq, "*makarios*," *TLNT* 2:441. Spicq gives an illustration of this principle—it is "not poverty as such that is blessed, but the poor; and poverty is not a matter of possessing nothing but of being detached from everything."

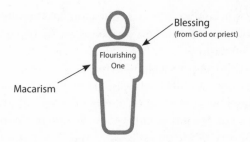

Confusion over the distinction between *'ašrê/makarios* and *brk/eulogētos* contributes to the failure to see that the former pair of terms communicates the idea of human flourishing and well-being. Herein lies the great problem of translating all of these terms with the same expression "blessed." *The English term "blessed" is so heavily loaded with the narrower sense of "divine favor" that the sense of human flourishing is almost always lost.*[35]

The reality that *'ašrê/makarios* is about human flourishing is precisely what creates the translation problem. We could say, then, that the solution is simply to come up with a gloss for these words that communicates this distinction. But the problem is exacerbated in that biblically there is in fact a close relationship between the two concepts even though they must also remain distinct: One can only flourish fully as a human when one is in a covenantal relationship with the creator God, which includes both ancient notions of what it means to flourish *and* a necessary orientation to God's revelation.

Thus, when the Psalms speak of the *'ašrê* state of the one who meditates on Torah (God's covenantal instructions), such as in Ps. 119, this is simultaneously a claim that this God-oriented person is in a state of flourishing *precisely because* he or she is experiencing the most direct means of grace that God has ordained to effect favor upon his people—meditation on God's self-revelation, or in short, knowing God. So, there is an inevitable, organic relationship between human flourishing and God's favor or blessing.

But, crucially, we must understand that despite this organic relationship, there is an important distinction. *'Ašrê* refers to the state of human flourishing in general (most fully but not exclusively in relationship with God),

---

35. It is not entirely clear whether earlier English speakers could have distinguished between "bléssed" and "blesséd," the latter an adjective more specifically referring to the state of "blessedness" rather than the action (and result) of a blessing from God. The morphological ambiguity of "blessed" as either a verb or an adjective in current English makes such a potential distinction almost certainly lost except on very few speakers. There was for a time in English a –*t* verbal ending form ("blest") that would have maintained the distinction, but aside from occasional poetic uses, this form has died out, especially in American English.

while *brk* speaks of God's effectual favor upon his creatures. And when we translate both of these with "bless" or "blessed" we collapse, conflate, and confuse this distinction.

I suggest that this creates a significant problem in many cases. A good example is in the foundational Ps. 1, which is an important *'ašrê* psalm. What is this foundational, wisdom-oriented First Psalm saying? An English reading (or even a Hebrew reading that fails to see the difference between *'ašrê* and *brk*) begins, "Blessed is the one who . . ." and communicates thus—"The person who delights in God's revelatory word and walks in the way revealed by God's word receives God's favor."

Unfortunately, many if not most readers will interpret this to mean, "If you do this (read the Bible), God will bless you." The more theologically attuned and sophisticated readers will immediately recognize the problem with this overly mechanistic reading and will need to provide an important qualification such as this—"It's not exactly that if we do X that God will respond and bless us, but rather that God is gracious in giving us the desire to read his Word and then blesses us with more favor and grace on top of what he already gave. It is all of God's grace. The desire to be blessed and the blessing all come from God." (Similar arguments are made about the Beatitudes, as we will see.)

I don't disagree with this more careful theological reading in a fundamental and overarching way. Holy Scripture teaches clearly that all flourishing is a gift from God and that he gives grace upon grace to his creatures. However, this theologically accurate statement is a fundamentally mistaken reading of what Ps. 1 is actually saying, and this misunderstanding is what creates the need for this complicated, convoluted explanation. Rather, a closer examination of *'ašrê* and *brk* makes clear that this whole reading is a self-inflicted dilemma and one that also makes readers miss what is actually being proclaimed.

Specifically, Ps. 1 is not making a claim about God's favor ("blessing" or *brk*) at all. Rather, it is an inspirational vision for the wise way of being in the world that will result in what all humans desire—human flourishing. It is a poetically crafted form of *implicit invitation* to consider what the best way of being in the world is and to pursue it. Psalm 1 is a wisdom psalm that has long played a central role in the canon.[36] It is like all the Wisdom literature, such as the book of Proverbs—a vision of human flourishing

36. In addition to being the intentional heading to the Psalter, from earliest Christianity Ps. 1 was seen as central. For example, Jerome stated that the main entrance to the mansion of the Psalter is the First Psalm, and Gregory of Nyssa wrote that the Psalter is arranged sequentially according to the logic of virtue, beginning with Ps. 1. These references come from Stephen J.

that is meant to effect change in people's lives by inspiring them to the good and the benefits that come from living a certain way. Psalm 1 is casting just such a powerful vision in saying "'Ašrê/makarios is the person . . ."—that is, "flourishing, fortunate, happy" is the one who doesn't go along the path of the wicked (cf. Proverbs) but instead focuses on God's revelation to guide him or her (vv. 1–2).

But the vision doesn't stop there; it provides a very vivid, future-oriented mental picture of what the consequences for one's quality (and quantity) of life will be based on how one chooses to live. The wise one who chooses God's revelation as his or her orientation rather than the paths of the wicked (note this wisdom imagery as well) will flourish like a well-watered tree (Could there be an image of human flourishing better than a fruit-bearing tree?), while the wicked ones will face judgment, rejection, and, to continue the metaphor, will not be rooted and fruit bearing like a tree but will be mere wind-blown, insignificant chaff (vv. 3–6). (The connections with the Sermon are remarkable.)

This is all a powerful, imaginative call *to be a certain way in the world* not just because God demands it,[37] nor out of Kantian altruism (it's the right thing to do and that's enough), nor out of a mechanistic tit-for-tat view of God (if you read your Bible and don't hang around with bad people, then God will bless you). But rather, this is based on the appeal to human flourishing for one's own sake.[38] Would you rather be a fruit-bearing tree or rejected chaff? Would you rather flourish (be happy, that is, 'ašrê) or face judgment? The answer is obvious, and thus the wise person will avoid the deceptive company of the wicked and instead orient his or her life around God's revelation. This is just like all other wisdom literature, biblical and extrabiblical: it is an appeal to one's own natural and good sense to pursue happiness. Yes, we might call this

---

Harris, "Happiness and the Psalms," in *Old English Literature and the Old Testament*, ed. Michael Fox and Manish Sharma (Toronto: University of Toronto Press, 2012), 301.

37. In *God and the Art of Happiness*, Ellen Charry has a fascinating discussion of the difference between "voluntarist" and "asherist" divine commands. The former are "single-occurrence or rarely occurring punctiliar orders that test obedience," while the latter are "guidelines that commend an ongoing way of life." She observes that while there are occasional voluntarist commands of God in the Bible, these are relatively rare; rather, most divine commands make an appeal to us via the evident personal and communal well-being that will result (170). Most biblical commands are based on wisdom appeals to what will result in our flourishing.

38. Note Charry's discussion of Joseph Butler's thoughtful arguments that this is the right sense of self-love (ibid., 132–53). In part this was the genius of John Piper's argument in *Desiring God: Meditations of a Christian Hedonist* (Portland, OR: Multnomah, 1986), which originally emphasized the idea of "Christian hedonism," or pleasing one's own greatest desires by desiring God above all else.

at the end of the day a kind of "blessedness," but I think that the translation of "blessed" more often than not causes confusion about what the basis of the appeal and argument is.

Thus, while it is important to realize that *'ašrê/makarios* casts a vision of human flourishing, it is equally important to see that this flourishing can never fully occur apart from a proper relationship with the creator God. All of the Bible's vision of human flourishing both now and in the age to come either assumes or explicitly states this fact. Recall the diagram of the relationship between *'ašrê/makarios* and *brk/eulogētos*:

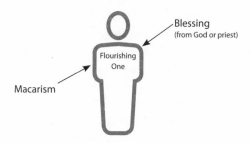

Blessings (and the corresponding negative, curses) are divine, effectual speech.[39] Macarisms (and the corresponding negative, woes)[40] are human, descriptive speech. Even though in a covenantal and theological context these are related, it is important to recognize the distinction. It is problematic if we treat macarisms and woes as promises and prohibitions, as blessings and curses, because this is not how they function in the divine economy. Macarisms and woes are invitations to living based on sapiential reflections, not divine speech of reward and cursing. This is in a sense a genre issue.[41] Even as we should not take proverbs as promises, so we must recognize the sapiential

---

39. A fascinating and comprehensive study of curses in the ancient Near East is found in Anne Marie Kitz, *Cursed Are You! The Phenomenology of Cursing in Cuneiform and Hebrew Texts* (Winona Lake, IN: Eisenbrauns, 2014). Kitz states that curses, like blessings, were not magic or superstitions, nor mere curiosities or trifles, but instead "were real and effective" (3).

40. In addition to the entries on "woes" in the assorted theological dictionaries, one may consult the somewhat dated but still helpful debate on the nature of woes in David Garland, *The Intention of Matthew 23*, SNTSMS 52 (Leiden: Brill, 1979), 64–90. Unfortunately, Garland did not see the connection between macarisms and woes, which would have strengthened the argument that woes are not maledictions but statements that imply sorrow and pity and an inherent invitation to repent.

41. Ceslas Spicq points out that macarisms are a way to frame exhortations to virtue and that this is a particularly OT habit. He goes on to say that "the biblical beatitude fits into the wisdom genre." He also observes that woes are not curses or maledictions, but a declaration of misfortune (*TLNT* 2:435n14).

nature of macarisms. They are sapiential invitations to the kind of life that will experience flourishing. To the extent that this wisdom is informed by God's law and covenant, the more fully it will align with reality. But we must not confuse the genre of a macarism with that of a promise or the giving of a blessing.

I have argued for the importance of keeping *brk* and *'ašrê* distinct conceptually and translationally. In the case of *brk* it seems that "bless" still works as a good English gloss, especially when describing God's activity in the world.[42] Likewise, the negative counterpart, "curse," is clear enough as a translation choice. On the other side of the ledger, "woe" works sufficiently as the negative counterpart of a macarism, though for some readers today it may not communicate much. However, the main idea under discussion here, *makarios*, proves perpetually difficult to translate into English.

Within Old Testament scholarship, this question does not seem to arise very frequently, and most English translations of texts like Ps. 1 continue the confusion of translating *'ašrê* as "blessed" and *brk* as "bless." In the New Testament, the question arises slightly more often because of the importance of the Beatitudes. There we find scholars occasionally wrestling with translation options for *makarios*. Some offerings include "happy," "fortunate," "how honorable," "congratulations," "wonderful news," "privileged," "Oh, the happiness!" My own choice, and what will be followed in this book, is "flourishing," even though I realize it is imperfect as well. As with all translation choices, there are pros and cons to a number of viable candidates. Each potential gloss highlights some aspect while de-emphasizing others.

Makarios-ness in Matthew and the Sermon

This survey of the concept of biblical macarisms has already cast rays of insight toward our interpretation of the Beatitudes; they are Jesus's macarisms, declaring with authority what is the true way of being that will result in happiness and human flourishing. They are Jesus's answer to the universal philosophical and religious question, how can one be truly happy? All of this will be revisited in the exposition of Matt. 5:3–12 in a subsequent chapter.

To round out our discussion of *makarios* it remains for us only to verify this understanding by a brief examination of its usage in Matthew more broadly, followed by some comments about how this idea frames and enlightens the Sermon overall.

42. When used in the sense of humans "blessing" God, I think most English speakers will remain perplexed by this odd, unclear usage.

Makarios *in Matthew*

Makarios occurs thirteen times in the Greek text of Matthew, out of a total number of fifty occurrences in the New Testament.[43] No other forms of the *makar* root occur in Matthew, though the verb form does appear two times elsewhere in the New Testament and the noun form three times.[44] By way of comparison, the distinct word for "bless" (Gk. *eulogeō*; cf. Heb. *brk*), which means something like "praise" or "give thanks to" or "honor," is found five times in Matthew.[45] The corresponding negative counterpart to a macarism, a "woe" (*ouai*), is found thirteen times in Matthew, most of which are in the Beatitudes-balancing woes of Matt. 23.[46]

The first thing to note about Matthew's uses of *makarios* stems from this last comment. In light of what a macarism is as opposed to a blessing, it is important to recall that what one expects in contrast to a macarism is not a curse but a woe. A woe (*ouai*)[47] is the opposite of a macarism in that it describes the result of a way of being in the world that does *not* result in flourishing but in loss, grief, and destruction. The Beatitudes (macarisms) in Luke 6:20–23 are part of a more expected pattern, being followed immediately by a comparable set of woes (6:24–26). Matthew has also chosen to give a set of woes to correspond with his macarisms, but he does so outside of the Sermon, in Jesus's climactic conflict with the Pharisees (Matt. 23:1–36).[48] This separation (for whatever literary and theological reasons) does not make his macarisms and woes any less of a literary pair. Matthew's Beatitudes lead off Jesus's teaching ministry, and the woes Jesus casts upon his opponents (whose lives are living testimony to the *opposite* of what he teaches in the Sermon) form a bookend with his final week of teaching.[49]

43. Matt. 5:3, 4, 5, 6, 7, 8, 9, 10, 11; 11:6; 13:16; 16:17; 24:46. The only NT book that contains more occurrences is the Gospel of Luke, with fifteen.

44. The verb *makarizō* means "to consider someone happy or flourishing" and is found only in Luke 1:48 and James 5:11. The noun *makarismos*, describing the state of happiness, occurs in Rom. 4:6, 9 and Gal. 4:15.

45. Matt. 14:19; 21:9; 23:39; 25:34; 26:26.

46. Matt. 11:21 (2x); 18:7 (2x); 23:13, 15, 16, 23, 25, 27, 29; 24:19; 26:24.

47. This word is rarely found in Greek outside of the Bible. It is a transliteration of the Hebrew *'ôy, hôy*, a kind of onomatopoeia, a cry of pain or distress, or a declaration of misfortune. The best translations into English are "Alas," "Ah," or "Woe." See Spicq, *TLNT* 2:442–44.

48. K. C. Hanson provides a helpful chart that shows the many parallels in wording between the macarisms of the Beatitudes and the woes of Matt. 23, including "theirs is the kingdom of heaven" (5:3, 10) / "you shut the kingdom of heaven" (23:13); "merciful . . . receive mercy" (5:7) / "neglected mercy" (23:23); "sons of God" (5:9) / "son of Gehenna" (23:15); and "so they persecuted the prophets" (5:12) / "sons of those who killed the prophets" (23:31) ("How Honorable! How Shameful!," 102).

49. On the debate concerning whether this means Matthew's fifth major discourse begins in Matt. 23 or 24, see chap. 5 in this book on the structure of the Sermon.

Outside of the macarisms in the Beatitudes (which will be dealt with in the exposition of that text), Matthew has four other ascriptions of *makarios*-ness. The next occurrence after the Beatitudes is in Matt. 11:6, where Jesus offers the aphoristic saying that the person who is not *scandalized* on account of him is *makarios*. The immediate context is the report of John the Baptist's imprisonment and his disciples' query about Jesus (11:2–6). Jesus responds by cataloging all the works he is doing and then offers this macarism. In light of how this word is consistently used, we can understand that this is once again a description of the kind of person who will flourish, not a promise that God will (actively) bless the person in question here. The *makarios* one is the person who is not offended at the arrival and behavior of Jesus. Notice also that in contrast to the *makarios* one at the beginning of Matt. 11 is the pronouncement of a *woe* upon those who *don't* respond positively to Jesus's miracles. In 11:21 Jesus pronounces woes upon Chorazin and Bethsaida for seeing the mighty deeds of Jesus (which were catalogued in 11:5) and not responding in faith. This is the opposite of being a *makarios* one a few verses earlier.

The next occurrence is in 13:16, in the midst of Jesus's Isaianically inspired explanation as to why he is teaching with vague and esoteric parables (13:10–17). Jesus contrasts unbelievers with believers. The eyes and ears and heart are metonyms for a certain kind of person, either a dull and closed person or one who is open to God's revelation. Again, there is no promise of blessing to those who have open ears and clear eyes; the whole point of the explanation is that some are given this and others are not (cf. 11:25–30). Jesus is saying that the person who *does* see and hear and listen and obey is the one who can be described as *makarios*, as experiencing true and full life, because of that person's alignment with Jesus's teaching.

Closely related is the next usage, in 16:17. As with the parabolic discourse in Matt. 13, the context is the discussion of God revealing himself to people *so that* they are able to understand, because mere human faculties are incapable of comprehending and receiving the mysterious realities of God (cf. 1 Cor. 2:6–16, which also uses Isaiah). Jesus proclaims that Simon Peter is *makarios* for being the recipient of God's revelation. We can acknowledge that while "Flourishing are you . . ." is a bit clunky of a translation, it does at least describe the function of *makarios* here, which is not a blessing. Jesus does not pronounce a blessing on Peter for having this revelation. He is saying that Peter's ability to see *is* the state of flourishing, or, if you will, "blessedness." It is an ascription, not a promise or blessing. This text is a prime example of the nuance necessary to understand the *makarios*/*eulogētos* relationship.

Jesus is not pronouncing or effecting a *blessing* on Peter, but he is declaring that the state of flourishing is upon those who are the recipients of God's ultimate blessing, the revelation of himself. Thus the ideas overlap, but we must not collapse the former into the latter.

Finally, the same sense comes across in 24:46, where Jesus describes as *makarios* the good and wise servant in the parable who is found to be faithful when the Lord returns. The faithful follower of Jesus will experience abundance of life and flourishing as a result of his or her wisdom. Interestingly, this *makarios* person is described with a term that also richly evokes the Greek virtue tradition. This faithful *makarios* person is called *phronimos*, or a wise one.[50] This is another key indicator that we are trafficking in the language and concepts of virtue and human flourishing, as *phronimos* is the Greek term used to describe the one who has learned and practiced wisdom over time through virtuous choices, resulting in true happiness. Further along this line of thinking, we can also note that Matthew has a propensity to use the negative counterpart to the *phronimos* one, the *mōros*, or foolish one. Six of the twelve New Testament occurrences of this term are in Matthew, usually paired as a foil with *phronimos*.[51] The significance of all this is deepened when one recalls that the contrast between the wise one and the fool is precisely the image used to conclude the Sermon (7:24–27),[52] rounding out the subject with the macarisms at the beginning (5:3–12).

Note that these other Matthean occurrences are very good examples of the nuanced view that we need to gain concerning the meaning and sense of *makarios*. Specifically, the point is that *makarios* statements are proclamations of a state of flourishing, not pronouncements of what to do and be to enjoy God's favor.[53] However, from the biblical perspective (and within the divine economy) there is no way to be ultimately *makarios* apart from God's blessing. Nevertheless, we lose a crucial and deep understanding of what redemption is about if we collapse *makarios* into divine favor.

50. This important term in Greek moral philosophy does not occur very frequently in the NT (14 times), but is apparently a Matthean favorite, with seven instances in that Gospel (7:24; 10:16; 24:45; 25:2, 4, 8, 9).

51. Matt. 5:22; 7:26; 23:17; 25:2, 3, 8. Notably, the other NT occurrences are found in strongly Greek cultural contexts, where this language was a common part of the virtue discussion (esp. 1 Cor. 1:25, 27; 3:18; 4:10).

52. See the helpful discussion of the Hellenistic context for this in Hans Dieter Betz, "The Sermon on the Mount (Matt. 5:3–7:27): Its Literary Genre and Function," in *Essays on the Sermon on the Mount* (1985; Minneapolis: Fortress, 2009), 6–7.

53. W. J. Dumbrell notes that all of Matthew's uses of *makarios* "are entirely consistent with the Old Testament background" that distinguishes between *brk* and *'ašrê* ("The Logic of the Role of the Law in Matthew 5:1–20," *NovT* 23, no. 1 [1981]: 8n25).

Contemporary Categories for Interpreting the Macarisms of the Beatitudes

The question of how to gloss *makarios* is important, but more significant is, of course, how we *interpret* or read the meaning of this expression in its context of Jesus's teachings, the Sermon, Matthew's Gospel, and the whole biblical canon.

It will be helpful to consider how an assortment of interpreters have both glossed and spoken about the meaning of the Beatitudes, specifically querying how sensitive they are to the sense of human flourishing that I have argued for. The principle at work here is that the gloss we choose both reflects and affects how we understand the Beatitudes, the Sermon, and even God's way of relating to his creatures. Each gloss is a metaphor that provides the frame of reference for the text, guiding what questions we ask and what answers we discover.

In general there are three main ways that contemporary interpreters have articulated an understanding of what is going on with the Beatitudes, some-times combining elements of these three. Each of these reflect and affect attention to the *makarios* issue, or lack thereof.

1. God's favor
2. Eschatological reversal blessings
3. Wisdom or virtue-ethics reading

"BLESSED" AS GOD'S FAVOR

In terms of glossing Jesus's Sermon macarisms, many commentators, re-gardless of what they say about the meaning, still continue to render the Beatitudes with the translation of "Blessed be . . ." These include Robert Gundry, Douglas Hare, Charles Quarles, Scot McKnight, D. A. Carson, David Turner, Frederick Bruner, Michael Wilkins, Grant Osborne,[54] J. Knox Cham-blin, and others, let alone the vast majority of English translations of the Bible. Of course, our English title for this section of "Beatitudes" comes from the Latin *beatus*, which means "happy or blissful," not "blessed" in the English sense, yet one will sometimes find commentators who mention *beatus* and then gloss it in English with "blessed."

---

54. Osborne has the slight variation of "God blesses . . . ," which is not entirely different from "Blessed are those . . . ," with the latter instinctively understood as a divine passive. Indeed, it makes the mistaken understanding most explicit. At the same time, Osborne does note that making a hard distinction between the Beatitudes as ethics and the Beatitudes as eschatological blessings (like Robert Guelich does) is too disjunctive because the Beatitudes are both moral mandate and promised reward (Osborne, *Matthew*, ZECNT 1 [Grand Rapids: Zondervan, 2012], 162n16).

Not all of these same people understand *makarios* as being about God's favor, but many do. This reading comes from failing to understand what I have been articulating, that there is an important distinction between *brk* and *'ašrê*. For many of these interpreters (if they follow the logical implications at all), especially the Protestants, this necessitates a kind of explanation similar to the one that I gave of Ps. 1 above—that while these Beatitudes speak of God's favor or blessing, this is not to be understood in a legalistic way of us earning God's favor but rather of God working these same things in us by grace or by the Spirit.

Charles Quarles's commentary on the Sermon is a good example. He is careful to observe that the Beatitudes are not entrance requirements, but rather they "define the character and conduct of those whom God has already claimed as his children. They describe the holy life that necessarily results from genuine salvation." The Beatitudes are pronouncements of divine blessing and describe "those to whom Jesus spoke as privileged recipients of God's favor."[55] The point seems to be that salvation as a gift/blessing *results* in these characteristics.

David Turner shows this same approach by reading *makarios* as divine favor. "The Beatitudes reveal key character traits that God approves in his people. These character traits are gracious gifts indicating God's approval, not requirements for works that merit God's approval. Those who repent receive these character traits in principle but must cultivate them in the process of discipleship."[56]

Not all interpreters work through the details or implications of this, but the few who do must face the question of how the two parts of these macarisms fit together. That is, we must wrestle with the syntactical issue of the protasis and apodosis of these statements.[57] What is the relationship between the two parts of "Blessed be . . ." and the "for theirs is the kingdom of heaven" or "for they will be comforted"?[58] In a God's favor/blessing reading, the interpretation is precisely what creates the dilemma of the grace reading. That is, if one understands the macarism as a statement about what God favors in the protasis ("Blessed is the one . . ." or "God blesses the one . . ."), then the apodosis naturally gives the reason or grounds for this. But if one reflects on

55. Charles L. Quarles, *Sermon on the Mount: Restoring Christ's Message to the Modern Church* (Nashville: B&H, 2011), 40–42.

56. David Turner, *Matthew*, BECNT (Grand Rapids: Baker Academic, 2008), 147.

57. I will use the terms *protasis* and *apodosis* to describe the two parts of a macarism, even though these are typically used with respect to "if-then" conditional statements. The protasis is the first half (beginning with *makarios*), and the apodosis is the second half (beginning with "because").

58. I will revisit this issue in the exposition of the Beatitudes in chap. 5 below.

this syntactical relationship, it becomes patently clear that this doesn't work and is precisely the problem. Paraphrasing—"God blesses the poor in spirit because they are part of the kingdom of heaven," or maybe "If you are poor in spirit you are blessed because you are part of the kingdom of heaven." "Blessed are those who mourn because they will be comforted," or "If you mourn you are blessed because you will be comforted." We can understand these renderings in part, and we are probably used to hearing them this way. But if one stops and asks what such a translation is really saying, the result is confusion. On the one hand, it could be understood legalistically, with a mechanistic, tit-for-tat view of God—if you are/do X then God will favor you and give you something else as well. On the other hand, these statements are just declarations of fact—if you mourn, are pure in heart, or hunger and thirst for righteousness, then you can take heart, you will have your needs met. Thus, at worst these are to be read in a mechanistic way (which most would avoid), or they are merely words of encouragement that things will work out. Neither understands the nature and function of a macarism.

Eschatological Reversal Blessings

Probably much more common now among scholars is the understanding that the Beatitudes are pictures of the blessing of a reversal of fortune that Jesus is promising and will bring about in the eschaton. Many have rightly observed that the primary subtext of the Beatitudes is Isa. 61 (also with the influence of several psalms), which does indeed greatly inform, shape, and color each of these macarisms.[59] The eschatological character and context of the Beatitudes is undeniable. Thus, language about the *makarios*-ness of "mourning" and "hungering and thirsting for righteousness," along with the promises of "inheriting the land" and "being satisfied," are examples of the thoroughly eschatological vision of Isaiah, which is so foundational to all the New Testament's self-understanding, including Matthew as much as any book.

Particularly helpful in this approach is an article by Benedict Viviano, which compares Matthew's Beatitudes with a collection of macarisms from Cave 4 at Qumran.[60] Among many other insights in this article, including a proper understanding of the distinction between *'ašrê* and *brk*, Viviano observes that

59. Robert Guelich was one of the first to emphasize this connection. See his *The Sermon on the Mount: A Foundation for Understanding* (Dallas: Word, 1982). Among the many commentaries that now make this connection, see esp. W. D. Davies and Dale C. Allison Jr., *A Critical and Exegetical Commentary on the Gospel according to Saint Matthew*, vol. 1, *Introduction and Commentary on Matthew 1–7*, ICC (Edinburgh: T&T Clark, 2004), 436–37.

60. Benedict Viviano, "Eight Beatitudes at Qumran and in Matthew? A New Publication from Cave Four," *Svensk exegetisk årsbok* 58 (1993): 71–84.

the Qumran macarisms are sapiential but *not* apocalyptic/eschatological. The subject is the general pursuit of wisdom, and these macarisms lack the eschatological reversal in the apodosis.[61] What makes the Matthean Beatitudes distinctive relative to these Qumran examples (as well as those in Sirach) is the eschatological, kingdom-oriented focus, where justice "includes an apocalyptic dimension of struggling toward the kingdom."[62]

This approach is good in many ways and is a vast improvement over the "God's favor" reading. Various commentators manifest this understanding of the eschatological background of the Beatitudes. How these interpreters gloss *makarios* varies; probably most still translate the term with "blessed" because the emphasis is on God rewarding or favoring.

Wisdom or Virtue-Ethics Reading

Yet there is another important and insightful way in which the Beatitudes have been read—probably the most common reading through most of church history and the one still most often found and clearly articulated in the Roman Catholic tradition (though not exclusively there)—an understanding of the macarisms as part of the wisdom tradition, particularly the Aristotelian virtue tradition that continues into Augustine and finds its apex in Aquinas.[63]

One example among many would be the Benedictine theologian Servais Pinckaers.[64] In his richly devotional exposition of the Beatitudes, he continues the Augustinian tradition and understands the Beatitudes as Jesus's answer to the great human question of happiness. As a result, most who read in this way are not afraid to gloss *makarios* with some form of "Happy" or "Fortunate"—even while acknowledging that this is not to be equated with a mere emotion.[65] A variation of this virtue reading is found throughout much of the

---

61. Ibid., 76. Examples of these macarisms from 4Q525/4QBeat are "Happy is he who speaks the truth with a pure heart and does not slander with his tongue"; "Happy are those who uphold his statutes and do not take to her paths of perversity"; "Happy are those who seek her with purity of hands and do not strive after her with a deceitful heart."

62. Ibid., 81. On page 83 he reiterates that the kingdom of God is the "theme which perhaps more than any other distinguishes the beatitudes of Jesus and the evangelists from those found at Qumran and in Ben Sira."

63. For a focus on biblical ethics as being about flourishing one may consult a number of works, including Charry, *God and the Art of Happiness*; Brent Strawn, ed., *The Bible and the Pursuit of Happiness: What the Old and New Testaments Teach Us about the Good Life* (Oxford: Oxford University Press, 2012); and Paul Wadell, *Happiness and the Christian Moral Life: An Introduction to Christian Ethics* (Lanham, MD: Rowman & Littlefield, 2012).

64. Servais Pinckaers, *The Pursuit of Happiness—God's Way: Living the Beatitudes* (Staten Island: Alba House, 1988).

65. Cf. the bold observation of Spicq: "Jesus is making an appeal to happiness. It is impossible to insist too strongly on the meaning of this *makarios*, repeated ten times (in Matt.) and

history of interpretation of the Sermon as seeing the Beatitudes as a picture of and guide on the journey of the soul or ladder of ascent to God.[66] This way of reading and applying the Beatitudes is not coextensive with a virtue reading, but it has much overlap and a shared worldview or engine of understanding.

There is a great deal to commend this way of reading the Beatitudes and indeed the entirety of the Sermon, something in fact that I am suggesting in this book over all. Among other arguments that can be made, this way of reading much more directly accords with and builds upon the proper understanding of the connection between *'ašrê* and *makarios*, unlike the "God's favor" view.

A Fourth Way and the Debate over Entrance Requirements or Eschatological Blessings

An issue that regularly arises in the literature on the Beatitudes is the question of whether the Beatitudes are to be read as entrance requirements or eschatological blessings. From a tradition-historical perspective, these two options are typically based on whether one sees the background to the Beatitudes as coming from the Jewish wisdom tradition or from the Jewish apocalyptic tradition. If the former, then the Beatitudes are read as ethical and therefore as entrance requirements. If the latter, they are read as eschatological blessings that make no demands on the hearers.[67]

These two categories become the primary means of interpreting and making sense of what Jesus is saying, and commentators fall on either side, though most commonly on the side of eschatological blessings. These categories, which are helpful in themselves as handles for different ways of reading the macarisms, have unfortunately been used to create a strong distinction, a dichotomy that, like most dichotomies in complex situations, proves to be false.

For example, one will often find comments such as that from Robert Guelich that the Beatitudes are *not* about wisdom ideals concerned with well-being but rather are prophetic.[68] Or, in the otherwise excellent article on "Blessing

---

intensified by the present imperatives 'Rejoice and be glad (*chairete kai agalliasthe*), for your reward is great in heaven'" (*TLNT* 2:437–38).

66. See the essays on John Chrysostom, Hugh of St. Victor, Dante and Chaucer, and C. H. Spurgeon in Jeffrey P. Greenman, Timothy Larsen, and Stephen R. Spencer, eds., *The Sermon on the Mount through the Centuries: From the Early Church to John Paul II* (Grand Rapids: Brazos, 2007).

67. Guelich, *Sermon on the Mount*, 63–65, 109–11, lays out the issue clearly.

68. Ibid., 110–11. See also Guelich, "The Matthean Beatitudes: 'Entrance-Requirements' or Eschatological Blessings?," *JBL* 95 (1976): 417, quoted in Glen Stassen, "Beatitudes," in *Dictionary of Scripture and Ethics*, ed. Joel B. Green (Grand Rapids: Baker Academic, 2011), 94.

and Woe" by David Garland, we find a very good discussion of the Beatitudes overall, including a gloss that reads "Happy are the unhappy for God
will make them happy," along with an understanding of the eschatological
context of these macarisms. Yet he goes on to write, "This condition [that
the recipients of the Beatitudes find themselves in] *has nothing to do with the
pursuit of happiness* or with fortunate external circumstances. It has to do
with openness to the gracious activity of God to save his people."[69]

Again, this is an unnecessary and unhelpful dichotomy. I fully agree that
there is a thoroughly Isaianic kingdom-restoring eschatological backdrop
to the Beatitudes (indeed, all of Matthew), but this in no way undercuts the
vision of human flourishing that the Beatitudes speak to. One is not forced
to choose between these or to put asunder what Second Temple Judaism has
joined together.

We can recall here briefly what was discussed in the previous chapter regarding the work of Grant Macaskill.[70] As noted, recent work has shown that
in the Second Temple period (clearly the context for Matthew) the strands of
the wisdom tradition and of the apocalyptic and eschatological traditions are
inextricably interwoven. That is, already in Matthew's conceptual and cultural
encyclopedia there is a significant (Venn diagram–like) overlap between the
Wisdom literature and its vision of human flourishing and the future-oriented
eschatological hope. There is a free exchange and interweaving of apocalyptic
and wisdom, a cross-pollination that is already occurring in Second Temple
literature, as *1 Enoch*, *2 Enoch*, and *4QInstruction* show.[71] As Macaskill skillfully argues, Matthew follows suit with this idea that the eschaton entails God
revealing his wisdom to an elect group. And in particular, in Matthew Jesus is
depicted as the eschatological revealer of wisdom. These insights prove very
significant for our understanding of the Beatitudes.

It is precisely in the eschaton that the ultimate human flourishing will occur,
as this can only come about when God restores his reign of justice, peace,
and rest. This central biblical vision and idea is precisely the backdrop for
the Beatitudes and makes their point become crystal clear: Jesus is offering
a vision for a way of being in the world that will result in true flourishing,

69. David Garland, "Blessings and Woes," *DJG*, 79 (emphasis mine).

70. Grant Macaskill, *Revealed Wisdom and Inaugurated Eschatology in Ancient Judaism and Early Christianity*, JSJSup 115 (Leiden: Brill, 2007).

71. Macaskill does not address the idea of *makarios*, but Klaus Koch earlier noted that *makarios* often appears in wisdom literature as a concluding statement and also in apocalyptic literature directed as a macarism to those saved in the last judgment (e.g., *2 Enoch* 52). Koch appears to see these occurrences as distinct rather than connected, while Macaskill's work shows that this dual appearance is not mere coincidence or surprising. See Klaus Koch, *The Growth of the Biblical Tradition* (New York: Scribner, 1969), 8, referred to in Dumbrell, "Logic," 6.

precisely in the context of forward-looking faith in God eventually setting the world to rights.

In light of this discussion we can also revisit the issue of the protasis and the apodosis: If we understand the macarisms as a sapiential proclamation of human flourishing, then the logic is clear and straightforward—flourishing/happy are those in these paradoxically lowly states (and who live in this way) because in reality now and eschatologically they are recipients of great blessing. Thus, when considering the various options for reading the Beatitudes—God's favor, eschatological reversal blessings, and a wisdom/virtue reading—I think that *the best reading of the Beatitudes combines the insights from the second and third ways above while also particularly emphasizing the aspect of human flourishing.*

A number of the best and most insightful commentators have recognized that there is a clear sapiential background to *'ašrê/makarios* that must not be lost while also noting the profoundly eschatological nature of Jesus's teachings. The eschatological focus is manifested in Jesus's teaching most clearly with the idea of the kingdom of heaven. The kingdom is a spatial metaphor or metonym for human flourishing.

Ulrich Luz certainly stands in this vein. He notes that in the Jewish wisdom tradition of which the Beatitudes are a part, macarisms/asherisms are sapiential paraenesis, a didactic genre. Yet as the tradition develops in the Second Temple literature, especially in apocalyptic literature, many beatitudes appear featuring an apodosis with an eschatological sense.[72] Thus, Luz argues, "Jesus' beatitudes are part of this transformation in apocalypticism of what was originally a wisdom genre" yet are also somewhat distinct, including in terms of the unexpected recipients of the macarism.[73]

Another good example is Ben Witherington, who sees Jesus presented in the Gospels as a prophetic sage who uses the Old Testament in sapiential ways and at the same time reveals wisdom from God. Witherington observes that the Sermon on the Mount is "a virtual compendium of the usual standing topics that sages would discuss," as can be seen when comparing it with Proverbs 1–8 or Sirach. "The difference here is that Jesus offers both traditional and counter-order wisdom, and all of the teaching is served up with the understanding that God's eschatological reign is breaking in, and so to some extent new occasions teach new duties, as well as reaffirming some of the old ones."[74]

---

72. Luz, *Matthew 1–7,* 187.
73. Ibid., 188.
74. Ben Witherington III, *Matthew,* SHBC (Macon, GA: Smyth & Helwys, 2006), 114. See also by Witherington, *Jesus the Sage: The Pilgrimage of Wisdom,* rev. ed. (Minneapolis: Fortress, 2000).

We might also place in this category Scot McKnight in his Story of God Commentary on the Sermon. McKnight notes the eschatological Isaianic background to the Beatitudes and how these teachings are a topsy-turvy reversal of the world's values. He also spends considerable time on the meaning and translation of *makarios* and shows that the good life or happiness is indeed in the background here. He writes:

> Furthermore, the entire history of the philosophy of the "good life" and the late modern theory of "happiness" is at work when one says, "Blessed are . . ." Thus, this swarm of connections leads us to consider Aristotle's great Greek term *eudaimonia*, which means something like happiness or human flourishing, but it also prompts us to consider modern studies of what makes people happy.[75]

I think this is spot-on. Yet at the same time I am a bit confused by McKnight's approach, which seems to want to maintain all aspects simultaneously. McKnight touches on many of the different ways that people have read the Beatitudes and seeks to keep them all together in a way that is not entirely clear to me.[76] Moreover, after all of this he still glosses *makarios* with "God's favor is upon . . ." and states that a "blessed" person "is someone who, because of a heart for God, is promised and enjoys God's favor regardless of that person's status or countercultural condition."[77] This throws us back into the *'ašrê/makarios* confusion.

Lastly, I will mention R. T. France, whose commentary on Matthew is a model of excellence. France titles 5:3–10 as "The Good Life: the Paradoxical Values of the Kingdom of Heaven" and glosses the Beatitudes with "Happy are those . . ." He acknowledges that *'ašrê* instead of *brk* is the background to the macarisms and states that while "happy" is certainly not fully adequate, it is better than "blessed," which has too theological a connotation in communicating that these people are "blessed by God."[78] At the same time, the eschatological background and "already but not yet" aspects are clearly at play in France's understanding as well. Thus, I find in France's commentary one of the most thoughtful and balanced treatments.

Indeed, when it comes to the great dilemma of how to translate *makarios*, I was pleased to find in France's commentary not only a thorough discussion but also one of the most novel and interesting translation suggestions. Thanks

---

75. McKnight, *Sermon on the Mount*, 32.
76. Cf. a similar critique that I made in chap. 1 regarding McKnight's otherwise helpful ethical categories.
77. McKnight, *Sermon on the Mount*, 36.
78. France, *Gospel of Matthew*, 160–61.

here must go to that particular version of English spoken by the Australians. France notes that in Australian English, people commonly use the unique expression "Good on ya/yer," which I myself have also heard during trips Down Under. This common cultural phrase is not easily definable, but in many contexts it means something quite close to what the Beatitudes are primarily communicating—a genuinely happy congratulations and acknowledgment of the favorable and happy state of another.[79] Unfortunately, "Good on ya/yer" will not likely work well as an English translation outside of an Australian context.[80] France also offers his own favorite gloss, coming from the traditional Welsh rendering of the Beatitudes, *Gwyn eu byd*, taken literally, "White is their world," meaning everything is good for the person.[81] This is beautiful and good, though again, helps us little as a current English gloss.

The point is that the best readings of the Beatitudes will combine and keep in balance the reality of two streams of tradition that are feeding into the encyclopedic background to Jesus's macarisms—the wisdom tradition (Jewish and Greco-Roman) and the Second Temple apocalyptic emphasis on the eschatological reversal of fortune. Unfortunately, even though a few scholars have seen the significance of both of these backgrounds, this has not made it into the translations or the general understanding. A significant reason why all of this makes sense is the many other ways in which the Sermon presents itself as eschatological wisdom teaching. From its opening *makarioi* statements through the various wisdom/ethics topics being discussed, through its sapiential aphorisms (such as the Golden Rule), to its final section of two ways (narrow and wide ways; true and false prophets), and especially its climactic call to be a *wise* life builder rather than a *fool*—the Sermon on the Mount presents itself as an eschatological wisdom teaching on virtue.

And this brings us back to where we began our discussion, to the Bible's meta-theme of human flourishing as the goal of God's redeeming work. Human flourishing is understood as the goal and result of pursuing and practicing virtue/practical wisdom. *This* Second Temple Jewish context— influenced by, trafficking in, yet also modifying Greco-Roman notions of

79. Closest in non-Australian English would probably be "Good for you," though this can have a snide sense in current parlance and so is imperfect.

80. Frederick Bruner's translation of the Beatitudes as "Blessings on the poor," etc., has some similarities to France's Australian suggestion. Bruner reflectively notes that while "happy" can seem banal, "blessed" can seem super-spiritual. He prefers "blessings on . . . ," which he says means compactly, "I am *with* you"; "I am on your side" (*Matthew: A Commentary*, vol. 1, *The Christbook: Matthew 1–12* [Grand Rapids: Eerdmans, 2006], 158).

81. In personal conversation the theologian Derek Thomas, also Welsh, informs me that a better translation of this traditional proverb might be "May their world be lit light."

virtue—is the encyclopedic cultural background for the Sermon and is key to reading it wisely and best.

Yet there is one other aspect of the Sermon's teaching—more than an aspect, another pillar—that I've not yet mentioned that also contributes to, supports, and explains how the Sermon is a picture of human flourishing: the idea of *teleios*-ity to which we may now turn.

3

Teleios

Wholeness throughout the Sermon

Introduction: A Track of Two Conceptual Rails

In chapter 1 I argued that the best reading and interpretation of the Sermon on the Mount is found through recognizing its cultural situatedness at the crossroads of the Second Temple Jewish world and the Greco-Roman virtue tradition. In chapter 2 I argued that this understanding rides on a track of two conceptual rails that can be summed up in two Greek words, *makarios* and *teleios*, which are themselves hooks for two large and important elements of earliest Christianity's cultural encyclopedia. The first of these rails, or to change the metaphor, columns upon which the Sermon is built, is *makarios*, which I argued is a vision-casting invitation to true human flourishing through Jesus. In this chapter we will examine the second and related concept of wholeness or singleness of devotion (*teleios*-ity), expressed through the word *teleios* and more broadly as a structural theme in the Sermon. Not only are these ideas (*makarios* and *teleios*) both foundational to the vision of human flourishing, they are, it turns out, also deeply integrated ideas. That is, these are not separate notions that both happen to support a virtue/flourishing reading, but rather they prove to be together at the core of the ancient vision for human flourishing.

Teleios: A Translation Problem

In our discussion of *makarios* we discovered a great translation dilemma in that there is no good, simple English gloss that communicates the conceptual world that *makarios* evokes in both the Greco-Roman and Jewish contexts. This creates a significant gap in our ability to interpret the Sermon as a Model Reader, since, as I have argued, *makarios* is a foundational concept.

Equally important to the Sermon is the concept of *teleios*, and in this instance the translation is not merely a dilemma, but even more, it has been the source of great misunderstanding for readers. That is, it *is* possible to provide some workable glosses for *teleios* (and a large family of *tel*-root terms), but the wrong ones have usually been used, resulting in much confusion as to Jesus's teaching. Specifically, *teleios* is usually translated into English with "perfect" (Matt. 5:48; 19:21), when a far better gloss is "whole," "complete," or even "virtuous."

The problem is that "perfect" communicates to the contemporary English ear the ideas of moral perfection, absolute purity, and even sinlessness. But this is not the idea of *teleios* in the Second Temple period or in the New Testament, nor even of its Hebrew equivalents in the Old Testament, as we will see. It is certainly not the sense of *teleios* that is functioning in the Greco-Roman virtue and Jewish wisdom traditions that serve as the seedbed for the vocabulary of the Sermon. This is no small matter because this translation decision has a substantive impact on one's overall reading of the Sermon as well as the theological construction of New Testament ethics and the notion of sanctification.[1]

Similar to *makarios*, part of the translation problem stems from the conceptual disjunction between our contemporary worldview and that of first-century Judaism and Christianity. A general principle is that to the degree that worldviews do not overlap, the more difficult the translation of certain ideas is. For example, one difficult issue today is how to conduct international business in different parts of the world that have developed different economic systems and have significantly different cultural values. Some words are simply untranslatable because the systems and cultures overlap so little.[2] The same thing occurs when a modern Western reader tries to understand *teleios* from an English perspective. The now-traditional gloss of "perfect" only adds to the confusion and inability of modern readers to discern the meta-theme of wholeness in the Sermon.[3] As with *makarios*, to understand how *teleios* func-

1. It is staggering to consider what negative impact the mistranslation "Be perfect as your heavenly Father is perfect" (Matt. 5:48) has had on countless Christians throughout the centuries, leading many to despair and others to a false sense of their own ability to live a sinless, "higher" life.

2. An interesting discussion of this issue can be found in John Blenkinsopp and Maryam Shademan Pajouh, "Lost in Translation? Culture, Language and the Role of the Translator in International Business," *Critical Perspectives on International Business* 6, no. 1 (2010): 38–52.

3. My student David Blackwell (unpublished paper) uncovers what seems to be the root of why English translations gloss *teleios* as "perfect," despite pervasive scholarly understanding that this translation is problematic. Like many of our English translation choices, they stem

tions in Matthew and the Sermon we need to examine its role in the Jewish
and Greek traditions.

Teleios in the Old Testament and Septuagint

The *tel*- word group, which includes *teleios*, and other conceptually related terms
are frequent in the Septuagint as well as in the Second Temple Jewish literature
that precedes the New Testament. Unlike the rare situation with *makarios*,
where there was a remarkable one-to-one correspondence between the Greek
makarios and the Hebrew *'ašrê*, *teleios* is used as a Septuagintal translation for
a variety of Hebrew terms. This does not make understanding the meaning of
teleios overly difficult; however, we can see that there is an important conceptual
overlap between the multiple terms involved, and this helps fill out the contours
of this important idea. There is a dominant and clear notion of "wholeness"[4] in
the *tel*- word group, and this is reflected in its appropriate use as a translation
for several Hebrew terms, especially *tāmîm* and *šālôm*. Our first pass at understanding the biblical notion of *teleios* will be an examination of the Hebrew
Bible's own important and nuanced theme of wholeness.

Tying the argument here to the preceding two chapters, we can note that
in the Hebrew Bible there is a recurrent theme of salvation as human flourishing. This is manifested in multiple ways, including with several weighty
concepts such as *'ašrê* (happiness; flourishing), *tāmîm* (wholeness), and especially *šālôm* (peace; flourishing). Having already discussed *'ašrê*, we will
address the latter two briefly.

Šālôm

A primary concept related to human flourishing is expressed by the Hebrew
term *šālôm* and its typical Greek equivalent *eirēnē*, both of which are usually translated into English as "peace." In the Hebrew Bible, forms of *šālôm*

---

from a conservative tradition dating back to the earliest translations from Latin into English by
Wycliffe, Tyndale, and the Coverdale and Geneva Bibles. The Vulgate uses *perfectus* in Matt.
5:48, which is a decent Latin gloss for *teleios*, both communicating wholeness or completion.
This came into the early English translations as "parfit," "perfecte," "perfite," and finally in the
Authorized Version, "perfect." This transliteration of the Latin term took on its own narrower
connotations as English developed, and now we continue to use this unhelpful gloss.

4. From his extensive study of the word group, F. M. J. Waanders concludes, "All the available evidence leads me to believe that the most frequent meaning of *teleios* ('having *telos*')
is 'complete'" (*The History of TELOS and TELEO in Ancient Greek* [Amsterdam: Gruner,
1983], 237; quoted in Patrick Hartin, *A Spirituality of Perfection: Faith in Action in the Letter
of James* [Collegeville, MN: Liturgical Press, 1999], 22n21).

occur many times and with a variety of related meanings. These many uses consistently center on the idea of *wholeness* with its natural consequence of *well-being* or *flourishing*. For example, a *šālôm* greeting is a kind well-wishing for another's prosperity; a state or relationship free from conflict is called *šālôm*; and most generally, one can be described as flourishing when all the parts of one's life—health, economics, interpersonal relations—are functioning together in harmony and completeness. All of these are com-municated in the Old Testament with the word *šālôm* (see, e.g., Gen. 26:29; 34:21; Ps. 122:6; Zech. 6:13).

Unfortunately, as is often the case when translating from one language to another, our English word "peace" is too narrow to communicate biblical *šālôm*. In English the word "peace" means either absence of conflict (espe-cially in a military sense) or one's inner serenity or tranquility. These notions are certainly not absent from *šālôm* but are too limited and distinct; absence of conflict and personal tranquility are natural benefits of *šālôm*, but not coextensive with it. Because of our more limited sense of English "peace," we have often missed the biblical message of *šālôm*, which is a robust picture of flourishing, described as wholeness.

Indeed, through its comprehensive nature and relationship to several other key biblical concepts, we may note that *šālôm* is a principal way the Bible describes God's entire redemptive work: God bringing his own *šālôm* to the earth. One can immediately think of images from the Old Testament's vision of the eschatological age, when God's reign is restored on the earth and the needy will be protected, the wolf will lie down with the lamb, the cow will feed with the bear, the child will play with the viper (Isa. 11:1–8), the poor will receive justice, and the lame will walk. All of this is *šālôm*, God's restoration of the world to full flourishing. As Nicholas Wolterstorff notes, the Bible has a clear vision of what God wants for his creatures, "a vision of what constitutes human flourishing and of our appointed destiny. The vision is not that of disembodied individual contemplation of God. . . . It is the vision of *šālôm*."[5]

Tāmîm

The other idea to be addressed here relates to *tāmîm*.[6] The Hebrew *tmm/tāmîm/tōm* and its related forms occur more than two hundred times in the

5. Nicholas Wolterstorff, *Educating for Shalom: Essays on Christian Higher Education*, ed. Clarence W. Joldersma and Gloria Goris Stronks (Grand Rapids: Eerdmans, 2004), 22–23.
6. The following paragraphs come from my essay "A Biblical Theology of Human Flourish-ing," the website for the Institute for Faith, Work, and Economics, March 4, 2015, https://tifwe.org/resource/a-biblical-theology-of-human-flourishing-2/.

Old Testament, communicating the idea of wholeness, integrity, and singleness. Because this is such a broad and important idea, the "boots on the ground" usage can vary quite a bit depending on context, conveying notions of completeness, blamelessness, justice, honesty, perfection, and peacefulness. A core idea related to each of these is genuineness and reliability. The adjectival form *tāmîm* denotes "whole, perfect, or blameless," used mostly in connection with cultic regulations pertaining to sacrificial offerings. Often used synonymously with *yāšār* (upright) and *ṣaddîq* (righteous), *tāmîm* also epitomizes the correct ethos among the righteous and wise (cf. Prov. 2:21). To be *tāmîm* also means to be pious and upright before the Lord. The nominal *tōm* (perfection) characterizes the nature and manner of an action or the attitude of the one who is performing it, thus meaning "in full measure" on the one hand and "integrity of heart" (1 Kings 9:4) on the other.[7] Often *tōm* is used to describe the state of the heart that is pure and has sinless conscience (e.g., Gen. 20:5, 6; 1 Kings 9:4; Ps. 78:72).[8] In Deut. 18:13, to be "blameless" before the Lord means to belong to him wholeheartedly without practicing idolatry (Deut. 18:9–12). This total surrender must be constant (Josh. 24:14). "To give one's whole heart in its purity, unblemished by alien thoughts and inclinations: this is what the substantive *tmm* expresses, and we might translate with 'innocence, simplicity.'"[9]

Tmm/tāmîm/tōm, understood as "completeness" and "wholeness," is a macroconcept that sums up the Old Testament's moral commands. This same understanding can be found in the subsequent Second Temple Jewish literature, where the idea of "wholeness of heart" (*tōm*, equivalent to the Greek word for "undivided" or "whole," *haplotēs*) is found, such as in the *Testaments of the Twelve Patriarchs*.[10] The Qumran community sees itself as the "perfect ones of the way," "those who walk perfectly," and "a house of perfection and truth in Israel." These "perfect ones" (the word is regularly collocated with "way" and "walk") see themselves as the holy remnant, the saints of the final age.[11]

7. J. P. J. Olivier, "םֹת," *NIDOTTE* 4:306–8.

8. Francis Brown, S. R. Driver, and Charles A. Briggs, *A Hebrew and English Lexicon of the Old Testament*, reprinted with corrections (Oxford: Clarendon, 1968), s.v. םֹת.

9. Rudolf Schnackenburg, *Christian Existence in the New Testament*, vol. 1, trans. F. Wieck (Notre Dame, IN: University of Notre Dame Press, 1968), 162.

10. In their commentary on *T. 12 Patr.*, Harm W. Hollander and Marinus de Jonge note the central virtue in Issachar is his character of being *haplotēs* (ἁπλότης) or "undivided." Repeatedly the phrase "to walk ἐν ἁπλότητι καρδίας/ψυχῆς ([*T. Reu.*] 4:1; [*T. Sim.*] 4:5; cf. [*T. Iss.*] 3:8; 4:1) means clearly: '. . . fear our Lord with your whole heart; and walk in simplicity according to all his law' ([*T. Levi*] 13:1)." *Haplotēs* (ἁπλότης) means "integrity, wholeness, whole-hearted obedience to God's commandments," the opposite of "doubleness." See Hollander and de Jonge, *The Testaments of the Twelve Patriarchs: A Commentary* (Leiden: Brill, 1985), 44.

11. Franz Mussner, "Perfection," in Johannes B. Bauer, ed., *Bauer Encyclopedia of Biblical Theology*, 3 vols. (London: Sheed & Ward, 1970), 2:663.

As one can see, the *tmm* root proves to be a very important one; but of course it does not stand alone in a vacuum-sealed bag. Rather it overlaps with, colors, and is colored by several other related and important concepts, including righteousness, well-being (*šālôm*), and holiness. Particularly interesting and important is the connection between wholeness, singleness, and *holiness*. One scholar who has thought carefully about this is Peter Gentry. He argues convincingly that despite the common assumption that "holiness" denotes "separateness, otherness, and moral purity," this view does not accord with the sense of "holy" in Hebrew or Greek (Heb. *qōdeš*; Gk. *hagios*). Based on close readings of Exod. 3 and 19 and Isa. 6, Gentry argues that the basic meaning of "holy"—for humans and for God—is *devotedness*. "The basic meaning of the word is 'consecrated' or 'devoted.' In scripture it operates within the context of covenant relationships and expresses commitment." Gentry carefully notes that this does not mean that "holy" is completely unrelated to moral purity, but instead "holiness should not be defined as moral purity, but rather purity is the result of being completely devoted to God as defined by the covenant."[12] Another scholar has discussed it as the difference between "separation from" and "separation to," with the latter, rather than the former, being the idea of holiness.[13]

We may follow the logical consequence one step beyond Gentry and note that his arguments get us very far in seeing that the idea of holiness (as devotedness) has great overlap and a mutually informing relationship with that of wholeness or completeness. All of this is predicated on God as one and the central place of the Shema in Israel's understanding. Indeed, one scholar who has made these connections very explicit is Mary Douglas. In her insightful work on purity in the Old Testament, she argues that "to be holy is to be whole, to be one; holiness is unity, integrity, perfection of the individual and of the kind."[14]

Teleios

Continuing in our trajectory of moving from the Hebrew Bible into the Septuagint, we see confirmation of this core idea of holiness/righteousness/

12. Peter J. Gentry, "The Meaning of 'Holy' in the Old Testament," *Bibliotheca Sacra* 170 (2013): 400–417.

13. Paul Johannes Du Plessis, *Teleios: The Idea of Perfection in the New Testament* (Kampen: Kok, 1959), 100.

14. Mary Douglas, *Purity and Danger: An Analysis of Concepts of Pollution and Taboo* (London: Routledge, 1966), 55, quoted in Jason Hood, *Imitating God in Christ: Recapturing a Biblical Pattern* (Downers Grove, IL: InterVarsity, 2013), 46. See also Gordon Wenham, *Story as Torah: Reading Old Testament Narrative Ethically* (Edinburgh: T&T Clark, 2004).

godliness as wholeness. Unlike the situation with *'ašrê/makarios*, we do not find a simple translational equivalency between *tāmîm* and *teleios*; but the conceptual connection is very strong nevertheless. Although the Greek *teleios* is not the only gloss for Hebrew *tāmîm*, this is because the latter is most frequently used with the narrower contextual meaning of an "unblemished" sacrificial animal.[15] For this specific usage of the idea of wholeness, there is a better Greek equivalent (usually *amomphos*), but the core idea behind both *tāmîm* and *teleios* is the same. As is often the case, we must look not only to individual words and their interrelationships but also to the range of meanings and conceptual understandings that overlap.

This overlap can be seen by examining the wide range of biblical meanings associated with *teleios*, which prove to be the same as those discussed above for *tāmîm*, *yāšār*, *ṣaddîq*, and *qōdeš*—the idea of wholeness, completeness, and perfection in the sense of wholehearted dedication to God. As Du Plessis observes, *teleios* "assumes the innate meaning of *tāmîm*."[16] Indeed, we may go so far as to say that the moral and religious call of the Old Testament is "a closely-knitted network revolving around a recurrent principle," that of the *tāmîm/teleios* idea.[17] The *teleios* person in the Old Testament—which is the ideal—is the one in total submission to God, who has an unimpeded relationship with Yahweh. Such a person is described as *tāmîm* or *šālēm*, like Noah, Abraham, David, and others.[18]

In the Septuagint all the instances of *teleios* mean "unblemished, undivided, complete, whole." The Hebrew expression *lēb(āb) šālēm* means "a heart that is whole or perfect"—the goal of humanity before God—and *šālēm* is translated with *teleios*.[19] For example, we hear the clarion call of Solomon to his people in 1 Kings 8:61 at the dedication of the temple to be "perfect" (*teleios*) or better, "singular in devotion" before God, walking before him and keeping his commandments; this is holiness. By way of contrast, we learn just a few chapters later in 1 Kings that Solomon's heart "was *not* true/devoted (*teleios*) to the Lord his God, as was the heart of David his father" (11:4).[20] We also see a Hebrew idiom that expresses this double-heartedness in Ps. 12:2, "with a heart and a heart," meaning one who lies to his neighbor and lacks integrity, whose lips are different from his heart.

15. *Teleios* is the translational equivalent for *tāmîm* only seven times and for *šālôm* another five times.
16. Du Plessis, *Teleios*, 97.
17. Ibid., 101.
18. Ibid., 241.
19. Hartin, *Spirituality of Perfection*, 24.
20. The same notion is repeated several more times: 1 Kings 15:3, 14; 1 Chron. 28:9.

Patrick Hartin summarizes his study of the use of *teleios* in the Old Testament by identifying three essential aspects:

1. the idea of wholeness or completeness;
2. the giving of oneself to God wholeheartedly, akin to *ṣaddîq* (righteous);
3. wholehearted dedication that is demonstrated in obedience to God's will, the idea of walking with God.[21]

Kent Browers, reflecting on the connection between righteousness and wholeness (*tāmîm*; *teleios*), makes an important distinction between blamelessness (wholeness) and flawlessness: "Blameless living is living according to the purpose of the Creator, in harmony with fellow creatures and with integrity, openness, and obedience toward God. The concept of *tāmîm/teleios* connotes blamelessness, not flawlessness, so that human righteousness in the OT is to be understood as a performance target."[22] This helpful distinction provides a segue into the Greco-Roman context for the idea of *teleios*.

Virtue, Human Flourishing, and *Teleios*

The usage of *teleios* discussed above comes from the Jewish tradition. As we have seen, the Second Temple period (including the translation of the Septuagint itself) overlaps in language, culture, and concepts with the Greco-Roman tradition. We have already noted in chapter 1 that *telos* and *teleios* are an important part of the Greco-Roman virtue discussion. We can touch on this topic again briefly en route to addressing *teleios* in the Sermon.

Plato considers the one who has moved from corporeal existence to the world of ideas to be *teleios*. The *teleios* one is the one who rekindles the memories of the true, unchanging ideas that he had before being united to the body. For Plato, the idea of the good is the highest of the ideas. Thus, the aim of philosophers was to contemplate the nature of the good. "In this way they perfect themselves by conforming themselves morally to the nature of the good."[23] All people should strive after virtue or inner harmony of the soul, which is to achieve this perfection or wholeness, and thus become like God.[24]

21. Hartin, *Spirituality of Perfection*, 26.
22. Kent Browers, "Righteousness," in *Dictionary of Scripture and Ethics*, ed. Joel B. Green (Grand Rapids: Baker Academic, 2011), 685–87.
23. Hartin, *Spirituality of Perfection*, 20.
24. Ibid., 20n14, referring to Hans K. LaRondelle, *Perfection and Perfectionism* (Berrien Springs, MI: Andrews University Press, 1971).

According to Aristotle, "perfect virtue" (*ho teleia aretē*) includes practical reason (*phronēsis*) and the natural inclination toward the good. The idea of "perfection" (*teleios*) is when the goal (*telos*), the end for which something exists, has been achieved. Aristotle saw a teleological principle at work in human nature that always drives it on the quest for the attainment of *teleios*.[25] The life of contemplative virtue is how to pursue and approximate *teleios*-ness. The result is *eudaimonia* or *makariotēs*. As Aristotle reasoned, this virtue entails or necessitates an intentional wholeness of person (*teleios*). We cannot be virtuous accidentally or in part. A virtuous action is that which includes all of who we are as humans—reasoning, affections, and embodied actions—our whole person.

The influence of this way of thinking is found throughout Greek philosophy in various forms and, not surprisingly, in hellenized Judaism, such as in Philo. For Philo, *teleion agathon* (the perfect good) is the highest form of ethical life (*agothetos*) in which all individual virtues are put into practice. In Philo *teleiotēs* means (quoting W. Volker) "nothing else than the summit of life, where the vision of God is associated with the most virtuous mode of life, where the whole of existence is conceived of as service of God and service of the brothers, where everything is received in experience as a gift of God and produced in act as a *mimesis theou*. This represents a synthesis of the Old Testament and Jewish ideal of perfection with that of the Greek Stoics."[26]

Teleios-ity in the Sermon on the Mount and the Rest of Matthew

All of the preceding discussion provides the encyclopedic background that the Sermon on the Mount would evoke for Matthew's readers (and any current Model Readers). In the preceding chapters I have been arguing that the Sermon is offering Jesus's answer to the great question of human flourishing, the topic that is at the core of both the Jewish wisdom literature and the Greco-Roman virtue tradition. As mentioned earlier, there are many ways in which the Sermon on the Mount clearly presents itself as a piece of eschatological wisdom literature, casting a vision for a way of being in the world in accord with God's coming kingdom. The macarisms are a large part of this. But so is the idea of wholeness or singular devotion. As noted, in Aristotle's terms this harmonious psychological functioning is and results in *eudaimonia*, human well-being or flourishing. This requires a learned

25. Hartin, *Spirituality of Perfection*, 21.
26. Mussner, "Perfection," 2:663.

and intentional wholeness and consistency in one's reasoning, affections, and actions.[27]

This background study of *teleios* is worthwhile because when we turn to the Sermon we find that the *teleios* idea is central to its whole structure and vision. This is seen in the crucial role that Matt. 5:48 plays as well as the thread of the whole-person virtue theme throughout each section of the Sermon.

Pride of place in this discussion goes to Matt. 5:48 and its famous declaration that Jesus's disciples must "be *teleios* as your heavenly Father is *teleios*." This verse comes at the end of the first part (5:17–48) of the central section of the Sermon (5:17–7:12). All of this is governed by the issue raised in the introduction (5:17–20), the greater righteousness that Jesus says is required to enter the kingdom of heaven. This introduction, or *kəlāl* heading (see chap. 5), is followed by six examples of the greater righteousness in relation to the law (5:21–47), culminating with the most shocking example of loving one's enemies (5:43–47). Matthew 5:48 then serves as the bookend to 5:17–20, saying in other terms the same thing, that God requires a greater righteousness. Matthew 5:48 then provides an ultimate definition of what this greater righteousness looks like: being like God the Father himself who is whole and loves his enemies (5:45).[28]

The language of "be *teleios* as your heavenly Father is *teleios*" is strongly reminiscent and allusive of the call to holiness in imitation of God in Lev. 19:2 and 20:26, with a nice allusion to Deut. 18:13.[29] But the change from the much more common *hagios* (holy) to the less frequent *teleios* is very significant.[30] The call to *teleios*-ity in Matt. 5:48 and throughout the Sermon is the same call to "holiness" that we see throughout the Old Testament (and the rest of the New Testament)—not moral perfection but wholehearted orientation toward God. Using a clever and provocative intertextual twist on the great holiness command from Leviticus, Jesus has restated Lev. 19:2 and 20:26 in terms of *teleios*-ity because "holiness" in the Pharisees' world had come to

27. See, e.g., the discussion of Aristotle in Julia Driver, *Ethics: The Fundamentals* (Malden, MA: Blackwell, 2006), 136–47.

28. In the *Didache*, a late first-century document that overlaps a great deal with Matthew conceptually and verbally and is either dependent on Matthew or sharing source material with Matthew, the word *teleios* is found twice. In the first instance (*Did.* 1.4) it describes one who behaves in a way that accords with Matt. 5:39–42. In the second instance (*Did.* 6.2a) it is ascribed to the one who is able to carry "the whole yoke of the Lord." See the discussion in Huub van de Sandt, "Essentials of Ethics in Matthew and the *Didache*: A Comparison at a Conceptual and Practical Level," in *Early Christian Ethics in Interaction with Jewish and Greco-Roman Contexts*, ed. Jan Willem van Henten and Joseph Verheyden (Leiden: Brill, 2013), 243–61.

29. The form of "be X as God is X" is more directly from Lev. 19:2 and 20:26, while the exhortation to be *teleios* is found in Deut. 18:13.

30. Luke has yet another rendering: "Be merciful as your Father is merciful" (6:36).

mean primarily external matters of purity and behavior.[31] The word "holy" was too loaded with the connotations that Jesus is arguing against to simply quote Lev. 20:26 directly. "Holiness" for the Pharisees was too easily defined as external obedience and cleanliness. Instead, as in 5:17–47, Jesus is giving a reappropriated, clear exposition of the true intent of the law, emphasizing the matter of the heart, the whole inner person who must match the outward behavior or it is not truly righteousness or virtue. The call to "holiness" in Lev. 19:2 and 20:26 is now properly explicated, as was its true intent always, as a call to "wholeness," or in short, Godward virtue. This will look like holiness or righteousness for Jesus's disciples, but not merely as outward behavior but inner cleanness (cf. Matt. 15:7–11).

By way of contrast, this makes sense of Jesus's constant attack on the Pharisees for being *hypocrites*.[32] The Pharisees are described as hypocrites, but not in the sense that we typically use that term, meaning someone who says one thing but lives a different way, such as a pastor who preaches marital faithfulness but serially commits adultery. That is one kind of hypocrisy, certainly, but it is not the kind that Jesus is addressing in the Sermon and with the Pharisees. They are hypocrites because they are not unified in heart and action; they actually *do* the right things, but they are not the right kind of people because their hearts are wrong.[33] In behavior they are righteous but inwardly they are not; hence, they lack what God cares about—as Aristotle would agree, they lack virtue. They are not "pure in heart" and therefore they cannot see God (Matt. 5:8). And overall this Godward virtue orientation is a radical eschatological vision—God is now in Christ Jesus bringing about the consummation of the ages and his redemptive work. In this way Jesus is like the prophets of the Old Testament, calling God's people not to more external obedience but to true righteousness, obedience that comes from the heart. Isaiah 29:13 speaks of God's people honoring him with their lips but having a *heart* that is far from him. Hosea 6:6 declares that God is more interested

31. Cf. Ellen Charry's insightful comments about the tendency for Tannaitic Judaism, which at least in part reflects Second Temple Judaism, to view purity as more an external than an internal matter, almost like a "germ theory" (*By the Renewing of Your Minds: The Pastoral Function of Christian Doctrine* [Oxford: Oxford University Press, 1999], 62).

32. This is a preferred Matthean term, occurring thirteen times out of a total of seventeen in the entire NT, concentrated mostly in the Sermon (6:2, 5, 16; 7:5) and the woes of chap. 23 (vv. 13, 15, 23, 25, 27, 29). It also occurs in Matt. 15:7; 22:18; and 24:51. See further discussion in chap. 4.

33. Michael Joseph Brown does not use the category of heart or virtue but understands hypocrisy similarly: The hypocrite is "not the person who is morally dishonest or a 'faker,' but the 'typical' religious person who prays, fasts, and gives without thinking" ("Matthew," in *True to Our Native Land: An African American New Testament Commentary*, ed. Brian K. Blount [Minneapolis: Fortress, 2007], 92).

in the heart of mercy and compassion toward others than he is in adherence
to his own system of explicit commands. Such an emphasis on wholehearted
obedience is very typical of the prophetic material. It is no accident that Matthew, who regularly highlights Jesus's prophetic role,[34] makes much of Isa.
29:13 (Matt. 15:1–11) and Hosea 6:6 (Matt. 9:13; 12:7).

This emphasis on wholeness or singleness of devotion is notable in Matt.
5:48, but its importance is highlighted by the fact that it is more than an isolated lexical occurrence. Rather, I suggest that one of the key ideas—if not
the key idea—that makes the Sermon hang together is that of "wholeness,"
"completeness," or "singular devotion." As Margaret Pamment observed,
for Matthew "the disciple is he whose dedication to God is *total, single*."[35]

Teleios *and Wholeness throughout the Sermon*

This emphasis on singleness or wholehearted dedication is seen in nearly
every part of the Sermon. The Beatitudes, as we have seen in our discussion
of *makarios* (see also chap. 6), focus on the virtues of the inner person as opposed to outward behaviors. Poverty of spirit, mournfulness, meekness, hunger
and thirst for righteousness, mercy and peacefulness, even joy in the midst
of persecution—these are whole-person virtues for which external obedience
can never serve as a substitute. Within the Beatitudes this can be seen most
clearly in the macarism of Matt. 5:8, which speaks of "purity of heart." As
H. Benedict Green points out, the Old Testament texts that this idea builds
upon are several psalms that use *tāmîm, teleios*, and other related terms.[36] In
the following six exegeses of Torah in 5:21–47, the consistent point is that
inward righteousness is necessary, not just outward obedience. Being angry,
lusting, making oaths, hating—these are heart matters that raise the bar
beyond what externally focused religious people might obey, the very people
Jesus calls hypocrites.

The next section of the Sermon (6:1–21) continues the internal, whole-
person theme by defining hypocrisy and lesser righteousness in terms of living
for the external only and not the internal. This lack of wholeness or integrity

34. Like the OT prophets, Jesus makes many declarations of truth and falsehood, blessing
and judgment (Matt. 5:3–11; 11:21–24; 12:31–32; 13:16–17; 23:13–29), and identifies himself
as a prophet (12:38–41; 13:57; 16:14; 22:34–40). See the exposition on 5:17, where "Law and
the Prophets" refers to a prophetic reading of the law.
35. Margaret Pamment, "Singleness and Matthew's Attitude to the Torah," *JSNT* 17 (1983):
73–86, here 74 (emphasis mine).
36. Green associates Matt. 5:8 with several OT texts, including Pss. 23:3–4; 119:1–2, 9–10,
which are all also connected to the Shema (Deut. 6:5) with its emphasis on the whole person
(*Matthew, Poet of the Beatitudes* [Edinburgh: T&T Clark, 2001], 235–38).

of personhood is described as living for the praise of people in public rather than recognition from God in private (6:1–18). This section then concludes with the same point made via a related metaphor: laying up foolish, destroyable treasures on earth rather than eternal, imperishable ones in heaven (6:19–21). All of this speaks to the necessity of singleness of devotion, seen by the climactic word—where one's treasure is, there one's heart or true person is (6:21).

The metaphor of earthly versus heavenly treasure then takes on a slightly different color in the following, overlapping section on earthly life as a citizen of the kingdom (6:19–34). Here the singularity of the person is not only extolled but also shown to be in reality a necessary thing. Because one's heart is the control center and seat of one's very person, one cannot be split in devotion: "No one is able to serve two lords, for the one he will hate and the other he will love, or he will be devoted to the one and think little of the other. You are not able to serve money and God" (6:24). Matthew 6:22–24 hangs together as a unit, contrasting the whole (*haplous*) person,[37] connected with light, with the evil (*ponēros*) person, connected with darkness. The whole person serves God singularly; the evil person tries to serve both God and the things of this world. The result is a splitting of the person's heart, a lack of integrity.[38] This unhealthy splitting of the person is also the problem of 6:25–34. The person who seeks to serve God and money (6:24) rather than seeking God's kingdom (6:33) experiences this splitting as anxiety. This is not the only cause of anxiety in life, certainly, but Jesus teaches that lack of wholeness does inevitably result in anxiety. The solution is to trust the heavenly Father (looking back to 6:8) and "seek first" God's kingdom, that is, to make God's coming reign the focus of one's whole life, reminiscent of the whole-person emphasis of the Shema.[39]

Wholeness as a theme is present in 7:1–12 mainly in the image of God the Father as one who can be trusted to give consistently and faithfully, who is good and therefore only gives good gifts. An early reception of this is seen in James 1:16–17, where God is described as the source of every good and perfect gift because he is not alternating like a shifting shadow. Matthew 7:12 also depends on the idea of wholeness and integrity in that one's treatment of others should be the same as one treats oneself.

37. This word is closely connected with *teleios* in Second Temple literature. See Mussner, "Perfection," 2:663. See also Hollander and de Jonge, *Testaments of the Twelve Patriarchs*, 44.

38. Green connects the central idea of the Beatitudes, understood as purity of heart, with 6:21–24, a repetition of the theme that then looks forward to the non-*teleios* young ruler in 19:16–22 (*Matthew, Poet*, 252).

39. See also the related teaching in the paradigmatic parable of the sower in Matt. 13:1–9, 18–23.

The final section of the Sermon ramps up the theme of dual-ness versus singleness/wholeness (7:13–27). In a threefold series of images, two ways are contrasted, emphasizing again (as in 6:22–24) that one's life is inevitably singular, either God directed or not. The inward theme is most explicitly unpacked in the middle of the three images (7:15–23). Here false prophets are contrasted with true ones, and the metaphors deal directly with the repeated topic of inward versus outward righteousness—wolves in sheep's clothing, and good and bad trees and their fruit. Both metaphors contrast the inner realities with the outward, noting that what matters is consistency or wholeness between the outward appearance and the inward reality. In this final section of the Sermon, Jesus ups the ante on this issue by tying it to the coming judgment. Trees that bear bad fruit and wolves that seem to prophesy will face judgment because they lack integrity. So too in the climactic image of the two builders. Both houses—the one built by the fool and the other by the wise builder—appear to be strong and beautiful. It is the eschatological divine judgment that reveals whether one's inner foundation is in place or whether one's righteousness is merely a façade (7:24–27).

We might describe this quick overview of the Sermon as a *cardiographic* reading. The point is that Jesus's consistent emphasis throughout is that whole-person righteousness (from the heart, in the inner person) is what real righteousness, godliness (godlikeness), and holiness look like.

Teleios *and Wholeness in the Rest of Matthew*

Confirmation of the importance of the wholeness theme in the Sermon can be found by examining the same concept in the rest of the First Gospel. The first place to start is in Matthew's version of the famous story of the rich young man who comes to Jesus asking about eternal life (19:16–22). We do not have space here for a full exposition of this interesting and important story. The reason for pausing here, however, is that it is the only other place in the Gospels (besides the two earlier instances in Matt. 5:48) that uses the word *teleios*. This invites the reader of Matthew to connect this story back to the Sermon, and the content confirms this inclination. This young man who fails to follow Jesus because of his wealth serves as a narrative foil to the teaching of the Sermon. He is one who *fails* to achieve the greater righteousness, the *teleios* state, that Jesus says is required to enter the kingdom of heaven. Assuming that the young man is not lying— and nothing in the story indicates this—he is a pious and faithful Jew and is sincere in his inquiry about what is necessary to enter eternal life / the kingdom of heaven.[40] He has kept all the commandments of a faithful Jew, but according to Jesus he still lacks something, he is not *teleios* (19:21). To get this *teleios*-ity, the man must sell his possessions and give to the poor. Unfortunately, he fails to do this. What is apparent from this story, especially when read in conjunction with the Sermon, is that the young man's problem is a heart, interior problem. He is pious and obedient, but he lacks the necessary wholeness that requires the proper *love*. His heart/love is disordered in that he ultimately values his wealth more than entering the kingdom, his treasure on earth more than his treasure in heaven (19:21; cf. 6:19–21). Interestingly, Matthew also provides us with another narrative foil in the pair of similes in 13:44–46. Here we have two men who rightly perceive the great value of the hidden kingdom (treasure in a field; pearl of great price) and, unlike the young man of 19:16–22, *sell everything they have to gain the kingdom*. The issue in all these scenarios is not money per se but wealth as a possible preventer of the heart-level wholeness required to be a disciple of Jesus.[41] All of this accords directly with the meta-theme of the Sermon. We should also note that there are once again several key terms in this story that, collated together, clearly evoke the virtue tradition. These include "the good," "having eternal life," "treasure" or "reward," and of course, *teleios*. Each of these has its own connotative meaning in a Jewish context, but they are simultaneously Greek terms that together evoke the virtue tradition.

The story of the wealthy young man who lacks *teleios*-ity is the most obvious place in Matthew to see the Sermon's heart/wholeness theme unpacked, but it is not the only one. We can note a few other hot spots for this theme. For example, the idea of singleness/wholeness provides the logic of the argument Jesus makes in 12:33–37. Using the tree-and-fruit metaphor again (cf. 7:16–20 and also the Baptist's usage in 3:8–10) but with a different application, Jesus argues that there is an inevitable wholeness to

40. This story reveals an important way that Matthew conceives of the relationship between "eternal life" and "the kingdom of God/heaven." These terms are all used interchangeably, showing their overlap. In 19:16 the young man queries about "having eternal life." In 19:17 Jesus calls this "entering life," which then becomes "enter the kingdom of heaven" in 19:23 and "enter the kingdom of God" in 19:24. It is not entirely clear whether "have treasure in heaven" (19:21, reminiscent of 6:19–21) is considered a synonymous expression or whether it has a different sense.

41. For a study of the history of interpretation of this passage with a view to the question of whether disciples are required to sell all their possessions, see Jonathan T. Pennington, "'Sell Your Possessions and Give to the Poor': A Theological Reflection on Jesus' Teaching regarding Personal Wealth and Charity," the website for the Institute for Faith, Work, and Economics, July 9, 2015, https://tifwe.org/resource/sell-your-possessions-and-give-to-the-poor-a-theological-reflection-on-jesus-teaching-regarding-personal-wealth-and-charity/.

humans—what comes out of the mouth is what is in the heart, whether good or bad (12:34–35). Another story that highlights this theme is found in 15:1–20, a very important and relatively long (by Matthean standards) pericope that sits in the trough between the high waves of the two wilderness feedings / water crossings (14:13–33; 15:32–39). The gist of this conflict story, complete with a damning Isaianic quote, is the difference between external and internal, whole-person righteousness. The Pharisees and scribes are very concerned about righteousness, which Jesus does not condemn in and of itself. Rather, Jesus opposes honoring the traditions of men over God's commands because the former can be manipulated for self-serving purposes. According to Jesus (quoting Isaiah), this is hypocrisy—external honoring of God when hearts and motives are aligned differently (15:8–9). Jesus goes on to explain this problem in external and internal terms. The metaphor is changed from a tree and its fruit to eating, but the point remains the same: the internal person is the true one, whether this is righteous or defiled (15:10–11, 17–20). Closely related is the lengthy set of woes upon these same Pharisees in Matt. 23. Overall this diatribe is best examined with the same lenses through which hypocrisy has already been defined in Matthew: as external righteousness without a pure heart. This serves as the substructure for all of 23:1–36 but comes to the surface most clearly in the fourth, fifth, and sixth woes. The fourth woe (23:23–24) emphasizes the weightier or deeper matters of the law, ones that accord with the heart. The scribes' and Pharisees' problem is that they do perform the minutiae of the law's requirements (tithing herbs) but they neglect true justice, mercy, and faithfulness. In the fifth and sixth woes, the internal-and-external issue becomes even clearer through two different metaphors. Matthew 23:25–26 speaks of the importance of the inside of the cup and plate being clean, not just the outside. In 23:27 these hypocrites are described as whitewashed tombs, which appear beautiful on the outside but inside are full of death and uncleanness. All of this is summed up with the statement of 23:28—"Thus, although you appear righteous before others on the outside, on the inside you are full of hypocrisy and lawlessness."[42]

42. The rest of the New Testament also witnesses to this same understanding, with forms of the *teleios/teleō/telos* word group occurring over seventy times. The book of James is one very clear example; multiple occurrences of *teleios* forms indicate a direct relationship with the Sermon (James 1:4, 17, 25; 2:8, 22; 3:2). Likewise, the idea of completion, maturity, and wholeness can be found repeatedly in Hebrews (2:10; 5:9, 14; 6:1; 7:28; 9:9; 10:1, 14; 12:23). It is also found in the writings of Paul, where the goal for every Christian is to reach maturity in Christ, which is a place of completeness and totality that accords precisely with the ideas already established in the OT (e.g., 1 Cor. 2:6; 14:20; Eph. 4:13; Phil. 3:12, 15; Col. 1:28; 4:12).

Conclusion

Taking this chapter and the previous one together, the point being made is that both *makarios* and *teleios* are key ideas for the best reading of the Sermon. Recognizing the importance of these dual conceptual rails serves a double purpose. On the one hand, it provides confirmation that the Sermon is trafficking in the ideas of Greco-Roman virtue as mediated through Hellenistic Judaism. At the same time, these dual ideas provide a framework for interpreting the Sermon holistically and with a consistent and pervasive internal logic. Chapters 2 and 3 have laid the groundwork for understanding the big ideas of *makarios* and *teleios*. The actual exposition of the Sermon in the following chapters will bear out the fruitfulness of these ideas even more.

4

Seven More Key Terms
and Concepts in the Sermon

Introduction

The first five chapters of this book aim to provide a foundational orientation to the best reading of the Sermon before engaging directly in its exposition. The preceding two chapters, on *makarios* and *teleios*, are lengthy and detailed because I am arguing that these two overlapping concepts are simultaneously two of the most important ideas for understanding the Sermon *and* the most misunderstood elements of the Sermon. They are, therefore, worthy of detailed exploration.

There are several other concepts that also prove essential to a good reading of the Sermon. These concepts are generally better understood and recognized in scholarly discussions of the Sermon, though not universally. The point of this chapter is to provide a brief survey of seven key ideas that appear in the Sermon and are important for understanding its cultural and conceptual encyclopedia. By discussing these ideas here, I provide a point of reference for these concepts in the later exposition of the Sermon, also eliminating the need for a lengthy discussion within my commentary. The seven themes or concepts under discussion here are: righteousness, hypocrisy, heart, gentiles/pagans, the Father in heaven, the kingdom of God/heaven, and reward/recompense/treasure.

Righteousness

Certainly one of the most important concepts in the Sermon is *dikaiosynē*, or righteousness. This is part of a larger theme in Matthew, but it is particularly

highlighted in the Sermon. The Greek root *dikai-* appears 26 times in Matthew.[1]
Very commonly this is in reference to "the righteous ones," an important category of people in Matthew. These righteous ones, or disciples, are often put
into contrast with other people and things, such as the unrighteous (*adikous*,
5:45), sinners (*hamartōlous*, 9:13), the evil ones (*ponērous*, 13:49), hypocrisy
and lawlessness (*hypokriseōs, anomias*, 23:28), and most interestingly, "those
of good repute" (*euōnymōn*, 25:41).[2]

Six of the occurrences of the root *dikai-* are in the Sermon (5:6, 10, 20, 45;
6:1, 33),[3] including two of Jesus's macarisms: those hungering and thirsting
for righteousness (5:6) and those persecuted because of righteousness (5:10).[4]
The frequency and importance of this root in the Sermon make it easy to see
it as an umbrella concept that envisages what Jesus expects of his disciples
so that they may enter the kingdom of heaven.[5]

Many scholars perceive that righteousness is one of the two main ideas
of the whole Sermon (along with kingdom).[6] Ulrich Luz notes that a fitting
title for the whole Sermon could be "Discourse on the Righteousness of the
Kingdom of Heaven."[7] Johan C. Thom's insightful analysis of the structure
of the Sermon based on the form of ancient speeches understands "exceeding

1. The root *dikai-* is manifested in the following forms in Matthew: the adjective *dikaios*
(17x); the noun *dikaiosynē* (7x); and the verb *dikaioō* (2x).
2. The other words contrasting with "righteous" are quite expected, but this last one is both
unexpected and classically Matthean. That is, to put the righteous ones (here it is the sheep
on the right in the parable of the sheep and goats [25:31–46]) in contrast with "those of good
repute/report" (the goats on the left) ties into the Matthean theme that the hypocrites are the
ones who *appear* righteous and are even praised by others in society but are not the ones who
are truly righteous and please God. Thus, "those of good repute" is not merely a euphemism
for "on the left" (as it is typically translated) but is a powerful Matthean piece of rhetoric
contrasting the seeming (Pharisaical) righteousness with true righteousness.
3. Of the seven occurrences of the noun *dikaiosynē* in Matthew, five are in the Sermon (5:6,
10, 20; 6:1, 33). The others are in 3:15 and 21:32. Matthew 5:45 has the adjectival form of the
same root, describing "righteous ones."
4. For those who structure the Beatitudes as two sets of four, this repetition of *dikaiosynē*
at the end of each of the two quatrains is an important structural indicator. See the classic
form-critical work of J. Dupont, *Les Béatitudes*, 3 vols. (Paris: Gabalda, 1973), 3:309–12; and
discussion of this option in H. Benedict Green, *Matthew, Poet of the Beatitudes* (Edinburgh:
T&T Clark, 2001), 26.
5. See Kari Syreeni, *The Making of the Sermon on the Mount: A Procedural Analysis of
Matthew's Redactoral Activity* (Helsinki: Suomalainen Tiedeakatemia, 1987), 207.
6. Glen H. Stassen, "The Beatitudes as Eschatological Peacemaking Virtues," in *Character
Ethics and the New Testament: Moral Dimensions of Scripture*, ed. Robert L. Brawley (Louisville: Westminster John Knox, 2007), 251. Robert Guelich sees the "greater righteousness"
as the theme of the heart of the Sermon, 5:17–7:12 (*The Sermon on the Mount: A Foundation
for Understanding* [Waco: Word, 1982]).
7. Ulrich Luz, *Matthew 1–7: A Commentary*, rev. ed., trans. James E. Crouch, Hermeneia
(Minneapolis: Fortress, 2007), 177.

righteousness" as the *propositio* or main theme (5:17–20).[8] Structurally, the central section of the Sermon (5:17–7:12) is clearly built on the idea of greater righteousness—righteousness in relation to the Torah (5:21–48), righteousness in personal piety (6:1–21), and righteousness in relation to the world (6:19–7:11). My own interpretation and structural analysis will affirm this idea of *greater righteousness* as the meta-category that makes sense of the whole Sermon, intimately connected as it is with both *makarios* and *teleios*. It is indeed the true *teleios* form of righteousness that will result in *makarios*-ness. The Sermon in many ways is an epitome of a moral philosophy on what righteousness is.

There has been no small debate about what "righteousness" means in Matthew.[9] Since the time of the Reformation, many have assumed that the Protestant understanding of "righteousness" in Paul's Letters as an imputed legal standing is also what Matthew means. Thus, for example, "hungering and thirsting for righteousness" is often interpreted as longing for God's imputed righteousness or the salvation he gives.[10] But careful study has shown that the Old Testament roots of the idea of righteousness are larger and more nuanced than merely forensic imputation. In the Old Testament, *ṣaddîq/ṣədāqâ* often has the idea of restorative *justice*,[11] understood in the context of covenant with God. This covenantal justice is ultimately God's work of setting the world to rights, his saving activity, though we are called to participate in this and are the beneficiaries of it. Relatedly, righteousness—both God's and humanity's—is a matter of honor.[12] Following suit, in the subsequent

8. Johan C. Thom, "Justice in the Sermon on the Mount: An Aristotelian Reading," *NovT* 51 (2009): 315. Robert Kinney, following George Kennedy, also understands 5:17–20 as the main proposition, identifying it with Quintilian's term *narration*. See Kinney, *Hellenistic Dimensions of the Gospel of Matthew* (Tübingen: Mohr Siebeck, 2016), 198, and Kennedy, *New Testament Interpretation through Rhetorical Criticism* (Chapel Hill: University of North Carolina Press, 1984), 50–51.

9. Benno Przyblyski's *Righteousness in Matthew and His World of Thought* (Cambridge: Cambridge University Press, 1980) has been very influential on subsequent Matthean scholarship.

10. See, e.g., Daniel M. Doriani, *The Sermon on the Mount: The Character of a Disciple* (Phillipsburg, NJ: P&R, 2006).

11. Stassen, "Beatitudes," 251.

12. See Jackson Wu, *Saving God's Face: A Chinese Contextualization of Salvation through Honor and Shame*, EMSDS (Pasadena, CA: William Carey International University Press, 2013); Jerome H. Neyrey, *Honor and Shame in the Gospel of Matthew* (Louisville: Westminster John Knox, 1998); David A. deSilva, *Honor, Patronage, Kinship Purity: Unlocking New Testament Culture* (Downers Grove, IL: IVP Academic, 2000); and Leland White, "Grid and Group in Matthew's Community: The Righteousness/Honor Code in the Sermon on the Mount," *Semeia* 35 (1986): 61–89. White points out that Jesus's disciples and Matthew's hearers are not considered "honorable" in their own society precisely because "the community claims Jesus the crucified as its leader. *Members of the community share the public esteem or blame in which the crucified is held*" (80). The Beatitudes (and the rest of the Sermon) provide a quasi-public forum where

Tannaitic literature righteousness "is uniformly a term for man's conduct in accord with God's will."[13] This is not to deny the theological construct of imputed righteousness, only to point out that more is going on with this term than that particular doctrine; and moreover, the theological concept of imputed righteousness is not in view in Matthew's usage.

The scholarly debate concerns whether "righteousness" in Matthew refers to God's saving activity or the ethical conduct required of Jesus's disciples.[14] In light of an overall reading of Matthew as well as the emphasis of the Sermon on human flourishing, it makes best sense to interpret *dikaiosynē* in Matthew not as imputed nor as something only God does, but in its natural ethical sense of what is expected of Jesus's disciples. In short, it is "doing the will of God" (7:21, 24; 12:50; cf. 6:10; 7:12; 18:14; 26:39, 42), that which is required to enter the kingdom of heaven (5:19–20; 7:21).[15] Outside of the Sermon, "righteousness" functions in the same way, as in 21:28–32, which contains a concatenation of the same terms—"doing the will of the father," "entering the kingdom of God," and "the way of righteousness" (in this case referring to the message that John preached).[16]

Yet at the same time, as Lee Irons rightly notes, while Matthew is not talking about Pauline justification, his ethical construal of "righteousness" is a "righteousness that rests upon the redemptive-historical and eschatological reality of the coming of the kingdom in the person of Jesus. This is what makes it the higher righteousness that exceeds that of the scribes and the Pharisees. In the words of Roland Deines, it is 'Jesus-righteousness.'"[17]

---

the disciples can be seen to be truly the righteous and honorable ones, despite what the society around them says. See also 5:11–12.

13. Syreeni, *Making of the Sermon*, 207, referring to Przyblyski, *Righteousness in Matthew*, 13–76.

14. An excellent survey and discussion can be found in Charles Lee Irons, *The Righteousness of God: A Lexical Examination of the Covenant-Faithfulness Interpretation* (Tübingen: Mohr Siebeck, 2015), 263–67.

15. In a very early reception of Matt. 7:12, 2 *Clem.* 4.2 glosses "righteousness" for "does the will of God"—"For he says, 'Not everyone who says to me, "Lord, Lord," will be saved, but only the one who does righteousness.'"

16. Dale Allison defines Matthew's "righteousness" as "Christian character and conduct in accordance with the demands of Jesus—right intention, right word, right deed" (W. D. Davies and Dale C. Allison Jr., *A Critical and Exegetical Commentary on the Gospel according to Saint Matthew*, vol. 1, *Introduction and Commentary on Matthew 1–7*, ICC [Edinburgh: T&T Clark, 2004], 499). Allison goes on to point out that the issue here is not a forensic or eschatological gift of God's righteousness as in Paul because the contrast is being made with the scribes' and Pharisees' righteousness. They do have a real righteousness, but it is deficient. The question is not whether they have a gift-righteousness, but what the nature and form (and heart) of that righteousness is.

17. Irons, *Righteousness of God*, 265–66, referencing Roland Deines, *Die Gerechtigkeit der Tora im Reich des Messias: Mt 5,13–20 als Schlüsseltext der matthäischen Theologie*, WUNT 177 (Tübingen: Mohr Siebeck, 2004).

This interpretation holds together well the strong ethical-discipleship sense of "righteousness" in Matthew with the eschatological orientation informed by Isaiah, in addition to the theological framing of the First Gospel, that Jesus has come to "save his people from their sins" (Matt. 1:21) through his death and resurrection. This fuller understanding accords with Benno Przybylski's insight into the ethical sense of "righteousness," but with a key difference: Przybylski wrongly argues that "righteousness" in Matthew has nothing to do with "getting in" but only "staying in" (covenantal nomism). For Matthew the "greater righteousness" is precisely what *is* required "to enter the kingdom of heaven" (5:20; cf. also 5:6, 10; 6:1–21; 7:13–14). For Matthew (and Paul), disciple-righteousness is not to be construed as the opposite of God's saving activity.

In Matthew, Jesus is the righteous one (27:19), he comes to bring about the consummation of righteousness (3:15, using "fulfillment" language), and he commends and exhorts others toward living that can be described as righteous (1:19; 10:41; 13:43, 49; 25:37, 46). All the while there is a subtle and powerful redefinition of what true righteousness is—it is not merely external piety but is the faithful purity and integrity of the inner person, the heart (23:27–28 describes the Pharisees, whose righteousness is only skin deep).

In sum, I define "righteousness" in Matthew as *whole-person behavior that accords with God's nature, will, and coming kingdom.* The "righteous" person, according to Matthew, is the one who follows Jesus in this way of being in the world. The righteous person is the *whole/teleios* person (5:48) who does not only do the will of God externally but, most importantly, from the heart. This is both radically continuous with the ethics of the Jewish Scriptures and radically in conflict with Jesus's interlocutors, the Pharisees.[18]

Hypocrisy

It is this functional definition of righteousness that provides the foil for the major theme in Matthew of hypocrisy/hypocrite. These English words are transliterations of the Greek *hypokrisis* and *hypokritēs*. The latter originally meant more neutrally an "actor" but took on a particularly negative connotation in the Septuagint (as a "godless one") and especially in Matthew's usage.[19]

18. For more discussion on how this idea of disciple-righteousness fits with grace and faith, see chap. 12.
19. *EDNT* 3:403.

Matthew particularly labels Jesus's enemies with this moniker.[20] Even though the scribes and Pharisees are not specifically called out as hypocrites in the Sermon, the strong collocation of ideas between Matt. 6:1–21 and Matt. 23, where they are repeatedly called "hypocrites," indicates that while hypocrisy is a more general phenomenon than Pharisaism, the Pharisees are a clear example.

As a result of Matthew's frequent use of this term and the First Gospel's influence on Christianity, "hypocrite" has become a significant entry in our own subsequent cultural encyclopedia. This creates a bit of a problem for reading Matthew, however, because his meaning is slightly different from how the word functions today. Typically in English usage today, this word refers to someone who says one thing but does the opposite. In common parlance, a hypocrite is one who lives a double life, contrasting actions and words, such as a politician taking bribes while running a campaign against corruption. This is not the sense of "hypocrite" in Matthew, however. Doubleness is a good way to describe hypocrisy in Matthew, but it is a doubleness of actions and the inner person or heart, not of words and actions. This is the opposite of being *teleios*, as was discussed in the previous chapter. Thus, hypocrisy is a very important idea for Matthew because it is the great enemy of true righteousness, defined as whole-person behavior. Jesus's hearers and Matthew's audience (both within and outside the church) were not being addressed on the issue of behavioral morality or external righteousness but rather on a matter of the heart or inner person. Because righteousness is whole-person virtuous living, for a religious community the most serious potential opposite to this is not blatant immorality but a skin-deep righteousness rather than true wholeness.[21] These two major themes in Matthew are mutually informing and function together as a foundational part of Matthew's vision.

Heart

Another very important and related idea in Matthew is the notion of the "heart." Forms of the Greek term *kardia* occur over nine hundred times in

20. The noun *hypokritēs*, referring to a person, occurs thirteen times in Matthew (6:2, 5, 16; 7:5; 15:7; 22:18; 23:13, 15, 23, 25, 27, 29; 24:51) out of a total of seventeen times in the NT. The abstract noun *hypocrisis*, "hypocrisy," occurs once (23:28). By way of contrast, Mark only uses *hypokritēs* once and Luke three times. This is a Matthean favorite. With only two occurrences in the Septuagint (Job 34:30; 36:13), *hypokritēs* does not appear to be a word that Matthew picked up from his Jewish tradition as much as from the realm of Hellenism.

21. Allison references the sentiment from Plato that "the greatest unrighteousness would be to appear righteous but not be" (my translation of the Greek) (Davies and Allison, *Matthew 1–7*, 581).

the Septuagint and are especially prominent in the Psalms (ca. 135x), Sirach (ca. 85x), Proverbs (ca. 75x), and most of the Prophets. It continues to be an important concept in the New Testament, where it is found more than 150 times, especially in Luke, Acts, Romans, and Matthew (16x).[22] There is a strong consistency in the meaning of this word throughout the Septuagint and New Testament, including in Matthew. Unlike in common English parlance, where "heart" becomes a metaphor for the seat of emotions, *kardia* in biblical usage refers more broadly to "human life in its totality."[23] Walther Eichrodt describes it as "a comprehensive term for the personality as a whole, its inner life, its character." It is what comes out of the heart that reveals the quality of the whole inner person.[24] As Birger Gerhardsson states, the biblical notion of the heart is an "inclusive term for man's inner nature, not only as the 'seat' of the animal instincts but also as the 'seat' of faith and knowledge of God."[25] Biblical *kardia* has overlap with "soul," "reasoning," and "mind" and is definitely closely associated with the seat of mental faculties, much broader and deeper than mere emotions.[26]

This important Greek and biblical notion proves important for reading Matthew and the Sermon well. In line with Psalms, Proverbs, and Isaiah (34x), Matthew puts great emphasis on the heart as the true inner person. This is seen especially in Jesus's teachings about the heart being the inner person from which all else flows, such as in Matt. 12:34 and 15:18–19. It is the heart that can become "fat," resulting in the inability to hear or see God (13:15), and people can continue to honor God with their lips while their inner person/heart is far away (15:8, quoting Isa. 29:13). Instead the disciple is called to forgive others "from the heart" (Matt. 18:35) and ultimately to "love the Lord your God with all your heart, with all your soul, and with all your mind" (22:37; cf. Deut. 6:5).

Within the Sermon *kardia* occurs three times (5:8, 28; 6:21). The "pure in heart" in the Beatitudes are given the remarkable promise that they will "see God" (5:8). It is difficult to imagine a higher commendation than the ability to see God, tied as it is with a unified (cf. *teleios*) or pure, undivided heart.

22. Walther Eichrodt, "*kardia*," *NIDNTT* 2:623, 2:625.

23. Ibid., 624.

24. Ibid., 624.

25. Birger Gerhardsson, *The Testing of God's Son (Matthew 4:1–11 & PAR): An Analysis of an Early Christian Midrash*, trans. John Toy (Lund: Gleerup, 1966; Eugene, OR: Wipf & Stock, 2009), 48. Discussed also in Green, *Matthew, Poet*, 238.

26. For an exploration of how the biblical idea of the heart relates to Christian psychology, see the insightful essay by Robert C. Roberts, "Situationism and the New Testament Psychology of the Heart," in *The Bible and the University*, ed. David Lyle Jeffrey and C. Stephen Evans (Grand Rapids: Zondervan, 2007), 139–59.

The eye as the lamp of the body is connected here as well because one's ability to see clearly is a reflection of one's inner state, whether it is light or darkness (6:22–23). Looking lustfully at a woman "in/from the heart" (5:28) is used in one of the representative exegeses of 5:21–47 to describe the greater righteousness that is required to be a disciple of Jesus—not just obeying externally but with the whole person. Finally, in 6:21, at a climactic moment in the discourse, Jesus gives an aphorism that connects one's inner person with one's treasure or reward: "where your treasure is, there will your heart be also." This is not merely a tautology, saying "what you value is what you love." Rather, it is a powerful challenge to say that what you value and love is who you really are; what you treasure is who your inner person really is.

Thus, this notion of the heart is yet another piece of the mosaic of biblical anthropology that Matthew is creating. The hypocrite is the one who lacks true righteousness because he or she does not have purity or wholeness in the inner person, the heart.

Gentiles/Pagans

Fundamental to the Jewish people's self-understanding was that they were the chosen people, God's own possession, and that all the varied peoples around them could be described with the generic term "the peoples" or "the nations," often taking on negative connotations. The Hebrew term *gôy* was translated into the Septuagint as *ethnos*, an important word that occurs nearly a thousand times and is found especially frequently in Isaiah and Ezekiel. This word continues in common usage to refer to the non-Jewish peoples 160 times in the New Testament, especially in Acts and the Pauline corpus, often quoting the Old Testament.[27] One lexicon defines it as "those who do not belong to groups professing faith in the God of Israel, *the nations, gentiles, unbelievers.*"[28]

Ethnos is also an important word in Matthew, appearing fifteen times, plus an additional three occurrences of a closely related adjective, *ethnikos.*[29] Most of the time *ethnos* functions rather neutrally to refer to peoples other than ethnic Jews (10:5, 18; 24:7; 25:32), sometimes with a rather negative sense (6:32; 20:19, 25; 24:9; the three uses of *ethnikos* fit here: 5:47; 6:7; 18:17), and other times, quite unlike the Jewish Scriptures, *ethnos* functions positively as the goal and focus of Jesus's ministry (4:15; 12:18, 21; 21:43; 24:14; 28:19).

27. Hans Bietenhard, "*ethnos*," *NIDNTT* 2:89.
28. BDAG, 276.
29. The occurrences of *ethnos* in Matthew are in 4:15; 6:32; 10:5, 18; 12:18, 21; 20:19, 25; 21:43; 24:7 (2x), 9, 14; 25:32; 28:19; and the occurrences of *ethnikos* are in 5:47; 6:7; 18:17.

The combination of the last two within Matthew—especially in light of the climactic gentile-inclusive Great Commission (28:18–20)—has caused much consternation and confusion for scholars who attempt to figure out how the First Gospel can be simultaneously so critical and positive toward "the gentiles."

I suggest that the solution to this puzzle comes from a broader reading of Matthew that recognizes the major theological emphasis in the First Gospel on *the redefinition of the people of God as based on faith-response to Jesus rather than ethnicity.* There are many ways in which this theme is unfolded throughout Matthew, beginning with gentile inclusion in the genealogy (1:1–17), the contrast of the pagan magi with the faithless Jerusalemites (2:1–12), and John the Baptist's claim that God can raise up descendants for Abraham from stones since his ethnic descendants are faithless and in danger of being cut off (3:7–12). These elements set the tone for the rest of the Gospel, which repeatedly makes bold statements such as that a centurion had a faith that Jesus found nowhere in Israel and that many "will come from east and west and recline at table with Abraham, Isaac, and Jacob in the kingdom of heaven, while the sons of the kingdom will be thrown into the outer darkness" (8:10–12 ESV). Often notorious gentile and sinful people are intentionally put into a contrastive relationship with Jewish people, such as by speaking of Tyre, Sidon, and Sodom as better off than Chorazin, Bethsaida, and Capernaum (11:20–24), and contrasting the Pharisees and scribes from Jerusalem with the faith (and the healing/salvation) of a *Canaanite* woman (15:1–28).[30] Many more examples could be given. The point is not that Matthew is somehow anti-Semitic but rather that, along with the rest of the New Testament authors, he understands through Jesus's teachings and death and resurrection that in the new covenant the people of God are defined along different lines, no longer in terms of ethnicity but based on whether one responds to Christ in faith. "There is no longer Jew or Greek" (Gal. 3:28 NRSV) does not mean there is no difference between the people of God and those outside but rather that the basis for this distinction is no longer ethnicity per se.

My understanding of what Matthew is saying is similar to the work of Graham Stanton. Stanton's influential book, *A Gospel for a New People: Studies in Matthew*, argues on both literary and sociohistorical grounds that Matthew is consciously writing to encourage the young church that the people of God now comprises both Jews and gentiles. Stanton prefers "new people"

---

30. The poignancy and rhetorical power of this contrast are heightened by Matthew's choice to anachronistically describe this Syro-Phoenician woman (Mark 7:26) as a *Canaanite*, clearly alluding to Israel's great enemies at the time of the exodus.

to "new Israel" or "true Israel" because the latter implies more continuity between the church and Israel than Matthew sees. Instead, Matthew's emphasis, in Stanton's view, is on the new people created out of both Jews and gentiles. A key verse in this understanding is Matt. 21:43, where Jesus warns that the kingdom will be taken away from the unfaithful tenants and given to a people (*ethnos*) who yield its proper fruit. This in effect creates a *tertium genus*, a third race of both Jews and gentiles.[31]

Matthew's appropriation of this understanding is subtle but powerful, and tied up in his use of *ethnos* and *ethnikos*. As noted, sometimes *ethnos* is neutrally referring to peoples of the world, but when it is used negatively, Matthew uses the word as part of his intentional redefining of who the people of God are. Matthew—who is writing some decades after the establishment of the church and this understanding—uses "gentiles" negatively to refer to anyone outside the people of God (the *ekklēsia*, another term adopted from the OT), regardless of ethnicity. That is, in a subtle but powerful way "gentile" has come to mean any Jewish person or (ethnic) gentile who does not follow Christ; the Jew-gentile distinction still exists, but the lines are now eschatologically drawn based on a faith-response to Jesus rather than ethnicity.[32] Any people outside the church can be said to be gentiles in need of evangelism and discipleship.

The Pharisees and other Jewish leaders particularly fall under this critique-through-redefinition-of-terms in Matthew. One of the most powerful ways is through identifying the raging gentiles who oppose the Messiah of Ps. 2 with the Jewish leaders. Five times in Matthew the Jewish leadership is said to gather together and take counsel on how to destroy Jesus.[33] This language is shockingly reminiscent of the same gathering together and counseling to destroy the Lord's anointed of the famous Second Psalm. This is a turning of the tables on the Jewish leadership—calling them the gentiles—that apparently was not unique to Matthew, as the same technique is used in Acts 4:23–28.

This understanding is important because, like the previous themes, it connects closely with Matthew's overall point. The new people of God, the truly righteous ones, the non-hypocrites, cannot be identified by ethnicity or the trappings of Jewish piety, but rather they are defined as followers of Jesus from the heart, the inner person. "Who is my mother and who are my brothers?"

31. Graham Stanton, *A Gospel for a New People: Studies in Matthew* (Edinburgh: T&T Clark, 1992), 11–12.

32. Matthew does not take the next logical linguistic step that Paul does in calling the church "Israel," though this is entailed in his own redefinition of "gentile." Cf. Gal. 6:16; Rom. 2:29; 4:12; 9:6–8; Phil. 3:3.

33. Matt. 12:14; 22:15; 26:3–4; 27:1; 28:12.

Jesus asks. The answer he gives is: "whoever does the will of my Father in heaven is my brother and sister and mother" (12:48–50 ESV). Thus, for Matthew's readers, the four references to "gentiles" in the Sermon, whatever connotations may have been evoked for those who heard the historical Jesus, can be understood as referring to those outside of the church.[34]

The Father in Heaven

Another very important theological concept for Matthew as a whole and the Sermon in particular is the emphasis on God as Father, particularly as "Father in heaven."[35] While the idea of God as Father was rare in ancient Israel, it was not completely absent. In the Second Temple period, however, it becomes more common, and this provided the backdrop for Jesus's own usage. The older notion that Jesus was unique in referring to God as Father has since been shown to be overstated. But it is true that understanding God as Father and addressing him in this way was *more frequent* and *characteristic* of Jesus and Christianity from its earliest days.

The Gospels refer to God as Father (*patēr*) over 170 times, most of them coming from the Gospel of John (109x). Second to John is Matthew, which refers to God as Father 44 times, much more frequently than the other Synoptics (Mark 4x; Luke 17x). This shows that for the First and Fourth Gospels (which prove to be the most influential on the church), God as Father is an important theme. God's fatherhood becomes a foundational idea for Christianity, no small part of which is the "Our Father" beginning to the Lord's Prayer. Paul also makes much of the idea that the Christian is *adopted* into God's community and thereby made a child of God and an heir of the Father's

34. A recent and increasingly well-received interpretation is that of Matthias Konradt, *Israel, Church, and the Gentiles in the Gospel of Matthew*, trans. Kathleen Ess (Waco: Baylor University Press, 2014). Konradt explores carefully the narrative of Matthew and concludes that the strong critique of the Jewish people in Matthew is directed primarily at the Jewish leaders, not the people in general. Moreover, for Matthew, Konradt argues, Israel remains the people (*laos*) of God in distinction from the *ekklēsia*. There is no opposition between these two groups, and Israel can only now find its salvation as part of the *ekklēsia* because of the death and resurrection of Jesus. However, the church does not supersede or replace Israel; rather, the church has a responsibility for an ongoing mission to Israel along with the gentiles. I am sympathetic to this view and find it has many strengths. At the same time, I think one can understand Matthew's redefinition of the people of God in a way that still respects the uniqueness, salvation-historical priority, and ongoing mission to ethnic Israel.

35. For a fuller discussion of the Jewish background to God as Father and Matthew's usage, see Jonathan T. Pennington, *Heaven and Earth in the Gospel of Matthew* (Leiden: Brill, 2007; repr., Grand Rapids: Baker Academic, 2009), chaps. 9–10. The following discussion is largely a summary of that material with some additions.

kingdom (Rom. 8:14–17; Gal. 4:4–7). Because of Matthew's frequent usage
of the idea of God as Father, H. F. D. Sparks concludes that Matthew "had a
special interest in the Divine Fatherhood," and Armin Wouters argues that "the
will of the Father" is a central idea in the whole proclamation of Matthew.[36]

Particularly distinct is Matthew's preference for referring to God as the
"Father in heaven" or with the synonymous "heavenly Father."[37] This too
becomes a common way for Christianity to conceive and speak of the First
Person of the Trinity. For Matthew it is part of an elaborate literary and theological theme of "heaven" and "earth" language that emphasizes the contrast
between God and humanity, using the metaphors of "heaven" and "earth."[38]

God's fatherhood revealed by Jesus would have been understood in the first-
century ear as communicating "both respectful dependence and affectionate
intimacy as well as obedience."[39] Ancient notions of fatherhood could create
juxtapositions somewhat lost in contemporary Western notions—intimacy
and awe, familial comfort and reverent respect. Donald Hagner suggests that
Matthew's "father in heaven" particularly communicates this juxtaposition
by combining "the personal, or immanent, element of fatherhood with the
transcendental element of God's otherness, 'in heaven.'"[40]

Jesus exhorts his followers to "call no one on earth father, for you have
one Father, who is in heaven" (Matt. 23:9). He also redefines the disciples'
biological relationships by calling people to leave their families if need be
(8:21–22; 10:34–37; 19:29) and providing them a new family identity based
on relationship with God through him (12:46–50; cf. 4:18–22).[41]

While God as Father is a recurrent theme in Matthew overall, it is especially important in the Sermon. The largest concentration of references to
God as Father is found in the Sermon (17x), including the first occurrence of

36. H. F. D. Sparks, "The Doctrine of Divine Fatherhood in the Gospels," in *Studies in the
Gospels: Essays in Memory of R. H. Lightfoot*, ed. D. E. Nineham (Oxford: Blackwell, 1967),
251; Armin Wouters, ". . . *wer den Willen meines Vaters Tut": Eine Untersuchung zum Ver-
ständnis vom Handeln in Matthäusevangelium* (Regensburg: Pustet, 1992).

37. Matthew's "Father in heaven" (*ho patēr en tois ouranois*) occurs thirteen times and
"heavenly Father" (*ho patēr ho ouranios*) another seven times. The only other time God is
referred to in these ways in the preceding Second Temple literature or the NT is Mark 11:25,
which closely parallels Matt. 6:14.

38. See my *Heaven and Earth*.

39. Craig S. Keener, *The Gospel of Matthew: A Socio-Rhetorical Commentary* (Grand
Rapids: Eerdmans, 2009), 216.

40. Donald Hagner, *Matthew 1–13*, WBC 33A (Nashville: Nelson, 1993), 101.

41. William Willimon and Stanley Hauerwas write, "For those who learn to pray like this,
our first family is not our biological family but those who have taught us to pray, 'Our Father'"
(*Lord, Teach Us: The Lord's Prayer and the Christian Life* [Nashville: Abingdon, 1996], 32). See
also Jonathan T. Pennington, "Christian Psychology and the Gospel of Matthew," *Edification:
The Journal of the Society of Christian Psychology* 3, no. 2 (2009): 39–48.

this language in Matthew, in 5:16.[42] Strikingly, in every instance but one Jesus speaks of God to the disciples as "*your* Father in heaven / heavenly Father."[43] Luz states that together the words "righteousness" and "Father" indicate the subject matter of the whole Sermon. Likewise, he observes that "Father in heaven" is the "guiding word" of the entire Sermon.[44] Similarly, R. T. France states that the Sermon is about the life and values of the followers of Jesus "who recognize God as their Father in heaven."[45]

Not only are the references to God as Father extremely frequent in the Sermon, they appear at crucial points. For example, the first occurrence in Matt. 5:16 comes as the conclusion to the first section of the Sermon (5:1–16), which summarizes the teaching with the exhortation to live in such a way that the disciples' lives lead others to honor their heavenly Father. Another crucial verse in the central section of the Sermon (5:17–7:12), 5:48 with its "be *teleios*" command, also uses "heavenly Father" language. On the other end of the Sermon, in the concluding unit (7:13–8:1), 7:21 makes clear that doing "the will of my Father in heaven" is the essential requirement for entering into the kingdom of heaven.

But going beyond these important verses, it is in the middle of the central section of the Sermon (5:17–7:12) where we find the greatest concentration of "Father" language. Here God is referred to as "Father" a full twelve times. Within this middle point of the Sermon (6:1–21) is built the contrast between laying up treasures with the Father in heaven versus humans on earth.[46] The constant refrain throughout this section is that the disciples should not practice their piety to earn the praise of others because they have a Father who sees from heaven and will reward them. In the very middle of this elaborate discourse is the famous Lord's Prayer (6:9–15), which begins with the invitation to address God as "Our Father," thus putting this notion at the very core of the Sermon. This section of the Sermon concludes by emphasizing the heavenly Father's knowledge of his children's needs and his abundant provision (6:26, 32).

Thus, throughout the Sermon a major aspect of the teaching is the notion that the disciples of Jesus have God as their heavenly Father. The major

42. The seventeen references to God as Father in the Sermon are 5:16, 45, 48; 6:1, 4, 6 (2x), 8, 9, 14, 15, 18 (2x), 26, 32; 7:11, 21.

43. The only exception is 7:21, where Jesus says that only those who do "the will of *my* Father who is in heaven" will enter the kingdom of heaven. In 6:9 Jesus tells the disciples to refer to their heavenly Father when praying as "*Our* Father who is in heaven," which I take as the plural equivalent of the expression in 7:21 used in the context of instruction.

44. Luz, *Matthew 1–7*, 352.

45. R. T. France, *Matthew: Evangelist and Teacher* (Eugene, OR: Wipf & Stock, 2004), 254.

46. See the exposition of these verses in chap. 8 below.

function of this "Father" language in the Sermon is to give the disciples a clear and distinct identity as the true children of the God of Israel, which is not unrelated to the redefinition of the people of God as discussed in the previous section.

The Kingdom of God / Kingdom of Heaven

There are few things in the scholarly discussion of Jesus that attain the lofty status of true consensus. One thing that does reach that height is that the historical Jesus preached and taught about the *kingdom of God*. What he thought about himself, whether his followers truly followed him, and why he died are all debated. But no one doubts that Jesus taught and preached regularly about God's reign or kingdom. All three of the Synoptic Gospels make this abundantly clear.

First among these is the First Gospel, which depicts Jesus's ministry as very much about God's kingdom both in action and in content of teaching.[47] As Donald Hagner has noted, the controlling theme for Matthew is the kingdom, and R. T. France observes that the kingdom of heaven functions "virtually as a slogan for the whole scope of the ministry of Jesus" in Matthew.[48] Matthew's unique contribution to the idea of the kingdom particularly comes through in his exclusive use of the phrase "the kingdom of heaven" (occurring thirty-two times), which is synonymous with "the kingdom of God" though different in connotative nuance.[49]

The Sermon on the Mount plays no small part in this kingdom emphasis, and many scholars see the kingdom as the Sermon's "principal theological concept."[50] We should not be surprised, then, to encounter references to the kingdom throughout the Sermon. We see this language immediately in the opening section of the Beatitudes. Indeed, "for theirs is the kingdom of heaven" serves as an *inclusio* in the first and eighth Beatitudes (5:3, 10), providing a framework and frame of reference for Jesus's macarisms.[51] The term "king-

47. A fuller account of the theme of kingdom in Matthew can be found in Pennington, *Heaven and Earth*, chap. 12.

48. Hagner, *Matthew 1–13*, lx; France, *Matthew: Evangelist and Teacher*, 262.

49. As I argue in *Heaven and Earth*, Matthew's unique verbiage of "kingdom of heaven" has particularly strong evocations that are a part of Matthew's elaborate theme, which contrasts God's heavenly ways with humanity's earthly ways.

50. This is the expression of Hans Dieter Betz in his "Cosmogony and Ethics in the Sermon on the Mount," in *Cosmogony and Ethical Order*, ed. Robin Lovin and Frank Reynolds (Chicago: Chicago University Press, 1985), 120.

51. As will be argued in the discussion of the structure of the Sermon in chap. 5, there are nine Beatitudes, spanning 5:3–11, not eight as some commentators have suggested, nor seven

dom" also appears six more times in the Sermon, at crucial junctures. Its three appearances in 5:19–20 are important because these verses serve as the proposition for the whole Sermon. The references to the kingdom of heaven here make clear that the issue at hand is whether one enters into the kingdom and is a part of God's people. The same idea is highlighted at the end of the Sermon in 7:21. No less important is the high-altitude, concluding exhortation of 6:33 to "seek first the kingdom and his righteousness." And even more central is the reference to the kingdom in the initial threefold petition of the Lord's Prayer (6:9–10). Here the kingdom is in a Venn diagram–like overlapping relationship with God's name and will, with the request that all of this reality now in heaven become our earthly experience.

All of these references to the kingdom invite the hearer to recognize that what Jesus is teaching in the Sermon is tied directly to his opening words and general message of "Repent, for the kingdom of heaven is at hand!" (4:17 ESV). Moreover, the entire literary frame for the Sermon and the narrative block that follows (Matt. 8–9) are demarcated by references to Jesus preaching and teaching "the gospel of the kingdom" (4:23; 9:35).[52] This prominence of the kingdom also orients the reader to understand that the macarisms and other wisdom being offered by the Sage Jesus in the Sermon are more than generalized, universal, human wisdom. Rather, these references to the kingdom of heaven set Jesus's teaching into the context of the Jewish story of God's reign and particularly the Jewish expectation of its eschatological consummation,[53] its coming from heaven to earth. To frame the Beatitudes and to open the Sermon with references to God's heavenly reign is to use a megaphone to communicate that Jesus's ministry is looking forward to the eschaton—in case there is any hearer who had not picked that up from Matthew's preceding four chapters.

Most importantly along these lines, we may note that the emphasis on the kingdom of God/heaven in the Sermon (and in Matthew more generally) is deeply interwoven with the vision of virtue and human flourishing. As I have argued earlier, in the ancient world, including in both the Jewish and Greek traditions, the ideal king was the example of a virtuous philosopher. The ideal king is the virtuous one who himself imitates the gods, becoming an animate

---

as was commonly argued in the premodern period. The ninth is set apart and highlighted by its repeating the content of the eighth and by its serving as a kind of add-on bonus feature to the *inclusio* structure of the first through eighth Beatitudes.

52. Luz observes that "the kingdom of heaven promised for the future stands over the entire Sermon on the Mount" (*Matthew 1–7*, 172).

53. Hans Dieter Betz describes the clause "for theirs is the kingdom of heaven" (5:3, 10) as "an anticipatory eschatological verdict" belonging to an account of the last judgment (cf. 25:31–46, esp. v. 34) (*Essays on the Sermon on the Mount* [1985; Minneapolis: Fortress, 2009], 26).

or living law, which then produces harmony for his subjects.[54] Matthew, rooted in his own cultural encyclopedia of linguistic associations for both "sage" and "king," is implicitly arguing that Jesus is the embodiment of both wisdom and the kingdom. The theme of the reign of God and human flourishing are not accidentally connected in the Sermon, but are organically intertwined.

Reward, Recompense, and Treasure

The final Matthean theme relevant to the Sermon is that of reward, recompense, and treasure. Matthew particularly highlights these overlapping ideas and uses the noun *misthos*, "reward, recompense," ten times, as compared to five times in the rest of the Gospels combined. Sometimes *misthos* is utilized negatively, warning against loss of payment/reward (6:1, 2, 5, 16), while at other times positively in terms of a promise (5:12, 46; 10:41–42; 20:8). So too with the closely related word "treasure," *thēsauros*, which occurs seven times in Matthew (6:19, 20, 21; 12:35; 13:44, 52; 19:21). Also connected: God the Father is frequently depicted as rewarding or recompensing people (*apodidōmi*) who are either good or bad (6:4, 6, 18; 16:27; implied in 18:35; 20:8; 21:41).[55] God is seen as one who pays back righteously. At the same time, people are required to recompense each other and God appropriately.[56] Many of these references are found in the Sermon, especially in the middle of the central section of the discourse (6:1–21), whose *kəlāl* heading and conclusion (see chap. 5) both emphasize this as the theme—true and lasting reward/treasure or not. Kinney notes that the demand of righteousness in the Sermon is set in relationship to the promise of eschatological reward, and, indeed, "these two concepts—righteousness and rewards—account for every verse of the Sermon on the Mount."[57]

The two main points relevant to interpreting the Sermon are these. First, the idea of receiving a wage, reward, or treasure is yet another piece of the

54. Josh Jipp, *Christ Is King: Paul's Royal Ideology* (Minneapolis: Fortress, 2015), 50–51.

55. *Apodidōmi* occurs eighteen times in Matthew as compared to one time in Mark and eight times in Luke.

56. Stephen Barton observes that wealth is a notably frequent and important symbol for the moral life/righteousness in Matthew: "The extent to which the nature of the moral life, or what constitutes 'righteousness,' is displayed in economic terms in the Gospel of Matthew is remarkable. This fits with Matthew's emphasis . . . on desires of the heart rightly ordered—in particular, the demand for total, undivided love of God and love of neighbor (cf. Matt 5:43–48; 19:19b; 22:35–39)." See Barton, "Money Matters: Economic Relations and the Transformation of Value in Early Christianity," in *Engaging Economics: New Testament Scenarios and Early Christian Reception*, ed. Bruce Longenecker and Kelly Liebengood (Grand Rapids: Eerdmans, 2009), 41.

57. Kinney, *Hellenistic Dimensions of the Gospel of Matthew*, 199.

wisdom/virtue background to the Sermon for which I have been arguing. The good and virtuous person expects an appropriate reward, not in a mercenary or self-aggrandizing sense but as the natural outworking of justice and God's just design of the universe. In light of the many other strong clues that the Sermon is a piece of eschatological wisdom/virtue literature, inviting people into true human flourishing, the theme of reward and recompense makes sense. Note, however, that especially in the Protestant tradition, with its built-in concern about the dangers of "works-righteousness," we often translate *misthos* with "reward," especially when used spiritually, rather than with "wages," "recompense," or "remuneration," even though these latter glosses do communicate the sense of the word. This is almost certainly a function of the difficulty the Protestant tradition has in maintaining a balance between the reality of just recompense for virtue and God's grace understood as an unmerited gift.[58]

Second, relatedly, any notion of Kantian altruism as part of Christian ethics is smashed by the dominance of this theme in the Sermon. That is, a significant part of how the argument of the Sermon is pursued is through an appeal to people to get true and lasting reward, to experience the flourishing they long for. This is no ethics of divine-command voluntarism nor a valuing of suffering for suffering's sake. Jesus continually offers great reward in heaven (Matt. 5:12), depicts the heavenly Father as one who gives blessings abundantly (6:33; 7:7–11), and warns people against the foolishness of not gaining an eternal treasure (6:1–21). For additional discussion, see the conclusion to the commentary on 6:1–21 in chapter 8.

Conclusion

The point of this chapter, in conjunction with the rest of part 1 of this book, is to provide a framework in which to understand the major themes and ideas of the Sermon. In addition to the ideas of *makarios* and *teleios*, which are typically the least understood aspects of the Sermon, I have identified here seven other ideas that prove to be frequent and framing concepts in the cultural encyclopedia of the Sermon. The Model Reader will keep these meta-level notions in mind when circling toward an understanding of the details of the individual teachings of the text.

58. For a thoughtful exploration of how this idea of recompense appears in Romans, see Jeff de Waal Dryden, "Immortality in Romans 2:6–11," *Journal of Theological Interpretation* 7.2 (2013): 295–310.

5

The Structure(s) of the Sermon
and Its Setting within Matthew

Introduction

The original subtitle to Robert Gundry's commentary on Matthew was "A Commentary on His Literary and Theological Art."[1] Gundry is not alone in recognizing the highly literary nature and complex artistry of the First Gospel. Readers and scholars alike have long appreciated—and been perplexed by—the intricacy of Matthew's literary prowess. As James Edwards has noted, Matthew is the "definitive" Gospel when it comes to structure. "The Gospel of Matthew displays greater design, balance, proportion, and order than any of the other three Gospels."[2]

Matthew's literary skills, notably, are not so much in the telling of epic and moving narratives; one unexpected observation about Matthew in comparison with his Synoptic brothers is that his narrative pericopes are generally much shorter and less detailed than theirs. Moreover, none of the Gospels fall into

1. Robert H. Gundry, *Matthew: A Commentary on His Literary and Theological Art* (Grand Rapids: Eerdmans, 1982). The second edition proceeded with a very different subtitle, one that clearly reflects the social-scientific and group-identity issues that were being hotly debated in Matthean studies in the 1990s: *A Commentary on His Handbook for a Mixed Church under Persecution* (Grand Rapids: Eerdmans, 1995).
2. James R. Edwards, *The Hebrew Gospel and Its Development of the Synoptic Tradition* (Grand Rapids: Eerdmans, 2009), 246.

the genre of epic story; they are biographies primarily.[3] Matthew appears
to be concerned less with the individual narratives per se than with how
these stories fit together in conjunction with major teaching blocks to tell a
larger story. Matthew's literary skill is all about *structure*. Many of the most
important aspects of Matthew can only be discerned by paying attention to
broader structures and themes rather than the individual story, noting how
various aspects of the material are structured together.

Therefore, in reading and rereading Matthew one begins to sense that there
is much more going on than first meets the eye in the arranging and crafting
of the stories into groups and patterns. I often think of Matthew as having
divine crop circles. To see the pattern, image, and message, one must get to
a higher elevation, an altitude of reading that provides perspective to see
larger patterns.[4] When walking in the midst of the fields of stories, following
along after Jesus, seeing him interact with others and hearing him teach, the
reader is amazed at his teaching and actions. This alone would be sufficient
and a contribution to our understanding of Jesus. But the evangelist is doing
more than data-dumping assorted stories. He is an artist and a theologian,
a theological artist and an artistic theologian. *Matthew's* voice—which is all
that we have access to in his Gospel[5]—is found in paying attention to how he
retells the individual pericopes, but much more in how he shapes and molds
and structures his many stories and teachings into the piece of theological
art that the First Gospel is. With Matthew the whole (communicated through
complex and beautiful structures) is always more than the sum of the parts.

The Sermon on the Mount is no exception to this habit in Matthew. Indeed,
the Sermon, while not the center of the Gospel or its entire message, does have
pride of place as the first of Matthew's five major teaching discourses, and it
does serve as the epitome of Jesus's teaching concerning true righteousness,
a primary theological truth. Moreover, of the five major discourses (to be
discussed below), the Sermon probably has the most complex and systematic
structure. To read the Sermon well requires close attention to how the parts

3. See my *Reading the Gospels Wisely: A Narrative and Theological Introduction* (Grand
Rapids: Baker Academic, 2012).
4. Cf. the Argentinian widower who planted trees to make a guitar shape in dedication to his
wife: Becky Evans, "Widow's Tribute to His Beautiful Wife: Stunning Forest Planted in Shape of
a Guitar That He Has Never Seen because He Fears Flying," *Daily Mail*, March 12, 2013, http://
www.dailymail.co.uk/news/article-2292155/Guitar-forest-Argentinian-widow-creates-tribute
-wife-planting-wood-seen-fears-flying.html. The shape can only be discerned from the air.
5. As noted in the first chapter, while historical setting and background information are very
valuable and helpful tools for reading well, our goal is not to get inside the mind of the historical
Matthew (something impossible to do) but instead to try to approximate the Model Reader of
the *text* of the Gospel according to Matthew, who is the implied author.

and the whole fit together. Before this, however, it will be helpful to make a few comments about the overall structure of Matthew and the Sermon's place in this larger work. We will then turn to a number of structural observations and suggestions about the Sermon itself.[6]

The Structure of the First Gospel

As noted above, the study of the structure of the Sermon is very old, demanded as it is by the literary form and skill manifested in Matthew and discernible by observant readers. While a literary-structural approach to interpretation was not of interest to most readers of the first millennium of the church, this is not a purely modern phenomenon either.[7]

Nonetheless, it was primarily in the latter half of the twentieth century that narrative and literary analysis of the First Gospel came into maturity.[8] There is no consensus, however, on this interesting topic within Matthean scholarship. One of the first scholars to move beyond a merely chronological structuring of Matthew was B. W. Bacon.[9] He observed and emphasized one important set of structural clues in Matthew, the repetition of the words "and it happened when Jesus had finished . . ." (7:28; 11:1; 13:53; 19:1; 26:1). As many scholars have since observed, this language stands out in Matthew and clearly is intended to provide important transitions in the material. This

6. It should be noted that in all of this I am assuming that Matthew the evangelist is responsible for the many structural elements throughout the First Gospel, including the final form of the Sermon, rather than ascribing them only to the historical Jesus. This is a reasonable assumption based on the different form and location that much of this same traditional material takes in other places in Luke, as well as clear evidence of heavy Matthean editorial activity in terms of wording and themes. This does not mean that the historical Jesus was incapable of such structuring or that *none* of the Sermon is dominical in form. Nor does this mean there was no actual sermon on the mountainside with this content preached by the historical Jesus. This would be a false dichotomy typical of the last couple of generations of Gospels scholarship: that "traditional/redactional" means "nondominical." But what we have to interpret now is the Sermon on the Mount as presented to us by Matthew. Throughout the remainder of the discussion I will often refer to Jesus saying or intending things. This should be understood as Matthew's redaction of the Jesus Traditions available to him.

7. For example, the very important medieval interpreter Nicholas of Lyra provided a structural outline of Matthew as part of his early fourteenth-century commentary. See Kevin Madigan, "Lyra on the Gospel of Matthew," in *Nicholas of Lyra: The Senses of Scripture*, ed. Philip Krey and Leslie Smith (Leiden: Brill, 2000), 204–5.

8. For a succinct and insightful analysis of this whole issue, see Dale C. Allison Jr., "Structure, Biographical Impulse, and the *Imitatio Christi*," in *Studies in Matthew: Interpretation Past and Present* (Grand Rapids: Baker Academic, 2005), 135–55.

9. B. W. Bacon, "The Five Books of Matthew against the Jews," *The Expositor* 15 (1918): 55–66. See also B. W. Bacon, *Studies in Matthew* (London: Constable, 1930).

formula is not only repeated five times, but each time it also clearly concludes
a major block of Jesus's teaching, or what is often called a discourse. The
result is an important insight into how Matthew was written, with five major
teaching blocks or discourses. Each of these contains a collection of material
gathered from the Jesus Traditions and crafted together into a memorable,
thematic unit that could easily be used as a catechetical piece. These five
major discourses in Matthew are the Sermon (chaps. 5–7), the mission/wit-
ness discourse (chap. 10), parables of the kingdom (chap. 13), the ecclesiology/
community discourse (chap. 18), and the judgment discourse (chaps. 23–25).[10]
This is a brilliant and powerful addition that Matthew makes to the more
strictly narrative biography of his predecessor Mark, and much more teaching
oriented and easily catechetical than either Luke or John.

This is not the only way to analyze the structure of Matthew, however, and
some scholars, starting in the 1970s, observed that the discourse approach to
Matthew ignored the fact that the Gospel is indeed a narrative with a plot, not
just a group of teachings hung loosely (and almost irrelevantly as some took it)
on a narrative thread. Thus, Jack Dean Kingsbury, as prototypical of this narrative reading, noted that there is another set of clues that structure Matthew, the
repetition of the phrase "from that time Jesus began to . . ." at 4:17 and 16:21.
Thus, Matthew's structure, according to Kingsbury, is more simply a threefold
plot development of the "Preparation of Jesus" (1:1–4:16), the "Proclamation of
Jesus" (4:17–16:20), and the "Passion and Resurrection of Jesus" (16:21–28:20).[11]
While this structure has some validity and benefit, it lacks a way to explain the
role and significance of the five major discourses. If the discourse reading of
Bacon and others fails to account for the narrative flow of Matthew, even more
does the plot-analysis approach fail to explain the discourses.[12]

10. There has been no small debate about the extent of the fifth discourse, whether it begins at
Matt. 23 or 24. I have recently become convinced that the arguments are superior for the longer
version of chaps. 23–25, including the recognition of the parallels between the macarisms of
chap. 5 and the woes of chap. 23. For a discussion of the length of the fifth discourse, see Jason
B. Hood, "Matthew 23–25: The Extent of Jesus' Fifth Discourse," *JBL* 128 (2009): 527–43.

11. J. D. Kingsbury, *Matthew: Structure, Christology, Kingdom* (London: Augsburg, 1991),
16–25.

12. There are several other important works that approach Matthew from a literary perspec-
tive, including Richard A. Edwards, *Matthew's Story of Jesus* (Philadelphia: Fortress, 1985);
David B. Howell, *Matthew's Inclusive Story: A Study in the Narrative Rhetoric of the First
Gospel* (Sheffield: JSOT Press, 1990). David M. Rhoads, Joanna Dewey, and Donald Michie,
Mark as Story: An Introduction to the Narrative of a Gospel, 2nd ed. (Minneapolis: Fortress,
1982); and R. Alan Culpepper, *Anatomy of the Fourth Gospel: A Study in Literary Design*
(Philadelphia: Fortress, 1983) are well-known literary analyses of Mark and John. See also the
discussion in Graham Stanton, *A Gospel for a New People: Studies in Matthew* (Edinburgh:
T&T Clark, 1992), 54–58.

Among many other commentators' suggestions for an outline[13] comes one of the most important, that of Dale C. Allison Jr. In his major commentary in the International Critical Commentary series, as well as in other essays, Allison provides a narrative-discourse approach that combines sensitivity to both the narrative flow of Matthew and to analyze the structure of Matthew, his major teaching blocks.[14] Allison argues for an intentional pattern that alternates between interconnected narrative and teaching blocks. There is a narrative flow while the discourses also naturally connect and help carry along the plot. This helpful analysis avoids the extremes of the discourse-only or plot-only approaches.[15]

My own interpretation of the structure of Matthew is influenced by Allison's but with an important modification. I see Matthew as structured with a set of five distinct discourse-narrative blocks rather than Allison's pattern of alternating narratives and discourses—D + N rather than N + D.[16] These DN blocks are all interconnected and together flow along the plotline of the Gospel story. That is, these identifiable DN blocks are not clunky impositions onto the plot (as Allison would agree) but instead are skillfully interwoven and carry the story along by tying in with both what precedes and what follows them.[17] Matthew has created five modules. Each consists of a discourse followed by a narrative that flows from it and leads to the next discourse, with the slight modification that the final unit reverses the order to conclude with the fifth discourse.[18] This set of DN units comprises the body of the main

13. Other helpful structural analyses include Warren Carter, *Matthew: Storyteller, Interpreter, Evangelist* (Grand Rapids: Baker Academic, 2004), 132–51 (narrative blocks); J. Edwards, *Hebrew Gospel*, 246n4; and esp. Wim J. C. Weren, "The Macrostructure of Matthew's Gospel: A New Proposal," in *Studies in Matthew's Gospel: Literary Design, Intertextuality, and Social Setting* (Leiden: Brill, 2014), 13–41.

14. See W. D. Davies and Dale C. Allison Jr., *A Critical and Exegetical Commentary on the Gospel according to Saint Matthew*, vol. 1, *Introduction and Commentary on Matthew 1–7*, ICC (Edinburgh: T&T Clark, 1998), 58–72, of which Allison wrote almost all; and Allison, *Studies in Matthew*, chap. 7.

15. Kari Syreeni provides a very helpful and thoughtful analysis of both the five major discourses and Kingsbury's plot analysis and argues that Matthew successfully weaves together the discourses with his broader plot structure by employing *both* the discourse-marker formula ("and it came about when Jesus finished these sayings . . .") and the narrative-plot formula ("from that time Jesus began to . . .") (*The Making of the Sermon on the Mount: A Procedural Analysis of Matthew's Redactional Activity*, part 1, *Methodology and Compositional Analysis* [Helsinki: Suomalainen Tiedeakatemia, 1987]).

16. This was anticipated by Philippe Roland, "From Genesis to the End of the World: The Plan of Matthew's Gospel," *Biblical Theology Bulletin* 2 (1972): 155–76. See the discussion in Weren, "Macrostructure," 16–18.

17. Helpful along these lines is David Barr, "The Drama of Matthew's Gospel: A Reconsideration of Its Structure and Purpose," *Theology Digest* 24 (1976): 349–59.

18. These five DN modules are 4:17–9:38; 10:1–12:50; 13:1–17:27; 18:1–20:34; and the reversed ND of 21:1–25:46.

story (4:23–25:46). This narrative is then bookended with an introduction (1:1–4:16) and conclusion (26:17–28:20), with two bridge passages that span between the introduction and conclusion and the body (4:17–22 and 26:1–16).[19]

The other significant difference in my structural understanding is that I believe that there is a consistent theme that ties all five of the discourses together, namely, the dual theme of revelation and separation. Each of the five major discourses has its own distinct teaching focus (righteousness, witness, kingdom parables, church community, and eschatology), but woven throughout each of these is a meta-theme that God is revealing himself in Christ and that this revelation results in or creates a separation of people into two groups, those inside and those outside, based on faith-response to Jesus. This theme is found throughout each of the discourses, including the Sermon, as we will see, but is most obvious and prominent in the central third discourse. Matthew 13, which serves as the chiastic center of the book,[20] is built entirely on the idea that God's revelation of himself creates a separation between peoples, as can be seen in the lead parable of the sower/four soils, in the Isaianic quotes about revelation to some (13:14–15 from Isa. 6), and in the parables of the wheat and tares and dragnet of fish.

The point of this discussion for our study of the Sermon is fourfold. First, simply, Matthew is clearly a skilled literary artist, and his meaning is often embedded in his structure. Paying attention to how the whole and the parts are structured is essential for a good reading of Matthew, including the Sermon.

Second, the five-discourse structure of Matthew helps us see that in addition to the chiastic center in Matt. 13, the first and fifth discourses manifest several mutually interpreting parallels. For example, both discourses end with a series of vignettes with characters who model either vice or virtue, foolishness or faithfulness. The Sermon concludes with a three-part series of stories (7:13–27) that contrasts two ways of being, while the fifth and final discourse presents a similar set of contrasting characters—wise and wicked slaves, wise and foolish virgins, good and bad servants—all summed up with the parable of the sheep and the goats (24:45–25:46). Interestingly, frequently repeated throughout all of these contrasts are several key words that tie both discourses

---

19. My structure has some overlap with Weren's but with some differences, the main one being that I see the first hinge or bridge passage as 4:17–22 as compared to him seeing it as 4:12–17.

20. That the Gospel of Matthew is an elaborate chiasm centered in chap. 13 has been argued with insight by Charles H. Lohr, "Oral Techniques in the Gospel of Matthew," *CBQ* 23 (1961): 403–35. See also J. C. Fenton, "Inclusio and Chiasmus in Matthew," in *Studia Evangelica I: Papers Presented to the International Congress on "The Four Gospels in 1957" Held at Christ Church, Oxford*, ed. Kurt Aland et al. (Berlin: Akademie, 1959), 174–79; Stanton, *Gospel for a New People*, 324.

together—"flourishing," "wise," "foolish," "good," "evil," and "faithful."[21] Even more striking, the sevenfold set of woes in 23:13–33 is clearly parallel to the macarisms of 5:3–12.

Third, the Sermon is but one of the five major discourses in the First Gospel. It simultaneously stands alone as a unit to be studied in and of itself, while also being one-fifth of the concentrated teachings Matthew has chosen to deliver. This means that while the Sermon does have a very strong, influential, and prominent place as the first teaching of the New Testament, it is also part of an overall teaching program that Matthew is presenting (which itself is part of a larger agenda of presenting a theological biography of Jesus). The Sermon is an epitome of Jesus the Sage's teachings, especially on the theme of righteousness (see discussion in chaps. 1 and 4); it is not the entirety of those teachings nor the only point Matthew is making, which must include the saving activity of God in Christ. While it is tempting to treat the Sermon as the most important unit, we must be careful not to overdo this. Not only are the discourses structured together in a chiastic manner, putting possibly the greatest weight on Matt. 13, but note also that in the final formulaic statement in 26:1 Matthew adds the word "all"—"when Jesus had finished *all* these sayings"—indicating that these five discourses are meant to be taken as one fivefold block of teaching material.[22] As Graham Stanton notes, "The interpreter of the Sermon who ignores the rest of Matthew's gospel misunderstands the evangelist's intentions and fails to do justice to the breadth of the evangelist's theological vision."[23]

Fourth and finally, the Sermon is part of a discourse-narrative unit (4:23–9:38) that taken as a whole is under the banner of the message of "the gospel of the kingdom." This section will be discussed more below. The point being made again is that the Sermon does not stand alone but is embedded in Matthew's broader structure. It is the didactic portion of the broader message of "the gospel of the kingdom," which is described in 4:23–9:38.

The Structure(s) of the Sermon on the Mount

As noted above, the Sermon is very much a part of the First Gospel in terms of its highly structured nature. We may even say that as the Sermon is the

21. Building off their previous usage in the Sermon, in 24:45–25:46 we find *makarios*, "flourishing," in 24:46; *pistos*, "faithful," in 24:45; 25:21 (2x); 25:23 (2x); *phronimos*, "wise," in 24:45; 25:2, 4, 8, 9; *agathos*, "good," in 25:21, 23; and *ponēros*, "evil," in 25:26. In addition to connecting these discourses to one another, we are also reminded of the Second Temple Jewish and Greco-Roman sapiential dual context of the Sermon. See chap. 1.

22. Stanton, *Gospel for a New People*, 323–24, argues the same.

23. Ibid., 324.

epitome of Jesus's teachings on righteousness, so it is the epitome of Matthew's structural skill.[24] This does not mean, however, that the complete structure of the Sermon is immediately apparent to all or without debates. Quite the contrary, there are several arguments about how best to organize the many teachings of the Sermon. The learned Matthean scholar Dale Allison has reviewed scores of approaches to the Sermon and concludes that, in his opinion, "the discussion has not yet run its course" and that "some interesting and important observations have been missed."[25] He goes on to offer his own, and I am following his lead in submitting mine.

It is important to note that of the myriad renderings of the Sermon's structure that have been offered by scholars, many are viable and beneficial; no one scholar has the corner on the market of insights, nor must we always choose one view over against another when several offer beneficial readings. This acknowledgment of multiple structures at play is based on the beauty and complexity of this material. While I will suggest some definitive structural units, which are important because of how they affect the interpretation of the Sermon, I can acknowledge simultaneously that some questions remain unanswered and some contrary suggestions are worth adopting for the insights they provide.

Additionally, these decisions regarding the structure are not mere academic wrangling but are eminently practical. This is because failure to regard the order and symmetry of the structure that Matthew has provided often causes readers to miss the main emphases. Moreover, each section of the Sermon is part of the larger whole, and the Model Reader will be cognizant of this. While each piece of the Sermon's discourse has its own integrity, beauty, cohesiveness, and preachability, the best and most beneficial reading comes from seeing the whole of the Sermon. At the same time it is necessary and fruitful to look with a keen eye at what is being said in each of the Sermon's units.

The first and most important point to make is that the Sermon is not a random collection of sayings put together haphazardly by Matthew. Rather, the Sermon is the work of an artistic theologian, inspired to take assorted teachings of his Master and present them in a coherent and rhetorically powerful and effective way. The Sermon is not a mere transcription of a speech devoid of any intentional structure or simply a historical record of what Jesus said that day on the hillside.[26]

24. Kari Syreeni suggests that the Sermon is a more carefully planned discourse than the other four, and this is to be explained as Matthew's setting forth a pattern in the first discourse with the assumption the others will be read accordingly (*Making of the Sermon*, 101–2).

25. Allison, "The Configuration of the Sermon on the Mount and Its Meaning," in *Studies in Matthew*, 173.

26. This opinion is not just a function of modern critical study of the Bible but can be found in premodern interpretations as well. For example, John Calvin reflected on the fact that

When we analyze the Sermon structurally, we need to get beyond thinking of the film versions or our mental re-creations of the historical event of the Sermon's delivery. While these re-creations have their own merit, the Model Reader will be able to separate this historical reconstruction from a wisdom-application approach, arguably what Matthew's intention was. A historical-reconstruction reading and an aretegenic (virtue-forming) reading are different approaches with different questions. All literary-historical retellings are necessarily stylized. How much more when it comes to reported dialogue and collected pedagogical discourses. Therefore, the best and most fruitful reading of the Sermon will focus on rhetorical structure and aretegenic reception, which affects structural decisions as well. For example, these different approaches affect one's analysis of Matt. 5:48 and its relation to 5:17–48. On a "picturing Jesus in my mind saying these things" (historical-reconstruction) reading, the "therefore" of verse 48 follows immediately and seems like nothing more than a concluding remark to the pericope of 5:43–47. But from a higher altitude, from a divine crop-circles reading, we see that the *oun*, "therefore," of 5:48 is a discourse marker that serves as the bookend to the introduction of 5:17–20 rather than as merely the concluding statement of 5:43–47. In what follows we will examine several ways the structure of the Sermon should be analyzed and what effect this has on an overall reading.

The Outer Structure of the Sermon: Two Concentric Circles

As mentioned above, within Matthew the Sermon is part of the first discourse-narrative block (4:17–9:38). This opening unit begins with a call to repentance because of the approach of God's heavenly reign through Jesus (4:17), followed by the calling of the first followers (4:18–22). These verses (4:17–22) are the prologue to the large section of 4:17–9:38.

After the prologue this unit has a clear two-part structure, with an *inclusio* of nearly verbatim wording in 4:23–25 and 9:35–38. These intentionally

---

although only four disciples had been called at this point in Matthew's narrative, clearly all the disciples were there listening to the Sermon. He writes,

> Those who think that Christ's sermon, which is here related, is different from the sermon contained in the sixth chapter of Luke's Gospel, rest their opinion on a very light and frivolous argument. . . . It is probable that this discourse was not delivered until Christ has chosen the twelve; but in attending to the order of time, which I saw that the Spirit of God had disregarded, I did not wish to be too precise. Pious and modest readers ought to be satisfied with having a brief summary of the doctrine of Christ placed before our eyes, *collected out of his many and various discourses.* (*Commentary on a Harmony of the Evangelists: Matthew, Mark, and Luke*, trans. William Pringle [Edinburgh: The Edinburgh Printing Company, 1859], 259 [emphasis mine])

overlapping passages both speak of Jesus's ministry with the power-packed, evocative phrase "the gospel of the kingdom" (4:23; 9:35) and describe Jesus's ministry in a threefold way: teaching and preaching, healing and restoration, calling of disciples. This two-part structure of the first discourse-narrative block proves to be a carefully crafted table of contents for the material found in Matt. 5–9. Chapters 5–7 give an epitome of Jesus's teaching and preaching while chapters 8–9 contain a collection of healing and disciple-calling stories. Matthew's clearly repetitive frame in 4:23–25 and 9:35–38 is a strong literary and aural indicator that this section is to be read as one unit, the theme of which is the call to discipleship (through repentance) that comes from the coming of the kingdom of heaven.[27]

This is an important point for our primary understanding of the Sermon. The Sermon is meant to be read as the explanation of what it means to live according to God's coming kingdom. It is the first, epitomical exposition of what repentance toward God and his Fatherly reign looks like (4:17), of what the life of discipleship looks like. Among other implications of this, we may note that any reading of the Sermon that disconnects it from Jesus's eschatological kingdom message on the one hand or his call to a real change of life on the other wrests the Sermon from its Matthean setting. Modern liberal readings have often done the former; the Protestant tradition is often guilty of the latter.

Moving in another level of concentric circles, there is one more outer structural layer (5:1–2 and 7:28–8:1) before the Sermon proper begins (5:3) and after it ends (7:27).[28] This outer crust of the Sermon is marked by a clear geographical and figural movement, ascending a mountainside in 5:1 and descending the same in 8:1, both accompanied by followers (crowds and disciples). Inside of this we have another beginning and ending with Jesus opening his mouth in 5:2 and "finish[ing] these words" in 7:28. Both 5:1–2 and 7:28–8:1 will be addressed in the exposition, so little comment is required here. The main point is Matthew's figural connecting of Jesus to Moses on the one hand (5:1–2) in stark contrast to the Jewish teachers of his day (who sit in the seat of Moses, 23:2) on the other (7:29).

27. Scot McKnight also notes that 4:23 and 9:35 are parallel and argues that Matt. 5–9 is "a *sketch of the mission and ministry of Jesus.* . . . The Sermon on the Mount, then, is a comprehensive sketch of the teaching and preaching message of Jesus. In the context of Matthew's narrative, the Sermon is a *presentation of Jesus' moral vision, his ethic*" (*The Sermon on the Mount*, The Story of God Bible Commentary [Grand Rapids: Zondervan, 2013], 20, emphasis original).

28. Notably, this kind of introductory setting is paralleled in each of Matthew's discourses: 9:35–10:4; 13:1–3; 13:36–37 (scene-shifting middle point of the third discourse); 18:1–3; and 24:3–4. See the chart in Davies and Allison, *Matthew 1–7*, 411.

The Inner Structure: Three Main Parts

The interior structure of the Sermon is more complex and therefore more debated. Most would agree that there is a basic—quite simple—threefold structure to the Sermon in terms of an introduction (5:3–16), body (5:17–7:12), and conclusion (7:13–27). Other than some disagreement and confusion over where to place 5:13–16,[29] this threefold basic structure seems patently clear. A slight variation on this—but one that still affirms it—comes from Johan Thom's insightful structural interpretation based on the parts of an ancient speech and centered on the theme of *dikaiosynē* (righteousness).[30] Thom sees four rhetorically structured parts:

- *Exordium* (Introduction; 5:3–16)
- *Propositio* (Summary statement of theme; 5:17–20)
- *Probatio* (Argument; 5:21–7:12)
- *Peroratio* (Conclusion; 7:13–27)

This is helpful and serves to confirm what a close study of the Sermon reveals, that *greater righteousness* is the major theme (see chap. 4). Thom's four-part structure corresponds to and does not contradict the basic three-fold analysis; it merely highlights that the introduction (5:17–20) to the body (5:17–7:12) can be featured separately as the *propositio* or thesis statement.

The Structure of the Introduction (Matthew 5:3–16)

Throughout many centuries of the church, the Beatitudes were interpreted as a group of seven, typically tied to the seven gifts of the Spirit discerned in Isa. 11:2.[31] This kind of intracanonical reading is rich and fruitful, but from a literary perspective it does not fully highlight Matthew's craftsmanship.

---

29. Allison argues that 5:13–16 is the introduction to the main body (5:17–7:12) and is in fact "a summation of the intended aim of the discourse, a broad characterization of those who obediently enter into 5:17–7:12" (*Studies in Matthew*, 181).

30. Johan C. Thom, "Justice in the Sermon on the Mount: An Aristotelian Reading," *NovT* 51, no. 4 (2009): 314–38. This is an improvement over an earlier application of rhetorical analysis to the Sermon in George A. Kennedy, *New Testament Interpretation through Rhetorical Criticism* (Chapel Hill: University of North Carolina Press, 1984), 49–62. See the critique of the latter in Charles Talbert, *Reading the Sermon on the Mount: Character Formation and Decision Making in Matthew 5–7* (Grand Rapids: Baker Academic, 2006), 23.

31. See the discussion of Augustine's reading in Robert Louis Wilken, "Augustine," in *The Sermon on the Mount through the Centuries: From the Early Church to John Paul II,* ed. Jeffrey P. Greenman, Timothy Larsen, and Stephen R. Spencer (Grand Rapids: Brazos, 2007), 43–58.

For much of modern scholarship the Beatitudes have been considered eight in number and delimited as Matt. 5:3–10. This interpretation is based on a number of factors, some subtler than others. The most obvious and strongest argument for eight Beatitudes is the *inclusio* that appears in both 5:3 and 5:10: both have an apodosis of "for theirs is the kingdom of heaven." This provides a frame for the Beatitudes and in terms of content this is certainly significant—the Beatitudes are set into the eschatological context of Jesus's kingdom message (which began in 4:17).

The other main argument for counting the Beatitudes as eight in number is the shift in form that occurs in 5:11–12. The eight Beatitudes of 5:3–10 each begin with the identical structure of *makarioi* followed by a nominative masculine plural article and adjective or participle (the poor, the merciful, the ones persecuted, etc.).[32] The result is a repeated rhythm. This pattern is broken in 5:11–12 in a couple of ways. Rather than "*makarioi* are the X," 5:11 switches to "*makarioi* are you." Additionally, 5:11 is much longer than the other Beatitudes in its explanation, and then, rather than being followed by a pithy apodosis, 5:12 supplies an exhortation in its place, encouraging the disciples to "rejoice and be glad" for their reward will be great in heaven.

These two observations are common among scholars. Some who have studied the Beatitudes more closely offer additional, subtler insights. For example, several comments have been made about the two sets of four Beatitudes, including the note that both sets end with reference to righteousness (5:6 and 5:10) and that the two sets relate as a complementary pair (see below).

All of these observations are helpful in our interpretation of the Beatitudes. However, on the issue of structure the best argument is that there are in fact *nine* Beatitudes, not eight. The clearest proponent of this view is Dale Allison, whose argument is based on an analysis of the many sets of threes in the Sermon as well as how ancient literature often adds a final, climactic item in a series that reiterates and highlights the main theme.[33] That is, as Allison points out, the ninth Beatitude is different in form and length *precisely because* it is an expansion of the eighth Beatitude, as is the custom in much of ancient literature. When Prov. 6:16 says there are six things that the Lord despises and seven that he hates, one does not find a list of thirteen abominations following but seven. The rhetorical power

32. Five of these eight are adjectives being used substantively and the other three are participles functioning as substantives, all introduced with the Greek article.

33. See Allison, *Studies in Matthew*, 174–80 on the number of the Beatitudes. Pages 198–205 deal with general triadic structures.

comes from the ramping up to the final, climactic saying in a list. This is what is happening in the Beatitudes as well. The ninth Beatitude expands upon the eighth, casting its shadow over the whole by this shift and expansion, all the while also providing a segue to the salt and light statements of 5:13–16. The repetition of the theme of persecution in both the eighth and ninth Beatitudes highlights this message and foreshadows the rest of the book.

Indeed, several proponents of the eight-Beatitudes interpretation also note that there is in fact an 8 + 1 structure at play here. For example, Jack Lundbom, following David Noel Freedman, David Daube, and his own research, notes that in Hebrew poetry, "the final line in a series often varies the repetition, is longer than the other lines, and shifts to direct address. This shift to direct address makes a heavier 'ballast statement,' which is another rhetorical feature in Hebrew poetry bringing discourse to a dramatic conclusion."[34]

It is odd, then, that scholars would continue to insist on eight Beatitudes rather than nine. This is to confuse the number of Beatitudes with how they are structured together. That is, to answer how many Beatitudes there are one must simply pause and ask the question, how many *macarisms* are there? The obvious answer is nine, not eight. Nine times in a row Matthew writes *makarioi*. Clearly there are nine Beatitudes. Whether the ninth is connected contentwise to and expanding upon the eighth is a further interpretive question, but this should not distract us from the obvious nine macarisms/*makarioi*. The ninth Beatitude does have a different form and moves beyond the "kingdom of heaven" *inclusio* of 5:3–10, but this is to highlight and repeat the theme of persecution (started in 5:10) and to structurally connect to the salt and light statements of 5:13–16 (see below).

Once we recognize that there are in fact nine, then we may query not only their relationship to each other but also their structure. With nine macarisms, the two best structural options are three sets of three or two sets of four with a final conclusion. There is indeed merit to both suggestions and there are scholars in both camps. Reading the Beatitudes as a complementary two sets of four, Mark Allan Powell suggests that the first four Beatitudes promise reversal for the unfortunate while the second four promise eschatological rewards to the virtuous, with verses 11–12 providing the concluding comment.[35] David Garland observes that the first four pertain to God and the

34. Jack Lundbom, *Jesus' Sermon on the Mount: Mandating a Better Righteousness* (Minneapolis: Fortress, 2015), 19.

35. Mark Allan Powell, *God with Us: A Pastoral Theology of Matthew's Gospel* (Minneapolis: Fortress, 1995), 119–40.

second four to relationships with others.[36] William Dumbrell notes the word "righteousness" concluding both sections of four, with the first set concerning attitudes and the second concerning conduct displayed.[37] In these cases, 5:11–12 is the concluding statement.

Alternatively, seeing the nine Beatitudes as three sets of three is also beneficial. Scot McKnight suggests three triads—three on humility of the poor (the poor in spirit, mourners, the meek); three on those who pursue justice (those who hunger and thirst for justice, the merciful, the pure in heart); three on those who create peace (peacemakers, the persecuted, the insulted). Thus, the three central moral themes of the Beatitudes are humility (of the poor), justice, and peace.[38]

Unique among these varied interpretations is that of H. Benedict Green, who makes many sophisticated and elaborate arguments about the structure and content of the Beatitudes, the Sermon, and Matthew overall. Green argues that all the Beatitudes relate to each other in a complex web of relationships. He sees the theme as purity of heart, which is expressed in the first macarism on the "poor in spirit" (5:3) and then most explicitly in the sixth on the pure in heart (5:8), "which is the real climax of the whole composition." These two alliterative expressions in Greek are the central idea and come from the Psalter;[39] they reappear as the idea behind 6:21 and 6:24, as well as in the story of the non-*teleios* ruler in 19:16–22. Green describes them as the tonic and dominant chords of the structure of the Beatitudes.[40] Yet another possible structure of the Beatitudes is that of Andrej Kodjak, who sees the first (5:3) and eighth (5:10) as both referring to internal and external poverty, with "poor in spirit" connected with "persecuted for righteousness's sake" as the frame and with the ninth as following up on the eighth.[41] The other structural issue

---

36. David Garland, *Reading Matthew: A Literary and Theological Commentary* (Macon, GA: Smyth & Helwys, 2013), 54.

37. Dumbrell ("The Logic of the Role of the Law in Matthew 5:1–20," *NovT* 23, no. 1 [1981]: 4) gets this from Howard A. Hatton and David J. Clark, "From the Harp to the Sitar," *Bible Translator* 26 (1975): 132–38. Two sets of four is also the view of Klaus Koch, *The Growth of the Biblical Tradition* (New York: Scribner, 1969), 8.

38. McKnight, *Sermon on the Mount*, 38.

39. In Greek, Matt. 5:3 reads *hoi ptōchoi tō pneumati* and 5:8 is *hoi katharoi tē kardia*. Green argues that it is not an accident that the central idea behind each of these Beatitudes is expressed in the Septuagint Psalter by a double beatitude—Pss. 31:1–2 and 118:1–2—and that each psalm concludes with the thought with which the other opens (31:11; 118:176) (*Matthew, Poet of the Beatitudes* [Edinburgh: T&T Clark, 2001], 252).

40. Ibid., 252–53.

41. Andrej Kodjak, *A Structural Analysis of the Sermon on the Mount* (Berlin: de Gruyter, 1986), 48–51. Working with a strongly structuralist framework, Kodjak offers a wide variety of comments about how the various parts of the Sermon work together, with varying degrees of insight and benefit. As is typical of structuralism, its exclusive focus on the text as a text limits

within the introduction to the Sermon (5:3–16) is the relationship between 5:3–12 and 5:13–16. Many scholars have stumbled in their interpretation of the structure of the Sermon in not knowing how to connect these two units. Often 5:13–16 is treated as separate from and unrelated to the Beatitudes, but this is a mistake. A fuller explanation of the conceptual connections can be found in the exposition of 5:1–16 below, but for now we can note that this is one unit both formally and conceptually. Formally, 5:13–16 is connected to 5:3–12 in a linchpin way. That is, 5:11–12 sits as a structural bridge between 5:3–10 and 5:13–16, sharing characteristics of both and indicating that 5:3–16 is one unit. Matthew 5:11–12 is the purple created from the blue of 5:3–10 and the red of 5:13–16. Or to change the metaphor, 5:11–12 is the area between two states—such as "Kentuckiana," Kentucky and Indiana on both sides of the Ohio River—that has characteristics of both 5:3–10 and 5:13–16. Specifically, the ninth Beatitude (5:11–12) breaks the pattern of the first eight so that structurally it can serve as the overlapping connection between the Beatitudes and the salt and light sayings that follow. In 5:11–12 we have an emphatic "you" (*este*) not found in the preceding macarisms. This prepares one for the "you are . . ." (*hymeis este*) salt and light statements. Conceptually, 5:3–16 together also serves as a unit in that all throughout it Jesus is casting a vision for the kingdom way of being for his disciples. The Beatitudes are an invitation to the way of being that will result in their flourishing, while the salt and light statements are the spreading of this flourishing to the world through witness, deed, and invitation to the same. Matthew 5:3–16 is an appropriate, consistent, vision-casting introduction to the Sermon.[42]

THE STRUCTURE OF THE BODY (MATTHEW 5:17–7:12)

The main body of the Sermon is marked clearly with an *inclusio* referring to "the Law and/or the Prophets" in 5:17 and 7:12.[43] As noted above,

---

the value of the overall interpretation, ignoring as it does the social and historical setting of the production of the text and its reception.

42. This is one area where I diverge slightly from Allison's structure. He treats 5:13–16 as part of 5:13–7:12 while also acknowledging that it is a "transitional passage, in which the speaker moves from the life of the blessed future, promised in 5:3–12, to the demands of life in the present, outlined in 5:17–7:12" (*Studies in Matthew*, 180–81). Not only does this fail to make the connections between 5:3–12 and 5:13–16, it also presents an infelicitous relationship of the Beatitudes to the present life, relegating them to a future ideal.

43. While nearly all scholars see 5:17–7:12 as the demarcated unit, Dumbrell has argued insightfully for a close connection between 5:13–20 and even 5:1–20 as a whole unit ("Logic," 1–2). He is right to point out the consistent law/covenant theme in 5:13–20 (even starting back in 5:1–2 with the allusion to Moses). Additionally, as Ulrich Luz and Robert Guelich have pointed out, the "good deeds" of 5:16 set the stage for 5:17–48, even serving as a potential

the main argument or *probatio* of the Sermon is found in 5:21–7:12, with its *propositio* or thesis statement in 5:17–20.[44] It is clear from this thesis statement that the central section of the Sermon is centered on Jesus's teaching about the necessity of having a "greater righteousness" to enter the kingdom of heaven (5:20).[45] The subsections within 5:17–7:12 apply this message to three different areas: greater righteousness in relation to the Torah (5:21–48); greater righteousness in personal piety (6:1–21); and greater righteousness in relation to daily life in the world (6:19–7:11).[46] Matthew 5:20 then stands as a heading over all and 7:12, the Golden Rule, as the concluding wisdom aphorism. The "therefore" that begins 7:12, which does not serve conceptually as the conclusion to 7:7–11, is Matthew's structural indicator that 7:12 "is a summary of and a conclusion to *all* the material in the central section of the Sermon."[47]

The structure of Matthew 5:21–48: Six exegeses of fulfilled Torah. Matthew's first unit in the central section consists of the famous "antitheses," as they are typically called because of the supposed contrast or antithesis being made between the teachings of Torah/Moses and Jesus, strung along on the series of "it has been said . . . but I say to you" statements. This traditional title is understandable but unfortunate. It leads one to misread this set of six

---

title for what follows (Luz, *Matthew 1–7: A Commentary*, rev. ed., trans. James E. Crouch, Hermeneia [Minneapolis: Fortress, 2007], 203; Guelich, *The Sermon on the Mount: A Foundation for Understanding* [Dallas: Word, 1982], 38). Nonetheless, the strong repetition in 5:17 and 7:12 proves to be a clearer structural marker, in addition to the triadic structure and clear thesis role of 5:17–20. We should not be surprised that there are consistent themes and close connections between the various units in this masterpiece of construction. But consistent themes and connections do not mean that there are also not clear structural units indicated by other formal clues. This is all the more understandable in light of Matthew's propensity for sectional overlaps. See below.

44. Another way of describing this structural pattern is that of heading and following explanation (*kəlāl ûpərāṭ*, "from the general to the particular"). This aspect of the Sermon's structure will be discussed further below.

45. Jack Dean Kingsbury goes even further and suggests that the theme of greater righteousness is consistent throughout the *whole* Sermon, including 5:3–16 and 7:13–27 ("The Place, Structure, and Meaning of the Sermon on the Mount within Matthew," *Int* 41 [1987]: 131–43). Others who see greater righteousness as the main theme include Guelich, *Sermon on the Mount*.

46. An alternative threefold structure can be found in Joachim Jeremias, *The Sermon on the Mount*, trans. Norman Perrin (Philadelphia: Fortress, 1972), 182–83. Jeremias argues that 5:21–48 is concerned with righteousness in the scriptural interpretation of the scribes, 6:1–18 with the piety of the Pharisees, and 6:19–7:27 with the new righteousness of Jesus's disciples. While my own interpretation differs, there is an attractive symmetry between the three Matthean groups of scribes, Pharisees, and disciples put into comparison, as well as an insight that the scribes and Pharisees are mentioned in 5:20 and thus outlined in what follows.

47. Stanton, *Gospel for a New People*, 303 (emphasis original).

examples of greater righteousness regarding the law as being Jesus contrasting his teaching with the law or even abrogating it, precisely what he insists he is *not* doing in 5:17–19.[48] As the exposition to follow will argue, the key word is that Jesus has come to *fulfill* the Law. Thus, better than thinking of 5:21–48 as "antitheses," they are better called "exegeses," or even "eschatological exegeses."[49]

Some have suggested that there are five examples in this section, but the best interpretation is to see a set of six split into two triads (5:21–32 and 5:33–48). The debate concerns the role of 5:31–32, with some taking it as part of the second example in 5:27–30.[50] But as Allison points out, this overlooks the extensive parallelism between 5:31–32 and the rest of the paragraphs in 5:21–48. Additionally, Matthew gives some editorial clues that the six examples are to be split into two sets of three. First, he uses the word *palin* (again) as a marker between the third and fourth exegeses in 5:33, which serves as an "editorial dividing line" between two triads that are nearly identical in length. Second, he uses the full phrase "You have heard that it was said to those of old" only in 5:21 and 5:33, at the head of each triad.[51]

Additionally, we may note that each exegesis is built on a three-part structure: giving of the Torah statement, Jesus's explanation of its true intent, and the practical application. The exact form and length of each part varies in the different exegeses, but this is the basic pattern. Similarly, Glen Stassen sees three parts but with a slightly different explanation: citation of traditional teaching, diagnosis of a vicious cycle, transforming initiative that maps the way of deliverance.[52]

Finally, we may observe that 5:48, a central verse (as was discussed in chap. 3), serves double duty as the end of the sixth exegesis (5:43–48) and even more as the conclusion to the entire section of 5:17–48. We will discuss below Matthew's sectional overlaps or use of verses in a dual sense. The main point here is that the exhortation to *teleios*-ity or whole-person righteousness in 5:48 is an appropriate conclusion to the theme set out in 5:17–20 as well as the six

48. Allison points out that 5:17–19 is a *prokatalepsis*, anticipating the incorrect interpretation of 5:21–48 and explaining this beforehand (*Studies in Matthew*, 181).

49. For further discussion see the commentary section below.

50. Bernard Brandon Scott and Margaret E. Dean, "A Sound Map of the Sermon on the Mount," in *Treasures Old and New: Recent Contributions to Matthean Studies*, ed. David R. Bauer and Mark A. Powell, SBL Symposium Series 1 (Atlanta: Scholars Press, 1996), 311, 378.

51. Allison, *Studies in Matthew*, 182–83. He points out that 5:21–32 and 5:33–48 have 1,138 and 1,133 letters respectively, adding to the symmetry of this section. Allison makes other observations about the structure of these two triads that confirm his argument.

52. Glen H. Stassen, "The Fourteen Triads of the Sermon on the Mount (Matthew 5:21–7:12)," *JBL* 122 (2003): 267–308; McKnight, *Sermon on the Mount*, 76n6.

examples given (5:21–47). In the exposition of that section in a subsequent chapter we will discuss the meaning of this section overall.

The structure of Matthew 6:1–21: Three areas of piety. The whole Sermon is elaborately constructed, but no part of it so much and so clearly as the center of the central section, Matt. 6:1–21. This unit is tightly structured and well crafted, with several key phrases repeated three times each: "Truly I tell you, they have received their reward"; "Your Father will repay you"; and "in secret" (twice in each of the triads).[53]

Similar to 5:17–48, 6:1–21 consists of an introductory heading followed by illustrative examples to explain the point practically. Matthew 6:1–21 gives three examples as compared with the six in both 5:17–48 and 6:19–7:12. At the same time, 5:17–20, as the heading for all of 5:17–7:12, also serves as the introduction to 6:1–21, with the latter giving three examples of the theme of greater righteousness expounded in relation to personal piety: the giving of alms (6:2–4), prayer (6:5–15), and fasting (6:16–18). The famous Lord's Prayer section (6:7–15) is an excursus inserted into the otherwise perfectly symmetrical structure.[54] Yet even the excursus follows a very similar pattern.

This unit is very stylized and polished, the apex of Matthew's literary skills. Each of the three examples of piety follows the same pattern of beginning with a negative statement about how *not* to behave, followed by how the area of piety should be practiced. Each of the three examples is introduced with the Greek word *hotan* (when) plus the verb (6:2, 5, 16), helping delineate the structure, while the excursus in the middle (6:7–15) breaks this pattern by beginning with a participle plus *de* (and/but).

Another structural issue concerns the extent of this section in chapter 6. While all Matthean scholars recognize the threefold structure of this section, notably, very few place a break at 6:21 but rather treat the section as 6:1–18 and the following one as 6:19–34.[55] Astute readers will notice that I have in

53. In Greek, the third of these includes a slight variation in vocabulary, which adds prominence and heightens the climax. *En tō kryptō . . . en tō kryptō* (in secret) in 6:4 and 6:6 becomes *en tō kryphaiō . . . en tō kryphaiō* (in secret) in 6:18.

54. In addition to the discussion of the broader structural issues here, specific comments on how the Lord's Prayer fits into the structure of the rest of the Sermon can be found in Davies and Allison, *Matthew 1–7*, 592–93; Birger Gerhardsson, "The Matthaean Version of the Lord's Prayer (Matt 6:9–13b): Some Observations," in *The New Testament Age: Festschrift B. Reicke*, ed. William C. Weinrich (Macon: Mercer, 1984), 1:207–20.

55. Nearly every commentary that I have surveyed begins a new section at 6:19, usually with no comment on how this section relates at all to what precedes it. R. T. France comments that 6:1–18 leads naturally into 6:19–20, but he still sees 6:19 as beginning a new section (*The Gospel of Matthew*, NICNT [Grand Rapids: Eerdmans, 2007], 138). Rare exceptions to this are J. C. Fenton, *Saint Matthew*, Pelican Gospel Commentaries (London: Penguin Books, 1963); Birger Gerhardsson, "Geistiger Opferdienst nach Matth 6,1–6. 16–21," in *Neues Testament und*

fact included the crucially important 6:19–21 in both sections because it is a clear example of a double-meaning sectional overlap for Matthew (see below on this phenomenon). Matthew 6:1–21 hangs together as a structural unit with a consistent theme of heavenly versus earthly rewards. The command to lay up treasures in heaven, not on earth, in 6:19–21 is the concluding restatement of the same instruction throughout 6:1–18: to practice righteousness to gain heavenly reward rather than the mere praise of earthly people.[56]

The reasons we should understand the structure as concluding with 6:19–21 rather than verse 18 are manifold.[57] First, we may observe that 6:19–21 clearly provides a verbal *inclusio* with verse 1 at several points: the word "heaven" appears in both as a frame, both contain a type of "heaven and earth" pair, and both have as their subject reward with God (*misthos* in 6:1, the closely related *thēsauros* in 6:19–21). Also, simply, 6:19–21 provides a needed conclusion to this highly structured passage. With a clear heading in 6:1 and three tightly arranged subsections, ending the pericope at verse 18 feels very inconclusive; a concluding exhortation on par with verse 1 is expected and even needed. Along these same lines, we may observe that the positive promise of verses 19–21 balances out the negative statement in verse 1. Birger Gerhardsson observes that verse 1 has only a negative declaration and that the positive-negative balance found throughout the pericope therefore finds its completion only in verses 19–21.[58] Finally, we may observe that the verbal and conceptual elements of 6:19–21 have strong connections with 6:1–18, even more than they do with 6:22–34. For example, the relatively uncommon word *aphanizō* (to ruin, destroy; disfigure)[59] appears in 6:16 in reference to what the hypocrites do to their faces when fasting and then is found immediately after in 6:19 and 20 to describe the destruction that comes upon earthly treasures.[60] Such a

---

Geschichte: Historisches Geschehen und Deutung im Neuen Testament; Oscar Cullmann zum 70. Geburtstag, ed. Heinrich Baltensweiler and Bo Reicke (Tübingen: Mohr Siebeck, 1972), 69–77.

56. This is the argument made in my *Heaven and Earth in the Gospel of Matthew* (Leiden: Brill, 2007; repr., Grand Rapids: Baker Academic, 2009). Fenton's comments are quite similar, even though I arrived at this conclusion independently: "To practice piety (alms, prayer, and fasting) in order to be seen by men is to lay up treasures on earth, in the praise and approval of men; but to practice piety in secret is to lay up treasures in heaven, with God, and to wait for his praise and approval at the last judgment" (*Saint Matthew*, 103). Thanks to Nathan Ridlehover for pointing me to Fenton's comments, which I had missed in my earlier argument in *Heaven and Earth*.

57. The following two paragraphs are a slight modification of my argument in *Heaven and Earth*, 245–46.

58. Gerhardsson, "Geistiger Opferdienst," 70–71.

59. *Aphanizō* is found approximately ninety-two times in the LXX, primarily with the meaning of "destroy" or "perish." It appears only five times in the NT, three of which are in Matt. 6, one in Acts 13:41 (a quote from Hab. 1:5), and one in James 4:14.

60. Luz, who recognizes verbal connections between vv. 1–18 and 19–21, still breaks the pericope at v. 18 with little comment (*Matthew 1–7*, 353).

powerful wordplay is no accident of the pen with a master such as Matthew. In contrast, the varied attempts at seeing 6:19–34 as a coherent unit are often quite contorted and inconclusive.[61] But for all the reasons just given, it is not difficult to see how 6:19–21 completes 6:1–18 in many ways.

Recognizing the structural break at verse 21 does not mean, however, that there are no connections with the verses that follow (6:22–34); indeed, there are some.[62] As one writer has observed, 6:19–21 is a "bridge" passage that connects the preceding and following texts and thus has somewhat of a dual referent.[63] The *thēsauros* of 6:19–21 alludes both to the *misthos* of 6:1–18 as well as to the "mammon" of 6:24. However, 6:22 does introduce a new idea and pericope, and the notional and structural connections are much stronger with 6:1–18. Thus, while we can acknowledge some links with 6:22–34, it is best to understand 6:1–21 as the primary structural unit.

All of this results in the following structure for 6:1–21:

I. 6:1 Introductory Heading: Pleasing the Father in Heaven, not Humans

II. 6:2–18 Three Areas of Piety

A. 6:2–4 Almsgiving

1. Negative instruction and statement of reward

2. Positive instruction and statement of reward

B. 6:5–6 Prayer

1. Negative instruction and statement of reward

2. Positive instruction and statement of reward

Central Excursus: 6:7–15 On Prayer

a. Negative instruction

b. Positive instruction

c. Promise and warning

C. 6:16–18 Fasting

1. Negative instruction and statement of reward

2. Positive instruction and statement of reward

III. 6:19–21 Concluding Exhortation: Rewards in Heaven, Not on Earth

61. Guelich deals with 6:19–7:12 as a unit but admits that it consists of six "apparently disjointed units of tradition" that do not "exhibit any visible interrelationship with each other" (*Sermon on the Mount*, 322–25).

62. See, e.g., Davies and Allison, *Matthew 1–7*, 625–26.

63. Blaine Charette, *The Theme of Recompense in Matthew's Gospel*, JSNTSup 79 (Sheffield: JSOT Press, 1992), 100. See also the discussion of "sectional overlaps" below.

As noted, the Lord's Prayer fits into this structure as a central excursus on the second of the three examples of greater-righteousness piety. Despite being an excursive addition, it does not overly disrupt the flow, and it has a formal structure similar to its surroundings, as the outline above shows. Very significantly, this structure puts the Lord's Prayer at the center of the center of the center of the Sermon, something that is certainly not an accident. A fuller exposition of the meaning of the Lord's Prayer can be found in the chapter to follow. For now the point is that the structure of the Sermon highlights the fundamental importance of the Lord's Prayer, even as the church has long practiced.

The Prayer itself is framed by an introduction (6:7–8) and concluding commentary (6:14–15). Within the Prayer we find seven petitions divided into two portions. Comparable to the Ten Commandments and the first and second greatest commandments, the seven petitions of the Prayer relate to both the divine and the human, the first part oriented toward God (6:9–10; petitions 1–3) and the second toward human needs and relations (6:11–13; petitions 4–7). Or, to describe it another way, the two parts of the Prayer relate to the heavenly and the earthly realms (6:9–10 and 6:11–13, respectively). Or yet again, the Prayer is a diptych with an eschatological orientation (6:9–10) and a focus on present needs (6:11–13).[64]

The first three petitions are really one idea described by three overlapping terms. It is the request for God's name, his kingdom, and his will to each receive the honor due them. All three are summed up with the phrase at the end of 6:10 that modifies and brings all three requests together—*as these are in heaven, let them be also on the earth*. This proves very relevant to the whole of the Sermon and provides the Christian with a fundamental orientation to the world. The Christian is to live now on this unredeemed earth in the way that corresponds to and honors God's coming reign.

The structure of Matthew 6:19–7:12: Six affairs of daily life. Even the most avid analysts of the Sermon struggle at points when they reach 6:19–7:12. The preceding parts are clearly organized into triads, and the conclusion likewise contains a threefold warning and exhortation (7:13–27). But every commentator encounters difficulty when trying to make sense of the structure of this penultimate unit. It is at this point in the Sermon where the material reveals some structure and a consistent theme but also seems to have a hodgepodge of aphorisms that are roughly inserted into an otherwise well-planned section. For example, the most difficult verse to interpret in the Sermon—7:6 with its

64. Craig S. Keener, *The Gospel of Matthew: A Socio-Rhetorical Commentary* (Grand Rapids: Eerdmans, 2009), 216n163.

reference to pearls before swine—feels a bit like a random appendage, as if a high school student has finished her research paper and then discovered an important note card under the dining room table that needs to be inserted into the paper right before turning in the final draft. Has editorial fatigue set in for Matthew at this point? I think not. More likely, this is a place where Matthew is remaining faithful to the Jesus Traditions/sources before him while also continuing to highlight his own theological emphases; the result is a slightly more fragmented section.

Regardless, while the structure of this section is not as immediately apparent as that of the other parts and while it does touch on a number of themes, there is a thread running through each of the subunits, which are structured as six examples of greater righteousness in relation to the world, broken into two triads (cf. 5:17–48).[65] This unit begins with 6:19–21, which, as noted above, serves double duty, referring to the praise of others versus God in 6:1–21 and to the goods/money and affairs of the world in 6:19–7:12. Matthew 6:19–21 thus serves as the introduction and is parallel to 7:7–11 near the end, with 7:12 as the conclusion both to 6:19–7:12 and especially the broader central section of 5:17–7:12. All of this is governed by the theme of greater righteousness as stated in 5:17–20.

We can easily break this unit into two subparts, greater righteousness regarding the things of the world (6:22–34) and regarding the people of the world (7:1–6), with the introduction in 6:19–21 and conclusion in 7:7–12. What else might be going on structurally is debated. Allison sees a parallel structure with three parts each in 6:19–24 and 7:1–6, with both ending with strongly paralleled words of encouragement about the heavenly Father's care (6:25–34 and 7:7–11).[66] All of this indicates that 6:19–7:12 is not a series of loosely related sayings.[67] Further discussion of how the parts of this unit

---

65. While not all scholars see 6:19–7:12 as unified, several do, including Allison, Luz, and Betz. For Allison this section can be classified as concerning "social relations," based in part on Davies's suggestion that Matthew has adopted and reinterpreted Simeon's three pillars that faithful Jews should focus on: Torah (5:17–48), worship (6:1–18), and deeds of loving-kindness (6:19–7:12). See Allison, *Studies in Matthew*, 173–216, and W. D. Davies, *The Setting of the Sermon on the Mount* (Cambridge: Cambridge University Press, 1964), 315. I remain ambivalent about Davies's argument, as do several other scholars, including Charles Talbert. See Talbert, *Reading the Sermon on the Mount*, 23. Allison does not appear to put as much weight on the consistent theme of greater righteousness that ties all of the central section together.

66. Allison, *Studies in Matthew*, 187–93. See also Davies and Allison, *Matthew 1–7*, 626.

67. Additionally, as was noted earlier, both 5:21–48 and 6:19–7:12 have six sections or topics, which seems far more than coincidental. Moreover, as Nathan Ridlehover has pointed out to me in personal correspondence, 5:21–48 and 6:19–7:12 have almost the exact same number of words, which again seems more than a coincidence.

relate to each other conceptually can be found in the expositions of both 6:19–34 and 7:1–12.

THE STRUCTURE OF THE CONCLUSION (MATTHEW 7:13–27)

The conclusion to the Sermon has a clear and powerful three-part structure based on three metaphors or parables that serve as warnings and exhortations to heed Jesus's teachings. Each of these three images utilize the common wisdom technique of exhorting listeners to pay attention to the consequences of two different ways of being in the world as the means of invitation to the way of true flourishing. Notably, as will be discussed in the exposition chapter, constant through all three subunits is the idea of singleness or wholeness, which is the consistency between the internal and external in the disciple.

The conclusion has three parts, the second of which is longer and more elaborate. The first (7:13–14) uses the image of the wide and narrow gates. The third (7:24–27) utilizes the picture of two house builders, one who builds foolishly on sand and the other wisely on rock.

The middle of these three (7:15–23) combines the two images of wolves in sheep's clothing and good and bad trees but within one subunit that is about true and false prophets. Many editions of the New Testament unfortunately break this middle paragraph into separate sections (7:15–20 and 7:21–23), but this fails to acknowledge the structure and consistent theme. Matthew 7:15–23 is more like the *kəlāl ûpərāṭ* structure that was used throughout the central section (see below). There is a heading in 7:15—beware of false prophets—and an unpacking of this exhortation with the two images of wolves and trees (7:15; 7:16–20). Rather than changing themes, the return to the teaching of false prophets in the latter half (7:21–23) shows that this is to be taken as one unit. Wolves in sheep's clothing and good and bad trees both teach that outer appearance is not sufficient but that over time the inner truth will come forth. This wholeness is what matters.

Taken together, these three concluding images of warning-exhortation match the introduction of 5:3–16. The opening section of macarisms (the Beatitudes) paints a picture of a way of being in the world that is an invitation to true human flourishing. After strong illustrative teaching on the necessity of a whole-person righteousness (5:17–7:12), the Sermon properly concludes with another invitation, this one darker and stronger in the form of wisdom warnings (cf. Prov. 1–9) to build one's life on Jesus's teachings lest destruction come. As has been noted earlier in our discussion, the technical woes counterpart to the Beatitudes' macarisms does not come until the fifth and final major discourse (Matt. 23), but there is still an appropriate and balancing symmetry in this sapiential-exhortatory conclusion to the Sermon.

Three Other Important Structural Notes

There are three other aspects of the structure of the Sermon that need to be addressed. I have mentioned each of these in passing in the discussion above. Each of these structural components is woven throughout the Sermon and affects our interpretation of it. These are (1) the *kəlāl ûpərāṭ* pattern, (2) the use of sectional overlaps, and (3) the question of the role of the Lord's Prayer as the center of the Sermon.

kəlāl ûpərāṭ

The famous Jewish teacher Hillel (active ca. 30 BCE–10 CE) preserved seven principles or hermeneutical rules for teachers of Torah to help them make systematic inferences based on the ancient text. Hillel did not make up these rules, of course, but his codification of them proved important and influential. Rabbi Ishmael, a third-generation mishnaic teacher (ca. 100–170 CE), expanded this list to thirteen by taking Hillel's fifth rule and subdividing it into eight different groups.

This fifth rule, the *kəlāl ûpərāṭ*, which means "from the general to the particular," gives guidelines about how to read Torah and apply it. The point is that a general principle may be restricted by a particularization of it in another text. At the same time, a particular rule may be expanded into a general principle. Thus, for example, instructions about how to handle the theft of one's ox, donkey, or sheep can be used as a particular that can be expanded into a general principle.

We can also think of the *kəlāl ûpərāṭ* principle as not just a hermeneutical rule for the *reading* of texts, but on the flip side, as a helpful guiding rule for the *production* of texts.[68] I contend that the Sermon reflects this *kəlāl ûpərāṭ* principle in terms of the production of its structure. Previous studies of Matthew have shown that this principle makes sense of other parts of Matthew's redaction. For example, Allison notes that this pattern is an ancient one (cf.

---

68. Ulrich Luz notes also that *kəlālîm* are not merely headings; they are combinations and generalizations at the beginning or at the end of a section, often with a pronounced transitional function (Luz, *Matthew 1–7*, 6). See also Donald Hagner, *Matthew 1–13*, WBC (Dallas: Word Books, 1993), 137; Stanton, *Gospel for a New People*, 297.

Lev. 18:1–24; Sir. 3:1–9; and rabbinic usage) functioning in Matthew.[69] In Peter Yaw Oppong-Kumi's elaborate study of the structure of Matthew's parables, he shows this pattern at work in various places, including Matt. 13.[70] In previous work and above I argued that Matt. 6:1 is the *kəlāl* for 6:1–21.[71]

I contend that this pattern of providing a general heading followed by specific examples makes sense of the whole of the central section of the Sermon. Throughout 5:17–7:12 we have a repeated pattern of a general heading followed by several particular examples, followed by a reiterative conclusion. The result is this analysis:

5:17–48
- *kəlāl* = 5:17–20
- *pərāṭ* = 5:21–47 (six examples)
- conclusion = 5:48

6:1–21
- *kəlāl* = 6:1
- *pərāṭ* = 6:2–18 (three examples + central excursus)
- conclusion = 6:19–21

6:19–34
- *kəlāl* = 6:19–21
- *pərāṭ* = 6:22–33 (in two parts: 6:22–24; 6:25–33)
- conclusion = 6:34

7:1–12
- *kəlāl* = 7:1–2
- *pərāṭ* = 7:3–11 (in two parts: 7:3–6; 7:7–11)
- conclusion = 7:12

The first two of these sections are easy to see as functioning with this kind of structure. The third one (6:19–34) likewise flows logically, recalling that 6:19–21 serves double duty as both the conclusion of 6:1–21 and the *kəlāl* of 6:19–34 (see below for fuller discussion). In terms of the latter case, this analysis provides the additional insight that 6:34 and its exhortation to not

69. Allison, *Studies in Matthew*, 181n21. See further David Daube, "Principles and Cases," in *New Testament Judaism*, vol. 2 of *Collected Works of David Daube*, ed. Calum Carmichael (Berkeley: Robbins Collection Publications, University of California at Berkeley, 2000), 173–75.

70. Peter Yaw Oppong-Kumi, *Matthean Sets of Parables*, WUNT 2/340 (Tübingen: Mohr Siebeck, 2013), 94–99, 104–5.

71. Pennington, *Heaven and Earth*, 242–47.

worry about tomorrow is a conclusion to the warning against storing up earthly treasures in 6:19–21. The most problematic portion of the Sermon is 7:1–12, as was mentioned above. This *kəlāl ûpərāṭ* explanation is not entirely satisfying, but no less so than other attempts to put 7:1–12 together, especially with the oddity of 7:6. In this structural reading the point that drives all of 7:1–12 is found in 7:1–2 with the idea of judging correctly (see the exposition in chapter 10). Yet at the same time, I have argued that the central section of the Sermon consists of three parts, and in this overall reading 6:19–7:12 is a unit, thus the *kəlāl* for all of this section is found in 6:19–21 and the conclusion in 7:12. I do not think these two structural observations are mutually exclusive. I have chosen to break 6:19–7:12 into two units here (and in the exposition to follow) because while they do hang together, there is also some distinction between the two parts of this unit.

OVERLAPPING SECTIONS

In the detailed discussion of the structure of the Sermon above, I have mentioned a number of instances of overlapping sections or verses that serve a dual purpose structurally. It is important to discuss this separately here because it occurs frequently in Matthew and the Sermon, yet it is unfamiliar to modern readers.

John Nolland rightly observes that while we can discern many clear-cut divisions in Matthew's material, there are also many times where a verse or section serves double duty, both as a conclusion to one section and as an introduction to the next.[72] Similarly, W. D. Davies and Dale Allison give several examples of how certain verses or passages serve multiple structural purposes, such as the first words (*biblos geneseōs*) in Matt. 1:1 being telescopic, expanding out to include the genealogy (1:1–17), the whole birth narrative (chaps. 1–2), the whole Gospel, and ultimately the new creation.[73] Likewise, 28:16–20 serves as the end not only to 28:1–20 but also to the entire Passion narrative and is a fitting capstone to the entire Gospel. In his later work on the structure of the Sermon, Allison points out that "many Matthean verses both end one section and introduce another. They are doors not walls."[74]

Matthew's use of this technique is part of a widespread and important way that rhetorical speech and literature were produced (and interpreted)

---

72. John Nolland, *The Gospel of Matthew: A Commentary on the Greek Text*, NIGTC (Grand Rapids: Eerdmans, 2005), 28.
73. Davies and Allison, *Matthew 1–7*, 154, leaning on the comments of J. C. Fenton, *The Gospel of St. Matthew* (London: SCM, 1977), 36.
74. Allison, *Studies in Matthew*, 176.

in the ancient world.[75] Ancient authors paid careful attention to transitions between blocks of material and regularly employed what can be called "chain-link transitions," wherein there is "the overlapping of material at a text-unit boundary in order to facilitate a transition."[76] This pervasive form of ancient rhetoric has been seldom seen by modern interpreters, resulting often in mis-interpretation of how ancient writings such as the Bible are structured.

There are many places where this insight helps us understand the Sermon. For example, 5:11–12 serves both as the conclusion to 5:3–12 and as a segue to 5:13–16. Similarly, 5:17–20, which we have seen as a *propositio*, is the heading for both the central section of the Sermon (5:17–7:12) as well as the smaller section of 5:17–48. Within the same unit, 5:48 serves as both the conclusion to the entirety of 5:17–48 and the natural ending to 5:43–48. As was discussed above, one of the greatest examples of the sectional-overlap technique is 6:19–21, which clearly serves as a dual-purpose text with respect to what comes before and after. Yet another example is the dual function of 7:12, which serves as the conclusion to both 7:1–12 and the larger unit of 5:17–7:12.

THE CENTRALITY OF THE LORD'S PRAYER

The previous two examples of meta-level structural techniques in the Ser-mon—*kəlāl ûpərāṭ* and sectional overlaps—are not difficult to discern. More debated, however, is the idea that the Lord's Prayer provides the structural framework for the whole sermon. I have argued already above that the Prayer intentionally sits at the center of the center of the center of the Sermon. However, some scholars have made an even stronger claim that the various petitions of the Lord's Prayer serve as a sort of table of contents for the rest of the Sermon's teachings. Various proposals along these lines have been made by Walter Grundmann, Günter Bornkamm, Robert Guelich, Daniel Patte, and Ulrich Luz.[77] While each of these provide some insight, and especially in the attempt to make sense of 7:1–12, most scholars are not convinced that the Lord's Prayer so neatly provides this organizing structure.[78] We should

75. The seminal work on this idea is Bruce Longenecker, *Rhetoric at the Boundaries: The Art and Theology of the New Testament Chain-Link Transitions* (Waco: Baylor University Press, 2005).

76. Ibid., 5.

77. See the discussion in Green, *Matthew, Poet,* 179; Stanton, *Gospel for a New People,* 298; and Talbert, *Reading the Sermon on the Mount,* 21–22. Syreeni evaluates Grundmann and Bornkamm and concludes that while their theories are not without some merit and insight, the connections between the Lord's Prayer and the rest of the Sermon are because of congeniality of themes, not because of an intentional structure (*Making of the Sermon,* 170–73).

78. Less ambitious but still leaving one with some questions is the attempt Kodjak makes to line up the Beatitudes with the petitions of the Lord's Prayer (*Structural Analysis,*

not overlook, however, the fact that the centrality of the Lord's Prayer conceptually does provide the disciple with a fundamental orientation to the
world and does connect with the frequent theme of the heavenly Father's
care (6:19–34; 7:7–11).

Overall Outline and Several Other Helpful Structural Images

The preceding discussion of the structure has, I hope, provided some interpretive insight. Putting all of these observations together, I can now present
my own outline of the Sermon.

I. Frame and Context: The Gospel of the Kingdom (4:23–25)

II. Ascending and Sitting (5:1–2)

III. The Sermon (5:3–7:27)

    A. Introduction: The Call to God's People (5:3–16)

        1. Nine Beatitudes for the New People of God (5:3–12)

        2. The New Covenant Witness of the People of God (5:13–16)

    B. The Body: The Greater Righteousness (GR) for God's People
(5:17–7:12)

        1. GR in Relation to God's Laws (5:17–48)

            a. Proposition (5:17–20)

            b. Six Exegeses/Examples (5:21–47)

            c. Summary (5:48)

        2. GR in Relation to Piety toward God (6:1–21)

            a. Introduction: Pleasing the Father in Heaven, not Humans (6:1)

            b. Three Examples (6:2–18)

                ** Central Excursus on Prayer (6:7–15)

            c. Conclusion: Rewards in Heaven, not on Earth (6:19–21)

        3. GR in Relation to the World (6:19–7:12)

            a. Introduction (6:19–21)

            b. In Relation to the Goods of This World (6:22–34)

            c. In Relation to the People of This World (7:1–6)

            d. Conclusion (7:7–12)

112–15). Some parallels are more convincing than others, such as the Beatitude for the merciful to receive mercy and the fifth petition of the Prayer to forgive us our debts as we have
forgiven others.

    C. Conclusion: Three Warnings Regarding the Prospect of Eschatological Judgment (7:13–27)

       1. Two Kinds of Paths (7:13–14)

       2. Two Kinds of Prophets (7:15–23)

       3. Two Kinds of Builders (7:24–27)

  IV. Descending and Action (7:28–8:1)

  V. Frame and Context: The Gospel of the Kingdom (8:2–9:38)

It should be noted, however, that underneath and throughout all of this analysis is the assumption of a flat, literary-outline approach. That is, due to educational habits in the Western tradition, we tend to think of literary structure as a two-dimensional outline with Roman numerals. This is one helpful approach. However, we cannot assume that this was in Matthew's mind or that this is the only beneficial way to represent the Sermon's structure. For example, Luz offers a pictorial diagram, which visualizes the centrality of the Lord's Prayer.[79] Allison's presentation of the structure is also more visually complex than a mere outline of the argument.[80] I think it is beneficial to consider other alternative ways of representing the Sermon's structure. I offer here a visual representation of the Sermon as the ascent and descent of a mountain. ("GR" means "greater righteousness.")

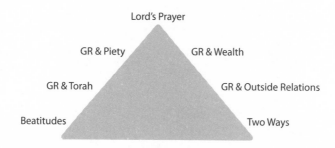

In this representation the journey begins with the macaristic invitation to human flourishing, proceeds through an exploration of the theme of necessary greater righteousness, and concludes with a return to the base of the mountain, exhorting hearers to heed what they have learned. At the apex of this journey, then, is the Lord's Prayer, providing the disciples with the high point of the Sermon's revelation. This pictorial representation provides several

79. Luz, *Matthew 1–7*, 173.

80. Dale C. Allison, *The Sermon on the Mount: Inspiring the Moral Imagination* (New York: Crossroad, 1999), 37.

vistas that more traditional outlines do not; namely, picturing the Sermon as a mountain emphasizes both the dramatic effect of the Sermon and that the life of discipleship, learned through the Sermon, is a journey. Additionally, it once again highlights the connection between the "Mount" of the Sermon and Mount Sinai.

Conclusion

This chapter serves as an important final step of orientation before beginning the exposition of the Sermon proper. Because Matthew apparently focuses so much of his creative energy on elaborate literary structures, the best readings of the Sermon will seek to note how the structures function and apply them appropriately to the interpretation of any individual text of the Sermon. We have seen that the structural analysis provided here indicates that the clear theme of the Sermon is the idea of greater righteousness, which for Matthew means a whole-person way of being in the world that can be simultaneously described as *makarios* and *teleios*.

PART 2

Commentary

6

Matthew 5:1–16

Introduction to This Exposition of the Sermon

Having laid a foundation for understanding the Sermon in the preceding five chapters, we are now ready to explore the contents of the Sermon proper. In the following chapters I will provide a theological exposition of the Sermon broken into units and subunits according to the structural decisions discussed previously. For each unit and subunit I will provide an original translation. I will then provide an exposition of the text, especially informed by the cultural encyclopedic context and meta-ideas discussed in the first section of this book. I will focus on the moves within the individual parts of the Sermon as understood from the vantage point of the larger theological vision and argument.

Matthew 5:1–2: Ascending and Sitting

> ¹*When he saw the crowds he ascended the mountain. And when he sat down his disciples came to him.* ²*And he opened his mouth and taught them, saying:*

Even though it leaves the reader at a bit of a cliff-hanger to break into our comments at verse 2, it is helpful to treat these first two verses separately from the rest. This is because verses 1–2 serve as the foundational introduction to the whole of the Sermon. They are not mere ornamental words to be skipped over quickly on the way to the real meat of the Sermon. As with nearly everything Matthew chooses to write, there are many levels of insight to be grasped for those who have eyes to see and ears to hear.[1] Or to use another Matthean meta-phor, there are treasures that the wise kingdom-scribe will continue to bring forth by digging around in the storehouse of Matthew's Scripture (13:51–52).

This is certainly true of these opening words of the Sermon. Kneaded in like yeast through a lump of dough are several biblical leitmotifs that Mat-thew wants his readers to discern. The greatest of these is the idea that Jesus is the fulfillment of Moses and his ministry of revelation to God's people. This is introduced with 5:1–2.

Matthew is clearly writing within the stream of the Jewish tradition, and this comes out in these verses with his implicit figural connection between Jesus and Moses. At the level of the basic narrative one can read Jesus's ascension to a mountainside as a simple auditory and pedagogical necessity due to the large crowd of followers. That is, for Jesus's proclamation to be heard and to reach the masses he needed to get some distance from them, and the higher elevation of a hilly slope is ideal. We may compare this to a very similar situation in Matt. 13:1–2, where Jesus is once again surrounded by massive crowds. In that instance he uses a fisherman's boat as a floating pulpit to get some necessary distance.[2]

But Matthew certainly is doing more with his selective and evocative sto-rytelling than reporting mere geographical movements. Jesus's ascent of a mountain speaks of divine revelation. More specifically, Matthew depicts Jesus's mountain visits as the place for the presentation of an eschatological event (5:1; 15:29; 17:1–13; 24:1–25:46; 28:16–20). Throughout the ancient world (and today) "high places" are understood as the location where gods speak and reveal.[3] Ancient Israel is no exception, and mountains played key roles in turning points in Israel's history, thereby making mountains potent theological symbols. One can think of Mount Ararat, Mount Carmel, Mount Gilead, Mount Moriah, Mount Pisgah, and Mount Zion. Each of these and many others are rich with evocations in Israel's history.

---

1. As H. Benedict Green points out, British and American scholarship tends to be quite re-served about puns and plays on words, but this is "an attitude at variance with those of almost all literary cultures, including the Hebraic" (*Matthew, Poet of the Beatitudes* [Edinburgh: T&T Clark, 2001], 21n19). Instead, as Dale C. Allison Jr. points out, "religious speech for [Matthew] was polysemous and heavily connotative" (*The New Moses: A Matthean Typology* [Eugene, OR: Wipf & Stock, 1993], 285).

2. See further discussion of this comparison in the following subsection.

3. As Erasmus writes, "When he had climbed the steep hill, he now began to play the role of the teacher of heavenly philosophy, indicating by the very height of the place that he was about to hand on nothing plebeian or lowly, but all the things that are exalted and heavenly" (*Paraphrase on Matthew*, ed. Dean Simpson and Robert Dick Sider [Toronto: University of Toronto Press, 2008], 83).

The most obvious and important revelatory mountain is Mount Sinai with its main character, Moses.[4] The connection of Jesus to Moses, who also ascended the mountain and from there taught the gathered people of God, has been long recognized and easily discernible.[5] As the subsequent sections of the Sermon will make even more explicit—especially 5:17–48—Jesus is presented as the new and final arbiter of God's law, thereby functioning as a new and final Moses.[6] The explicit discussion in 5:17–48 is hinted at here with the depiction of Jesus ascending the mountain and sitting down to teach. As Allison notes, Jesus is seeking a place "befitting his weighty words. That is, the revelatory character of the discourse demands a site consistent with its content. The 'mount of the beatitudes' is, therefore, a symbolic mountain, 'the mount of revelation.'"[7] With this interpretation Allison stands in the long line of ancient interpreters who understood the theological and spiritual implications of Jesus's mountain location.[8]

Indeed, the preceding four chapters of Matthew have also prepared one to think of Moses here in 5:1. The events of Moses's and Jesus's lives line up remarkably—dreams connected to their births, the slaughter of children from which they were spared miraculously as infants, flight from the land only to return later at God's direction, temptation in the wilderness, forty days and

4. Many scholars have observed that Matthew uses the otherwise unneeded Greek article before the word "mountain" here (*eis to oros*) to evoke a particular mountain, Sinai. See, e.g., Charles L. Quarles, *Sermon on the Mount: Restoring Christ's Message to the Modern Church* (Nashville: B&H, 2011), 35; W. D. Davies and Dale C. Allison Jr., *A Critical and Exegetical Commentary on the Gospel according to Saint Matthew*, vol. 1, *Introduction and Commentary on Matthew 1–7*, ICC (Edinburgh: T&T Clark, 2004), 423–24.

5. Dale Allison notes the clear connections made with Moses's ascent of Sinai in Exod. 19:3; 24:15, 18; 34:1–4. Also, Allison makes the interesting observation that in the rabbinic tradition the reference to Moses "remaining" on the mountain to receive the law in Deut. 9:9 was read as "sitting," which may indeed be what Matthew is thinking of here (Davies and Allison, *Matthew 1–7*, 424). See also Quarles, *Sermon on the Mount*, 36. Even though Ulrich Luz does not go as far as Allison in making the Moses connection, he still acknowledges that this ascending of a mountain and teaching is reminiscent of Israel's story and that now through Jesus God is speaking to Israel as he did at Sinai (*Matthew 1–7: A Commentary*, rev. ed., trans. James E. Crouch, Hermeneia [Minneapolis: Fortress, 2007], 182–83).

6. It should be noted that while the connection with Moses is dominant, this in no way eliminates a cultural encyclopedia evocation of Jesus as a hellenistic sage, as sitting to teach was also typical when Greco-Roman philosophers were presented. See Robert Kinney, *Hellenistic Dimensions of the Gospel of Matthew* (Tübingen: Mohr Siebeck, 2016), 175–79.

7. Davies and Allison, *Matthew 1–7*, 423.

8. For example, John Chrysostom contrasts heavenly and earthly teachings, Jerome sees Jesus as bringing people to a higher life, and Augustine says that the mountain points "toward the gospel's higher righteousness . . . higher precepts to a people to whom it is fitting to be set free by love" (Augustine, *Sermon on the Mount* 1.1.2, quoted from Manlio Simonetti, ed., *Matthew 1–13*, ACCS [Downers Grove, IL: InterVarsity, 2010], 77–78).

nights of fasting on a mount of revelation (see esp. Deut. 9:9), and passing through the Jordan River.[9] We also can see that all of Matt. 1–9 is even more broadly construed than a Mosaic typology—a new exodus typology that includes the figural parallels between Jesus and Moses but goes beyond to see the Moses story as part of something bigger—God rescuing and forming for himself a people (ekklēsia) through the exodus. Thus, "when Jesus goes up on the mountain to utter the sermon on the mount, he is speaking as the mosaic Messiah and delivering messianic Torah."[10] The Sermon stands in the place that the Law did on Mount Sinai, not as a mere substitute, but as its eschatological fulfillment. Additionally, as Charles Quarles observes, Moses is not only a lawgiver, but for the Jews he was also their redeemer, deliverer, and savior, a role that Jesus will play for the Jews and the gentiles.[11] All of these connections are being made in line with Matthew's constant refrain in the first four chapters, namely, that all these things happened as a fulfillment.[12] This means that Jesus is not merely being presented as another Moses. Rather, in line with but greater than Moses, Jesus is being presented here as the Messiah who fulfills God's ancient and promised purposes. While the Sermon will cast a vision of how disciples should live, it is first of all a christological statement.[13]

Jesus's sitting down on the mountainside is part of the regular depiction of Jesus in Matthew as the teacher. In addition to 5:1, Jesus sits down to teach in 13:1–2; 15:29 (a mini-redo of the Sermon); 24:3; and 26:55. Also, Matthew tells us that in the future Jesus will sit on a throne (19:28; 25:31; cf. 20:21–23).

Another way in which the Jewish tradition is evoked here is with the subtle connection of Matthew's redundant phrase "and he opened his mouth" to Ps. 78:2. We are safe to assume that the reason for this phrase is not for Matthew to contrast Jesus's open-mouthed teaching with a ventriloquistic style: "with his lips not moving he began to teach them . . ." Rather, this unexpected and unnecessary phrase sets a tone of solemnity for what is about to be said and

9. Scot McKnight, The Sermon on the Mount, The Story of God Bible Commentary (Grand Rapids: Zondervan, 2013), 22.

10. Davies and Allison, Matthew 1–7, 427.

11. Quarles, Sermon on the Mount, 37. Eusebius was one church father who particularly highlighted the shift to both Jews and gentiles. As he writes in his Demonstration of the Gospel 3.2, "Moses was the first to teach the Jewish race, Jesus Christ has been the first to publish them to the other nations by His disciples in a far diviner form. So that Moses may properly be called the first and only lawgiver of religion to the Jews, and Jesus Christ the same to all nations" (quoted in McKnight, Sermon on the Mount, 23).

12. The idea of fulfillment may be rightly seen as the framing motif of Matthew, who organizes the first four chapters of his Gospel along these lines. See 1:22; 2:15, 17, 23; 4:14.

13. See Douglas R. A. Hare, Matthew, IBC (Louisville: John Knox, 1993), 34.

also points us to other weighty sayings from the Old Testament.[14] It is possible, of course, that no specific Old Testament connections are being suggested by this phrase but rather only the tone of solemnity. However, the use of the same expression in the parallel passage of Matt. 13:35—which includes a quotation from Ps. 78—makes the intentional connection much more likely. In Matt. 13:35 one of Matthew's ten fulfillment quotations appears, with Ps. 78:2 being used to explain Jesus's teaching style. The same connection may very well be at work here.

The connection with Matt. 13 is intriguing in many ways, especially how Jesus's teaching on the mountainside contrasts with his teaching on the seashore from a boat (13:1–2). In Matthew's third major discourse (chap. 13) Jesus is still being followed by massive crowds, and again, as in chapter 5, he must get some physical distance in order to be heard. But the contrast between the response of the crowds to the Sermon (7:28–29) and the reception of the parables discourse could not be more stark. The crowds and disciples recognize that Jesus has wisdom, but they are perplexed, confused, and even scandalized by Jesus's parabolic teaching, which is far from clear in its meaning (13:10–17, 53–58). Could the locational difference between the mountainside in 5:1 (and 24:3) and the seaside in 13:1–2 be part of how this contrast is being communicated? The revelatory teachings on the mountainsides (Galilee and Jerusalem in chaps. 5 and 24, respectively) contrast with the concealing teachings at sea level of chapter 13. This comes full circle at the end of the Gospel when Jesus commissions *from a mountain* his disciples to go out and teach all that he has taught them (28:16–20), where Jesus's *authority* (7:29; 28:18) is emphasized again.[15]

This also highlights the important observation that mountainsides are the significant symbolic setting for several other events in Jesus's life. Before we get to Matt. 5:1–2, there is a rich heritage of revelatory mountain scenes throughout the history of Israel. Matthew continues to evoke this tradition by informing us of the mountain location of Jesus's place of prayer (14:23), of healings (15:29), of visions (17:1; 28:16), and of teaching (24:3). Of particular note is the final and abiding scene of the First Gospel with its mountainside Great Commission (28:16–20)—the sending of Jesus's disciples out into all

14. The same phrase occurs in Acts 8:35; 10:34; 18:14 and is described by several commentators as a solemn formula appropriate for introducing an address. See, e.g., A. B. Bruce, ed., "The Synoptic Gospels," in *The Expositor's Greek Testament*, ed. W. Robertson Nicoll (Grand Rapids: Eerdmans, 1956), 95.

15. Kari Syreeni uses this special connection between the Sermon and the Great Commission to suggest that for Matthew the Sermon might have a special role and status even among the five "great discourses" (*The Making of the Sermon on the Mount: A Procedural Analysis of Matthew's Redactoral Activity* [Helsinki: Academia Scientiarum Fennica, 1987], 101).

the world to do all that he did, especially *teaching* all that he commanded, certainly including the greatest summary of this in the Sermon. What makes this connection particularly intriguing is the unexpected definite phrase in 28:16—the disciples went to "*the* mountain to which Jesus had directed them." Which mountain this was we do not know for certain. Many early Christians assumed it was the Mount of Olives because of its great significance. But many of the early commentators observed that this did not fit with Matthew's setting in Galilee. Thus, a likely candidate was Mount Tabor.[16] Regardless, we know that the disciples were following Jesus's directions to return to Galilee (see Matt. 28:10) and meet him on a specific high place. This appears to be pointing back to the Sermon and wrapping up the Gospel's story by simultaneously bringing the book to a close and creating this open-ended beginning with the disciples' mission beginning where Jesus's began.

One last Jewish encyclopedia evocation to note is that of Isa. 40:9, which reads, "Get you up to a high mountain, O Zion, herald of good news; lift up your voice with strength, O Jerusalem, herald of good news; lift it up, fear not; say to the cities of Judah, 'Behold your God!'" (ESV). This passage is particularly significant because it is the second part of Isaiah (chaps. 40–66) that serves as the primary backdrop for all of the Gospels[17] and for the Beatitudes particularly. We have already seen Isaiah appear as a key backdrop for Matt. 1–4.[18] Going back to the beginning of Isaiah also proves enlightening—Isaiah prophesies that in the latter days the mountain of the house of the Lord will be established. People from all the nations will flow to it saying, "Come, let us go up to the mountain of the Lord, to the house of the God of Jacob; *that he may teach us his ways* and that we may walk in his paths" (Isa. 2:3 ESV).[19] All of this makes the reference to the good news or gospel being proclaimed eschatologically from a high mountain more than coincidental for any Jewish or Christian reader.

Finally, a common question regarding 5:1–2 is, for whom is the Sermon intended, and who heard it? Matthew 5:1 mentions the crowds (of 4:25), but then Jesus specifically calls his "disciples" to himself to teach them. Yet at the conclusion to the Sermon the crowds have apparently been hearing as well

16. This is the view of at least Jerome (*Commentary on Matthew* 1.5.1). Some modern interpreters have identified the site as Tagbah near Capernaum, a high ridge overlooking the Sea of Galilee and its surrounding villages. See Michael J. Wilkins, *Matthew*, NIVAC (Grand Rapids: Zondervan, 2003), 191, following Bargil Pixner.
17. See Jonathan T. Pennington, *Reading the Gospels Wisely: A Narrative and Theological Introduction* (Grand Rapids: Baker Academic, 2012), chap. 1.
18. Isa. 7:14 in Matt. 1:23; Isa. 40:3 in Matt. 3:3; and climactically, Isa. 9:1–2 in Matt. 4:15–16.
19. This insight comes from Frederick D. Bruner, *Matthew: A Commentary*, vol. 1, *The Christbook: Matthew 1–12* (Grand Rapids: Eerdmans, 2007), 153 (emphasis original).

because they are astonished at his teaching and authority (7:28–29). While elsewhere Matthew does distinguish between the crowds as people who hear him and the disciples as those who both hear *and are given understanding* (11:25–27; 13:10–17), here all are hearing Jesus's teaching and all are welcome to respond. Additionally, we may note that this idea of a dual audience also appears in two other of Matthew's five major discourses. In both chapter 13 and chapters 23–25 the audience consists of both full disciples and interested hearers, the former being given the revelatory ability to understand.[20]

In light of this it is unhelpful when interpreters constrain the meaning of the Sermon to be only for "believers" because Jesus specifically calls the disciples to himself. Rather, the concluding reference to the crowds shows that the Sermon is to be understood as a general call to all people, an epitomizing of Jesus's teaching concerning the kingdom, and that "he who has ears to hear" should respond. The hearing, understanding, and obeying moves one from being part of the crowd to being a disciple.

Matthew 5:3–16: Introduction: The Call to God's People

Matthew 5:3–12: Nine Beatitudes for the New People of God (A Vision for True Human Flourishing)

> [3]*Flourishing are the poor in spirit because the kingdom of heaven is theirs.*
>
> [4]*Flourishing are the mourners because they will be comforted.*
>
> [5]*Flourishing are the humble because they will inherit the world.*
>
> [6]*Flourishing are the ones hungering and thirsting for righteousness because they will be satisfied.*
>
> [7]*Flourishing are the merciful because they will be given mercy.*
>
> [8]*Flourishing are the pure in heart because they will see God.*
>
> [9]*Flourishing are the peacemakers because they will be called the children[21] of God.*

20. Recognition of the dual audience of these three discourses comes from Graham Stanton, *A Gospel for a New People: Studies in Matthew* (Edinburgh: T&T Clark, 1992), 320–21.

21. This is a very difficult translation decision that must be made from Greek into English. The Greek word here (*huioi*) can be rightly translated "sons," but in many contexts like this the sense of gender specificity (sons, not daughters) is not intended. Yet "children," which does eliminate the male-only appearance, loses the emphasis on inheritance that "son" would communicate in an ancient culture. Thus, the translator, as is often the case, is on the horns of a dilemma as to which gloss to provide; each option cuts off part of what is being communicated. For a helpful discussion of the translation issues surrounding "son" in the Bible, see chap. 3 of D. A. Carson, *Jesus the Son of God: A Christological Title Often Overlooked, Sometimes Misunderstood, and Currently Disputed* (Wheaton: Crossway, 2012).

>[10]*Flourishing are the ones persecuted on account of righteousness because the kingdom of heaven is theirs.*
>[11]*Flourishing are you whenever people revile and slander[22] and speak all kinds of evil things against you on account of me.*
>[12]*Rejoice and be glad because your reward is great in heaven. In this same way people slandered the prophets who came before you.*

These verses make up the justly famous Beatitudes. This striking and memorable series of nine *makarios* statements (macarisms) is intentional in form and has great importance for our overall understanding of the Sermon's purpose. As was discussed in chapter 2 on the meaning of *makarios*, all such "flourishing" statements or macarisms cast a vision for life that includes an implicit invitation. "Beatitudes are description, and commendations, of the good life."[23] As prophet and sage, Jesus is offering and inviting his hearers into *the way of being in the world that will result in their true and full flourishing now and in the age to come.* Through his authoritative and eschatological claims he is more than an ancient philosopher of happiness, but he is not less than this. By beginning his message with macarisms, Jesus follows squarely in the ancient tradition of Jewish sages who offered practical wisdom for living according to God's rule and reign. As Servais Pinckaers states, leaning heavily on Augustine, "The beatitudes are Jesus' answer to the human question about happiness, an answer given in the form of a series of promises and challenges."[24] At the same time, the Beatitudes offer "a radical revisioning of the people of God," as Scot McKnight calls it.[25] Jesus presents not a list of heroes of the faith nor a list of moral behaviors that describe the truly pious but rather a redefinition of who the people of God are—they are ones whose lives look like this beatitudinal way of being (and like Jesus himself).

In the following discussion, rather than provide a verse-by-verse commentary of the Beatitudes, I will take this series of macarisms as a whole, exploring their background, their relationship to the rest of the Sermon and to Matthew, as well as how they function as wisdom literature. More could be said about

22. This word (*diōxōsin*) is usually translated with the English gloss "persecute," and in a general sense this is a reasonable and valid connection to make. However, the series of three verbs being used here all concern speech. The first (*oneidizō*) and third (*legō*) expressions are clearly so, and it seems this is also the sense being communicated with the second (*diōkō*). This is a series of statements that concern those outside attacking and criticizing Jesus's disciples via verbal assaults, hence "slander" is a better gloss here than the generic "persecution."
23. R. T. France, *The Gospel of Matthew*, NICNT (Grand Rapids: Eerdmans, 2007), 161.
24. Servais Pinckaers, *The Pursuit of Happiness—God's Way: Living the Beatitudes*, trans. Mary Thomas Noble (Eugene, OR: Wipf & Stock, 1998), viii.
25. McKnight, *Sermon on the Mount*, 31.

the content of each of the individual Beatitudes, but I have chosen to treat them thematically and according to their function as a whole—providing Jesus's vision for what true human flourishing in God's coming kingdom looks like. For more information on the nature of macarisms and the structure of this collection, see chapters 2 and 5 above.

The Eschatological Isaianic Background to the Beatitudes

It is enormously valuable to understand that the main subtext for this series of macarisms is Isaiah's prophetic vision.[26] Isaiah provides the context and frame for the Beatitudes. Isaiah's overall impact on the self-understanding of the New Testament authors, and especially on Matthew, has been long recognized and not difficult to discern. In Matthew 3–4 (immediately preceding the Sermon), Isaiah is used as the explanation for and interpretive framework to describe the actions of both of the main characters in these chapters, John the Baptist and Jesus. John's role and ministry are portrayed as fulfilling[27] the prophetic vision of Isa. 40:3 (Matt. 3:3). Jesus's ministry is likewise described as the fulfillment of what Isaiah had spoken: Jesus's travel movements and gentile-focused light bearing/proclamation is explained as happening "to fulfill that which was spoken through the prophet Isaiah" concerning Galileans who are sitting in darkness and death, upon whom the Light is now dawning (4:14–16). The events of Matt. 5–9 will later be summed up as a concatenation of Isaianic promises when Jesus explains his ministry to the imprisoned John the Baptist (Matt. 11:4–5, based on Isa. 26:19; 29:18–19; 35:5–6; 42:7–18; 61:1–3).

We should not be surprised, then, to recognize Isaiah as the source for much of the verbiage in these opening words of proclamation from Jesus, the

26. While Isaiah plays the leading role in the background to the Beatitudes, it is not surprising that there are also many other texts and underground streams that rise to the surface in Matt. 5:3–12. E.g., several Psalms are evoked at key points, particularly Pss. 1 and 36, but also Pss. 33, 39, and others. H. Benedict Green has particularly highlighted Ps. 119 as part of the background to the Beatitudes in both structure and content (*Matthew, Poet*, chap. 2). The Beatitudes also call to mind several important characters from Jewish history, including Moses (humble, meek; sees God) and several other prophets, esp. the suffering prophets such as Jeremiah. The connection to prophets who stood for God and suffered at the hands of God's own covenantal people is strongly highlighted by the tailpiece of this section, Matt. 5:12. After his detailed analysis of the Beatitudes, Green concludes that apart from the phrases "theirs is the kingdom of heaven" and "persecuted for righteousness' sake," "every detail of the wording of the Beatitudes has its counterpart somewhere in the LXX text" (*Matthew, Poet*, 264). See his chart of Greek word connections between the LXX and the Beatitudes on pp. 266–67.

27. While the fulfillment of Isa. 40:3 in John's ministry is clearly being argued, Matthew interestingly does not use one of his ten technical "fulfillment quotation formula" statements here ("this happened to fulfill the word of the prophet . . ."). This is likely because, although John is fulfilling Isaiah's words, Matthew wants to reserve this special formula for Jesus.

Beatitudes; the Model Reader has already been thinking of Isaiah all along. Several passages from Isaiah serve as clear subtexts for the Beatitudes,[28] but it is especially the central section of Isa. 61 that appears to be the main encyclopedic background.[29]

The significance of this is not difficult to discern: here at the fount of his teaching, Jesus is evoking the great promises of the eschatological deliverance that God has foretold. Jesus is the new Moses, but his message is appropriated through the eschatological vision of the prophets, especially Isaiah. This eschatological emphasis receives another shot of support if indeed Matthew considered the Psalms to be prophetic as well (cf. the "prophet" speaking in Ps. 78:2, quoted in Matt. 13:35), which seems to be the case.[30]

In a way that is both brilliant and beautiful, the Beatitudes simultaneously invite Jesus's disciples into these flourishing virtues and comfort them with the promise of God's coming deliverance and setting of the world to right. As Glen Stassen describes it, the Beatitudes are virtues of participation in grace-based deliverance.[31] Thus, for the careful reader this opening to Jesus's teaching is both macaristic and eschatological, combining the vision for true human flourishing and the context of God-centered eschatological hope.

The Beatitudes in Connection with the Rest of Matthew

Throughout the church's history the most common mistake in interpreting the Sermon has been the tendency to extract it from the narrative and

---

28. One can consult the chart in Davies and Allison, *Matthew 1–7*, 436–37.

29. In addition to Davies and Allison, this understanding is supported by many scholars, including Matthew Black (*An Aramaic Approach to the Gospels and Acts*, 3rd ed. [Peabody, MA: Hendrickson, 1998], 158), who notes that in Luke 4:16–21 Jesus opened his public ministry with these verses, and he also replied with these same verses to the question of John's disciples (Matt. 11:5; Luke 7:22), after which he says, "and *makarios* is the one who is not scandalized by me" (Matt. 11:6; Luke 7:23).

30. Green notes:

   Matthew, like some other New Testament writers, seems to have reckoned the Psalter among the prophetic books; and since he apparently knows nothing of any further subdivision of the scriptures beyond Torah and prophets, he may well have seen the prophetic strain as continuing in at least some of the books that the rabbis assigned to the Writings. However that may be, the fact that he placed at the head of what he meant to be seen as the definitive messianic reinterpretation of Torah a composition that was overwhelmingly prophetic in inspiration [the Beatitudes] should shed some light on his own understanding of his preferred expression "law and prophets." (*Matthew, Poet*, 265)

31. Glenn Stassen, "The Beatitudes as Eschatological Peacemaking Virtues," in *Character Ethics and the New Testament: Moral Dimensions of Scripture*, ed. Robert Brawley (Louisville: Westminster John Knox, 2007), 246.

theological context in which it has been set. But when taken as part of Matthew's Gospel as a whole, we see many ways in which the Beatitudes are deepened and explained throughout the rest of his Gospel account. For example, we can note how many of the themes highlighted in the Beatitudes are picked up and reiterated in other passages in Matthew. There are especially four such themes worth noting. They are the *kingdom of God / heaven, righteousness, persecution,* and *mercy.* The first and second of these have already been addressed as important topics in chapter 4 above and so they do not need much explanation. It remains only to point out that the Beatitudes use these ideas as an important part of their vision.

(1) In the case of the *kingdom,* we see that "for theirs is the kingdom of heaven" serves as an *inclusio* in the first and eighth Beatitudes (5:3, 10), providing a framework and frame of reference for Jesus's macarisms.[32] The kingdom also appears in 5:20; 6:10, 33; and 7:21. This repeated reference to the kingdom invites the hearer to recognize that what Jesus is about to teach is tied directly to his opening words and general message of "Repent, for the kingdom of heaven is at hand!" (4:17 ESV). Reference to the kingdom in the Sermon is part of the larger kingdom message in Matthew overall.

(2) With regard to *righteousness,* as noted earlier, this theme is the overarching idea of the Sermon. Two of the nine Beatitudes mention *righteousness:* flourishing are those hungering and thirsting for righteousness (5:6) and those persecuted because of righteousness (5:10). These evoke Isaiah (Isa. 61:3, 8, 10, 11) and also resonate throughout the rest of Matthew, which contains 26 forms of the *dik-* root, including several other references in the Sermon (5:20, 45; 6:1, 33).[33]

(3) Another important theme that appears in the Beatitudes and then reappears throughout the Gospel is that of *persecution.* Overall, the subject of suffering (for the sake of this Jesus-righteousness) proves to be the main emphasis, feel, and flavor of the Beatitudes. This is accomplished by Matthew with his 8 + 1 *makarios* structure and the expansion of the final macarism in the Sermon.[34] This Matthean structural choice places great stress and weight on the theme of persecution by making it the repeated and climactic note. These eighth and ninth Beatitudes paint a particularly pointed picture of

---

32. As was noted in the previous discussion of the structure of the Sermon, there are nine Beatitudes, spanning 5:3–11, not eight as some commentators have suggested, nor seven as was commonly argued in the premodern period. The ninth is set apart and highlighted by its repeating the same content as the eighth and by its serving as a kind of add-on, bonus feature to the *inclusio* structure of the first through eighth Beatitudes.

33. See chap. 4 above for more discussion of righteousness in Matthew and the Sermon.

34. See chap. 5 above on the structure of the Sermon.

unanticipated flourishing—it is a flourishing in the midst of suffering and persecution. Throughout the rest of Matthew, Jesus anticipates that his disciples will experience persecution precisely because they are following him and his way of righteousness (10:16–23). Moreover, his life (and death) will be marked by persecution, even as the life of many righteous prophets before him (e.g., Jeremiah; cf. Matt. 23:29–36).[35] This is in many ways the greatest example of the key principle of discipleship—no disciple is greater than his or her master (10:24–25); what is true for the master will be true for the disciple. This includes suffering and persecution.[36] Thus, once again, the Beatitudes prove to highlight a theme that is particularly important for Matthew's overall teaching and theological understanding.

(4) Finally, we can also note that another topic raised in the Beatitudes proves to be of great importance in Matthew more broadly—that of *mercy*, manifested by the state of the heart that makes peace, shows compassion, and forgives others. "Mercy is about an action, that is, a generous action that delivers someone from need or bondage."[37] This could be deliverance from the bondage of guilt or deliverance in the sense of healing or giving. This comes out in the Beatitudes with the macarisms about showing mercy (5:7) and making peace (5:9). Examining Matthew more broadly shows that this in many ways typifies Jesus's way of righteousness, especially as it fulfills the second greatest commandment, love for others (22:34–40). For example, the great weight placed on showing compassion to others is highlighted twice with Matthew's strategic use of Hosea 6:6 (Matt. 9:13; 12:7). Even more frequently, Jesus speaks of the necessity and beauty of forgiving other people who have sinned against us (6:14–15; 18:15–20, 35). Additionally, disciples are exhorted to help those in need (6:3; 25:35–36), an exhortation connected to mercy (*eleos*) in terms of the word for "giving alms to the poor" (*eleēmosynēn*). In addition to highlighting these key Matthean themes, the Beatitudes serve another crucial Matthean purpose: providing a framework for understanding Jesus's own way of being in the world. The purpose of writing a biography is largely (though not exclusively) to inspire followers to model their lives after the *biographee*, the subject of the biography.[38] This happens through modeling—through showing how a great person lived, the outcome of his or her life, and its inherent beauty. This appeal-by-example is the most important,

35. See Michael Knowles, *Jeremiah in Matthew's Gospel: The Rejected Prophet Motif in Matthean Redaction* (Sheffield: JSOT Press, 1993; repr., London: Bloomsbury, 2015).

36. For example, "to persecute" (*diōkō*) occurs six times (5:10, 11, 12, 44; 10:23; 23:34) and "to kill" (*apokteinō*) twelve times (10:28; 14:5; 16:21; 17:23; 21:35, 38, 39; 22:6; 23:34, 37; 24:9; 26:4).

37. Stassen, "Beatitudes," 251.

38. See Pennington, *Reading the Gospels Wisely*, chap. 2.

powerful, and lasting way of effecting change and inculcating virtue in others.[39] The Gospels are more than biographies, but they are not less. Jesus is clearly depicted as one to *follow*.

Christianity is not just a set of doctrines added onto or even fundamentally altering Judaism. It is the revelation of God himself *in a person*. To be godly, godlike,[40] has always meant to act in accord with who God is and how he acts. Now this is made clearest and most pointed with the revelation of God in the flesh, Jesus the Christ. We now have a complete image of what it means to be like God, and hence, at this unique point in salvation history the biography[41] of God can be written.

Here at the beginning of the Sermon Jesus gives a vision of a way of being in the world that will result in our flourishing. We would be suspicious and disappointed if he were teaching this cerebrally but did not *know* or experience or model it himself. Matthew helps us see that nothing could be farther from the truth. In his carefully crafted and thoughtful work, Matthew takes pains to show that Jesus models precisely what he commends to us in the Beatitudes. Jesus is humble and poor in spirit (11:28–29; 21:5), mourns and grieves (23:37), hungers and thirsts with longing for God's kingdom to be manifested (9:38), is pure in heart (4:10), shows mercy (12:1–21; 14:13–21; 15:32–39; 20:30–34), and brings peace (28:10). And even as the primary sense of the Beatitudes proves to be the emphasis on unjust suffering and persecution for righteousness' sake, so too Jesus serves as the greatest example of the same. Indeed, one could say that this beatitudinal flavor matches the overall sense of the Gospels, which are tilting and careening toward the inevitable darkness of Jesus's suffering and unjust death. Thus, in each of these ways the Beatitudes relate intimately with the entirety of Matthew, and the Beatitudes and Matthew as a whole illuminate one another in a mutually informing way.[42]

39. Dale C. Allison Jr. notes, "The disciples not only confront his [Jesus's] words but study the Messiah himself. 'Learn of me' (Matt. 11:29) means, in effect, 'Follow me' (Matt. 9:9). One learns not just with the ears but also with the feet. Education is much more than heeding an infallible wordsmith. It additionally involves the mimetic following of Jesus, who is virtue embodied" (*Studies in Matthew: Interpretation Past and Present* [Grand Rapids: Baker Academic, 2005], 153).

40. Jason Hood points out in his excellent book on imitation that "godly" is a shortened form of "godlike" (*Imitating God in Christ: Recapturing a Biblical Pattern* [Downers Grove, IL: IVP Academic, 2013]).

41. Even though there are four Gospel accounts, the singular "biography" is appropriate here, even as the early church understood the fourfold book to be *the* (singular) Gospel according to four inspired witnesses.

42. Contra Hans Dieter Betz, who sees the Sermon as a jewel only later fitted into a very different setting in the Gospel of Matthew and best read apart from that context (*Essays on the Sermon on the Mount* [1985; Minneapolis: Fortress, 2009], 19).

The Beatitudes as Head of the Sermon: Some Key Observations

As was discussed in the previous chapter that analyzed the structure of the Sermon, there is nothing that appears by accident in this masterful artwork that is the Sermon on the Mount. The placement of the Beatitudes at the head of this masterpiece is worth paying attention to, even as the first paragraph of a novel or sermon is. H. Benedict Green and others suggest that the Beatitudes stand at the head of the Sermon even as the Decalogue stands as the first installment of the Mosaic law.[43] Some interpreters have even said that the Sermon is the summary of the whole Gospel, and the Beatitudes are the summary of the Sermon.[44] There is some truth to this, even if we might desire a bit more nuance in its theological outworking. Nonetheless, the crucial fact that is obvious yet often not weighed sufficiently is that the opening salvo of the Sermon is a series of macarisms. This Matthean choice is very instructive in several ways for our overall understanding of the Sermon.

The first and most striking thing to observe is that the Sermon presents itself as virtue- or flourishing-oriented wisdom literature. I have argued earlier that the two key pillars of the overall point of the Sermon are *makarios* and *teleios*. These two concepts are deeply rooted in the traditions that precede the Sermon and evoke these traditions in terms of both Greco-Roman notions of virtue and Second Temple Jewish wisdom literature, the very nexus at which the Sermon lies. This sets up for Matthew's hearers a powerful matrix and lens through which to interpret and receive the Sermon—it is *flourishing-oriented, eschatological wisdom exhortation* (now with a radically Christocentric orientation).

In this we are relying on the arguments already made in the earlier exploration of *makarios*. We need not reargue those here except in a short summary. Macarisms are proclamations that invite the hearers into a way of being in the world (a vision of virtues) that promise human flourishing. This has a rich heritage in the Jewish Scriptures (especially the Psalms) and the Greco-Roman virtue tradition. In the former it is the vision of the asheristic life. In the latter it is synonymous with *eudaimonia*. In this, Jesus is stepping into the stream of the great universal human question of how one can attain true happiness and flourishing. His answer is simultaneously Jewish in origin (rooted in divine revelation), Greek in context (the language and engine of virtue), and radically new in emphasis (eschatological kingdom orientation).

43. Green, *Matthew, Poet*, 284.
44. Pinckaers, *Pursuit of Happiness*, 25, is one such example, himself citing Jacques Bénigne Bossuet.

Central to this Old Testament wisdom-flourishing is Ps. 1. It is not a mere coincidence that Ps. 1 and the Sermon have so much in common. There is a real sense in which the Sermon is an eschatological, Jesus-given expansion of Ps. 1. Both are macaristic wisdom, and the content of the Psalm overlaps with the conclusion to the Sermon (7:13–27) in remarkable ways: they both invite hearers onto the path of wisdom (Ps. 1:1; Matt. 7:24); they contrast two paths or ways of being in the world (Ps. 1:1, 6; Matt. 7:13–14); they use fruit-bearing trees as a key metaphor (Ps. 1:3–4; Matt. 7:16–20); they both speak of final judgment and separation of the righteous from the wicked (Ps. 1:5–6; Matt. 7:13, 21–23, 26–27); they both contrast those whom the Lord "knows" and those he does not (Ps. 1:6; Matt. 7:23); and they both emphasize hearing and heeding God's revelation (Ps. 1:2; Matt. 7:24).

On the basis of this foundation we may make a few additional observations about how these Beatitudes function in the Sermon. The first thing to note is that there is a structure to the Beatitudes.[45] Various interpreters have offered different analyses of what this structure is. Throughout much of the church's history they were seen as a progressive ladder to be climbed toward God.[46] Some Reformed Protestants have emphasized "hungering and thirsting for righteousness" as the center.[47] Hans Dieter Betz suggests that the first Beatitude is the key, with the rest of the Sermon as an outworking of it.[48] Mark Allan Powell sees the first four Beatitudes as promising reversal for the unfortunate (5:3–6) and the second four as promising eschatological reward to the virtuous (5:7–10), with a closing comment (5:11–12).[49] Scot McKnight suggests three sets of three, showing the three main moral themes of the Beatitudes: humility (5:3–5), justice (5:6–8), and peace (5:9–12).[50] From a more distinctly literary and structural analysis, we may observe the intentional alliteration (in Greek) and the fact that each of the quatrains have exactly the same number of letters.[51] Each of these interpretations offer

45. See additional discussion in chap. 5 on the structure of the Sermon.
46. See, e.g., Hugh of St. Victor's *De quinque septenis*, discussed in Boyd Taylor Cameron, "Hugh of St. Victor," in *The Sermon on the Mount through the Centuries: From the Early Church to John Paul II*, ed. Jeffrey P. Greenman, Timothy Larsen, and Stephen R. Spencer (Grand Rapids: Brazos, 2007), 59–80.
47. See, e.g., Daniel M. Doriani, *The Sermon on the Mount: The Character of a Disciple* (Phillipsburg, NJ: P&R, 2006).
48. "The rest of the SM [Sermon on the Mount] is nothing else than the concretization and elucidation of the first macarism" (Betz, *Essays*, 35).
49. Mark Allan Powell, *God with Us: A Pastoral Theology of Matthew's Gospel* (Minneapolis: Fortress, 1995), 119–40.
50. McKnight, *Sermon on the Mount*, 37.
51. See Allison, *Studies in Matthew*, 174–75; Green, *Matthew, Poet*, 39–40. Originally, Christine Michaelis, "Die P-Alliteration der Subjektsworte der ersten 4 Seligpreisungen in Mt.

insight and benefit from their own line of sight. I would also suggest seeing
a parallel with the two tablets of the Decalogue, with the God-centered focus
followed by other-centeredness. The first four Beatitudes thus have a vertical
emphasis (relating to God; 5:3–6) and the remainder are horizontal (relating
to others; 5:7–12).[52] But overall, as discussed in chapter 5 above, it is best to
see the Beatitudes as three sets of three, setting a triadic pattern that will be
repeated throughout the Sermon.

Secondly, we can observe how these macarisms function in the symmetrical structure of the Sermon. It has often been argued that these opening
nine Beatitudes correspond to the closing three warnings, modeled after a
blessings-curses pattern in Deuteronomy, a "choose this day whom you will
serve" (Josh. 24:15 ESV) kind of moment. This interpretation is not entirely
wrong—there is some element of truth here—but it is not primary and is
in fact based on the typical confused conflation of macarisms and blessings
(see chap. 2).

Far better is to understand this parallel structure more broadly as a symmetry of nine invitations and three warnings. As has been argued above,
macarisms are not "blessings" in the *brk*, blessings-cursings sense. Macarisms
are exhortatory invitations to flourishing whose counterparts are *woes*. And in
fact Matthew does provide precisely this counterpoint of woes, in chapter 23,
during the last week of Jesus's life and teaching. There we find a remarkably
similar poetic pattern of anti-macarisms or declaratory warnings about the
way of nonflourishing and its consequences (23:1–36). Interestingly, confirmation of this way of linking the macarisms with the woes (rather than with
curses) is found in Luke 6:20–26, where we find a direct fourfold macarism-
woe series, what one typically finds in wisdom literature. Matthew apparently has reasons for putting his fuller set of woes in the narrative of Passion
Week in Jerusalem rather than in the manifesto that is the Sermon. From a
literary perspective this provides a powerful set of bookends that demarcate
the beginning and end of Jesus's teaching ministry. But this separation of
seventeen chapters does not alter the clear point that macarisms and woes
are the contrastive pairs. Indeed, if Charles Lohr is correct that the whole
structure of Matthew is chiastic based on the five discourses, this strengthens

v 3–6 und ihre Bedeutung für den Aufbau der Seligpreisungen bei Mt., Lk. und in Q," *NovT*
10, no. 2 (1969): 148–61; and Julius Schniewind, *Das Evangelium nach Matthäus* (Göttingen:
Vandenhoeck & Ruprecht, 1962), 270, on letter counting.

52. Charles Talbert, *Matthew*, Paideia: Commentary on the New Testament (Grand Rapids:
Baker Academic, 2010), 75; David Garland, *Reading Matthew: A Literary and Theological
Commentary* (Macon, GA: Smyth & Helwys, 2013), 54. Green does not see the structure of
the Beatitudes as working out directly in this way, even though he does see the horizontal and
vertical aspects of the Decalogue at play (*Matthew, Poet*, 287–88).

the interpretation even more, with the first and fifth discourses matching each other with macarisms and woes.[53]

Thus, in the Sermon itself, rather than emphasizing blessings and warnings, it is better to simply observe that the natural and even expected structure of the message entails an invitation at the beginning *and* the end. The initial invitation is a positive one that operates by casting the vision of the virtuous way of being in the world that will result in one's flourishing. The invitation at the end is the same, with a more negative bent, with a dash of warning kneaded in: beware that you must take this whole message seriously lest you find yourselves on the wrong side of the equation. Hearers are exhorted to enter by the narrow gate (the way of Jesus's teachings, not the Pharisees') and to build one's house with wisdom (by listening to Jesus's words, not the Pharisees') *lest the hearer end up in a state of desolation and destruction* (7:13, 27), a truly woeful state, the opposite of human flourishing. It is precisely this state of destruction that stands as the contrast to the Beatitudes, not cursings per se, which are not actually found in 7:13–27. And at a broader literary level, the Beatitudes as macarisms are paired with the woes of Matt. 23.

The Beatitudes as Paradoxical Suffering-Flourishing

When we drill down even further into Matthew's series of nine macarisms, we find a rich reservoir of "black gold." It is divine gold of priceless worth, but it appears to be only darkness. And herein lies the genius of the Beatitudes: they are situated in a Christ-centered apocalyptic and eschatological understanding of the world; *they present true human flourishing as entailing suffering as Jesus's disciples await God's coming kingdom that Jesus is inaugurating.*

Jesus's macarisms provide a powerful shock by the way in which they describe flourishing with ironic, paradoxical, future-oriented hopes. Implicit in any proclamation about what it means to flourish is an invitation for hearers to reorient their thinking and sensibilities about what it means to thrive and live fully. But what is unexpected and most important about Jesus's

---

53. Charles H. Lohr, "Oral Techniques in the Gospel of Matthew," *CBQ* 23 (1961): 424–34. Jack Lundbom suggests that this pattern shows that Matthew is presenting his work as a new-covenant document (*Jesus' Sermon on the Mount: Mandating a Better Righteousness* [Minneapolis: Fortress, 2015], chap. 2). While I agree with the idea, the argument is unfortunately based on the common mistaken conflation of blessings and macarisms. Lundbom notes rightly that Matthew's "blessings and woes" are different in several significant ways from the Deuteronomic "blessings and curses," but he fails to see that this is because they are not the same thing. Instead he resorts to suggesting that these differences are the difference between the old covenant and the new (42–43).

macaristic invitation is its vision that appears—at least from a human and natural perspective—to be profoundly *non*flourishing in nature. As Servais Pinckaers beautifully reflects:

> We can compare the work of the beatitudes to that of a plow in the fields. Drawn along with determination, it drives the sharp edge of the plowshare into the earth and carves out, as the poets say, a deep wound, a broad furrow. . . . In the same way the word of the beatitudes penetrates us with the power of the Holy Spirit in order to break up our interior soil. It cuts through us with the sharp edge of trials and with the struggles it provokes. It overturns our ideas and projects, reverses the obvious, thwarts our desires, and bewilders us, leaving us poor and naked before God. All this, in order to prepare a place within us for the seed of new life.[54]

As John Calvin observes, most people hold to the erroneous belief that the happy person is the one who is "free from annoyance, attains all his wishes, and leads a joyful and easy life"; the mistaken idea is that true happiness is about our present emotional state. However, in these Beatitudes, Calvin continues, Christ exposes this belief as false, lest Christians think that calamities and reproaches are at variance with the happy life. They are not because of the conviction that "we are happy in the midst of miseries for our patience is *blessed* by the Lord, and will soon be followed by a happy result. . . . The disciples of Christ must learn the philosophy of placing their happiness beyond the world, and above the afflictions of the flesh." Calvin concludes by arguing that the point of the Beatitudes is to show that "those are not unhappy who are oppressed by the reproaches of the wicked, and subject to various calamities."[55]

Today's readers, now two thousand years into Christian history, are so accustomed to thinking positively about the content of the Beatitudes that we often fail to look directly at their darkness. But when we do, we see that the protasis of each macarism is not immediately and apparently a vision of positive human flourishing, despite what *makarios* would initially indicate to any ancient reader. Rather, what Jesus proclaims as being a state of flourishing includes many things that humanity naturally and even vehemently seeks to avoid—poverty of spirit, mourning, humility,[56] hunger and thirst, merciful-

---

54. Pinckaers, *Pursuit of Happiness*, 36–37.

55. John Calvin, *Commentary on a Harmony of the Evangelists: Matthew, Mark, and Luke*, trans. William Pringle (Edinburgh: The Edinburgh Printing Company, 1845), 259–60 (emphasis original).

56. A prime example of the way the Christian tradition has understandably but unhelpfully clouded our perspective on Jesus's teaching here is that Christianity has long embraced the good

ness, and peacemaking (things that are only required toward those who have wronged us), and especially suffering through persecution (which is the climactic and emphatic note of the Beatitudes, as we have noted). The only state of being in the list of protases that does not appear to be completely negative is purity of heart (5:8). It is difficult to say if this one stands apart from the others for this reason or if instead there is yet something unexpected in this macarism. Regardless, the overall and overwhelming sense of the Beatitudes is that Jesus is *authoritatively yet perplexingly commending states of being in the world that are the opposite of flourishing, despite introducing them with the standard* makarios.

And herein lies the key to interpreting these macarisms—paying attention to the relationship between the protasis and the apodosis. Unfortunately, in the history of interpretation of the Beatitudes this aspect has been little discussed.[57] But reflection on this provides crucial insight into how these macarisms function in Jesus's teaching and vision.

I have translated the flexible word *hoti* that links the two halves of each Beatitude with "because." This translation makes sense of the whole of each Beatitude and communicates the paradoxical nature of the content. This is a much clearer gloss than the ambiguous and unhelpful translation of "for" that is often found in English translations. *"Because" shows that the apodosis provides the essential explanation or causal grounds for the radical paradox being claimed in the protasis.* The unexpected claim of flourishing found in each protasis needs an explanation or else it makes no sense. The apodosis of each Beatitude explains why the paradoxical protasis is true and not meaningless.[58]

---

and beauty and desirability of humility and "poverty of spirit." But in the ancient world rarely was such humility and self-deference valued and praised. Humility is a distinctly Christian virtue, especially in contrast with the Greco-Roman tradition, such as in Aristotle. But also more broadly in an honor-shame culture (including ancient Judaism), the lowly person is in a lower place in society—not something to rejoice in or consider a state of flourishing. Hence, herein lies the paradox of Jesus saying that a lowly and humble person is flourishing and happy.

57. One exception is George Kennedy, whose knowledge of Greco-Roman rhetorical style leads him to the conclusion that the Beatitudes' form of *makarios* plus *hoti* is that of an *enthymeme*. An enthymeme is a three-part syllogism (major premise, minor premise, conclusion) in which one of the premises is omitted but assumed. Kennedy suggests that the major premise in each of the Matthean Beatitudes, which appears to be a summation of the minor premise and conclusion, is assumed. See Kennedy, *New Testament Interpretation Through Rhetorical Criticism*, 49–50. Whether Kennedy is correct or not does not affect my suggestion of the logical and conceptual relationship of the protasis and apodosis. See the discussion in Kinney, *Hellenistic Dimensions of the Gospel of Matthew*, 197–98.

58. One interpreter who, unlike most others, considers the relationship between the first and second parts of the Beatitudes is Andrej Kodjak. He rightly observes that the relationship between them is one of "inverse equity, according to which those qualities subject to suppression

The reason Jesus can boldly claim that the poor in spirit are truly flourishing is *because*, despite appearances, these lowly ones are actually possessors and citizens of God's heavenly kingdom. "Poor in spirit" may seem like a positive Christian virtue, but in an ancient Near Eastern and Greco-Roman setting of honor and shame, the poor in spirit are in low places in society, not identified as the possessors of God's kingdom. So too, the humble are flourishing—despite appearances in society and the world—*because* they are the true inheritors of the world. Likewise, those in mourning (evoking from Isaiah the image of those suffering and longing for God's reign to come)[59] are truly flourishing *because* God will be their comforter. Those who forgive and show mercy to their enemies and those who wrong them (5:7, 9) are truly flourishing *because* they will receive mercy and will be given the greatest moniker—the children of God. Flourishing are those whose lives are marked by hunger and thirst for righteousness, that is, for God to set the world to right. This is not apparently a good state to be in—to be dissatisfied because of an awareness of how *not* right the world is, and to be in a place of longing and need for God to return. Yet it is precisely these who are described as flourishing *because* of the great promise that this hungering and thirsting for righteousness will be satisfied. This macarism is richly evocative of the great Isaianic hope of God's restoration and also finds connections with Jesus's work as described in Matthew, such as in the stories of his miraculous wilderness feedings (14:14–21; 15:29–38). Those who are pure in heart are flourishing *because* they will see God. And finally—and most radically and unexpectedly—flourishing are the ones who suffer and are persecuted on account of righteousness. Is there any worse suffering than being attacked and slandered and cut off from community precisely when one is innocent, true, and living according to God's righteousness? No. Yet Jesus claims this is true flourishing *because* these are the inheritors of God's kingdom and recipients of a great reward. Because of this true promise, those suffering in this state can actually rejoice and be glad, have a taste of flourishing now. This is not a "grin and bear it" approach to simply "keep calm and carry on" in the midst of difficulties, but an invitation to rejoice due to the realization that this state is true human flourishing now and in the age to come.[60]

---

in the temporal realm of existence generate the highest possible state of bliss and identify those blessed with the kingdom of heaven and God. This system of inverse equity dominates not only in the Beatitudes, but is consistently reiterated in the remainder of the Sermon on the Mount" (*A Structural Analysis of the Sermon on the Mount* [Berlin: de Gruyter, 1986], 71).

59. Isa. 60:20; 61:2–3.

60. In their own powerful and poetic way the Jewish Scriptures wrestle with flourishing and suffering most poignantly through the story of Job. As David Ford points out, Job 1:1–3 and Job 42:10–17 are pictures of human flourishing that are intentionally paralleled as the bookends to

This understanding is significantly different from how the Beatitudes are typically presented, as if a blessing from God is being offered in the protasis and the consequence in the apodosis. That is, without considering closely the relationship of the protases with the apodoses, most interpreters read the Beatitudes as if God is giving a blessing first and then on the basis of this blessing giving another blessing. In addition to the foundational problem of macarisms not being active blessings, this makes little sense of the relation between the first and second parts of each Beatitude. Is God *blessing* the poor in spirit and then giving them something else as a result, the kingdom of heaven? Thus, God is giving poverty of spirit and then blessing that blessing with another one? This sounds very nice and in one foundational sense is even true; all good things, of course, do come ultimately from God alone. However, this is not what macarisms are, nor how they function. It would require a very convoluted theological paradigm to understand the Beatitudes in this way—something I might humbly suggest Jesus's or Matthew's hearers did not possess.[61]

An even more problematic interpretation sees these Beatitudes as flat-footed conditional statements, with the protasis giving the "if" and the apodosis the "then." In this reading the first part is a command to do something—be humble, mourn, be meek, hunger and thirst (an odd thing to exhort), and so on—with the second part as the divine consequence. If you are poor in spirit, you will get the kingdom of heaven; if you mourn, you will get comfort; if you are merciful, you will get mercy. Again, this is founded on the fundamental confusion about the nature of a macarism versus a blessing. Moreover, as many scholars and teachers (especially Protestant ones) are quick to point out, this mechanistic "do this and you'll get this from God" interpretation does not accord with the overall emphasis on the grace and succor that Jesus is providing in his teaching and actions; that would be idealistic religion, not grace-based Christianity. As was discussed in chapter 2, this "entrance requirements" reading of the Beatitudes does not accord with the rest of Matthew or the New Testament.

The solution for these problematic readings is to understand anew that macarisms are invitations to a way of being in the world that will result in flourishing,

---

Job's story of great suffering. The pivotal moment is Job 42:5 where Job exclaims that before his suffering, in his flourishing he had only heard of God, but that afterward, "now my eyes see you." David Ford, "God's Power and Human Flourishing: A Biblical Inquiry after Charles Taylor's *A Secular Age*," paper presented at the Yale Center for Faith and Culture, http://faith .yale.edu/sites/default/files/david_ford_-_gods_power_and_human_flourishing_0_0.pdf. See also Elenore Stump, *Wandering in Darkness: Narrative and the Problem of Suffering* (Oxford: Oxford University Press, 2010), 177–226.

61. Recall the discussion of this way of reading Ps. 1 in chap. 2 above.

while understanding that Jesus is redefining flourishing as suffering while awaiting the eschaton. This is not the opposite of grace but the means of it. What is
radical and unique about Jesus's macarisms is the unexpected eschatological
twist that human flourishing is now found amid suffering in the time of waiting for God to bring his just reign from heaven to earth (see the Lord's Prayer).

THEOLOGICAL APPROPRIATION OF THE BEATITUDES
BEYOND THE SERMON

The history of the interpretation of macarisms, and especially these Beatitudes, does much to confirm our reading here. As was discussed in chapter 2
above, macarisms are certainly not unique to Jesus but have a strong precedent
in ancient Near Eastern literature, including Second Temple Jewish writings,
of which the New Testament is a part.

In the Second Temple period two important Jewish genres are being wed
together—*apocalyptic* writings and *wisdom* instruction. One of the key ways
these two genres are joined is through macarisms (and the corresponding eschatological woes). As Ulrich Luz points out, beatitudes in Jewish literature
were mostly wisdom paraenesis that instructed by expressing "the connection
between a person's deeds and what happens to the person."[62] In the time of the
Second Temple, when Jews are largely persecuted and producing apocalyptic
writings, these macarisms particularly emphasize the apodosis, giving hope
that by living wisely now a good promised future from God will come. In
this context we see that Jesus's beatitudes are very much the same.[63] They are
invitations to flourishing in light of God's coming eschatological kingdom.

When we examine the early Christian reappropriation of these Beatitudes,
we also see the same focus on an invitation to flourishing, especially the paradoxical emphasis that this flourishing comes to us in the midst of suffering and
persecution. One strong example is found in 1 Pet. 4:14, a letter whose whole
theme and tenor can be summarized as joy and flourishing in the midst of
trial—"If you are slandered for the name of Christ you are flourishing, because
the glorious and divine Spirit rests upon you." The precise historical-literary
relationship between 1 Pet. 4:14 and Matt. 5:10–12 is impossible to determine,[64]

---

62. Luz, *Matthew 1–7*, 187.
63. Ibid., 188. See also Davies and Allison, *Matthew 1–7*, 432.
64. The close repetition of theme and specific verbiage in both Matthew and 1 Peter speaks
loudly to the relationship that exists between these texts. The possible logical relationships are
(1) Matthew is using 1 Peter; (2) 1 Peter is using Matthew; (3) both are using a common source/
tradition (written or oral). I am inclined to think that the epistles are consciously drawing from
these Jesus Traditions, which did exist at least orally and often in some written form before
the writing of the epistles. Determining which of these is historically the case is impossible yet

but there is no doubt that the same message is being communicated—true human flourishing is found in the midst of (and even in a mysterious way because of) persecution and suffering.

Finally, it is helpful to consider broadly the various ways these Beatitudes have been read in Christian history. Many have understood Jesus's opening to the Sermon as a word of grace, often specifically emphasizing that grace comes before the high ethical demands of the rest of the Sermon, succor before command.[65] In contrast to this, others have either embraced or created as a foil the reading of the Beatitudes as entrance requirements. Many others, especially in the earliest days of the church, saw the Beatitudes as some form of ethical exhortation—the royal stairway from repentance to perfection; a mountaintop of virtues to climb in sequence, beginning with poverty of spirit. A variation on these themes is that the Beatitudes provide regulation for the life of the community, particularly the life (macarisms 5–8) that comes from grace (macarisms 1–4).[66]

Each of these has something to commend it, but they fail to see that the overriding sense being communicated and the picture being painted is an *invitation to flourishing*. We create a self-inflicted dilemma that cannot make sense of the entirety of Scripture's witness when we pit grace and virtue against each other. Macarisms, including these Beatitudes, appeal to hearers to find fullness of life by orienting themselves toward a certain way of being in the world (specific images of virtue). All of this, according to Matthew, is by and through the grace that alone comes from Jesus's saving work (1:21; 26:28). Thus, these Beatitudes are *more* than appeals to an individual's virtuous choices and the flourishing that will result, but they are not *less* than this. The Sermon is a manifesto or constitutional document for the life of the individual follower of Christ in the midst of the community of his followers. As Benedict Green concludes:

> The Beatitudes, then, are a summary description of the character of the true disciple; they encapsulate both the kind of person the disciple will be seen to be if he or she faithfully follows the requirements of the Sermon on the Mount, and, conversely, the kind of person the disciple will need to be if he or she is to rise to its demands and to persevere in the right (and narrow) path (7.13–14). They spell out what is involved in obedience to the double commandment of love.[67]

---

ultimately irrelevant to the benefit that comes from seeing the common theme and interpretation found here.

65. For a succinct summary of the history of interpretation, see esp. Luz, *Matthew 1–7*, 188–91.

66. According to Luz, this seems to be the view of Christoph Burchard (1978), Georg Eichholz (1984), and Wolfgang Trilling (1969).

67. Green, *Matthew, Poet*, 288.

Therefore, one misreads the Beatitudes if they are taken as mere statements of God's blessing without recognizing that inherent in a macarism is an appeal to live a certain way that will result in our flourishing.[68]

One of the ways that the failure to perceive this sense and function of the Beatitudes has appeared in the interpretation of the Sermon is the debate that commentators have had regarding who Jesus's *audience* is for the Sermon. As noted above, it is often observed that 5:1–2 pictures the recipients of this first and greatest of Jesus's instructions to be his already-called *disciples*. On the other hand, however, many note that at the end of the Sermon the audience is obviously more than the narrowly defined category of the disciples; the crowds respond with awe and amazement (7:28–29). Thus, commentators have often stumbled over the question of who Jesus's and/or Matthew's intended audience is—believers/followers of Jesus or, much more broadly, anyone who will listen?

This is a relevant question worth raising again because it relates to the big issue that interpreters have wrestled with in the Sermon, especially in the Beatitudes: Is the Sermon giving entrance requirements for the kingdom of heaven or instructions for those who already believe? This common way of approaching the Sermon—understandable as it is, especially for Protestants who are sensitive to the issue of justification by faith versus works—deals with the big idea of grace. If the Sermon is read to be a list of entrance re-quirements, then this seems for many to be the opposite of grace (especially in a Protestant understanding). As a result, because of a desire to correct this seemingly wrong reading of Jesus's statements, emphasis is put on the fact that Jesus is speaking to his *disciples* here, not just to anyone. This, it seems, will clarify that one does not earn God's favor or enter the kingdom through Jesus's instructions given here. For some who read the Sermon this way, this means that Jesus's Beatitudes can be taken seriously as commands because they are given in the context of a blessing or grace. For others the interpreta-tion is the opposite—these are pronouncements of the blessings upon the disciples precisely because they are already disciples.

The problem is that this understanding of what it means to be a disciple or believer is anachronistic and theologically confused, at least from the perspective of Matthew's presentation. As noted above, while Matthew does distinguish between the crowds and disciples in part, there is always a fluidity and dynamic

68. In his otherwise very insightful essay, and with a proper understanding of the meaning of *makarios*, William Dumbrell unfortunately perpetuates an unhelpful dichotomy: the Beatitudes are "not designed to call a new state into being but rather to describe a state which exists and to describe it from the standpoint of recommendation" ("The Logic of the Role of the Law in Matthew 5:1–20," *NovT* 23, no. 1 [1981]: 8). He is correct on the latter but this does not necessitate a rejection of the former.

7

reality at work in anyone's life. Discipleship in the Gospels is portrayed as it really is in real life—the life of being an imperfect human who is following Jesus with limited understanding and many mistakes (see Matt. 14:31; 15:16; 16:23; 17:17; 20:24; and esp. 26:69–75). All humans are always being invited to hear and understand Jesus's words with greater depth and application. Macaristic invitations to flourishing are not only for one set of people, "believers," over against another; they are casting a vision with the understanding that the ones with ears to hear and eyes to see will follow as a result.

The other problem with this typical reading of the Beatitudes is what I have stated above—that it is based on a misunderstanding of what macarisms are and how they function. The Beatitudes do not present a dilemma of grace versus entrance requirements.[69] This is a self-inflicted problem based on not understanding that *Jesus's macarisms are grace-based, wisdom invitations to human flourishing in God's coming kingdom.*[70]

Eugene Peterson's words about how the Bible instructs readers overall apply very insightfully to the Beatitudes as well:

> Scripture does not present us with a moral code and tell us "Live up to this," nor does it set out a system of doctrine and say "Think like this and you will live well." Rather the biblical way is to tell a story and in the telling invite: "Live *into* this—this is what it looks like to be human in the God-made and God-ruled world; this is what is involved in becoming and maturing as a human being."[71]

Matthew 5:13–16: The New Covenant Witness of the People of God

> [13]*You are the salt of the earth. But if this salt ceases to be salty,[72] with what will it be made salty again? This salt is good for nothing except being thrown away, where it will be trampled by people.*

69. See further the discussion in chap. 12.
70. In his levelheaded and practical discussion, David Wenham explores how to preach the Sermon, including pointing out the Sermon's strong note of grace throughout. This is seen in the opening words of the Beatitudes, the emphasis on the forgiveness of sins in the Lord's Prayer, and the promises that God will answer prayer as a Father responds to his children. See David Wenham, "Preaching the Sermon on the Mount," in *Preaching the New Testament*, ed. Ian Paul and David Wenham (Downers Grove, IL: InterVarsity, 2013), 73–86.
71. Eugene Peterson, *Eat This Book: A Conversation in the Art of Spiritual Reading* (Grand Rapids: Eerdmans, 2009), 43–44.
72. This phrase is very difficult to translate because there is a play on words in the Greek that is impossible to bring across in English. The word used here (*mōranthē*) is a form of the word for "foolish" (*mōros*) and the phrase here reads, "If this salt is made foolish" or "shown to be foolish." As an idiom this expression can communicate "cease to be salty" or "become tasteless," hence the translations as such. But we as English readers lose the other evocation of this phrase—that our saltiness can cease to be wise and wisely distributed, thereby losing its

> ¹⁴*You are the light of the world. A city that is built upon a moun-*
> *tain cannot be hidden.* ¹⁵*Neither do people light a lamp and then put*
> *it under a basket. Rather, they put it on a lampstand and then it gives*
> *light to everyone in the house.* ¹⁶*In this way let your light shine in the*
> *presence of everyone such that they see your good works and glorify*
> *your Father who is in heaven.*

This short section is one of the many portions of the Sermon that have
provided memorable and oft-used phrases to the Christian (and non-Christian)
vocabulary—such as "salt of the earth" and "city set on a hill." Several comments are in order.

The first note to make is that these verses are clearly connected to 5:1–12,
more so than to 5:17 and following.[73] As was discussed in the previous chapter on the structure of the Sermon, commentators have often been unsure
or confused about how these verses fit into the flow of the Sermon. This is
because the Beatitudes (5:3–12) form a clear unit of thought, as does 5:17–48
(in the broader structure of 5:17–7:21). As a result, 5:13–16, memorable and
pithy as it is, may appear to stand outside this structure and serve as a floating, free agent.

However, despite this initial appearance, 5:13–16 actually flows logically
from 5:3–12 and serves as a fitting conclusion to this opening portion of
the Sermon. The logical flow comes from the emphatic and climactic theme
with which the Beatitudes end—suffering and persecution for the sake of
righteousness and the subsequent instruction to rejoice in the midst of this
(5:11–12). It is precisely this negative and potentially anxiety-inducing picture
(cf. 10:26–33) that provides the background for and even requires the teachings on salt and light.

An important textual clue that 5:11–12 and 5:13–16 are meant to be taken
together in a logical relationship is the abrupt shift to the second-person plural
pronoun "you" in 5:11–12. This emphatic "you" that represents a shift in the
last macarism continues now in these "you are . . ." salt and light statements.
Indeed, the redundant Greek construction of *hymeis este* not only provides
this connecting link but also highlights 5:13–16 as emphatic in the whole unit
of 5:1–16. Thus we see that 5:11, rather than being a mere comment on the
eighth beatitude, is a perfectly designed ninth beatitude that serves as the

effectiveness. The reference to "foolish" also connects with the Sermon's concluding image of
wise and foolish builders (7:24–27), the latter of which also faces destruction.

73. Yet, at the same time, one could see the reference in 5:16 to "good works" as a sort of title
for 5:17–48. See Luz, *Matthew 1–7*, 203. Also, Dumbrell, "Logic," offers several insights about
the connections within 5:1–20 as a unit, specifically regarding the law and new covenant (see
below). Nonetheless, to recognize connections does not mean that a new section has not begun.

linchpin between the Beatitudes and 5:13–16; it provides the perfect contact point by mimicking the vocabulary of both sections that it connects, the Beatitudes (*makarioi*) and 5:13–16 (*este*).

Jesus's teachings in 5:13–16 are instructions to go forth into the world as heralds of the new covenant that Jesus is effecting. To be a disciple means to be an outward-focused agent of the kingdom, inviting people to honor/glorify God (5:16). Yet the disciples have just been told that this kind of kingdom living will clearly result in suffering. This was the climactic conclusion of the Beatitudes. Thus, the images of being salt and light, complete with warnings and exhortations, are like a pushing of the young birds out of the nest to fly. It is required because the prospect of injury is quite fear inducing. Who wants to suffer? Jesus's disciples need to be clearly exhorted (and even warned) to go forth into the world as his heralds *precisely because* of the certain prospect of persecution.

This reading makes sense of the structure of 5:1–16 and shows how Matthew is unfolding his argument. The biggest question of 5:13–16 remains: What do these metaphors mean? Regarding the symbolic meaning of salt, one will find a wide assortment of opinions because of how ubiquitous a metaphor this was in the ancient world. Most commentators today acknowledge the difficulty of determining which symbolic sense of salt is at play here and then offer some generalized understanding. Opinions range from salt as a preservative, as tastiness, as that which endures, as a purifying agent, or most generally, the disciples' influence on the world.[74] Interpreted in isolation, it is difficult to know which of these is the connotation of "salt" here.

However, this salt metaphor does not stand alone; it is not a random pearl on the Sermon's string that has been roughly thrown next to another in Matthew's redaction. Rather, salt is put into clear parallel conjunction with another, much clearer metaphor, that of light. Verses 13 and 14 are structurally and conceptually parallel. They both begin with rhythmically identical phrases with analogous lines:

> *Hymeis este to halas tēs gēs*
> You are the salt of the earth
> *Hymeis este to phōs tou kosmou*
> You are the light of the world

74. Assorted views can be found in the commentaries. Davies and Allison survey eleven possibilities (*Matthew 1–7*, 472–73). Both Scot McKnight and David Turner opt for the general idea of influence (McKnight, *Sermon on the Mount*, 57–58; Turner, *Matthew*, BECNT [Grand Rapids: Baker Academic, 2008], 154–56). The most comprehensive study can be found in James E. Latham, *The Religious Symbolism of Salt* (Paris: Beauchesne, 1982).

The intimate connection between these two metaphors is seen by the analogous expressions that conclude each of them—"earth/land" and "world." That these are corresponding terms is obvious. The question is whether some distinction can be discerned between these parallel words or whether they are meant to be seen as synonyms. Most commentators see them as an example of synonymous parallelism.[75] One potential implication of this is that Matthew has expanded the land promises to Israel into a worldwide promise to all who believe. Other sections in Matthew confirm this interpretation.[76] Regardless, the parallel structure is clear. Each is then followed by an explication of the impact of this metaphor, specifically, what the opposite of the metaphor would look like—useless salt and a hidden light, both of which are really impossible (5:13b, 14b–15). Matthew 5:16 then serves as the concluding exhortation for the whole paragraph: let your "good deeds" (*kala erga*)—another term for "righteousness"—affect people such that the heavenly Father would be honored. Thus, in every way 5:13–16 is communicating one message.

This cohesiveness enables and even requires the reader to interpret the salt metaphor as part of the overall message, specifically in how it relates to the other metaphor, light. This is good news for the interpreter because while light is a potentially broad metaphor as well, its sense in Matthew's unfolding account is very clear. Light in the Old Testament symbolizes many overlapping ideas, such as revelation, instruction, the law, righteousness, and God's presence. One of the most important places where light appears is in Isaiah.

75. An exception is Scot McKnight, who likewise sees the parallel but distinguishes "earth/land" and "world" in the two metaphors, the first speaking of the disciples' role in relation to Israel and the second to the gentile world (*Sermon on the Mount*, 57). Thus, the two parts of the early Christian mission—to Jew and gentile—are alluded to here. While this dual mission is a reality in Matthew and early Christianity, I think the greater emphasis in Matthew is on the redefinition of the people of God based not on ethnicity but on faith response to Jesus, from among Jews and gentiles. Therefore it is entirely appropriate for Matthew to equate "land" (a concept very important to Judaism) with the broader concept of the whole "world." The synonymizing of the Jewishly important word "land" with the broader concept of "world" (a negative term for ancient Jews) is precisely the point, not their remaining distinction. See also the macarism of 5:5 that promises to all those aligned with Jesus the inheritance of the land/earth.

76. Closest to hand is obviously the Beatitudes, which have already been redefining the true people of God in terms that are based on faith-virtues, not Torah observance or ethnicity. Quarles, reflecting on the Isaianic connections (see below), observes that "the designation of Jesus' disciples as the 'light of the world' identifies His disciples with Zion and marks them as the new Israel" (*Sermon on the Mount*, 85). Similarly, Lundbom notes that Jesus is telling his disciples, who constitute the new Israel, that they are the light of the world (*Jesus' Sermon on the Mount*, 133–34). John the Baptist's words in 3:9–10 are very important thematically for Matthew—"And do not think you can say to yourselves, 'We have Abraham as our father.' I tell you that out of these stones God can raise up children for Abraham. The ax is already at the root of the trees, and every tree that does not produce good fruit will be cut down and thrown into the fire" (NIV).

As Charles Quarles notes, "Throughout the prophecies of Isaiah, the shining light is a metaphor of the Messiah and His people fulfilling the missionary purpose of manifesting the glory of God among the nations."[77] By the time the astute reader gets to this metaphor, Isaiah has already been evoked countless times in Matthew, including throughout the Beatitudes, as was discussed above. Most clearly Matthew has primed the pump for this way of reading by the long Isaianic quote right before the unit of chapters 5–9 begins. In 4:15–16 we are given another fulfillment quotation, which emphasizes that all the nations of the world, the gentiles, have been sitting in darkness but are now, with the coming of Jesus, about to see a great light (*to phōs*), to have the light shine upon them (4:16; from Isa. 9:2). Several other texts in Isaiah use this metaphor as well, such as 42:6 ("a light for the nations") and 49:6. Isaiah 60 is built on the light metaphor and concludes with reference to God's people inheriting the land and being righteous, with the result that people glorify God (60:21). (Recall also the predominance of Isa. 61 in Jesus's ministry and the Beatitudes.) It is difficult to miss that these are the references at work in Matt. 5:13–16. Even as Jesus is the true light that comes to bring salvation to all the world through his ministry in life and death (cf. John 1:9), so too, through identification with the Master, the disciples are now described as light. This corresponds not only with the idea of the disciples' imitation of their master but also is specifically unpacked in Matt. 10, where the disciples are commissioned to do on their own all that Jesus taught and did in Matt. 5–9.

So the sense of the metaphor of light and its application to the disciples is clear, as is the paralleling of the salt and light images. Putting it into the context of Isaiah, a vision emerges that makes an important salvation-historical and theological point: *Both the salt and light metaphors are communicating the same idea, that Jesus's disciples are now the heralds of the new and lasting covenant being effected by Jesus.*[78]

As noted, salt by itself is very open to metaphorical evocations. Light is as well. Is there a place where the two metaphors overlap conceptually? Yes, in the area of covenant. One of the uses of salt in the ancient world was in the solemn event of enacting a lasting covenant. As a sign of loyalty, salt was eaten by itself or with bread to commit to a covenantal agreement (Lev. 2:13; Num. 18:19; 2 Chron. 13:5; cf. Ezra 4:14).[79] James Latham's extensive study

---

77. Quarles, *Sermon on the Mount*, 84.

78. Thanks goes to a PhD student in my seminar on the Sermon on the Mount, Colin Smothers, whose fine paper first suggested this idea to me and which provided several of the sources cited below.

79. These references come from Quarles, *Sermon on the Mount*, 78, though the argument presented here is not his view.

of the ancient usage of salt concludes that the most fundamental idea is that of permanence. When applied in the Old Testament context this refers to the permanent covenant between God and his people. Latham concludes that in Matt. 5:13 "the disciples are a sign of the New Covenant, uniting Christ and those who are called to salvation."[80] Likewise, Don Garlington, following the work of Paul Minear and William Dumbrell, argues that it is this cohesive salt-covenant idea in the Old Testament that informs Matthew: "salt" is a covenant term and is the point of the metaphor in 5:13.[81]

We can now return to the idea of light and its Isaianic background in Matthew. As noted, several passages in Isaiah clearly provide the setting for Matthew's language. Isaiah 42:6 is particularly important for Matt. 5:14. Isaiah's "light for the nations" becomes Matthew's "light of/for the world." Very importantly, note that this phrase in Isaiah is put into direct parallelism with God speaking of a covenant going forth to the nations/gentiles. The full verse reads, "I am the LORD; I have called you in righteousness; I will take you by the hand and keep you; I will give you as a covenant for the people, a light for the nations" (ESV). What follows is the emphasis on God doing a *new* thing, the old passing away and a new era dawning (cf. 42:9–10). In Isa. 42 and beyond, the Spirit-filled servant (42:1) is liberating the nations, establishing justice/righteousness, and is given by God as a covenant for the people and a light for the nations.

Taken together, the salt and light metaphors, with the flavors of Isaiah everywhere, result in a clear and powerful statement about the eschatological new covenant coming through Jesus. This combination of the metaphors of salt and light and Isa. 40–66 together evoke the biblical story line and hope for the new-covenant time when God will return and bring his comfort and beauty throughout the world. Jesus is the great prophet and suffering servant spoken of in Isaiah, bringing light and grace to all the world. By extension, then, Jesus's disciples are likewise the heralds of this new-covenant message, the sons of the prophet, the friends of the bridegroom. The promise of coming persecution in 5:11–12 and the specific connection of Jesus's disciples with the persecuted prophets before them put all of this discussion in the context of the Old Testament prophets, who were heralds and reinforcers of the covenant.[82]

80. Latham, *Religious Symbolism of Salt*, 241.
81. Don B. Garlington, "'The Salt of the Earth' in Covenantal Perspective," *JETS* 54 (2011): 715–48; Paul S. Minear, "The Salt of the Earth," *Int* 51 (1997): 31–41; Dumbrell, "Logic," 1–21.
82. Dumbrell puts it well: "prophetic sufferings indicate a prophetic-type ministry, and a prophetic-type ministry understood in Old Testament terms is a ministry which operates within the framework of covenant" ("Logic," 10).

Additionally, considering the broader context reveals that these covenant-evoking metaphors are not alone. The Sermon began with Jesus ascending a revelatory mount, suggestive of Sinai, where Moses received and delivered the covenant. Furthermore, the following verses (5:17–20), which introduce the central section of the Sermon, raise the issue of the law, which becomes the focus of 5:21–48. Mention of the law highlights the covenantal question being discussed in 5:13–16. As Dumbrell insightfully points out, the New Testament's many references to a "new covenant," "new commandment," and "law of Christ" make it difficult to separate law from covenant in early Christianity. Moreover, "in the argument of the Sermon on the Mount where law is re-emphasized and radicalized, the covenant relationship may plausibly be understood as implied."[83] Therefore, this whole section on salt and light is communicating the message that Jesus's disciples are the prophets and adjudicators of the new covenant, an idea that will be expressed in several other ways throughout Matthew, including in the second and fourth discourses, which highlight the disciples' authoritative role in the world.[84] Like their Old Testament counterparts, the disciples are "covenant witnesses and guarantors to their age."[85] This is the meaning of being salt and light.

This section ends with the powerful exhortation of 5:16: *In this way let your light shine in the presence of everyone such that they see your good works and glorify your Father who is in heaven.* Even as the conclusion to the conclusion of the Sermon will do (7:24–27), the conclusion of the introduction highlights the need for a real, whole-person, active behavioral response to Jesus's teaching. This fits well within the encyclopedic context of first-century Judaism wherein rabbis commonly stated that good deeds sanctify the Holy Name while bad deeds dishonor it.[86]

This "salt and light" heralding of the new covenant by disciples is described as good works that glorify the heavenly Father. We have already noted in chapter 4 the importance of the theme of the Fatherhood of God in Matthew, and this is its first occurrence in the Sermon. Matthew 5:16 is reminiscent of the exhortation to be like the heavenly Father in terms of *teleios*-ity (5:48). The main point to be made here is that the whole of 5:3–15 can be summed up with 5:16 as an exhortation to a way of being in the world that is visible

---

83. Ibid., 5n14.

84. The second major discourse (Matt. 10) emphasizes that how people receive the disciples and their message determines whether they are part of God's kingdom or not, while the fourth major discourse (Matt. 18) highlights that the disciples have the authority to "bind and loosen," that is, to determine who is in and out of the assembly of God's people.

85. Dumbrell, "Logic," 13.

86. J. D. M. Derrett highlights this aspect of rabbinic teaching in his *Law in the New Testament* (London: Darton, Longman & Todd, 1970), 203.

as deeds and dispositions (even if this kind of "good work" is disliked and persecuted) that honor the disciples' heavenly Father, thereby proving their shared identity, precisely what Jesus will promise and offer repeatedly during the rest of his earthly ministry.

Matthew 5:1–16: Wholeness and Human Flourishing

These opening verses paint a richly evocative background and set the tone for the rest of the Sermon about to come forth from Jesus's mouth. The evocations are steeped in the ancient Israelite tradition of mountains as places of solemn revelation. At the very least, then, Jesus is being depicted as a prophet of God sent to announce a message from God. And as Matthew continues his story this prophetic nature of Jesus will continue to be a theme. But starting here in the Sermon we already find hints that Jesus is *more* than a prophet, even more than the prophet Moses. Like many of the prophets before him (especially Isaiah), Jesus is pronouncing that a new era is coming and is in fact here (4:17). But unlike these prophets, Jesus is doing more than faithfully delivering a message he received from God. He will be depicted as the arbiter of this message, not just its messenger (see 5:17–48). He is not wandering the courts of the temple pronouncing judgment nor setting up a baptistery in the wilderness around the Jordan; he is seated as a teacher on a mountain while people stream to him. Here at the beginning of the Sermon we see that he is intentionally gathering crowds, calling people to leave what they are doing to follow him (4:17–25). He will later clarify that he has in fact created a new community (see esp. 18:1–20). Although it is not yet explicit in these first two verses, the Sermon will provide the vision for this new *politeia* or community of the people of God in Christ.[87] Every community is seeking to flourish, and this founding document will offer a vision for just that.

---

87. We will return to this important idea of the Sermon as the foundation document for the community of Jesus followers. For now we can note that this way of reading the Sermon as the charter for a *politeia* was common in the early history of the interpretation of the Sermon, such as in Chrysostom. See Margaret Mitchell, "John Chrysostom," in Greenman, Larsen, and Spencer, *Sermon on the Mount through the Centuries*, 19–42.

7

Matthew 5:17–48

Overview

We have now entered the central part of the Sermon that spans from 5:17 to 7:12, marked conveniently by the *inclusio* reference to "the Law and the Prophets" in the first and last verses of this lengthy unit.[1] I have titled this main body of the Sermon, "The Greater Righteousness for God's People." This central section has three major subsections (5:17–48; 6:1–21; 6:19–7:12), each of which can be helpfully broken up into yet smaller units. This first portion of the central section of the Sermon contains a general introduction (5:17–20), followed by six examples of the point being made in the introduction (5:21–47), and concluding with a summarizing statement (5:48). All of this concerns the "greater righteousness" theme that is set forth in 5:17–20. As is often the case in Matthew, the introductory verses of 5:17–20 serve double duty: they provide the introduction to both 5:21–48 and the broader section of which they are a part, 5:17–7:12.

I have argued earlier that the whole of the Sermon relates to the call to repentance in 4:17.[2] The Sermon in many ways is an unpacking of what this call

---

1. The slight variation of "the Law *or* the Prophets" in 5:17 and "the Law *and* the Prophets" in 7:12 is insignificant, not only because of the overlap in meaning of the particles used but also because the "or" of 5:17 (rather than "and") is necessitated by the negative clause "do not think." Typical of Matthew's style, he uses a variety of overlapping expressions to communicate the same thing. See also "the Prophets and the Law" in 11:13 and "the whole Law and the Prophets" in 22:40.

2. See chap. 5 on the structure and setting of the Sermon.

170   Commentary

to repentance looks like. This is true for the Sermon as a whole, but especially in 5:17–48 with its call to holiness as wholeness, as we will see. Repentance is about the whole person turning back to God and devotedness to him.³ We will see this as the key idea throughout 5:17–48.

Matthew 5:17–48: Greater Righteousness in Relation to God's Laws

Matthew 5:17–20: The Ethos of the Ethics of the Kingdom of Heaven—Greater Righteousness

¹⁷Do not think that I have come to abolish the Law or the Prophets. I have not come to abolish but to fulfill. ¹⁸Truly I say to you that until heaven and earth pass away not an iota or one pen stroke of the Law will pass away, until all is accomplished. ¹⁹Whoever, therefore, lessens one of the least of the commandments and teaches others in this way, that person will be called least in the kingdom of heaven. But whoever does these commandments and teaches others will be called great in the kingdom of heaven.

²⁰For I tell you that if your righteousness does not surpass that of the scribes and Pharisees then you will never enter into the kingdom of heaven.

As has been noted in the discussion of structure, 5:17–20 is the *propositio* or main thesis statement of the Sermon. Not only is this passage crucial to the whole of the Sermon, Jesus's statements condensed into this compact paragraph also sit at the core of one of the greatest and most contentious questions of broader Christian theology—What is the relationship of Christianity to Israel/Judaism, or the new covenant to the old covenant? This is still hotly debated today, and many versions of contemporary Christianity are different precisely because of how they answer this question.⁴ But the debate was even more heated (and deadly) at the birth of Christianity. It was Jesus's apparently lax interpretation of certain Mosaic laws, as well as his claims to be the arbiter of a greater law, that irked the religious leaders to the point of

---

3. Deut. 30:2; 1 Sam. 7:3; 2 Kings 17:13; 2 Chron. 7:14; Isa. 31:6; Jer. 25:5; Hosea 6:1–3; Joel 2:12–13; Mal. 3:7.

4. On one end of the spectrum is a denomination such as the Seventh Day Adventists, who see the specifics of the Mosaic law as an essential part of Christian experience, hence their strict dietary and worship rituals. The dispute between the Reformed tradition and the much younger dispensationalist tradition rests largely on this issue as well, the latter rejecting any replacement of Israel by the church. Within the Reformation, many of the differences between the Calvinist/Reformed tradition and that of the Lutherans also rests on a different rendering of the relationship between the law and the new covenant.

instigating his execution.[5] This conflict continues in just the same way with the first generation of Christian disciples, who likewise were persecuted and even killed for their claims that Jesus overturned and replaced the Mosaic covenant/law with something else (Acts 4:1–3; 5:17–42; 6:8–8:1, etc.).[6]

Matthew 5:17–20 does not provide a complete answer to this vexed and multilayered question (other canonical texts must be examined as well), but this is one of the most important texts in this discussion, and it holds pride of place situated in the first teaching block in the first book of the New Testament. The compactness of 5:17–20 is at once its power and its difficulty. By virtue of its pithy, contrastive statements we get a large-scale snapshot of the issue. But its brevity and super-concentrated collection of weighty terms and ideas mean that every sentence is a spark that sets off a fire in a different direction. Like good poetry, this short passage is thick with meaning and in need of deep reflection. We can address the meaning of this paragraph overall by concentrating on the key issues that various phrases and terms raise.

The first issue is what "the Law or the Prophets" means. In general this is a phrase used in the first century to refer to all of God's written revelation, with "Law" referring to the Pentateuch or Books of Moses and "Prophets" meaning the rest of the Jewish Scriptures, everything understood as having been spoken and written by prophets, including the Psalms.[7] This is slightly different from the later, more technical canonical distinction we make about the genre and portion of the Hebrew Bible concerning the

5. Erasmus's sixteenth-century paraphrase of Matthew renders 5:20 in this interesting way: To enable you to understand how great a difference there is between Jew and Christian, between a disciple of Moses and one of mine, I say to you unequivocally: if you fulfill whatever the Law prescribes, whatever the Pharisees fulfill (men who are now thought to possess a sort of absolute justice and think so themselves), but you add nothing further of a more perfect kind, so insignificant will you be in this religious profession that in the kingdom of heaven not even the right of admission is to be given." (*Collected Works of Erasmus: Paraphrase on the Gospel of Matthew*, ed. Robert D. Sider, trans. Dean Simpson [Toronto: University of Toronto Press, 2008], 97)
6. Claims for Jesus's divinity and/or messianic fulfillment certainly were often the cause of persecution of early Christians by the Jewish leadership, but it seems that the perceived disregard for and even attacks on the Mosaic law caused the most vehement emotional and violent reactions.
7. There is debate concerning when the divisions of the Jewish Scriptures were codified and categorized, but certainly it was occurring over time and by the first century had some clear distinctions. H. Benedict Green points out that "Matthew, like some other New Testament writers, seems to have reckoned the Psalter among the prophetic books; and since he apparently knows nothing of any further subdivision of the scriptures beyond Torah and prophets, he may well have seen the prophetic strain as continuing in at least some of the books that the rabbis assigned to the Writings" (*Matthew, Poet of the Beatitudes* [Edinburgh: T&T Clark, 2001], 265).

Major and Minor Prophets (Isaiah through Malachi in our English canonical order), which we now often refer to as "the Prophets." The phrase
"Law and the Prophets," used in a general and comprehensive way to refer
to all of the Jewish Scriptures, was common and convenient and shows the
central role that the books of Moses and therefore the Mosaic covenant
played/plays in Jewish understanding. "The Law" is supreme shorthand for
the whole foundation story of Israel, explaining both the creation of the
world and the creation of Israel as God's beloved covenant people. There
is no more important reality for a Jewish person, today or two thousand
years ago, than the stories and commands of the Pentateuch. The rest of
the Jewish Scriptures (whether called "the Prophets and the Writings" or
more generally, "the Prophets") looks back to and reappropriates the Law
into subsequent settings.

But in Matt. 5:17–20 "the Law or the Prophets" seems to be providing
more than a reference to the whole canon. Instead, by adding reference to the
"Prophets" Jesus indicates that he is talking about the Law interpreted "not
only as it was given in its essence but as it was prophetically interpreted."[8]
That is, it is Torah understood within the context of the whole canon, with
the prophets as interpreters of the Law, calling people back to wholehearted
and eschatologically oriented faithfulness to the covenant.[9] As Green notes,
Matthew is invoking the prophets to provide a new interpretation of Torah,
one that can be observed outside of the Sermon as well, where Hosea 6:6,
for example, is used to identify the weightier matters of the Law in Matt.
9:13 and 12:7.[10] Additionally, as Kari Syreeni points out, Matthew's favorite
expression of "the law and/or the prophets" has become for him a *terminus
technicus* for "the fulfilled law."[11] This "fulfilled law" is in effect Jesus's own
teachings that will follow; with authority (7:28–29) Jesus is explicating what
this new-covenant, "fulfilled law" now means. The addition of "Prophets"
evokes this forward-looking, eschatological rereading of the Law, the promise

8. W. J. Dumbrell, "The Logic of the Role of the Law in Matthew 5:1–20," *NovT* 23, no. 1
(1981): 17. For a similar argument, see also J. P. Meier, *A Marginal Jew: Rethinking the Historical Jesus*, vol. 4, *Law and Love* (New Haven: Yale University Press, 2009), 73, 165.

9. Alexander Sand argues similarly that the addition of the reference to "the Prophets"
shows that Matthew is concerned not only with the legal and casuistic interpretation of the
Law like many of his contemporaries but also with the prophetic understanding of the Law, as
well as the Law *and* the prophetic message together as the manifestation of God's will for his
people. See Sand, *Das Gesetz und die Propheten* (Regensburg: Pustet, 1974), as summarized by
Kari Syreeni, *The Making of the Sermon on the Mount: A Procedural Analysis of Matthew's
Redactoral Activity* (Helsinki: Suomalainen Tiedeakatemia, 1987), 187, though Syreeni does
not fully agree with Sand.

10. See Green, *Matthew, Poet*, 289.

11. Syreeni, *Making of the Sermon*, 188.

of it being renewed and written on the heart (Jer. 31:31–34). All of this fits precisely with Jesus's own eschatological and new-covenantal emphasis.[12]

Moving further into the issue of what "the Law" means, we encounter a significant translation and interpretation problem. In English "the Law" evokes images of lawyers, judges, and police officers making decisions about what is right and wrong and enforcing this (usually to our detriment). When we hear "law" we think of legal cases or rules that must be obeyed. We don't think about "covenant," even though this is certainly what the term would have conveyed to any first-century Jew. A covenant includes restrictions and rules, certainly, but the latter are understood as part of the former, not a separate and impersonal government.

"Law" is an English translation of the Greek *nomos*, which itself is the Septuagint translation for the Hebrew *tôrâ*. At each stage of this transmission and translation process, a slippage of gears inevitably occurs. Or to change the metaphor, as the vessel of this idea sails across times, cultures, and languages, it both gathers some unwanted barnacles and springs a few leaks. In short, the issue is that *tôrâ* means all of the Pentateuch—the story of Israel and the instructions that accompany God's covenant with his people. *Tôrâ*, even in its occasional narrowest sense of "commandments," comes to us in the context of a bilateral covenant made between the rescuing, saving God and his chosen people. This is a far cry from the images of dusty old law books, large marble-filled rooms, and powerful judges standing coldly and objectively over us as we sit fearful in a box awaiting sentencing. *Tôrâ* is covenantal and relational. Thus, when Jesus talks about "the Law and the Prophets," he is talking about the whole gracious story and Mosaic covenant with Israel. This has an ethical/commandment dimension, certainly, but the issue of "the Law and the Prophets" is much bigger than the question of which commandments or rules one must obey; we are dealing here with the question of the relationship of Jesus's person and work to the whole covenant God made with Israel through the mediation of Moses. This ups the ante on the discussion and also reorients it to a covenantal discussion instead of a *merely* ethical one.

This insight gives us a firmer ground for understanding the language of "abolish" versus "fulfill" that leads off the discussion in Matt. 5:17. From the

12. Note that my emphasis here is somewhat different from that of Calvin, who emphasized that Jesus was criticizing the Pharisees' interpretation of the Law, not the OT commands themselves, thus preserving a place for the old-covenant teachings in the church. I agree that Jesus is in continuity with the intent of the OT commandments, but I think that Matthew is putting great emphasis on the transformation that happens through the coming of the new covenant, the fulfillment of God's plan, which results in a more radical break with the Mosaic covenant. Jesus's main critique is of the Pharisees' lack of wholeness in applying the Law to themselves, not of their wrong interpretation of it.

historical perspective of Jesus's ministry and/or Matthew's situation, these verses likely serve as an important clarification and even *apologia* for the Christian understanding of Judaism and the Mosaic covenant. Matthew's Jesus is striking at the knees of any misunderstanding of Christianity as anti-Semitic, antinomian, or unrefined and flat-footed. Jesus has not come haphazardly, irreverently, or thoughtlessly to attempt to abolish, overthrow, disregard, and snidely ignore the Mosaic covenant and God's work among his chosen people in the past. He is not a sophomoric or lunatic revolutionary proclaiming freedom from all moral and ethical constraints. This would be a gross misrepresentation of Christianity—one that apparently Paul had to fight against as well ("shall we sin so that grace may abound . . ."; Rom. 6:1; cf. James 2:14–26). This kind of view would have been easy to promulgate by both well-meaning, immature Christians as well as the "Judaizer" opponents of the earliest Christian leaders such as Paul (cf. Gal. 2). But here in Matthew we have a clear opening statement that naïve rejection of God's former saving work and covenant was *not* Jesus's view.[13] As William Dumbrell points out, there was no question for any Jew (or Christian) of whether Torah, as God's revelation, would continue in the eschatological age. The question, rather, is *how* it will function.[14] What follows in 5:21–48 (and beyond) is Matthew's answer to that question.

Operative is the word "fulfillment." And herein lies a great difficulty in interpretation that is not easily solved. The streams flowing into this discussion are many and the rivers flowing out from it are rushing and widespread. Dale Allison offers nine different ways to understand the word "fulfillment" and what it might mean here. He rightly opts for a view that understands Jesus's "fulfillment" to be eschatological and a transcending of the Mosaic law, not simply explaining it or enabling others to do it.[15] Dumbrell, following Rudolf Schnackenburg, helpfully describes this word as meaning "bringing to fulfillment a prior scriptural pronouncement or body of teaching by giving to it full validity. . . . The law finds its prophetic centre in Jesus but not necessarily its end."[16]

The single most important factor in understanding this saying in 5:17 is also the one often least considered—the fact that Matthew has already used

---

13. Dale Allison calls this a *prokatalepsis*, a text that anticipates objections and wards off misunderstanding. See W. D. Davies and Dale C. Allison Jr., *A Critical and Exegetical Commentary on the Gospel according to Saint Matthew*, vol. 1, *Introduction and Commentary on Matthew 1–7*, ICC (Edinburgh: T&T Clark, 2004), 481.

14. Dumbrell, "Logic," 19.

15. Davies and Allison, *Matthew 1–7*, 485–86.

16. Dumbrell, "Logic," 19. See also Rudolf Schnackenburg, *The Moral Teaching of the New Testament*, trans. J. Holland-Smith and W. J. O'Hara (London: Seabury, 1964), 56–59.

"fulfill" as the main idea of the story he has told in the preceding four chapters. The opening portion of this Gospel account gives us a series of stories about Jesus's conception and childhood, each of which contains a repeated, formulaic saying that this story "fulfills" what the prophets spoke of beforehand (1:22–23; 2:5–6, 15, 17–18, 23). It is easy to see from these examples that this biblical idea of fulfillment does not mean the completion of a previous prediction, even though this is what the English word often means. Rather, the kind of fulfillment in view here is that of figuration or typological interconnectivity. To say that these events of Jesus's early life "fulfill" previous words and events from Israel's past means that these events figurally connect to each other; they model or imitate each other, with an added edge of consummation and completion. Fulfillment is a powerful biblical idea that does not depend on prediction per se, while it still leans forward to a time when God will bring to full consummation all his good redemptive plans. Prediction is really a subset of the bigger idea of fulfillment.

These five "fulfillment quotation" stories in Matt. 1–2 are followed by two more important references to fulfillment in chapters 3–4 (bringing the total to seven). In Jesus's first recorded words in the New Testament he tells John the Baptist that it is indeed appropriate for him to receive John's baptism because this will "fulfill all righteousness" (3:15). Chapter 4 and the extended introduction to Matthew ends with the seventh reference to fulfillment, which introduces a long quote from Isaiah (4:14–16). In light of this and a broader reading of Matthew as a whole, the respected Matthean scholar R. T. France argued persuasively that "fulfillment" is actually the closest thing we can get to describing the overall theology and theme of Matthew's whole Gospel.[17]

This sevenfold fulfillment theme, then, provides the crucial background to Jesus's words in 5:17. When Jesus says that he did not come to abolish but to *fulfill* the Law and the Prophets, he means this in the same way that the preceding chapters have used the concept—in great continuity with God's preceding, saving, covenant work, Jesus is bringing to completion all that God began to do in ancient times. The contrast with "abolish" highlights the sense of continuity; the subsequent phrase "until all is accomplished" (5:18) emphasizes the sense of completion and consummation.

This is why in 5:18–19 Jesus stresses the abiding witness and importance of God's Mosaic revelation. He is not offering a plan B or a self-contained new revelation, nor a simple explanation of the true intent of the Law that was easily recognizable. But rather Jesus brings and gives the true consummated

17. R. T. France, *Matthew: Evangelist and Teacher* (Eugene, OR: Wipf & Stock, 1989), 166–205.

or fulfilled understanding of the Law and the Prophets. This emphasizes the continuity of Jesus's work with what came before while also leaving the door open for the understanding that things are changing through his own advent.

Allison points out a couple of important implications of this understanding. First, we must keep in mind that the entirety of the Gospel is about who Jesus is before it is about how to interpret properly the Law and the Prophets. Jesus is the center of attention in Matthew; "the thing signified (Jesus) is naturally more important than the sign (the law and the prophets) pointing to it."[18] Matthew 5:17–20 is a christological statement above anything else. Second, while Jesus is the promised eschatological prophet (17:5; cf. Deut. 18:15–20) and therefore speaks with God's authority, the emphasis on the fulfillment of the Law means that it cannot be merely set aside as irrelevant ("abolished"). "Fulfillment can only confirm the Torah's truth, not cast doubt upon it. And while Jesus' new demands may surpass the demands of the OT, the two are not contradictory."[19] This is an important point and makes sense of 5:19, which maintains the abiding witness of *tôrâ*, even if it has undergone a necessary eschatological transformation.

This speaks to the continuity in God's revelation and salvific work. The sense of "fulfillment" as discontinuity will be continually unpacked in the teachings and narrative to follow but is noted somewhat cryptically here with reference to heaven and earth passing away and all being accomplished (5:18). At first glance, 5:18 might be read as saying that the teachings of the Law and the Prophets will *never* pass away, and many have interpreted it this way. "Heaven and earth" are taken here as a reference to eternal reality. But this reading misses the meaning of "fulfillment" just discussed and also fails to understand the apocalyptic background evoked by this reference. Heaven and earth passing away is an image that refers to the age to come and the cataclysmic events that will occur when God's reign returns to earth. This is why Jesus is speaking in the same context about entering the kingdom of heaven (5:19–20), a forward-looking idea. Moreover, "until heaven and earth pass away" and "until all is accomplished" are put into a strongly parallel structure (easier to see in Greek than in English), indicating that these are mutually interpreting phrases: when all is accomplished heaven and earth will pass away, and vice versa. Further confirmation of this is found in the reuse of the language of "heaven and earth passing away" in the final discourse (24:29–35). In 24:29–35 Jesus speaks of his own death and resurrection as a time of cataclysmic events involving heaven and earth (cf. the darkness and

18. Davies and Allison, *Matthew 1–7*, 487.
19. Ibid.

events in heaven and on earth at Jesus's death in 27:45–53), which will also describe the time of the eschaton or new age. According to Matthew's narrative plot it is the suffering, death, and resurrection of Jesus that accomplishes God's saving work through Jesus. It is finished. Notably, in the closely parallel wording in 5:17–20 and 24:34–35, it is very significant that the teachings of the Law and the Prophets have now been replaced by "my words" (Jesus's) that will not pass away.

In short, the best explanation of the *when* of all these things being accomplished is first at Jesus's death and resurrection and then again finally at his second coming. Therefore, the Mosaic covenant per se has come to its perfect, completed end/goal through Jesus's life, death, and resurrection. This is the same argument that Paul makes in Galatians. The promise to Abraham, which is older, has been fulfilled now in Christ, thus making and showing the Mosaic covenant to be what it always was, a temporary tutor (Gal. 3:10–29). Now the "law of Moses" has become the "law of Christ" (Gal. 6:2).

This eschatological, salvation-historical understanding of Jesus's saying about heaven and earth passing away does much to help explain the six sample exegeses that follow (5:21–48). We do not need to debate or worry about whether Jesus is addressing the actual Mosaic covenantal demands or only later scribal reinterpretations of them, as is often the discussion. Whether it is one or the other—or more likely some of both—is irrelevant because Jesus is inaugurating a new era, the final time, a new covenant in which God's Torah revelation (and any traditions built upon it) is superseded, not in terms of rejection but fulfillment in a full mode of interiorization of the law, the law written on the heart, as the prophets foresaw (Jer. 31:31–34; Ezek. 11:19; 36:26).[20] What matters now are *his* words, his covenantal teaching (cf. again the switch from "the Law and the Prophets" to "my words" in Matt. 24:35).

The final declaration (5:20) of this super-condensed paragraph both concludes the argument being made and provides the thesis statement for the rest of the central section of the Sermon, through 7:12. The key word here is "righteousness," and as with the interpretation of "fulfillment," there is an essential Matthean context preceding the Sermon that makes sense of what is being said.

As has been discussed in chapter 4, righteousness is a key idea for the whole Sermon and can be defined in Matthew as *whole-person behavior that accords with God's nature, will, and coming kingdom*. There are two places in the preceding narrative where this notion occurs and that are especially important for Jesus's saying in 5:20. The first is the description given about

---

20. Dumbrell, "Logic," 20, makes a similar point.

his adopted father Joseph in 1:19. Joseph is described as *dikaios*, righteous, in how he handles the news that his betrothed wife is pregnant. Even before the angel appears to him with instructions, Joseph the Righteous decides not to condemn Mary but rather to break off the relationship quietly so that she does not come into shame and reproach. This is a very significant point in the very first story in the Gospel. Righteousness is portrayed not as justice but as mercy. Joseph is being commended for his forgiveness and grace—whole-person behavior that accords with God's nature, will, and coming kingdom.

The other important "righteousness" passage for understanding 5:20 is the same one that proved significant for "fulfillment," 3:15. Jesus receives John's baptism because it was fitting "to fulfill all righteousness." This is a supercharged and power-packed expression worthy of more exploration than I can provide here. The main point is that Jesus's obedient reception of the baptism of the prophet John the Baptist is an action or behavior that is in accord with God's nature, will, and coming eschatological kingdom. This is just what is being argued in 5:20. There is a kind of whole-person behavior or way of being in the world that can be called "righteous." One must "do and teach" Jesus's commands to be part of God's kingdom (5:19). This taps into the broader theme of doing the will of God throughout the Sermon and Matthew (7:21; 12:50; 21:28–32; 26:39, 42; cf. 6:10; James 1:22; 2:22). Jesus models this and subsequently calls his disciples to do the same. The rest of the Sermon, the six exegeses of applying the Law in Matt. 5:21–47, the three examples of piety in 6:1–21, and the six applications to daily life in 6:19–7:12 all unpack what this whole-person righteousness can and should look like. The concluding, summarizing statement of 5:48 likewise points to the necessity of righteousness that is defined as wholeness (see below).

At the same time there is an added personal punch and eschatological urgency to Jesus's declaration here. This true and greater kind of righteousness is not just an option for the super-spiritual or a chosen few; it is a matter of entering God's coming kingdom or not (5:20). This is what the otherwise confusing language of 5:19 communicates. The reference here to being "least in the kingdom of heaven" is a play on the loosening or disobeying of the "least" of the commandments. Being "least in the kingdom of heaven" is not a reference to ranking in the kingdom or getting in by the skin of one's teeth but rather is a poetically parallel way of saying that one does *not* get in, as 5:20 makes clearer.[21]

---

21. It is possible that another parallel is implied by the structure of Matt. 5:19. The positive "does and teaches" of the second half of this verse does not specify what should be done and taught, even though English translations typically add "them," making it seem that the reference is to "the least of these commandments." This may indeed be correct, but the parallelism in the first half of this verse (i.e., he who loosens the least will be the least) makes me wonder if

Jesus gives a shocking reference point for what this necessary righteousness looks like: it must be greater than that of the scribes and Pharisees. On the one hand this is shockingly bad news, because in Jesus's day the scribes and the Pharisees *were* the righteous untouchables who were obviously far superior in righteousness to the mere masses. They were, as one children's Bible rightly pens them, the "extra-super-holy people."[22] To have a righteousness that surpasses these holy and pure ones is nearly impossible, especially for the average Jo(seph) of Jesus's audience. This point will prove to be very important for how this true righteousness is to be understood and practiced. Here is a hint: as with the Beatitudes, the priority of internal disposition over external purity is the vital issue. So even though the righteousness of the scribes and Pharisees was by all accounts very high, Jesus declares as inferior precisely these same people. Their righteousness is not sufficient to enter the coming kingdom of heaven.

As noted, from a historical perspective it is not difficult to understand the role that these verses played in earliest Christianity—they serve to explain the nuanced position that true Christianity holds regarding the relationship between the old and new covenants, mitigating any misinterpretation of what Christians were teaching relative to Judaism and the Law. This section anticipates and answers the objection that Jesus and his followers are radical antinomians or are breaking from the ancient traditions. Quite to the contrary, Matthew is at pains throughout his Gospel to show that Jesus *fulfills* all that God promised, particularly showing how Jesus is the ultimate son of both Abraham and David (1:1).

In their literary and theological context in the Sermon these verses introduce the central section of the Sermon, in which multiple examples are given to explain what true, *makarios* righteousness looks like in a real-life, boots-on-the-ground way.

Matthew 5:21–48: Greater Righteousness in Relation to the Law in Real Life[23]

The introduction concluded, what follows is a practical working out of what Jesus has just said. As a wisdom *teacher*, Jesus does not just make general

---

the object of the "doing" and "teaching" in the latter half of the verse is instead the "great" or "weightier" teachings (cf. 23:23)—he who does *the greatest* "will be called great." This would then refer to those who obey Jesus's interpretation of the Law and obey its weightier or greater matters, the matter of the heart.

22. Sally Lloyd-Jones, *The Jesus Storybook Bible: Every Story Whispers His Name* (Grand Rapids: ZonderKids, 2007), 211, 213.

23. As has been argued in chap. 5, the threefold structure of 5:17–48 is introduction/kəlāl (5:17–20), six exegeses (5:21–47), and conclusion (5:48). In the commentary below, 5:48 will be addressed separately, though it is included here in the larger unit of 5:21–48.

proverbial statements; he offers real-life examples of what his wisdom teaching looks like in practice. Wisdom is "caught more than taught," meaning here that it is truly only understood through practice and seeing models and examples. As the first-century Roman philosopher Seneca put it, "The way is long if one follows precepts, but short and helpful, if one follows patterns."[24] Jesus gives illustrations of the countless ways that this way of being in the world can and should be worked out in the hearers' lives.

This means that these illustrations are not the only possible applications, nor are they to be taken as if they *are* the teaching per se, resulting in an overly literal reading. The kingdom-oriented wisdom Jesus has just taught is that to enter into God's coming kingdom one must have a deep and high righteousness—higher even than the manifest righteousness/piety of the scribes and Pharisees. With bated breath, the open-eared and openhearted learner now listens to hear what this utterly shocking teaching really means. This is what Jesus then provides in six meaningful examples.

As was discussed in chapter 5 on the structure of the Sermon, like every section of this discourse there is much intentionality and significance in the way that the subunits are structured. So too in 5:21–47. These six examples are broken into two sets of three (5:21–32 and 5:33–48). The key is recognizing the repetition and variation in the opening words in each of the six examples (5:21, 27, 31, 33, 38, 43). Each time Jesus provides auditory anchors and mental memory hooks by repeating "You have heard that it was said."[25] This is followed by an example from Israel's Scriptures and practice, on which Jesus comments and applies his teaching from 5:17–20.

Traditionally these illustrative examples have been called the "antitheses," emphasizing a discontinuity between what the Jewish Scriptures taught and Jesus's words. On a first reading this is an understandable interpretation. "You have heard it said . . ." followed by Jesus saying, "but I say to you . . ." certainly sounds like an antithetical pair—"this is true, not this." In this reading, then, Jesus is understood as providing a new, different teaching that is opposed to what the Jews believed and understood; it is antithetical.[26]

---

24. Seneca, *Ad Lucilium* 6.5. Translation comes from Richard M. Gummere LCL 75 (Cambridge, MA: Harvard University Press, 1961), 26–27.

25. There is a slight variation in this language that helps indicate Matthew's structuring of the sayings. In the third exegesis, the shortened form "it was said" is used. This leads to the fourth example, where the longer "You have heard that it was said to the people of old" (5:33), combined with a typical Matthean transition marker, the word *palin* (again). This is the structural marker Matthew provides to show that the six exegeses are broken into two triads (5:21–32 and 5:33–48). See the discussion in chap. 5.

26. For some who follow the "antithesis" reading, there is still a sensitivity to the fact that Jesus would not be contradicting the Old Testament, and therefore they argue that the "you

But this fails to take into account the emphatic words of introduction in 5:17–20. Jesus did *not* come to oppose or present an antithetical alternative to God's revealed word. He is doing something eschatologically new, for sure, in his own person, as we will see. But the wisdom, ethics, and vision of his teaching are *not* new or antithetical to what God has said. Jesus has come to *fulfill*, not abolish. As Allison notes, Jesus's purpose here is twofold, showing through six examples "(i) what sort of attitude and behavior Jesus requires and (ii) how his demands surpass those of the Torah without contradicting the Torah."[27] An ancient way of saying this can be found in this explication: "Christ's commandment contains the law, but the law does not contain Christ's commandment. Therefore whoever fulfills the commandments of Christ implicitly fulfills the commandments of the law."[28]

These six examples, then, are not antitheses but exegeses. They are illustrations that interpret, or exegete, both the Old Testament teachings and Jesus's words together, showing how the fulfillment-not-abolishment of 5:17–20 is worked out. The only sense in which they could be considered antithetical is that, unlike any other rabbi or prophet, Jesus is not simply repeating the words of God and calling people to repentance/renewal. Rather, he is making a bolder claim than this—he is now the arbiter of the truth of God (cf. 7:24, 29; 21:27; 24:35; 28:18–20). No prophet or rabbi would ever say—without getting killed—"you have heard it was said but I say to you . . ." regarding God's revelation.[29] So there *is* an important antithesis here, but it concerns the speaker and interpreter, Jesus, not the content of the revelation. The antithesis is eschatological and christological. In terms of heart-level, internal righteousness, Jesus stands in continuity with the prophetic tradition, as we will see.

Matthew 5:21–26

21You have heard that it was said to the people long ago, "You shall not murder, and whoever commits murder will be liable to judgment."

---

have heard it said" portion of each antithesis is not really a scriptural teaching per se but the wrong, rabbinic *interpretation* of the saying, complete with its many human traditions added on by legalistic accretion. I do not think this does justice to how the text reads, nor is it necessary.

27. Davies and Allison, *Matthew 1–7*, 508.

28. Scot McKnight, *The Sermon on the Mount*, The Story of God Bible Commentary (Grand Rapids: Zondervan, 2013), 72, anonymous author quoted from Manlio Simonetti, ed., *Matthew 1–13*, ACCS (Downers Grove, IL: InterVarsity, 2001), 101.

29. Ulrich Luz, *Matthew 1–7: A Commentary*, rev. ed., trans. James E. Crouch, Hermeneia (Minneapolis: Fortress, 2007), 230–32, discusses Jesus's authority as expressed in the "antitheses," noting how remarkable it is that Jesus's authority rests on an appeal to nothing else but simply what he himself says.

> ²²*And I say that everyone who is angry with his brother or sister will*
> *be liable to judgment. And whoever says to his brother or sister, "You*
> *moron!" will be liable to the court. And whoever says, "You fool!"*
> *will be liable to the fiery hell.*
>
> ²³*Therefore if when you are offering your gift at the altar you re-*
> *member that your brother or sister has some issue with you,* ²⁴*leave*
> *your gift there before the altar and go and first be reconciled to your*
> *brother or sister and then go and offer your gift.*
>
> ²⁵*Quickly make things right with your adversary, even as you are on*
> *the way to court, lest your adversary hand you over to the judge and*
> *the judge hand you over to the guard and you are thrown in prison.*
> ²⁶*Truly I say to you that you will certainly not get out of there until*
> *you have paid back the last cent.*[30]

This first example/exegesis is the longest and in many ways the most complicated. It sets the example of the "Law and the Prophets" reading that is
being taught through six illustrations. It invites readers to learn by imitation,
and the following five exegeses can be shorter as a result. This is a typical
Matthean pattern.

Like each of the exegeses in the Sermon, 5:21–26 has three parts: the Torah
statement, Jesus's explanation of the true intent, and the practical application.
The first portion comprises verses 21–22 and is the focal point as an example
of the "greater righteousness" theme throughout 5:21–48. In these verses we
see the principle at work: Jesus takes up a command from the Jewish tradition and, without overturning it, shows the true intent and practical reality
of the commandment, all the while driving home his point with urgency in
light of his own coming.

In this instance, all would agree that God has prohibited murder and that
Jesus is *not* offering an alternative, "antithetical" reading—"Murder is really
OK," or "God has never really been concerned about murder, so relax a bit,
friends," or even, "The issues surrounding murder are complex ethically."

---

30. A few comments are in order regarding the translation I have provided here. First, in the
six exegeses, I have chosen to translate the flexible Greek *de* as "and" rather than "but" to better
communicate this idea: "You have heard that it was said . . . And I say to you." Unfortunately,
English has no way to communicate a subtler sense that straddles both the intended contrast of
"but" and the continuity of "and." I am choosing "and" because it is the more ambiguous of
the options. In 5:22 I have chosen to translate (not just transliterate as is often done) the Greek
rhaka as "moron" and *synedrion* as "court" since these make more sense to today's English
reader, even though inevitably some of the Jewish and Greek context is lost. In 5:23–24 I have
rendered *adelphos* as "brother and sister" since this word was often used in Greek to refer in
general terms to kin, without specifically limiting the idea to male brothers. For today's reader,
"brother and sister" better communicates this idea.

Without abolishing but rather showing the deepest sense and consummated reality of the commandment (= fulfillment), Jesus gets to the heart of the matter by saying that the real issue underneath murder is not the act itself—as wrong and devastating and consequential as it is—but the *heart* or *inner disposition* of the moral agent. Being angry and insulting another person made in God's image (cf. James 3:8–10), not just the outward physical act of murder, is wrong and worthy of judgment.

With rhetorical flourish Jesus delivers a threefold series of images to make his point:

- Whoever is angry with his brother = liable to judgment
- Whoever calls his brother "moron" = liable to the Sanhedrin/court
- Whoever calls his brother "fool" = liable to fiery Gehenna/hell

We would overread and miss the point if we tried to slice the differences too finely here. There is not a different condemnation intended for "fool" versus "moron" or yet another for being angry; being liable to judgment, standing before the court/Sanhedrin, and entering fiery Gehenna/hell are not to be distinguished for the point being made here. Together these three images demonstrate that God sees and cares about something deeper than just the physical act of murder: God sees and cares about the heart, the inner person.[31] The teaching here does not consist of the gradation of images. These are all escalating metaphors harnessed for the bigger point. Being angry and insulting someone are seen as the heart issue; judgment, court, and hell are seen as the consequence.

Again, Jesus is not abolishing the law against murder but bringing out its fullest and truest sense. To "fulfill all righteousness" and to have a "righteousness that surpasses the scribes and the Pharisees," disciples must face the issue of the inner person. Not committing the physical act of murder is good and right, of course, but it is not the true litmus test of piety and alignment with God's nature, will, and coming kingdom; examining one's attitudes and speech are just as important as refraining from homicidal violence.

In this there is great continuity between what Jesus is teaching and what the old-covenant commands also prohibit. A common misinterpretation of 5:21–48 is that Jesus is somehow deepening or expanding the commandments here. These verses are often treated as if there is discontinuity here, as if Jesus is upping the ante on God's righteous standards. In a Rehoboam-like way

---

31. Recall that the "heart" in Greek and Hebrew idioms refers to the inner person and one's identity, not affections per se as in current English usage. See the discussion in chap. 4.

Jesus is saying, "You think murdering was bad, now God is getting even more hardcore! You better not even hate someone else!"[32]

Just a bit of reflection reveals that this is not what Jesus is arguing. Never in the Mosaic covenant (or at any other time) did God ignore or disregard the ethical state or inner disposition of the person. The point of the Ten Commandments was never "just do these things outwardly and don't worry about your hearts." Quite the opposite. The message of the prophets is largely one of calling God's people to pursue righteousness and to do it from pure, whole hearts.[33] Sometimes God's people are called to repentance and turning away from outward physical acts—sins of omission and commission—but the issue of the heart or inner person is always present even there. Any repentance that happens must be more than merely external behavioral change, or else it is not true repentance. And many times the prophets do not reprove the people for external acts but for going through the motions with a heart that is not aligned with God.[34] In short, God has always seen and cared about the posture of the heart. Repentance can include nothing less.

This is precisely what Jesus the Prophet is saying. He is pulling back the veil on outward ethics and reminding God's people—especially the "extra-super-holy" ones—that true righteousness cannot be construed as mere outward obedience. It must be understood as *wholeness* (5:48). He is not changing the ethics of the old-covenant commands; he is revealing them as any good prophet does. Yet, as has also been noted, Jesus's role is *more* than prophetic; it is also eschatologically consummating. He did come to *fulfill* the law, not just to reiterate.

Matthew 5:21–22 is the main point of the passage and would have been sufficient to serve as an exegesis/example of 5:17–20. But there is a second part to this teaching, found in 5:23–26. Jesus gives further practical application of the principle.[35] He gives two examples of how to work out this ethical issue of not "murdering" with anger or words. The first concerns interpersonal relationships in the church (5:23–24). In teaching that foreshadows other texts in Matthew (see esp. 18:15–35), Jesus exhorts his hearers to be reconciled with a brother

---

32. The reference to Rehoboam comes from his strong and memorable words that caused the ten northern tribes to break away from Judah and Benjamin—"My father made your yoke heavy; I will make it even heavier. My father scourged you with whips; I will scourge you with scorpions" (1 Kings 12:14 NIV).

33. 1 Sam. 15:22; 16:7; 1 Kings 8:61; 1 Chron. 28:9; Pss. 26:2; 40:6–8; 139:23; Prov. 21:3; Isa. 1:11–13; 29:13; Jer. 32:39; Ezek. 11:19–20; Hosea 6:6; Mic. 6:6–8.

34. 1 Sam. 15:22; Pss. 40:6; 51:16–17; Eccles. 5:1; Isa. 1:11; Hosea 6:6; Amos 5:21; Mic. 6:6–8.

35. This is in fact the pattern in this first of the two triads of exegeses—(1) statement of the understood ethical norm, (2) explanation of the true ethical issue at its heart ("But I tell you that . . ."), (3) further example and/or implication.

or sister who might be angry, with one who might have "something against you," which could certainly include (but is not limited to) a conflict involving name-calling and accusations (cf. "moron" [*rhaka*] and "fool" [*mōros*]). The inward-outward and divine-devotional aspects of this commandment are still in play. The exhortation to be reconciled horizontally with one's brother or sister is tied intimately to worship and devotion to God vertically.[36]

The second practical application (5:25–26) of the teaching in 5:17–20 is even more universalized and stark; indeed, it seems out of place at first. It is a step or two removed in generalization from 5:21–22. The connection stems from the two ideas that occur consistently throughout the whole paragraph—judgment and interpersonal conflict.[37] The exhortation is to realize that conflict with others—not just the extreme prohibition of murder—is a serious matter that will often result in destruction. Therefore, reconciliation should be sought lest judgment be experienced.

Matthew 5:27–30

> [27]*You have heard that it was said, "Do not commit adultery." *[28]*And I say to you that everyone who looks at another man's wife with lustful intent has already committed adultery with her in his heart. *[29]*But if your right eye creates a stumbling block for you, then pluck it out and cast it away from you. For it is far better if you lose part of yourself rather than your whole body be cast into hell. *[30]*And if your right hand creates a stumbling block for you, cut it off and cast it away from you. For it is far better if you lose part of yourself rather than your whole body go into hell.*[38]

36. There are a couple of other NT texts that are figurally related, either as refractions of the Sermon's teaching or as coming from a common source: 1 Cor. 11, where unity at the Lord's Table is essential and disunity warned against in dire terms; 1 Pet. 3:7, where Peter exhorts husbands to honor their wives and live with love and understanding, lest one's prayers be hindered. Looking backward to the OT context for Matt. 5:23–24, Dale Allison has shown the likely connections with the Cain and Abel story of Gen. 4. See his "Murder and Anger, Cain and Abel (Matt. 5:21–25)," in *Studies in Matthew: Interpretation Past and Present* (Grand Rapids: Baker Academic, 2005), 65–78.

37. The parallel teaching appears in very similar form in Luke 12:57–59. In both cases the direct connection with the surrounding verses is not as apparent as in other instances.

38. I have chosen to translate *gynaika* in 5:28 as "another man's wife" rather than the more general "woman" because the focus here seems to be on marriage in particular and the prohibition against the destruction of marriage through adultery, not just general unchasteness or sexual immorality. This is certainly not to say the latter is acceptable, of course, but only that in this particular exegesis, which is but one of any number of examples that could be given, the focus is on adultery, which is with another man's *wife*; adultery is the breaking of marriage through sexual immorality. See Luz, *Matthew 1–7*, 244. Some commentators and translations have argued that the sense of 5:28 is that the man looks at a woman in a flirtatious way that

This second exegesis of the Torah by Jesus follows the same formulaic pattern of the statement of the well-known commandment (5:27) followed by Jesus's explanation of its true intent (5:28) and practical outworking (5:29–30). Moving from murder to adultery, Jesus addresses two monstrous, destructive sins, and ones that come straight from the Ten Commandments (here the seventh commandment against adultery, Exod. 20:14, is in view). In both cases the true righteousness is revealed.

In this second exegesis nearly every man is brought under the spotlight of God's all-knowing sight, not just those who might struggle with "anger issues" as described in Matt. 5:21–26. This second example addresses a universal part of male sexuality, both in its created and broken sense. The focus on the heart comes to the fore again because while many people in the ancient world, including Jews, did commit adultery, most did not. In first-century Judaism, especially under the influence of the Pharisees, with their strong religious character, honor-shame cultural values, and strict laws and punishments concerning sexual immorality, actual adultery probably did not occur with great frequency, even as murder did not.

However, this is precisely the point that Jesus drives home. Adultery has already been committed (at least in one sense) when a man looks with the purpose of coveting or desiring *in his heart*.[39] The explicit language of the "heart" here is one of the clearest examples of the deep and consistent theme of inward purity that pulses through all of the Sermon. God sees and cares about the inner person. Because of this the ethical command here is based not just on the explicit action of adultery but much more pervasively, on adulterous intent. This is Jesus preaching again a whole-person, greater righteousness to be pursued by God's people, without which they cannot enter the kingdom of heaven. As St. Methodius of Olympus wrote, Jesus is not counting as clean someone who avoids only the act of adultery; he wants the heart to be clean as well, "for it is not the fruit of adultery that he commands us to cast out, but its seed."[40]

---

makes *her* lust for sexual immorality. While this is grammatically possible in the Greek text, as Charles Quarles has shown, this interpretation is mistaken (*Sermon on the Mount: Restoring Christ's Message to the Modern Church* [Nashville: B&H, 2011], 117–18).

39. The Greek *pros* + infinitive used in 5:28 communicates the idea of purpose or intention, thus my translation as "with lustful intent." Admiring beauty or experiencing the natural attraction to beauty is not the issue here, but rather using the creational gift of the imagination (which functions in the "heart") for the purpose of fantasizing about and objectifying another man's wife as a sexual partner.

40. Methodius of Olympus, "On Leprosy—An Allegorical Explanation of Leviticus 13," trans. Ralph Cleminson and Andrew Eastbourne, http://www.roger-pearse.com/weblog/wp-content/uploads/2015/09/Methodius-De-Lepra-2015.pdf.

Two important notes should be made in this regard. First, once again, as with the preceding example, Jesus's exhortation is in strong continuity with the ethical teaching of the Old Testament. Not only does the Decalogue have the command against adultery, which Jesus is in no way overturning, but it also contains a command that makes it clear that the issue is more than the action, but the heart. This comes from the final, tenth commandment to not covet, which includes specific mention of not desiring another man's wife. In this Jesus is saying nothing new but is calling God's people back to heart-driven repentance.

Another important note is also consistent with the previous example. Even as we should not think of Jesus as raising the bar relative to Old Testament ethics, so we must not err in the other direction and think that Jesus is now equating all sins. That is, in this saying, just as with his discussion of murder and anger above, Jesus is *not* creating a new sin syllogism that equates lust to adultery in a coextensive way. One will often hear interpreters suggest that Jesus is saying that being angry is just as bad as murder, or more commonly, that lust is just as bad as adultery (5:27–30). But this is to flatten out important distinctions and to miss the point of the teaching. Jesus is not making all sins equal; murder and adultery are indeed worse sins with greater social and personal consequences than hating and lusting. The point is not a great equalization of all sins—beating one's spouse *is* indeed worse than a biting spousal remark; sexually abusing a child *is* truly worse than neglecting their need for affection, and so on. Not all sins are equal. Jesus's point is not to bring murder down to the level of fallout from anger, nor does he equate adultery with lust, thus removing all distinctions.

Rather, these heart-focused exegeses reveal the true depth of the matter. They are a strong push against the human tendency to focus on external actions and make godliness a matter of appropriate behavior regardless of the heart's intent. The broad and easy way is the way of external religion, not that of whole-person righteousness (7:13–14). At the most practical level, if anger and lust are to be understood coextensively as the same as murder and adultery, then at best we would have no leaders or pastors (who would be excluded on these grounds), and at worst we would need to stone most men, after they have been imprisoned for murder. These ridiculous (but logical) extrapolations reveal that we must not overread the point of Jesus's teaching here.

After teaching and explaining this point, Jesus gives us one further sapiential exhortation stemming from it: the strongly worded metaphors about plucking out one's right eye and cutting off one's right hand so as to avoid stumbling into adulterous sin (5:29–30). If indeed it is true that God sees and cares about the heart, and therefore adulterous lust is a serious matter, then the disciples' greater righteousness requires that they take radical action to avoid falling into such sin. Eye plucking and hand amputating are appropriate responses to pursue kingdom-oriented ethical practice.[41] While some in the history of the church have applied such commands physically/literally (cf. the idea of being a "eunuch for the kingdom" in 19:11–12), most have understood these allegorically or figurally. The most common such interpretation has been to cut off evil thoughts and a covetous spirit, but many have also read these verses as commands to stay away from and even expunge any friends or members of the church who might lead one to stumble in these sins.[42] This latter interpretation has much to commend it in light of the intratextual overlap with Matt. 18:7–20, where the same language of "cutting off hand or foot" and "plucking out the eye" is used more generally to refer to the radical necessity to avoid stumbling (18:7–9). This same passage goes on to discuss "church discipline," or the church's authoritative decisions to exclude some from the assembly of the disciples (18:15–20). We also see the apostle Paul speak similarly, referring to the body of Christ as having many parts (1 Cor. 12:12–30), exhorting Christians to put to death the earthly "parts," defined as sexual immorality, lust, and so forth (Col. 3:5), and to rid the church body of rebellious sexual sinners (1 Cor. 5:6–13), all likely reflecting the Jesus Traditions underneath his paraenesis.

MATTHEW 5:31–32

> [31]It was said, "Whoever sends his wife away must give her a certificate of divorce." [32]And I say to you that everyone who divorces his wife except on account of sexual immorality makes her commit adultery, while everyone who marries such a divorced woman commits adultery.

Jesus's third exegesis of Torah continues the pattern of the others yet is unique in several ways. At the basic level we can note that this example is much shorter than the others, has an opening that is slightly different from the formulaic pattern of the other five,[43] and is closely related in content to

---

41. The call to eliminate the *right* eye and *right* hand likely has to do with the metaphorical value of the right eye and hand as the most important or valuable. Hence, the point is that "in order to avoid sin one is to give up everything, even what is most important and most treasured" (Luz, *Matthew 1–7*, 247).

42. See discussion of the history of interpretation of these sayings in ibid., 247–48.

43. All of the other examples begin with "you have heard that it was said" while 5:31 alone has only "it was said." The rest of the pattern is the same, however, including the following "and I say to you . . ." The reason for the slight variation in pattern here may be because this is the conclusion to the first of the two triads, as indicated by several other clues: the use of *palin* in

the preceding one. All of this has led some interpreters to group 5:31–32 with the preceding set of verses, making five examples rather than six, with all of 5:27–32 being the second one. But on balance there is convincing evidence that we should understand 5:31–32 as separate and as the third of the first of two triads of instructions.

At a deeper level there is one other particularly unique aspect to this exegesis—the theological and moral issues of divorce, remarriage, and adultery comes up specifically again and are treated later in Matthew's Gospel (19:1–12). Each of the themes and teachings of the Sermon appear in other places in Matthew, but none of the other exegeses has such a reiteration and unpacking as 5:31–32 does. Maybe this also partially explains the brief treatment divorce gets in the Sermon. In Matt. 19:3–12 the reader is given another opportunity to understand both the heart of what Jesus is teaching and some of its implications. In chapter 19 the Pharisees attempt to test and entrap him in a theological and/or rhetorical blunder that they hope will result in the decline of his popularity at least and, at most, his imprisonment and execution, as happened to his similarly prophetic forerunner, John the Baptist.[44] Jesus's answer is brilliant and insightful. He sagaciously responds by challenging his learned opponents to reconsider what in fact is going on in Deuteronomy when Moses allows for divorce. By pointing them to another text of Scripture, the creation account (Gen. 1:27; 2:24), Jesus once again models how to properly fit together the many mosaic pieces of Scripture's witness. He does so by making just the same kind of argument he is making in 5:21–48—there is a matter of the *heart* that underlies the mere outward instruction. It is because of heart sclerosis,[45] hardness of heart, that Moses ever allowed divorce; it was never God's intention for a marital union to be broken (19:8). Thus Jesus uses the same kind of argumentation that he is employing in the six exegeses of 5:21–47—understanding God's ethical

---

5:33 to start the second triad, the similarity and difference between the first triad and the second regarding what follows "you have heard it said" (see below on 5:33–37), and the symmetry of the two triads in terms of length. On all of this, see Allison, "The Configuration of the Sermon on the Mount and Its Meaning," in *Studies in Matthew*, 181–87; and chap. 5 on structure above.

44. The parallels between Jesus's and John the Baptist's lives are many and not mere coincidence. This was not lost on the Pharisees, who were increasingly desperate to end Jesus's growing popularity. It was the issue of divorce, remarriage, and the accusation of adultery that finally got John arrested and beheaded. Jesus's opponents would have been quite relieved if Jesus met the same fate.

45. Matthew uses a powerful compound word *sklērokardia* to communicate this idea. This word is used in both Deut. 10:16 (LXX) and Jer. 4:4 (LXX) to describe the heart of Israel and the need for the circumcision of their heart. The related noun, *sklērotēs*, occurs just once in the NT in Rom. 2:5 to indicate a hardness of heart that is storing up wrath.

commands requires thinking about the inner person, or the virtue at hand.[46] This insight helps us conclude that while 5:31–32 could initially seem like a different kind of argument than those surrounding it in 5:21–48, it is clear that we are meant to understand it in the same way: focusing on the heart.

Despite the unique elements of these verses, the teaching on divorce, remarriage, and adultery in 5:31–32 still follows the same tripartite pattern of the other exegeses. Its basic shape is the same as those that precede it, albeit in a shorter form. The statement of the original teaching is in verse 31, followed by the explanation of its true sense in verse 32a, using the same "and/but I say to you that . . ." phrase preceding the right ethical understanding. As we have noted above, it is not as immediately apparent that this explanation follows the same external/internal, outer-person/inner-heart pattern of the murder-anger and adultery-lust example before it, but the revisiting of this paraenetic topic in chapter 19 helps us see that the same interpretation is at play in Jesus's/Matthew's ethics.

The most debated portion of this teaching is Matthew's inclusion of the famous "exception clause," giving at least one situation in which divorce *is* valid in Jesus's otherwise radically and shockingly strict view on divorce.[47] Part of the dispute concerns what the Greek word *porneia* means in the exception clause. Most scholars have argued convincingly that *porneia* is a general term for a wide variety of forms of sexual immorality. Adultery (*moicheia*) is a subset or specific form of *porneia* that is committed by anyone who is married. Thus in 5:32 "adultery" is the functional sense of *porneia* (because the context of the discussion is married people), which is a broader term that can have different meanings elsewhere (such as "incest," "bestiality," etc.).[48]

The third part of the formulaic structure—the further example/implication— is found in verse 32b. Again, the reiteration of this teaching in Matt. 19 helps fill out our understanding and application here. The apparent oddity of Jesus's

46. It is also significant to remember the story of Joseph, Mary's husband, who is the only character in the Gospels who is shown to pursue a valid divorce, because of the (apparent) adultery of his betrothed, Mary. Matthew wants to make sure his readers understand that Joseph would have been completely *righteous* in divorcing Mary (1:19) because this appeared to be a clear case of *porneia*, or sexual immorality. Some have erroneously used this valid connection between Joseph and the *porneia* exception clause in Matt. 5:32 and 19:9 to suggest that only in the case of betrothal is divorce acceptable. Even though this was indeed Joseph's situation, it is a logical non sequitur to conclude that betrothal is the *only* case where the exception applies and divorce is valid.

47. Frequently it is noted that by the time of Jesus's day divorce was often allowed within Judaism on nearly any grounds, as summed up in the school of Hillel's approach in the Mishnah. (See Quarles, *Sermon on the Mount*, 125–27 for a survey of the many ridiculous grounds for divorce.) This makes Jesus's very conservative stance all the more striking.

48. The clearest discussion of this can be found in Luz, *Matthew 1–7*, 253–55.

saying that divorcing a woman for any reason except for sexual immorality "makes her commit adultery" is somewhat clarified by the understanding that the issue here is ultimately remarriage. It is not divorce—valid or not—that makes a person an adulterer, but subsequent remarriage in the case of an invalid (non-*porneia*) divorce. It would be extremely difficult for a formerly married woman in first-century Judaism to survive economically and socially without being married, thus the assumption is that most divorced women would get remarried. Hence, while initially Jesus's statement seems to put the burden unfairly on the woman, in fact he is pushing the male perpetrator of an invalid divorce to realize that he is actually the cause of his former wife's adultery, not her, by virtue of forcing her into a remarriage situation when she was wrongly divorced. The teaching ends by also putting the emphasis squarely on the man's shoulders: men should not presume that they are free to remarry either, for they too will commit adultery by remarrying such divorced women (5:32b; cf. 19:9).

These are hard teachings, today as much as in the first century. And we see that even Jesus's own faithful disciples wrestled with what this strong stance might mean, realizing it is best not to remarry lest one fall into adultery (19:10). In all of this we are reminded what the point of Jesus's exegeses of Torah is—Jesus models both the continuity and discontinuity of what his life and ministry mean. The continuity is found in following the pattern of the prophets, who summon God's people back to wholehearted repentance and ethics. The discontinuity is manifested in the authority that Jesus has as the new Moses, last Adam, and Son of God, who is the arbiter of God's will on the earth.[49]

MATTHEW 5:33–37

> [33]You have heard that it was said to the people long ago, "You shall not break your vow, but instead, fulfill whatever vow you have made to the Lord." [34]And I say to you, do not make vows at all, neither by heaven, which is the throne of God, [35]nor by earth, which is the footstool of his feet, neither by Jerusalem, which is the city of the great king. [36]Neither should you make a vow by your head, because you are not able to make even one of your hairs white or black. [37]But instead let your word be "Yes" or "No." Anything that goes beyond this is from the evil one.[50]

49. On the complex and emotionally fraught issues of divorce and remarriage in the church today, see Scot McKnight's thoughtful, pastoral reflection in *Sermon on the Mount*, 104–9.
50. A few translation notes are in order: I have chosen to use the term "vow" rather than "oath," by which I mean the general idea of making a verbal commitment to do something,

The first example in the second triad of exegeses (5:33–48) concerns the making and fulfilling of oaths or vows. Behind this statement is a concatenation of several Old Testament commands, especially Lev. 19:12 and Deut. 23:23. Indeed, these verses are probably the best interpretation/explication of what the original Decalogue commandment means (Exod. 20:7). That is, the second or third commandment (depending on how they are counted) is not so much against spouting divine titles when using profanity (e.g., on the golf course), but instead is a commandment against using God's name *in vain*—making an oath or vow of any sort (including profanity) while invoking God if one is not able or going to perform the vow. Also relevant here are Zech. 8:17 and Num. 30:3–16.

In our current culture, oaths carry little weight except in specific legal situations. But in much of the ancient world, including in ancient Israel and early Judaism, swearing that one was going to do this or that was ubiquitous.[51] We are not exactly sure why this was so, but it could reasonably be connected to the much higher value that was placed in the ancient world on one's speech or words having great power to affect reality. God is a speaking God, and, not insignificantly, he *creates by speaking*. This extends to God's ongoing creative work through blessing, which is an effecting of reality through speaking, as well as to its destructive counterpart, cursing.[52] Examples of important and good oaths in the Bible include God initiating his covenant with Abraham (Gen. 22:16–18; cf. Ps. 105:9), God establishing his covenant with David (2 Sam. 7:10–16; cf. Pss. 89:3–4, 19–37; 132:11–12), and finally, God promising David his priesthood (Ps. 110:4). The apostle Paul himself takes a Nazirite vow (Acts 18:18). The abiding power of words appears repeatedly in the church's authority to declare who is in and out of the kingdom (through declarative binding and loosing: Matt. 16:19; 18:18) and to pronounce the forgiveness of sins (John 20:23; cf. 1 Pet. 4:11).

---

whether to God or other people. I have also avoided the language of "swearing" an oath that often appears in translations because the meaning of "swear" in current parlance has come to mean primarily the use of profane language. Finally, I take the Greek *ek tou ponērou estin* in 5:37 as "from the evil one," in concord with Matthew's typical usage of the articular *ho ponēros* as reference to "the evil one" (6:13; 13:19, 38).

51. See Luz, *Matthew 1–7*, 263n33.

52. Note that the only form of American Christianity that seems to have retained this pre-Enlightenment notion of the power of speech is the Pentecostal and charismatic branch, where prophetic utterances and announcements of blessing or judgment are a regular part of Christians' experience and are heeded with great authority. The extreme and clearly perverted sense of this is found in the "Word of Faith" or "Health and Wealth Gospel" movement, which turns the power of effecting speech into a baldly manipulative mechanism by which one gains physical prosperity (at least those at the top of the "Word of Faith" hierarchy) in the name of God but devoid of God's control and in submission to his will.

Prone to wander as humanity is, this understanding of the power of words is easily perverted and twisted into a mechanistic understanding and simultaneously a way to evade true, ethical, whole-person living. This is the matter at hand here in Matt. 5:33–37. Vow making had become an elaborate way to wiggle out of doing what one promised and what Scot McKnight calls "scaling honesty in words,"[53] that is, a way to only partially fulfill one's vows. We see this clearly later in Matt. 23:16–22. Similar to the return to the topic of divorce and remarriage in 19:1–12, 23:16–22 provides a fuller explanation and application of the pithy aphorisms provided in 5:33–37. In one of the strong woes upon the Pharisees in 23:1–36, Jesus gets to the heart of the matter of vows, showing that the Pharisees' attempt at slicing a very thin argument—of making an oath by the gold of the temple rather than the temple itself, or vowing by the gift on the altar rather than the altar itself—are all foolish wrangling and evasion.

This is the essence of the teaching in 5:33–37 as well. Using the now-familiar threefold pattern of the exegeses, Jesus states the original ethical command (5:33) followed by the inner-person, whole-person, true sense of this teaching (5:34–36). The simple summary application is then given in verse 37.

As with the other exegeses, Jesus is not overturning or abolishing the original commandment. He is not opposed to oath or vow taking,[54] and he would certainly affirm the importance of following through with integrity on what one vows to do, in accordance with several Old Testament texts. Instead, using hyperbolic, poetic speech, Jesus is speaking to the heart issue of trying to get out of fulfilling one's vows by semantic and technical arguments about the supposed differences between the objects upon which one based their vow.[55] If one is going to do this, he or she should not make any vows at all. With strong and persuasive images Jesus shows that this way of practicing vows is not the way of being in the world that accords with God's nature, will, and coming kingdom; this is not a righteousness greater than that of the scribes and Pharisees.

53. McKnight, *Sermon on the Mount*, 112.
54. It is well known that some Christians throughout history have indeed read Jesus's statement in this totalizing and literalistic way. This was one of the significant differences between the Lutheran/Reformed and the Anabaptist readings of the Sermon in the sixteenth century. This continues to affect the life and practice of the descendants of the Anabaptists in the Mennonite and Amish traditions. Their separation from society is in part undergirded by a literalistic reading of precisely these verses, requiring them to avoid any sort of vow or oath that would bind them. The result is no house mortgages, military service, holding government office, etc. This necessarily results in the need to create a separate, non-oath-laden society.
55. Quarles sums it up this way: "Jesus prohibited the use of misleading oaths, but he did not intend to prohibit all use of oaths. Oaths in court, marital vows, oaths of office, and the use of other oaths on solemn occasions to emphasize one's truthfulness comport both with biblical teaching and Christian practice" (*Sermon on the Mount*, 144).

If anyone is left with doubt about how to live out this heart-level righteousness in the matter of oaths and vows, then Jesus the Wisdom Teacher makes it simple and applicable—Don't make your vow complicated; just say "Yes" or "No" and then do what you've said. Anything else is evil, coming from the evil one, not God.

Along these same lines, James 4:13–17 provides another early wisdom application of Jesus's saying. In an appropriation of the teaching of Matt. 5:33–37, James exhorts his hearers not to boast arrogantly about plans made with one's speech but instead to qualify all such assertions with the humility of trusting the Lord's sovereignty (James 4:15). Saying you are going to do something and then not doing it is a sin for the speaker (4:17). This is followed up in the summative statement of James 5:12, which is clearly a refraction of the Jesus Tradition behind Matt. 5:33–37—"But above all, my brothers, do not make any vows, whether by heaven or by earth, or any other vow. But instead let your 'yes' be yes and your 'no' be no, in order that you don't become liable to judgment."

The issue in this exegesis is once again the greater righteousness that is *wholeness of the inner person*. The external matter of vow making is but an illustration of the real issue, being people of integrity, singleness, or wholeness in our speech, actions, and intentions. Ultimately, humans must be truthful and faithful to their commitments because God himself is faithful to his oaths. These exegeses will be concluded by making this same connection—Jesus's disciples are to be *teleios* even as the heavenly Father is *teleios*.

MATTHEW 5:38–42

[38] *You have heard that it was said, "An eye for an eye and a tooth for a tooth."* [39] *And I say to you that you should not resist an evildoer, but if someone slaps you on the right cheek, turn and offer the other cheek as well.* [40] *And if someone sues you and desires to take your coat, give him your shirt as well.* [41] *And if someone forces you to go one mile, go two miles with him.* [42] *Give to anyone who asks you and do not turn away from anyone who wants to borrow from you.*[56]

56. In 5:39 a nice play on words in Greek is unfortunately lost in translation. Matthew's uncommon verb choice (*antistēnai*) serves as a foil to the *lex talionis* statement of "an eye *anti* an eye" and "a tooth *anti* a tooth" in 5:38. Also in 5:39 the Greek *tō ponērō* can be rendered either as "evil," "the evil one" (referring to Satan), or "the evil person/evildoer." Various scholars and translations have chosen each, but the third is best in light of Matthew's usage and contextual considerations. A few scholars have instead understood *tō ponērō* very differently, as an adverbial instrument of means—thus, do not retaliate or seek revenge *by evil means*. See Glen Stassen, *A Thicker Jesus: Incarnational Discipleship in a Secular Age* (Louisville: Westminster/John Knox, 2012), 189. While this does connect well

I have been arguing throughout that the consistent theme of the six exegeses is that true righteousness means that in addition to external-behavior morality, the disciple of Jesus must seek and possess internal/heart-level virtue. Entailed in this interpretation is the understanding that Jesus's teaching here is in general continuity with the ethical teaching and prophetic messages of the Old Testament, albeit in its eschatologically fulfilled form.

The final two examples of Jesus's reading of Torah, however, appear at first glance to contradict this interpretation on both counts. In 5:38 and 5:43 Jesus quotes from an Old Testament commandment and then seems to contradict it or at least change its meaning to a deeper sense. These two examples are the strongest reasons why many have described 5:21–47 as "antitheses," as if Jesus is saying the opposite of the Old Testament teaching or at least modifying it significantly by expanding its application. I have argued above that this antithetical reading does not accord best with how these exegeses function. The initial reading of 5:38 and 5:43, however, may give us pause as to whether this anti-antitheses reading is indeed accurate.[57]

Further examination reveals that, even in these last two examples, what appears to be an antithetical interpretation of Torah is actually more of the same way of reading that is found in the preceding exegeses. Even in 5:38 and 5:43 Jesus is affirming the basic validity of the original command but pushing and expanding the understanding to its true and deep inner-person sense. We will explain how this works out in the analysis of each passage in turn.

As with the other exegeses of Torah, 5:38–42 follows the tripartite pattern of statement, explanation of its true intent, and practical applications. The Old Testament statement in this case is the expression "an eye for an eye and a tooth for a tooth," which can be found in several biblical texts: Exod. 21:24; Lev. 24:20; Deut. 19:21. This is what has long been called the *lex talionis*, or law according to kind. The point of this seemingly harsh and violent language is actually positive, not negative. The rule of *lex talionis*, which is also found outside the biblical witness in many other ancient cultures,[58] was designed to prevent two wrongs—severe retribution that did not fit the crime

---

with commands such as Rom. 12:19–21 and teaching against retaliation, I am not convinced this is the best rendering here.

57. Many thoughtful commentators do indeed see Jesus as overturning the OT law here. E.g., Scot McKnight states that Jesus "overtly ends the Mosaic command to 'show no pity' in the appropriation of the *lex talionis* and in its place orders his followers to be merciful" (*Sermon on the Mount*, 124). I understand this interpretation and respect the dilemma of putting this puzzle together, but for the reasons argued here and especially in light of the overall interpretation of the exegeses, I respectfully disagree.

58. It can be found, e.g., in the Code of Hammurabi as well as in classical Greek sources (Luz, *Matthew 1–7*, 275n41).

and self-appointed vigilante action. It is all too easy for revenge to quickly get out of hand, for the one(s) seeking justice to be controlled by passions, and for well-intentioned responses to become violent reactions that often end up doing more damage than the original crime and spiraling into more violence and instability. This is why the *lex talionis* exists and why it continues to be a part of our own justice system in the West.

As with the other examples, Jesus is not contradicting the good of this good command. It will only appear so if we think of this as a negative command or a command that we *must* exact retribution on our enemies. This is not the original sense or goal of the *lex talionis*. It is good for society as a *prevention* of violence; it fights against people taking justice into their own hands. Jesus does not contradict this, but in the second part of this exegesis he offers the true and heart-level virtue that corresponds precisely with this command. As lust is to adultery and anger to murder, Jesus speaks to the heart matter—do not be a vengeful, vigilante, self-justified distributor of justice. There is a righteousness greater and more beautiful than self-justice—letting God be the judge and righteousness maker, the one who puts the world to right.[59] This is a consistent theme in the Old Testament regarding interpersonal relations—do not take your own vengeance but let God be the one who sets things to right (1 Sam. 24:12; 25:26, 39; Ps. 18:47; Jer. 5:9; 23:2; Hosea 4:9; Joel 3:21; cf. Rom. 12:19).[60]

So again, rather than abolishing or abrogating Torah (cf. Matt. 5:17), Jesus is offering a holistic reading that explains the true intent and righteous interpretation of the Old Testament teaching. This is found in its simple form in 5:39a—"And I say to you that you should not resist an evildoer."

What follows in 5:39b–42 is the third part of the formulaic structure, the practical illustrations. Jesus gives four representative applications: turning the other cheek, giving one's shirt and coat, going the extra mile, and giving

---

59. It is one of the unfortunate accidents of linguistic history that English does not have a verbal form for "righteous" as Greek does. We must use the Latin-derived "justify" as the verbal correspondent to "righteous," thus losing the obvious connection between the words, even though in Greek "righteous," "justice," and "justify" are all from the same root. Though it is a bit clunky, I like to use "righteousize" to communicate the biblical idea of "set the world to right" or "make the world righteous, in accord with God's nature, will, and coming kingdom." The alternative "justify" in English now communicates almost exclusively a forensic legal meaning that is narrower than the biblical sense.

60. This is similar to what Allison has suggested. There is no contradiction between the rejection of personal *lex talionis* and belief that God will eschatologically bring judgment. "What Jesus rejects is vengeance executed on a personal level. . . . So the law of reciprocity is not utterly repudiated but only taken out of human hands to be placed in divine hands" (Davies and Allison, *Matthew 1–7*, 540). Cf. 1 Thess. 5:15 and Rom. 12:9–21, which almost certainly show the influence of the Jesus Traditions on Paul.

to the one who asks. These four examples of nonretaliatory righteousness provide the Judeo-Christian heritage of Western civilization with phrases that are familiar and well worn, even if they are often misunderstood.

While each of these illustrations inevitably has its origin in first-century Judaism, taken together their point is clear and applicable across time—often the right(eous) thing to do is to be wronged by another; often the just thing to do is not to seek one's own justice. In this we hear again the echoes of the topsy-turvy, eschatological virtue vision of the Beatitudes (5:3–12). The place of flourishing is, unexpectedly and ironically, the place of poverty of spirit, mourning, meekness, hunger and thirst, mercifulness, purity of heart, peacemaking, and suffering for righteousness' sake. Or to sum it up as Paul does in his own practical application regarding Christians' interpersonal conflicts, "Why not rather be wronged?" (1 Cor. 6:7 NIV).

In all of this we see once again that a virtue-ethics approach makes sense of what is being presented in the Sermon. As Ulrich Luz notes, what is being offered here is not the formation of a new *legal* principle (one that is overturning the Mosaic one), but instead an *ethical* principle is being contrasted with a legal one.[61] Charles Talbert rightly argues that 5:38–42 is a key text where a virtue-ethics approach contrasts with a deontological and/or literalistic reading as found in some branches of the Anabaptist tradition, the latter of which will often result in absurdity (becoming nude if someone asks for your clothing, etc.). A literal reading of these verses cannot give us the wisdom needed for decision making in all kinds of real-life situations that do indeed require the resistance of evil. Instead, this strong language shocks and jolts us into seeing the situation in a new way. Talbert calls this kind of teaching a "'verbal icon' through which one sees the divine will and in the contemplation thereof is changed."[62] That is, Jesus's teachings are a call to a way of being in the world that teaches us to look inward and become a different kind of people, a vision of virtue. A radical reorientation to our thinking often requires hyperbolic speech (cf. the parables).

It is important to note at this point that as with all ethical teaching, the practical outworking of these principles—even these specific illustrations of cheek turning, coat giving, and mile walking—requires *localized wisdom*. Without neutering the challenge of this virtue vision, we must acknowledge that these illustrations are just that; they are not to be applied literally and without wise exceptions. The command to turn the other cheek does not

61. Luz, *Matthew 1–7*, 276.
62. Charles Talbert, *Reading the Sermon on the Mount: Character Formation and Decision Making in Matthew 5–7* (Grand Rapids: Baker Academic, 2006), 91.

apply to the situation of rescuing a child from abuse, nor does the example of giving to those who beg require me to hand over the keys to my car to the homeless man who approaches me in the grocery store parking lot. This kind of literalistic interpretation not only misses the point of this exegesis (nonretaliation)[63] but also misunderstands the nature of paraenesis or ethical teaching—it gives a vision of virtue, of how to be in the world, that accords with God's righteousness; but the working out of this in the individual's life is inevitably localized. This is wisdom.

Two final observations are in order. First, in line with the entire virtue tradition we see here once again that this invitation to virtue is accompanied by the idea of emulation and modeling. Matthew shows us that Jesus is the model par excellence of the virtue being presented here. He of all people did not resist evil done against him, nor did he seek his own vengeance, but entrusted himself to the Father (cf. 1 Pet. 2:21–23). Not only is this conceptually clear, but Matthew also gives several verbal hints that invite the attentive reader to connect 5:38–42 with Jesus's own passion, such as in 26:67 and 27:35.[64]

Second, we should note that 5:38–42 is also connected to other important texts in both the Old Testament and Matthew. Several scholars have noted the many interesting points of contact between 5:38–42 and the suffering servant in Isa. 50:4–9. In addition to the general use of Isaiah in Matthew, these two texts show many striking verbal connections, including the suffering servant offering his cheek to be slapped.[65] These connections indicate that Matthew almost certainly employed this text in his own theological reflections when crafting the Sermon's teachings. Also related, Matt. 5:38–42 evokes other passages in Matthew such as the Beatitudes' promise of persecution (5:10–12) and the emphasis on suffering in the midst of the disciples' mission (10:16–25), not to mention the final exegesis, which exhorts disciples to "pray for those who persecute you" (5:44). Combining all these texts together, we see that there is much to the argument that Joachim Jeremias made that in 5:38–42 the difficulties envisioned are largely persecution resulting from following

63. Allison sums it up well:
   The import of the following sentences is lost if one attempts to take them literally. Jesus often resorted to extreme exaggeration in order to drive home his points and to get his hearers to ask questions and see their world from a new perspective. The command to turn the other cheek cannot be understood prosaically. Rather, it is Jesus calling for an unselfish temperament, for naked humility and a will to suffer the loss of one's personal rights. He is declaring two wrongs don't make a right, that revenge is poison. (Davies and Allison, *Matthew 1–7*, 541)
64. Matthew 5:39 and 26:67 both refer to being struck (*rhapizō*) on the face, and in 27:35 Jesus's clothes (*ta himatia*) are taken from him (cf. *to himation* in 5:40).
65. See esp. Davies and Allison, *Matthew 1–7*, 544.

Jesus.[66] In the midst of the disciples' salt-and-light witness in the world they should expect dishonor, physical suffering, and even imprisonment, and they must not retaliate in kind. As with all teachings, this initial setting does not limit the application only to this instance.

MATTHEW 5:43–47

[43]*You have heard that it was said, "Love your neighbor and hate your enemy."* [44]*And I say to you, love your enemy and pray for those who persecute you* [45]*in order that you may be the children of your Father in heaven, who shines the sun on both evil and good people and brings rain to both the righteous and unrighteous.* [46]*For if you only love the ones who love you, what reward will you have? Do not even tax collectors do that?* [47]*And if you only love your brothers and sisters, how are you doing more righteousness? Do not even gentiles do that?*

This sixth and final exegesis is climactic both in its structure and in its content. Structurally, the reference to the righteous (5:45) and the idea of a righteousness that is *more* than others (5:47) tie back into the same themes in the introduction (5:17–20), indicating we are reaching a conclusion. With regard to content, the call to *love* is an appropriate final, culminating ethical command, as this becomes central to all of Christianity's moral teaching and vision. Additionally, it wraps back around to the first exegesis and its prohibition of murdering/hating.

As with the other portions of the exegeses, we discern a threefold structure: statement of the original saying (5:43), Jesus's explanation of the deepest sense (5:44–45), and practical application (5:46–47). These can be examined in turn. As previously noted, 5:48 is in one sense a part of this pericope, but in a stronger sense it is the conclusion to all of 5:17–48. For reasons explained below, I have chosen to treat 5:48 separately.

The statement of the original saying in this sixth example is perplexing in a way that the preceding ones were not. This is because while the first part of the saying ("you shall love your neighbor") is clearly from the Jewish Scriptures (Lev. 19:18), the second half's command to "hate your enemy" is not found in the Old Testament.

Scholars have long debated how to understand this matter. It is best to understand that "hate your enemies" was an inevitable view (though ultimately unbiblical) that derived from putting together a number of other biblical texts

---

66. Joachim Jeremias, *The Sermon on the Mount*, trans. Norman Perrin (Philadelphia: Fortress, 1963), 29.

and ideas. These include various texts wherein individuals speak of hating their personal enemies and those who oppose the things of God (Pss. 97:10; 119:113; 139:21–22; more generally, Eccles. 3:8), as well as the understanding that allowing God's enemies to live and thrive in the promised land will be a snare to the faithful (Deut. 7:12–16). None of these statements, which are descriptive rather than prescriptive, command the hating of one's enemies. And even the rare order to hate evil (Amos 5:15) speaks to hating injustice, not exacting hell-bent destruction on individuals.

Nonetheless, especially for a people long oppressed and who were currently living under the heavy cultural and financial boot of the Roman Empire, hating one's enemies seemed not only natural but divinely patriotic (cf. a modern-day notion of "Christian" America that is interpreted as standing up against certain aspects of culture and government). As Jeffrey Gibbs describes it, this view in the first-century Jewish context "could readily have grown its twisted fruit out of a misuse of canonical soil."[67] We know, for example, that those in the Qumran community did explicitly teach the hatred of one's enemies.[68]

Thus, at least in part Jesus is addressing a misunderstanding of God's commands. In this sense, then, one might argue for a valid *antithetical* reading at play here, though it is not an abrogation or overturning of Torah but of Jewish misappropriation of God's commands.[69]

However, this antithetical reading would miss the consistent and bigger note that this sixth exegesis is giving that accords precisely with preceding ones. In Jesus's explanation (5:44–45) and then further illustrations (5:46–47), we see that the same theme of whole-person, heart-level righteousness is what drives this teaching. The command to love and pray for one's enemies—primarily defined as those who persecute you—is about consistency and about righteousness that pervades every part of the disciple, not just the external, behavioral part. Loving those who outwardly love you already and who are already your "brothers and sisters" is a righteousness that does not rise above that of tax collectors and gentiles and is therefore not truly love (5:46–47).

With a deeply ironic twist that occurs other places in Matthew (cf. 18:17), Jesus pushes his enemies, the Pharisees (and by extension, anyone in the church who acts like them), to see that their righteousness is on the level

---

67. Jeffrey Gibbs, *Matthew 1:1–11:1: A Theological Exposition of Sacred Scripture*, ConC (St. Louis: Concordia, 2006), 306.

68. Allison notes that 1QS 1:10–11 and other references encourage the "sons of light" to hate all the "sons of darkness" (Davies and Allison, *Matthew 1–7*, 549–50).

69. Luz states that 5:43b is not directed against a particular group or position within Judaism but in general against a common Jewish tendency to limit the love commands to Jews only. "For all practical purposes hating enemies is what happens when one understands the love command in a particularistic or popular ethical sense" (*Matthew 1–7*, 288).

of those whom they deem as the *least* righteous—the gentiles and the tax-collecting, sellout Jews. He does this with two poignant questions: "Do not even tax collectors do this? . . . Do not even gentiles do this?" (5:46, 47). Jesus's challenge-invitation is to see that this is inconsistency, a lack of integrity, because this is mere outward obedience. To enter the coming kingdom of the heavenly Father, one must have a greater righteousness than this (5:20): one must be *like* the heavenly Father, who in his own perfect righteousness loves and cares for *all* peoples, the righteous *and* the unrighteous (5:45). Thus, once again, true, surpassing, kingdom-entering righteousness is seen as that heart-fueled way of being in the world that accords with God's nature, will, and coming kingdom.

Going beyond this issue of the consistent nature of the six exegeses, we can also note that the choice of the specific *content* of this final, climactic example is not arbitrary or a mere accident. The vision of virtue that Jesus gives in the Sermon and in Matthew overall has a certain color, shape, sound, and feel. The dominant hue and tune is undoubtedly *love for one another*.

Love is, as is well known, the great message and vision of Christianity. Christians are to be known in the world by their love for one another (John 13:35). Leviticus 19:18, quoted by Jesus here, reappears in many places and in many forms throughout the New Testament, including Matt. 19:19; 22:39; and James 2:8 (the "royal" law). The apostle Paul speaks for earliest Christian theology in echoing the same sentiment and casting the same vision—the greatest and most important truth to pursue is the practical truth of loving one another, the true fulfillment of the Torah (Rom. 13:9–10; Gal. 5:14). Though not without some precedent in Judaism, Jesus's command to love one's enemies is unique and new in claiming "universal validity beyond religious and national boundaries."[70] It is the high point of God's demands upon his people. So the choice to put love—even love for one's enemies—as the final example of the greater righteousness is more than mere coincidence; it accords with the same meta-theme in all of Christ's teachings and the New Testament witness.[71]

70. Georg Strecker, *The Sermon on the Mount: An Exegetical Commentary*, trans. O. C. Dean (Nashville: Abingdon, 1988), 177.
    71. Strecker goes on with the following pointed observation:
        The commandment of love of enemy is of such unambiguous precision and radicality that it has plainly become the epitome of Christian teaching far beyond the realm of the church. By this first principle of Christian ethics, the followers of the Preacher on the mount have been repeatedly measured and—as history shows—found guilty of their failure vis-à-vis Jesus' claim. In the nature of this extreme demand of Jesus lies the reason why the history of the church—like the history of humankind in general—can be written as a history of closing oneself off from this commandment. (Ibid.)

But one need not go further than Matthew to see the same, and recognizing the significance of the content of this sixth exegesis helps us see the deeply woven web of interconnections that the First Gospel creates and hangs upon. It has been recognized by many students of Matthew that *mercy* is a foundational idea throughout the book.[72] Pulling on this thread reveals its connections with many passages and themes in Matthew, including the necessity of forgiving one another (5:23–26; 6:12, 14–15; 18:15–20, 21–22). Mercy itself is highlighted on several occasions (9:13; 12:7; 23:23), as is the explicit command to love one another (22:39; cf. 5:43–45). To end this sixth exegesis of Torah with the same strongly Matthean and Christian theme should come as no surprise, then.

Even closer to home, in the immediate context of the Sermon we can see that this message of love for enemies relates closely to what has already been said. Several of these wisdom sayings have dealt with interpersonal relationships, but now this one encompasses them all with the great command to love one's enemy. There is no higher apex of virtue than this command.[73] It also relates closely to the preceding teaching, the command against personal retaliation (5:38–42). It also satisfyingly wraps back around to the first of the examples, the command not to hate one's brother in word or deed (5:21–26), providing the positive counterexample/virtue to pursue. And notably, it also has a strong connection with the Beatitudes (5:3–12), which also speak of being sons of God (5:9; cf. 5:45), emphasize the experience of persecution (5:10–12; cf. 5:44), and cast a distinct vision for being people of humility, meekness, mercy, and peacemaking. Thus, the first and second major sections of the Sermon (5:3–12 and 5:17–48) both end with the emphasis on suffering persecution and doing so righteously.

The idea of being/becoming the "sons/children of God" (language that speaks of kinship identity) has already occurred in the seventh Beatitude: "Flourishing are the peacemakers, because they will be called the children of

72. Cf. Jesus's double use of Hosea 6:6 (in Matt. 9:13; 12:7), which shows the centrality of the virtues of mercy and compassion toward others, even over obeying the sacrificial laws. See also the discussion in Richard Hays, "The Canonical Matrix of the Gospels," in *The Cambridge Companion to the Gospels*, ed. Stephen Barton (Cambridge: Cambridge University Press, 2006), 66.

73. It is well known that Augustine rooted his ethical and hermeneutical approaches in the double love command (Matt. 22:37–39). This was also intimately connected to Augustine's understanding of virtue and human flourishing in that he redefined all the virtues in terms of proper love and particularly love oriented toward God. For example, he writes, "If, then, virtue leads us to a happy life, I should assert that virtue is nothing other than the greatest love of God" (*De moribus* 1.25, trans. Tornau). See the discussion in Christian Tornau, "Happiness in This Life? Augustine on the Principle That Virtue Is Self-Sufficient for Happiness," in *The Quest for the Good Life: Ancient Philosophers on Happiness*, ed. Øyvind Rabbås, Eyjólfur K. Emilsson, Hallvard Fossheim, and Miira Tuominen (Oxford: Oxford University Press, 2015), 272–74.

God." It is also closely connected with 5:48 to follow, with the exhortation to be the same *teleios*-ity as that of the heavenly Father. Interestingly, this combination of imitation of God and being people of love occurs multiple times in the New Testament. For example, Eph. 5:1–2 exhorts believers to "be imitators of God, as beloved children, and walk in love." First John 4:7–12 connects our loving others directly with the model of God's love for us. And 1 Pet. 1:13–25 combines the exhortation to "be holy as I am holy" with the command to love one another earnestly from the heart. As Allison notes, "Apparently there is embedded in Matt 5, Eph 5, 1 Pet 1, and 1 John 4 a paraenetic pattern common to early Christian moral teaching: as God's children, imitate him in his love."[74]

MATTHEW 5:48: THE SUMMARY CALL OF THE ETHICS OF THE KINGDOM

48 *Therefore, you shall be whole as your heavenly Father is whole.*

We now come to the final saying of this foundational "greater righteousness" section of the Sermon and the conclusion to the whole unit of 5:17–48. As was discussed in chapter 5, 5:17–48 is clearly the first unit of the central section of the Sermon (5:17–7:12). This section appropriately opens the instruction segment of the Sermon, following the vision casting of 5:3–16. As we have seen, the teaching is that there is a righteousness necessary for entering the coming kingdom and that this righteousness is in both continuity and discontinuity with the revelation of Torah. This was laid out in the crucial introductory verses of 5:17–20, followed by six examples of what this looks like via six heart-level exegeses of Torah (5:21–47/48).

It would be poor rhetoric and odd teaching if this weighty matter had no reiterating and summarizing conclusion. "Tell them what you're going to say, tell them, and tell them what you told them" is conventional pedagogical wisdom that is as old as teaching itself. Such a summary is precisely what we find in 5:48. The teaching of 5:48 makes sense of the whole unit in concluding the discussion of the greater righteousness begun in 5:17–20, and in doing so it pushes us to one more level of understanding.

Though short, this verse is power-packed and must be opened up carefully. Perhaps it will be best to note several *wrong and unhelpful* observations one might make about this verse by means of getting to its most beneficial exposition:

1. Matthew 5:48 is simply the conclusion to 5:43–47, based on the word "therefore."

74. Davies and Allison, *Matthew 1–7*, 554.

2. The word *teleios* should be translated as "perfect."

3. This verse is showing us the impossible demand of being like God and therefore is meant only to show us our need for grace.

I will respond to each of these mistaken understandings in turn. First, as I have just argued, 5:48 serves as the conclusion to the whole section, not just 5:43–47. The "therefore" (*oun*) of 5:48 may cause some Greek or English readers to think otherwise, and this is understandable. A deeper understanding of Matthew's way of writing as well as consideration of the nature of this discourse enable us to see that this "therefore" does not necessitate reading 5:43–48 as one unit with 5:48 only connected to 5:43–47. Matthew, like many other ancient authors, uses the great variety of discourse markers that Greek affords to communicate section and unit breaks. The "therefore" here is indicating a larger structural unit.

Second, as was discussed extensively in chapter 3, *teleios* is a key theological, virtue-related word that does not correspond well enough with our English "perfect" to make the latter a good gloss. Building on the argument made already, we can note how this key word in 5:48 serves as a perfect (whole) summary of what has just been argued in 5:17–47.

Matthew 5:48 relates to the Jewish Scriptures with the same balanced mixture of continuity and discontinuity that the rest of 5:17–47 does. I argued above that Jesus's teaching in this section does have an important eschatological and christological *discontinuity* relative to the old covenant that comes from his nature and the new era and covenant he has inaugurated. At the same time, however, in terms of the ethical instruction and call to virtue, the teachings of 5:17–47 are completely *continuous* with the instructions of Torah; God has always seen and cared about holiness that is whole, about integrity/righteousness that is throughout the entire person—mind, heart, and body. The clever and profound wording of 5:48 reflects this same approach.

As with the six exegeses of Torah, Jesus is *not* giving a new law of super-ethics and *more* requirements to enter God's kingdom—"adultery was bad before; now adultery *and* lust are bad," and so on. Rather, the same Jesus who says his yoke is easy and his burden is light (11:28–30) is emphasizing the internal over the external and proclaiming that God sees and cares about who people are at the heart level. To say that disciples must be *teleios* as God is *teleios* is to say that they must be whole or virtuous—singular in who they are—not one thing on the outside but another on the inside. The call to *teleios*-ity in 5:48 and throughout the Sermon is the same call to holiness that we see throughout the Old Testament (and the rest of the New Testament)—not moral perfection but having wholehearted orientation toward

God. Indeed, 5:48 is clearly a reappropriation of (or intertextual twist on) the great holiness command from Lev. 19:2 and 20:26 ("Be holy as I am holy"), with the likely influence of Deut. 18:13 as well.[75] I believe Matthew/Jesus has chosen to restate Lev. 20:26 in terms of *teleios*-ity because "holiness" in the Pharisees' world had come to mean primarily *external* matters of purity and behavior.[76] The word "holy" was too loaded with connotations to quote Lev. 20:26 directly, so he playfully but profoundly swaps out *hagios* (holy) for *teleios* (whole). As in 5:17–47, Jesus is giving a reappropriated, clear exposition of the true intent of the Law. The call to "holiness" in Lev. 19:2 and 20:26 is now properly explicated—as was its true intent always—as a call to "wholeness," or, in short, Godward virtue. At the same time, by emphasizing wholeness Jesus is showing that a casuistic approach to God (through obedience to Torah) will not produce the greater righteousness because it is all too possible to refrain from adultery and still lust, to refrain from murder and still hate. Thus, to obtain *teleios*-ity one must have something deeper, a purity of heart (Matt. 5:8) and poverty of spirit (5:3), and so on. As Allison notes, obedience to rules "does not automatically produce the spirit that Jesus requires of those who would follow him."[77] We will see in the following teachings of the Sermon that this is the essence of Jesus's attack on the Pharisees for being hypocrites—not that they were externally or behaviorally unholy or ungodly but that they lacked consistency, wholeness, and true virtue.[78]

Third, and finally, we must cast a line out toward the much bigger issue of the nature of salvation, grace, and virtue ethics that the Sermon on the Mount is wrestling with—or better, that the Sermon presents and causes readers to wrestle with. Full discussion of this matter must be deferred to the final chapter of this book, but we can note here that, in accord with the entirety of the instruction in 5:17–48, we are not dealing here with hypotheticals or mere "law" that condemns and shows our need for grace. Grace and virtue are friends, not enemies. The command that is present in 5:48 and throughout

---

75. Deuteronomy 18:13 in the LXX exhorts the Israelites to "be *teleios* before the Lord your God."

76. See Ellen Charry, *By the Renewing of Your Mind: The Pastoral Function of Christian Doctrine* (Oxford: Oxford University Press, 1999), 61–67.

77. Davies and Allison, *Matthew 1–7*, 509.

78. McKnight, following the clues of several other thoughtful interpreters, concludes that *teleios* here means being "perfect in loving," that is, "to love all humans, Jews and Romans, as neighbors" even as God does (cf. Luke 6:36: "Be merciful as your Father is merciful") (*Sermon on the Mount*, 145–47). While I think this is the appropriate interpretation of *teleios* in the specific context of 5:43–48, we cannot narrow *teleios* to only "loving fully" in light of the role that this term plays in the virtue tradition and the fact that 5:48 is doing more than concluding 5:43–47 but is summing up the broader teaching of 5:17–47.

this section is an invitation to flourish like God the heavenly Father, or to put it in macaristic form, of being called the sons of God (5:9, 45). Note that in all six exegeses God the Father is known to be *teleios* with respect to the topic in each paraenesis—God does not murder, but is forgiving; God is faithful to his marriage covenant (with Israel; cf. the extensive allegory in Hosea); God is honest and keeps his covenant oath; God forgives and gives even to those who dishonor him; and God loves even his enemies.

All of this life in the imitation of God comes only in and through grace, but the command for the necessity of greater righteousness is not thereby muted or emasculated. It will not do to punt here to an imputed righteousness; despite the reality of this imputation through union with Christ, this is *not* what 5:17–48 is talking about at all. Paul helps us understand more explicitly than the Gospels that it is through the regenerating and empowering work of the Holy Spirit that all God-glorifying good works are wrought, but Paul agrees wholeheartedly with what Jesus is saying here—the Christian's life must be marked by a way of being in the world that accords with God's nature, will, and coming kingdom (i.e., righteousness; cf. 2 Cor. 5:10; Gal. 5:16–21). The requirement of wholeness or heart-affections-behavior righteousness in 5:48, in imitation of God the Father, is a great summary of the gracious invitation of the gospel, not its enemy. As one contemporary Christian poet and songwriter has put it, "This is grace—an invitation to be beautiful."[79]

Matthew 5:17–48: Wholeness and Human Flourishing

The immediately preceding discussion leads us into the higher-level theological interpretation of this portion of the Sermon. My aim in this book is not to force a virtue or human-flourishing reading onto the Sermon but instead to show that understanding these themes—particularly flourishing through wholeness ("greater righteousness")—makes the most sense of the theology of the Sermon and gives us clear footholds to ascend its heights.

This first major unit of the central section of the Sermon is dominated by the theme of wholeness and defines righteousness in terms of God-centered behavior that virtuously comes from an internal consistency. This is true holiness. This is Matthew's understanding of righteousness—whole-person behavior that accords with God's nature, will, and coming kingdom.

This reading of 5:17–48 makes the best sense of its details and overall argument. But it is strengthened even more when considered in light of the flow of

79. Sara Groves, "Add to the Beauty," in *Add to the Beauty*, INO Records, 2005.

the whole Sermon to this point. As we have seen, the entire tone of the Sermon was set in the opening vision of the Beatitudes. There it was made clear that Jesus is presenting the true, divine perspective on human flourishing, framed with reference to being participants in the kingdom of heaven. He is inviting those who have ears to hear to *makarios*-ness. What follows that orientation is this first set of instructions about how to be in the world and align oneself with God's coming kingdom, the kingdom of heaven. One must have a greater righteousness or virtue of wholeness to enter this kingdom.

8

Matthew 6:1–21

Overview

Most chapter divisions in our modern Bibles are at once both helpful and misleading. When determined correctly they are helpful in making transitions of content and theme more apparent to the reader. They are simultaneously misleading (even when determined correctly) in that they regularly create and perpetuate an atomistic reading of Scripture. That is, chapter breaks, such as the beginning of Matt. 6, provide an overly convenient way for the reader of the Bible to jump in, insensitive to the flow of the whole, and read a portion of the text. But in doing so the overall message is often lost, or at least the breadth of the argument is undetected.

This is the case with 6:1–21. Having just exposited the necessity and content of the greater righteousness that is required to enter the kingdom of heaven, the Sermon now moves to a practical outworking of what this looks like in the realm of personal piety. In this sense, then, 5:17–20 serves as the introduction not only to 5:17–48 but more generally also to 6:1–21, and as we have already suggested, all of 5:17–7:12. If the six examples in 5:17–47 were exegeses of Jesus's "greater righteousness" Torah reading, then the three examples of 6:1–21 continue the pattern by providing representative illustrations of what greater righteousness looks like in personal religious practices. The six exegeses of 5:17–48 are kingdom-oriented, Torah-interpreting righteousness; the three examples of 6:1–21 are kingdom-oriented devotional righteousness or piety. Matthew 6:19–7:12 will continue the application of 5:17–20 to daily life in the world.[1]

---

1. As was discussed in chap. 5 above, 6:19–21 functions in the Sermon in two ways—as the conclusion to 6:1–21 and as the introduction to 6:19–34—and will be addressed in both sections of the commentary below.

As with the Sermon as a whole and particularly 5:17–48, 6:1–21 is again highly structured. It follows the expected pattern of a thematic introduction or *kəlāl* (6:1), followed by three examples (6:2–4, 5–6, 16–18), and wrapped up with a reiterating conclusion (6:19–21). Both the introduction and conclusion focus on prohibitions, while the three examples in the middle each begin with a prohibition—how *not* to practice the specific type of piety—followed by the positive alternative. Each of the three examples begins with the Greek word *hotan* (when) plus the verb (6:2, 5, 16), helping delineate the structure. The artistic and fitting addition to this basic structure is an excursus directly in the middle of this unit (6:7–15), indicated by a break in the otherwise strong pattern, using a participle plus *de* (and, but) in 6:7.[2] This central excursus flows naturally from the second of the three examples, expanding and expounding upon its same theme of prayer. This is, of course, the Lord's Prayer, arguably the most famous portion of the entire Bible. It is no accident that the Lord's Prayer appears in the center of the center of the center of the Sermon, being the excursus in the middle of this unit, which itself is the middle (6:1–21) of the larger central section of the Sermon (5:17–7:12). We will address 6:1–21 in subunits following its own threefold structure.

Matthew 6:1–21: Greater Righteousness in Relation to Piety toward God

Matthew 6:1: Introduction

> [1]*Be careful that you don't perform this righteousness for the purpose of being seen by others. For if this is the case you will have no reward with your Father who is in heaven.*

This opening instruction at once communicates a sense of continuity regarding the matter at hand and introduces a new topic. The continuity is found in the issue of righteousness. Jesus is continuing the discussion about the greater righteousness that is necessary to enter the kingdom of heaven, the topic with which he began in 5:17–20.[3]

Consistent with all that he said in 5:17–48, Jesus highlights the issue of the heart/inner person and internal/external righteousness. He warns his would-be

---

2. It should be noted that I do not mean by "excursus" that the Lord's Prayer plays a secondary role or is an afterthought in 6:1–21. Quite the opposite: it is the intentional center of the center of the center of the Sermon. But in terms of the highly structured, tripartite arrangement of 6:1–21, it stands apart from the rest of 6:1–21.

3. Greek readers will notice the anaphoric use of the article in 6:1, which I have rendered as "this righteousness," referring back to the preceding discussion of 5:17–48.

disciples that there is a heart issue at stake not only in *what* righteousness is (anger, not just murder; lust, not just adultery) but also in *how* one lives this out in daily life. Specifically, there is the ever-present temptation to be righteous *so that others will see it and think well of the doer*. Jesus is not condemning here the public practicing of righteous behavior, as if only secret, anonymous acts can be righteous (see below on 6:3–4). Rather, he is warning against righteous behavior that has a wrong heart/motive, the praise of others rather than the praise of God. Once again we see that righteousness, which is real behavior, is defined as truly righteous only if it is done with a right heart. New-covenant kingdom righteousness—that which is necessary for entering the coming kingdom of heaven—is a matter of internal motives, not just external actions; it is a matter of the whole (*teleios*) person; it is virtue.

This consistency of argument has one added flavor or accent—the matter of rewards or recompense. I have already discussed this theme in chapter 4, and it will come up below in the concluding comments, but for now we can observe that in 6:1–21 Jesus returns to an idea that was hinted at in 5:12 and then again at the end of the preceding section (5:46)—the matter of reward or recompense for virtue. The theme of recompense becomes the consistent focus throughout this section of the Sermon. This idea of gaining a reward for true righteousness kills any notion of altruism that might linger in a modern interpretation of Jesus's commands. It also serves as yet another clue to the hellenized Second Temple Jewish context of the Sermon—"reward/recompense" is language that stems from the worldview of honor and virtue and is consistent with many of the writings of Second Temple Judaism.[4] Throughout 6:1–21 the invitation to heart-deep righteousness is based on the appeal to gaining a lasting reward from the heavenly Father. We will see this important idea reappear in the bookend conclusion of 6:19–21, and it will be further discussed in the conclusion below. This recompense is "with" the Father (6:1), not "from" as is typically translated, speaking to an incorruptible, stored-up reward that will be given to Jesus's disciples at the end.[5]

The other important notion that is highlighted in 6:1 is that of God as heavenly Father. Of the seventeen references to God as Father in the Sermon, ten occur in 6:1–21, including at the beginning (6:1), in the final part of each

4. On the latter point in particular, see Nathan Eubank, "Storing Up Treasure with God in the Heavens: Celestial Investments in Matthew 6:1–21," *CBQ* 76, no. 1 (2014): 77–92, who shows that the idea of storing up rewards with God through faithful righteousness is frequent in Second Temple literature. It is also related to the idea of sin as debt (see Gary A. Anderson, *Sin: A History* [New Haven: Yale University Press, 2009]), with righteousness understood in equally economic terms. See Eubank, *Wages of Cross-Bearing and Debt of Sin: The Economy of Heaven in Matthew's Gospel* (Berlin: de Gruyter, 2013).

5. See Eubank, "Storing Up Treasure," 77–78. The Greek phrase is *para tō patri*.

of the examples (6:4, 6, 18), and four times in the center of the Sermon in the Lord's Prayer, called the "Our Father" in many traditions (6:8, 9, 14, 15). This super-concentration of "Father" references in the center of the central section of the Sermon (6:1–21) accentuates the vital role this understanding of God plays in earliest Christianity. As with the idea of reward, we have discussed this key Matthean and Sermon on the Mount theme more fully in chapter 4 above.

So as the introduction to this section frames the discussion in an important way that is both entirely consistent with the preceding argument and that extends it naturally to another realm of human life, religious practices. The teaching of 6:1–21 is a good and necessary application of the principle of 5:17–20 to the realm of personal piety. The six examples of 5:21–47 speak to the necessity of the match between internal and external behavior, with the focus on general interpersonal relationships that the Law addresses. The three examples of 6:2–18 do the same regarding religious and devotional practices.

Unfortunately, the realm of personal devotion and piety is not beyond the potential for the perversion and distortion of the heart. As Andrej Kodjak observes, generally accepted religious practices (such as almsgiving, prayer, and fasting) serve a double function, connecting people with God and also establishing a social norm. Because such practices establish a social norm, one's honor and reputation in society become intimately connected with such religious activities. This is a recipe for disaster, as this makes it easy for pious practices to get directed not toward God but toward establishing one's safety and security in society.[6] This is precisely what seems to be happening with these first-century opponents of Jesus. In what follows Jesus identifies three specimens of behaviors that fall under the requirement of a greater righteousness, examples that can be applied to all acts of piety.

Matthew 6:2–4: First Example—Almsgiving

> [2]*Therefore, when you are giving to help the needy, do not sound a trumpet before you, as the hypocrites do in the synagogues and in the streets so that they might receive glory from others. Assuredly I tell you that this is their only reward.* [3]*But when you are giving to help the needy do not let your left hand know what your right hand is doing,* [4]*such that your giving to the needy is done in secret. And your Father who sees what happens in secret will reward you.*

6. Andrej Kodjak, *A Structural Analysis of the Sermon on the Mount* (Berlin: de Gruyter, 1986), 104.

For the first example of religious piety done virtuously, Jesus uses almsgiving or giving to help the needy. In our own church experience two thousand years later, especially in the affluent West, many think of (alms)giving as tithing or the weekly offering-plate donation that goes to support the pastoral staff, operating expenses, and some missionary efforts. The same principles of whole-person virtue would certainly apply to this kind of financial sacrifice.

However, the issue addressed here is a more specific kind of giving that was far more common and accepted as essential to personal piety in ancient Judaism and Christianity—giving directly to help the poor and needy. In a time and place with great poverty and subsistence living (like first-century Palestine) and no government assistance, the needs of the needy were met by the community. This was more than just custom; it finds specific instruction in the Scriptures and was considered essential to what it means to be a faithful person.[7] Thus, in this sense, once again Jesus is unpacking what true righteousness has always looked like.

The emphasis that is new, or at least particularly highlighted by Jesus, is the question of the *motive* for performing this standard act of community and religious righteousness. The contrast made between the "hypocrites" and what is expected of Jesus's disciples is that the goal or inner motive of the almsgiving should be reward from God rather than glory from others. Notice that the issue of whether disciples should be giving to help the needy is not on the table; the assumption is that *all* religious people, hypocritical or not, are performing this act. The difference that is highlighted is at the level of the inner person or the heart, even as it was in the six exegeses of 5:17–48. Whereas the preceding passage emphasized that the disciple must look inward and deeper when facing certain sins, 6:1–21 emphasizes that even regarding positive acts disciples must look inward and deeper.[8]

7. Deuteronomy 15:11 reads, "For there will never cease to be poor in the land. Therefore I command you, 'You shall open wide your hand to your brother, to the needy and to the poor, in your land'" (ESV). Note also James 1:27, "Religion that is pure and undefiled before God, the Father, is this: to visit orphans and widows in their affliction, and to keep oneself unstained from the world" (ESV). See also the commands for the people of Israel to leave grain for the poor and aliens: Exod. 23:11; Lev. 19:10; 23:22; Deut. 14:28–29; 15:7, 11. Also see more generally Exod. 22:22; 23:6; Lev. 19:15; 25:35; Pss. 10:18; 41:1; 82:3–4; Prov. 11:12; 14:21; 21:13; 22:9, 16, 22; Isa. 1:17; Jer. 22:3, and many others.

8. While this is clearly Jesus's great emphasis, and such inwardness becomes the gold standard for Christian ethics, this is not to suggest that Jesus was unique or different from all of contemporary Judaism, which at times also emphasized the importance of inward motive (cf. the rabbinic notion of *kawwānâ*) and the heart (cf. Sir. 17:15; 23:19; 39:19). In the case of almsgiving in particular, several rabbinic and Second Temple texts offer similar teachings, emphasizing that giving in secret is important and that acts of charity should be done with modesty. See assorted references collected in W. D. Davies and Dale C. Allison Jr., *A Critical and Exegetical*

Receiving praise or glory from others is an ever-present temptation when doing good religious acts, and it is precisely this creeping motive that disqualifies one from living in the greater righteousness. This is how Jesus in Matthew defines a hypocrite, not as a supposedly religious person who is actually living an immoral life but one who is indeed righteous in outward behavior but doing so with the wrong motives, the wrong heart.[9]

It is interesting to note that here in the Sermon these hypocrites are not identified as the Pharisees, even though they are the obvious candidates and the constant enemies of Jesus in Matthew. This generic reference to hypocrisy (not specifying the Pharisees), defined here with respect to wholeness and virtue, may be so that the Sermon can easily be applied and appropriated more universally in the church, not only as a historical critique of Jesus's contemporary enemies. Nevertheless, from the perspective of Matthew's overall narrative it becomes clear that the hypocrites par excellence in Jesus's own day (and apparently in Matthew's situation) were indeed the scribes and Pharisees, as Matt. 23 makes clear. In the beginning of the fifth discourse (Matt. 23–25), in the woes (23:13–36) that match the macarisms of 5:3–12, "scribes and Pharisees" is put into regular, mutually defining apposition with "hypocrites" (23:13, 15, 23, 25, 27, 29; cf. 23:28; see also 15:7; 22:18). Additionally, the charges laid against the scribes and Pharisees in 23:1–36 significantly overlap with the instructions of the Sermon, both in 6:1–21 and beyond.[10] So, reading Matthew as a whole, it becomes abundantly clear that in the first instance the hypocrites of 6:1–21 are the scribes and Pharisees, while leaving open the appropriate application of this to any person who likewise practices piety for the sake of the praise of others.[11]

Commentary on the Gospel according to Saint Matthew, vol. 1, *Introduction and Commentary on Matthew 1–7*, ICC (Edinburgh: T&T Clark, 2004), 579–80. Also, in light of the argument of this book that the teachings of the Sermon sit at the intersection of Second Temple Judaism and the Greco-Roman virtue tradition, it is interesting to note that in several Hellenistic texts the teaching is comparable. See, e.g., Epictetus, *Dissertationes* 4.8.17: "Whatever I did well, I did so, not on account of the spectators, but on my own account . . . ; it was all for myself and for God" (quoted in Ulrich Luz, *Matthew 1–7: A Commentary*, rev. ed., trans. James E. Crouch, Hermeneia [Minneapolis: Fortress, 2007], 301).

9. See the discussion of hypocrisy as a theme in the Sermon in chap. 4 above.

10. There are many enlightening connections between the Sermon and Matt. 23. These include the scribes and Pharisees' love for public honor (6:1–21; 23:6–7) and their elaborate evasions of vow taking (5:33–37; 23:16–22). (The rest of the woes find other connections throughout Matthew as well.) In addition to all of this, there is the general condemnation that they outwardly appear beautiful but inwardly are dead and unclean (23:27–28). It is difficult to imagine a more apt summary of the Sermon's exhortations to wholeness.

11. Several scholars have made the intriguing suggestion that Matt. 5:21–48 is a critique of the scribes that matches a critique of the Pharisees in 6:1–21. Davies and Allison (*Matthew 1–7*, 581n14) reference Theodor Zahn and Joseph Fitzmyer. While it is probably not ultimately viable

Continuing with the strong theme of reward that marks this whole unit, Jesus warns with a backhanded, ironic statement that the hypocritical alms-giver already has the only reward he or she will receive. This reward is the praise of others (probably the shallow praise of other hypocrites) rather than reward from God. Similar to the ironic statement that those who disobey will be "least in the kingdom of heaven" (5:19), meaning they will be excluded from the kingdom, the point here is that this reward is really no reward at all. The powerful conclusion to this section (6:19–21) will drive home poignantly why this is *not* a good idea or not a good deal—because this human praise is fleeting, temporal, fickle, and earthly.

Following the consistent pattern of each example, the alternative to this foolish exchange and the way to fight the temptation of wrong-motive righ-teousness is given in 6:3–4. The disciple of Jesus is told not to let his or her left hand know what the right is doing and to give in secret. Both of these are idiomatic phrases that should not be applied with the mind-set of the literalist. Not letting the left hand know what the right is doing is simply a metaphor for different members of the body not performing deeds for the purpose of recognition.[12] Giving in secret is meant not as a new prescription requiring cash-only gifts (rather than checks used for tracking tax-deductible giving), or that when helping a homeless person the helper must wear a ski mask lest he or she be recognized. The countless impossibilities and absurdities of a literalistic reading are easily recognized. Rather, the "in secret" is a memorable, stark contrast to the "trumpet blowing" almsgiving of the hypocrite. While it is possible that some religious people literally blew trumpets before giving to the poor, this seems like not the most common practice and misses the point of Jesus's teaching—"trumpet blowing" and "in secret" are evocative, poetic, memorable images meant to communicate the heart matter of *motive*, whether the deed is being done for the praise of others or praise from God.

This first example of piety concludes in the formulaic way that each illus-tration will. After instructing what not to do in acts of piety (6:2), followed by the proper way to be (6:3), verse 4 gives the consistent incentive (cf. 6:6b, 18b) for obeying what Jesus teaches: if disciples practice their righteousness in *this* way—not for the praise of others but unto God in wholeness—then the

---

or helpful from Matthew's perspective to split up these two overlapping groups, it is insightful that the first two units of the central section of the Sermon address topics of specific interest to scribes and Pharisees—Torah for the scribes and acts of piety for the Pharisees.

12. See Charles L. Quarles, *Sermon on the Mount: Restoring Christ's Message to the Modern Church* (Nashville: B&H, 2011), 177. There is debate on what "right" and "left" specifically refer to here, but the overall point of the metaphor seems clear from the context. Luz likewise states that we should not press the image, which "has become a household saying," too far (*Matthew 1–7*, 300).

heavenly Father *will* indeed reward them, a reward that cannot be lost (6:19–21). Disciples can have confidence that non-self-promoting, secret acts of piety will be rewarded because that confidence is based on the reality that their God is a heavenly Father who sees what happens in secret; that is, he knows all things.[13] While humans look at the outward appearance, God looks into the heart (1 Sam. 16:7). Thus, based on a belief in God's power and ability, the disciple is free to pursue virtue apart from the need for praise and honor in society.

Also relevant, we see that this focus on inward piety—emphasized by the *en tō kryptō* (in secret) repeated multiple times (two times each in 6:4, 6, 18)—is not only Matthean but also has currency in other parts of the New Testament. Particularly relevant is the use of this same phrase (*en tō kryptō*) by Paul in Rom. 2:28–29, where we find a radical redefinition of the people of God in language very reminiscent of Matthew's: "For the Jew is not the one who merely appears to be one, nor is circumcision what it merely appears to be in the flesh. But the Jew is the inward [*en tō kryptō*] one, and circumcision is of the heart by the Spirit, not the letter of the Law. This person's praise does not come from other people but from God."

Matthew 6:5–6: Second Example—Prayer

> [5]*And when you pray do not be like the hypocrites because they love to pray standing in the synagogues and at the corners of the main streets so that they might be seen by others. Assuredly I tell you that this is their only reward.* [6]*When you pray go into your private room, shut the door, and pray to your Father who is in the secret place. And your Father who sees what happens in secret will reward you.*[14]

This second example is governed by the same principle of 6:1 and follows the same formulaic pattern as the first example (6:2–4). The principle, again, is a

---

13. Many other texts depict God as one who sees into dark and secret places, such as Ps. 90:8; Philo, *On Providence* 35; Josephus, *Jewish Antiquities* 9.3; *2 Baruch* 83:3; *b. Soṭah* 3a, 9a (Davies and Allison, *Matthew 1–7*, 584).

14. There are two translation matters of note. First, in 6:5 I have rendered *en tais gōniais tōn plateiōn* fully as "at the corners of the main streets" to communicate the intentionally public nature of this hypocritical praying, which the text itself seems to emphasize. Second, "your Father who is in the secret place" presents a real translation dilemma (so also in 6:18). It is tempting to interpret this as elliptical, with the verb "see" from the following phrase implied here as well, thus, "pray to your Father who sees in secret." The repetition of the Greek article makes this difficult, however, which may have resulted in its loss in some manuscripts. The situation is the same for the other option, taking the phrase adverbially, "pray to your Father secretly," which corresponds with its parallel in 6:4, "so that your almsgiving may be done in secret," that is, secretly. Acknowledging the potential of these options, I have chosen to render the phrase as "the Father who is in the secret place."

warning that people will have no reward if they are being righteous for the praise of others. The second example, concerning prayer, closely follows the one regarding almsgiving. The same characters, setting, and plot appear. The hypocrites are the ones whose motive is the praise of others. They perform their supposedly righteous behavior in the same conspicuous public places, the synagogues and the street corners. The problem is not only their location but also their motive—"so that they might be seen by others," which is a poetic parallel to receiving glory from others in 6:2. And the result is the same—there is no true reward because there is no true righteousness.

The solution or alternative course of action given is the same as with the almsgiving instructions: watch your motives when you pray. It may appear at first that Jesus is giving definitive instructions regarding how to pray. Specifically, prayer, it seems, must be private, secret, and closeted. Taken literally, then, the instructions prohibit corporate prayer meetings (unless the same ski masks used in almsgiving are worn by all), prayers in church, and outdoor devotional times. It is apparent from all of Scriptures' commands and modeled practices, including Jesus himself praying outside and in front of others, that this is not the case. The point of Jesus's saying is *not* to provide instructions on the proper mode of praying. Rather, the contrast being made is public versus private *in terms of heart motives*. As the ancient exposition of Theophylactus says with poetic punch (lost in English), "It is not the place [*topos*] that harms, but the nature [*tropos*] and the purpose [*skopos*]."[15]

This instruction on prayer is not all that Jesus wants to say about prayer, and Matthew provides a well-placed excursus on this topic immediately following. But the formulaic example of wholehearted, greater-righteousness prayer ends as the others do, not just with the warning, but with the hope-giving promise that when disciples do pray in humility and authenticity to the Father, he will hear and reward them.

Matthew 6:7–15: The Center—The Lord's Prayer

> [7]*In your praying do not babble on like the gentiles, for they reason that with their many words they will be heard.* [8]*Do not be like them, for your Father knows what you need before you ask him.*
> [9]*Therefore, you shall pray in this way:*
>
> Our Father who is in heaven,
>   Let your name be sanctified,
>   [10]Let your kingdom come,

---

15. Theophylactus, *Ennaratio in Evangelium Matthaei*, 204, quoted in Luz, *Matthew 1–7*, 302.

Let your will be done,
As these are in heaven, let them be also on the earth.
¹¹Give to us our daily bread
¹²And forgive us our trespasses¹⁶ as we also forgive those who tres-
pass against us.
¹³Do not lead us into temptation, but deliver us from the evil one.¹⁷

¹⁴For if you forgive others their trespasses against you, your heavenly
Father will forgive you. ¹⁵But if you do not forgive others, your heavenly
Father will not forgive you.

Volumes have been and should be written on this most central Christian text, the Lord's Prayer. A separate chapter in this book would certainly not be inappropriate. But for the purposes of our overall reading of the Sermon, it will have to be sufficient to make a few comments on the Lord's Prayer as it exists within the Sermon's overall teaching and vision.

Structurally, as has been noted, this section consists of an introduction (Matt. 6:7–8) and a conclusion (6:14–15) with six petitions inside. Taken as a whole it is a comprehensive image. To use the poetic language of Bruner: "The Lord's Prayer stretches from the Father at the beginning to the devil at the end, from heaven to hell, and in between in six brief petitions everything important in life."¹⁸ The content of the Prayer itself occurs in verses 9–13.

16. The Greek word here (*opheilēmata*) is more commonly translated as "debts," and this would not be inappropriate. However, I have chosen "trespasses" because "debts," rather than communicating a financial matter (as this word indicates in contemporary English), was a metaphor in an honor-shame culture (such as that of first-century Palestine) for things owed to another because of dishonoring/sinning against them. In the addendum to the Prayer in 6:14–15, which is a commentary on 6:12, a different word is used, a word that more clearly and less metaphorically refers to trespasses (*paraptōmata*). Thus, I have chosen to translate these two different words with the same English gloss in 6:12 and 6:14–15 so that the intended connection is made clear; this would not necessarily be the case with "debts" as the translation of 6:12. See also note 39 below on the overlap between "debts" and "trespasses." Frederick Bruner helpfully suggests "failures" as a gloss here, seeking to bridge the gap between "debts" and "trespasses" (*Matthew: A Commentary*, vol. 1, *The Christbook: Matthew 1–12* [Grand Rapids: Eerdmans, 2006], 308).

17. The traditional liturgical form of the Lord's Prayer has the familiar ending, "For thine is the kingdom, and the power, and the glory forever, Amen." This is found in many later manuscripts, including several later uncials and minuscules, but is missing in the earliest ones and is almost certainly not original. Bruner suggests that the ragged ending to the Prayer with its reference to the devil was too rough for many hearers and so scribes added the more polished "for thine is the kingdom" (*Matthew*, 1:315). Interestingly, the *Didache*, which shows a clear connection to Matthew and the wording of the Lord's Prayer, does have a similar conclusion: "for yours is the power and the glory forever" (*Did.* 8.2). Christian readers' familiarity with this longer version in the *Didache* may be one of the reasons why it later appears in manuscripts of Matthew as well.

18. Bruner, *Matthew*, 1:315.

The framing introduction (6:7–8) and conclusion (6:14–15) both give us additional insight into the best reading of the Prayer.

The introduction (6:7–8) prepares the hearer for the actual prayer by framing the issues and tying the Prayer into the flow and argument of 6:1–21. That verses 7–15 serve as an excursus on the larger argument of 6:1–21 is shown not only by the highly structured form of this section but also by how 6:7 begins with a reference to praying similar to 6:5, albeit in a different form.[19] The setting of the Prayer relative to the larger structure is seen in how 6:8 echoes the prohibition of 6:5—"Do not be like the hypocrites. . . . Do not be like them . . ."—both of which also allude to the important conclusion to the preceding section of 5:48 ("You must be whole as your heavenly Father is whole").

The Prayer's introduction also recalls the consistent message of the Sermon regarding internal and external wholeness and its application in this section to performing one's righteousness for the praise of others. The prohibition against many-worded, gentile-like prayers is not a new law outlining the word length or time length of all praying—something for which we can find counterexamples in the rest of the New Testament (e.g., Jesus praying all night in Luke 6:12; the prayer in the garden of Gethsemane in Matt. 26:36–46; Acts 16:25) as well as the history of the church. But rather, it is a call for simplicity over rhetoric, for clarity over piled-up repetition. The rare Greek word *battalogeō*, used here in combination with "many words" (*polulogia*), is likely referring to the habit of pagan prayers, which "by accumulating epithets for God or also words of magic give the impression of babbling."[20] From the Jewish tradition one thinks of the story of Elijah and the prophets of Baal, who engage in meaningless, babbling prayer for hours, along with cutting themselves, but are not heard (1 Kings 18:26–29). By contrast, Elijah offers a simple and direct prayer, and God immediately appears with fire (18:36–38). We know in the first-century world that many ritualistic prayers and magical incantations contained repeated phrases, often stirring the individual or the masses into a religious frenzy. One biblical example of the latter is when the Ephesians gathered together to protest Paul's anti-idol influence and cried out "Great is Artemis of the Ephesians" for two solid hours (Acts 19:34). Calling it "like the gentiles"[21] is the strongest, most evocative language Jesus could use

19. In a break from the repetitive pattern of *hotan* plus a finite topic verb in 6:2, 5, and 16, 6:7 begins with a participle, translated here temporally as "when you are praying."
20. Luz, *Matthew 1–7*, 305.
21. This reference to not praying "like the gentiles" is deeply ironic in Matthew, where the people of God are constantly redefined according to faith in Jesus, not ethnicity. As throughout the OT and the Second Temple period, "the gentiles" or "the nations" becomes the code word for those who are *outside* the people of God. Matthew also uses the term in this way but with the profoundly ironic shift of referring to the gentiles or outsiders as anyone who does not

with his Jewish opponents. The heaping up of many words in (public) prayer *appears* to be external righteousness but lacks the internal connection with God that Jesus is seeking and commending. The Lord's Prayer provides an alternative to this kind of externally focused, get-the-praise-of-others praying.

The ultimate reason Jesus's followers are not supposed to pray like the babbling gentiles is because they have a heavenly Father who knows their needs before they even present them (Matt. 6:8). This is not meant to add confusion to the mystery of prayer, discouraging or eliminating the need for prayer because God already knows; after all, Jesus offers a model prayer immediately following. Rather, the point is that because of the disciples' child-parent relationship with God made available through the divinely revealed Son, a follower of Jesus does not need to try to persuade or manipulate a reluctant god. Instead, prayers can be simple and direct because they are already predicated on an established familial relationship. The reader may refer back to chapter 4 for more discussion on the meaning of God as Father.

Jesus's model, alternative prayer is found in 6:9–13. In terms of the Prayer's historical Jewish context, we may make a few observations. Of course, Jesus's offering of a formal prayer pattern is not new or unique to him. In addition to various extemporaneous prayers found recorded throughout the Jewish Scriptures, we know of several well-used formal prayers in the Jewish tradition, including the Eighteen Benedictions and the Kaddish. The exact dating of these traditions is impossible to determine, but there is sufficient evidence to assume that something like these was already in use at the time of Jesus.[22] These prayers have some overlap of content and ideas with the Lord's Prayer, particularly the future orientation of the prayers, asking God to let his name be honored and to bring his will and kingdom to the earth. For example, the oldest form of the Kaddish reads: "Exalted and hallowed be his great name in the world, which he created according to his will. May he establish his kingdom in your lifetime and in your days, and in the lifetime of the whole household of Israel, speedily and at a near time."[23]

---

follow Jesus, whether Jew or gentile (cf. 18:15–20). In this Matthew is consistent with the early church, which speaks the same way, e.g., by describing the Jewish leaders opposed to Jesus as the nations/gentiles raging against the Lord's anointed from Ps. 2 (Acts 4:24–26).

22. Craig Keener cites a host of scholars who assume some connection between the Lord's Prayer and other Jewish prayers. He also points out that while the specific links between the Lord's Prayer and the Kaddish must be more than coincidental, they both also reflect features that were standard among Jewish prayers in general such as the Eighteen Benedictions (*The Gospel of Matthew: A Socio-Rhetorical Commentary* [Grand Rapids: Eerdmans, 2009], 215nn161–62).

23. This translation comes from J. D. G. Dunn, "Prayer," *DJG*, 617, following Joachim Jeremias, *New Testament Theology*, pt. 1, *The Proclamation of Jesus*, trans. John Bowden (1971; repr., London: SCM, 2012), 198–99.

These points of conceptual overlap do not mean that Jesus adds nothing new to his model prayer—the framing and form reveal important teachings—but it does confirm that Jesus sits in the stream of faithful Second Temple Judaism, which was longing for God to return and establish his earthly reign, as understood through the prophets' lens and language.

Matthew's version of the Prayer is also worthy of comparison with two other early Christian versions, those of Luke and the *Didache*. In the case of *Did*. 8.2, a late first-century or early second-century document, the version is very close. There has been recurrent debate about the direction of the literary and historical relationship between Matthew and the *Didache*, but there is no doubt that we have in these two documents witnesses to a dominant Christian version of Jesus's teaching on prayer.[24] In comparison with Luke, Matthew's version is longer and manifests several typical Matthean themes and emphases. Luke 11:2–4 is much shorter and lacks three phrases: "Let your will be done," which for Matthew creates a poetic triad; "As these are in heaven, let them be also on the earth," which is part of Matthew's recurrent "heaven and earth" theme; and "but deliver us from the evil one," another frequent Matthean idea.[25]

Regarding the form and structure of the Prayer itself, we may first note that, comparable to the Ten Commandments and the first and second greatest commandments, the seven petitions of the Prayer are broken into two sequential parts—the divine and the human, the first part oriented toward God (6:9–10; petitions 1–3) and the second toward human needs and relations (6:11–13; petitions 4–7). Or to describe it another way, there are two parts, each with a different orientation, the heavenly and the earthly realms (6:9–10 and 6:11–13, respectively). Indeed, the Prayer is built upon the strong Matthean theme of heaven and earth as a contrastive pair. Yet again, closely related and not in contradiction with these diptych readings, the two parts

24. See Clayton N. Jefford, ed., *The* Didache *in Context: Essays on Its Text, History, and Transmission* (Leiden: Brill, 1995). For the view that Matthew is dependent on the *Didache*, a view with which I disagree, see Alan Garrow, *The Gospel of Matthew's Dependence on the* Didache (New York: Bloomsbury, 2013).

25. This has been recognized by several commentators, including Davies and Allison, *Matthew 1–7*, 591; Robert Guelich, *The Sermon on the Mount: A Foundation for Understanding* (Dallas: Word, 1982), 290; and Robert H. Gundry, *Matthew: A Commentary on His Literary and Theological Art* (Grand Rapids: Eerdmans, 1982), 106. Graham Stanton, *A Gospel for a New People: Studies in Matthew* (Edinburgh: T&T Clark, 1992), 334, cites these as an example of Matthew's expansion of Q according to his own emphases. Interestingly, most contemporary and comparable Jewish prayers (such as the Kaddish) use the term "world" where Matthew has "heaven and earth." This subtle difference highlights the emphasis that Matthew placed on this phraseology. See my *Heaven and Earth in the Gospel of Matthew* (Leiden: Brill, 2007; repr., Grand Rapids: Baker Academic, 2009).

of the Prayer can also be described as eschatologically oriented (6:9–10) and
focused on present needs (6:11–13).[26]

The first divine or heavenly half begins with Jesus's familiar and familial
moniker for God, "Our Father in heaven." In much of the Christian tradition
these first two words become shorthand for the Prayer, the "Our Father,"
or in Latin, the *Pater Noster*. This is now the ninth occurrence of God as
Father (*patēr*) out of seventeen total in the Sermon and forty-four in Matthew.[27] There is much to the argument that God as (heavenly) Father is a focal
theme throughout the whole Sermon.[28] It is to be expected, then, that we find
this theme highlighted especially in the midsection of the central unit of the
Sermon, including in the epicenter of the Prayer.

As the center of the center of the center of the Sermon, we should expect
that the Lord's Prayer has much to teach us about the whole, and such is the
case. As we have seen in the earlier discussion of the structure of the Sermon,
some have understood the Lord's Prayer as the key to understanding the entire Sermon or even the entire Gospel, calling it a "compendium of heavenly
doctrine" (Cyprian) or an "abridgment of the entire Gospel" (Tertullian).[29]
The Prayer is not the only prayer that a Christian can or should pray, but
rather it is a model of what kind of petitions and God-orientation should
mark the Christian life. It is the scaffolding around the tower of prayer[30] or
the guiding handrails along which the disciple walks in forming his or her
own prayers.[31]

In the first instance we may note that this exemplary prayer speaks to the
corporate reality of Christians' lives. The Prayer does not instruct in an individual way—"*My* Father . . . *my* daily bread . . . *my* trespasses . . ."—but
with the community of Jesus's disciples in view: "*Our* Father . . . *our* daily
bread . . . *our* trespasses." As Willimon and Hauerwas note: "There may be
religions that come to you through quiet walks in the woods, or by sitting
quietly in the library with a book, or rummaging around in the recesses of
your psyche. Christianity is not one of them. Christianity is inherently communal, a matter of life in the Body, the church. Jesus did not call isolated
individuals to follow him. He called a group of disciples."[32]

26. See Keener, *Matthew*, 216n63.
27. See further discussion of this theme in Matthew and the Sermon in chap. 4 above.
28. N. T. Wright suggests that a title for the whole Sermon might be "What it means to
call God 'father'" (*Matthew for Everyone* [Louisville: Westminster John Knox, 2004], 58–59).
29. Luz, *Matthew 1–7*, 312.
30. Wright, *Matthew for Everyone*, 58.
31. Bruner, *Matthew 1–12*, 292.
32. William H. Willimon and Stanley Hauerwas, *Lord, Teach Us: The Lord's Prayer and the
Christian Life* (Nashville: Abingdon, 1996), 28.

Moving on we observe that the content of the first half of the prayer consists of three overlapping petitions, all summed up with the catchphrase at the end—"as these are in heaven, let them be also on the earth."[33] Matthew 6:9–10 is often treated as three petitions, but it is best to understand the three parallel verb-requests as one threefold prayer.[34] That is, there is a significant, mutually informing overlap between the three initial requests, making them in effect one cohesive idea. The entreaties for God's name to be sanctified ("hallowed" in the English tradition), for his kingdom to come, and for his will to be done are slightly nuanced versions of the same request. They might best be summed up as the desire for God's honorific reign to become a full reality.[35] As W. D. Davies and Dale Allison state: "The coming of the kingdom, the hallowing of God's name, and the doing of God's will on earth as in heaven are in essence all one: each looks at the *telos* of history, each refers to the fitting culmination of God's salvific work."[36]

This understanding is strengthened and explicated by the phrase at the end of 6:10 that modifies and brings all three requests together—*as these are in heaven, let them be also on the earth.* This climactic phrase gets at the very heart of the Christian's future-oriented, eschatological hope, vision, and orientation to the world. Followers of Jesus are defined as those awaiting the time and place in which God will make the realities of the heavenly realm (where God dwells) the reality on the earth (the place of humanity). There is nothing more fundamental than this soul-situatedness for the people

33. Several commentators are in agreement with my assessment that the final phrase, "as in heaven so also on earth," refers to all three of the preceding petitions together. This is explicitly the view of R. T. France, *The Gospel of Matthew*, NICNT (Grand Rapids: Eerdmans, 2007), 134–35; Floyd Vivian Filson, *A Commentary on the Gospel according to St. Matthew* (Peabody, MA: Hendrickson, 1987), 96; H. Benedict Green, *Matthew, Poet of the Beatitudes* (Edinburgh: T&T Clark, 2001), 86; Alfred Plummer, *An Exegetical Commentary on the Gospel according to St. Matthew* (London: Eliot Stock, 1909), 99. Gundry, *Matthew*, 107, is the only one to express disagreement with this interpretation, though no reason is given. Davies and Allison (*Matthew 1–7*), Leon Morris (*The Gospel According to Matthew*, PNTC [Grand Rapids: Eerdmans, 1992]) and Guelich (*Sermon on the Mount*) do not give an opinion on this question.

34. Furthering the idea that 6:9–10 is to be treated as one thought, several scholars have noted that these verses are marked by an *inclusio* of references to heaven (*ouranos*). See Davies and Allison, *Matthew 1–7*, 606; Green, *Matthew, Poet*, 79; Gundry, *Matthew*, 106; John P. Meier, *The Vision of Matthew: Christ, Church, and Morality in the First Gospel* (New York: Paulist Press, 1979), 61.

35. Quarles points out that this petition may be behind what apparently became a widespread prayer in the early church, rendered in its Aramaic form as "Maranatha!" meaning "Come, Lord!" (cf. 1 Cor. 16:22; Rev. 22:20; *Did.* 10.6) (*Sermon on the Mount*, 198).

36. Davies and Allison, *Matthew 1–7*, 603. Similarly, Guelich, *Sermon on the Mount*, 289, observes that the first three petitions "are not only formally parallel but also materially interrelated." Keener, *Matthew*, 220, states that they "are all variant versions of the same end-time promise: everything will be set right someday."

of God. This is the orientation to the world that can be seen throughout the Scriptures—not a rejection of or apathy toward the earth, nor a longing to "get out of this world that's going to hell in a handbasket." Rather, the believer in God the Creator and Redeemer is depicted as one who longs for God to make his de jure righteous ruling of the world de facto or completely real and manifested on the earth, with no remainder. This is the vision of the prophets (Isa. 9:1–7; 35:1–10; 40:9–11) as well as the New Testament witness (Rev. 19–21). It is also, naturally, the foundational center to prayer and the Lord's Prayer.

The threefold petition that is summed up with this "on earth as it is in heaven" phrase is all about God's rule or real reign. Disciples are instructed to affirm and pray that God's name be honored and set apart (the sense of the old "hallowed be"), that his reign or kingdom come, and that his will become reality. These are deeply interrelated ideas that could be depicted as a tightly conjoined Venn diagram—the time and place where God the King is honored, where his reign is clear and absolute, and therefore, his sovereign will happens. The essence of the Prayer is that these overlapping ideas, which *are* the full reality now in the heavenly realm, would become patently and fully so on the earth. It is not as if God is *not* the King over the earth, but the reality in this broken and rebellious age is that while God is sovereign, his perfect, peaceful righteousness has not yet consumed all of his creation. This heavenly age, time, space, and experience are what every believer is looking forward to and what provides the fundamental orientation for the Christian life.

Even as the Decalogue and the first and second greatest commandments have a complementary pairing of the divine and human—orientation toward God and orientation toward others, both with a focus on love—so too the two halves of the Prayer. The first part orients the one praying to how he or she should think about God and his reign over the earth. The second part is on the more mundane, earthly level of daily needs and relationships with others.

There are three aspects to this earthly/human side of the great Christian Prayer.[37] First is recognition of the disciple's dependence on God for the meeting of daily needs. To pray for the provision of our "daily bread"[38] or what is needed for sustenance more broadly is the necessary humble stance that the believer should have toward God. Thoroughgoing neediness and dependence on God for life, breath, and sustenance is the case for every human, believer or not, whether it is realized or not. The allusion to the manna of Exod. 16 and the Israelites' dependence on God's provision in the wilderness is clearly intended. To pray with this mind-set both reflects and inculcates the virtues of humility and faith. It is reminiscent of the whole tone of the Beatitudes, which portrays the virtues of meekness, humility, and even hunger. As Craig Keener observes, "this is not the prayer of the complacent and the self-satisfied, but of the humble, the lowly, the broken, the desperate . . . the 'meek' who will 'inherit the earth.'"[39]

Like much of prayer, the praying is as much about the attitude and development of the one praying as it is about the actual request. Like all prayer, there is a great mystery here. Jesus began the Prayer by stating (and will shortly say again) that God the Father actually knows all needs *before* he is asked and he provides for his creatures continually (6:8, 25–34), even apart from their asking. Indeed, he even provides for rebels in his kingdom by giving them sun and rain (5:45). So it is not as if human's daily-bread needs are contingent on their faithfulness in praying. Rather, believers are invited into the experience of the Father's care and the necessary orientation of humility and dependence by praying for God's daily provision. This heart orientation is, as the Beatitudes expressed, the state of true flourishing.[40]

37. Rather than seeing the Lord's Prayer as having a 3 + 3 pattern as I am suggesting, David Wenham argues for a sevenfold structure, splitting 6:13 into two parts. See Wenham, "The Sevenfold Form of the Lord's Prayer in Matthew's Gospel," *ExpTim* 121, no. 8 (2010): 377–82. I think the two parts of 6:13 are best seen as one concluding petition.

38. The translation of the Greek *ton epiousion* is notoriously difficult and ultimately retains some necessary ambiguity. Allison calls it "one of the great unresolved puzzles of NT lexicography" (Davies and Allison, *Matthew 1–7*, 607). This is because the word only occurs here and in *Did.* 8.2 in all of ancient literature. Etymologically it may derive from "substance, essence," "to be," thus communicating "today's bread," or "to come," thus "bread for the future" (Dunn, "Prayer," in *DJG*, 622). Keener argues that "bread for tomorrow" understood eschatologically is probably the most dominant view among scholars currently (*Matthew*, 221). Interestingly, in his commentary on Matthew, Jerome understands this rare adjective as meaning "of the future" because he states that in the so-called Gospel according to the Hebrews he found the word *maar*, which means "of tomorrow" (*Commentary on Matthew*, trans. Thomas P. Scheck, FC 117 [Washington, DC: Catholic University of America Press, 2008], 88).

39. Keener, *Matthew*, 216.

40. Cf. especially the macarisms of poverty, mourning, meekness, and hungering and thirsting for righteousness.

In addition to this, bread is a pervasive and powerful biblical image worthy of a fuller exposition than we have space for here. One thinks immediately of God's provision of bread (manna) in the wilderness (Exod. 16). Closer to home, in Matthew we have already seen that one of Satan's temptations of Jesus was the turning of stones into bread (Matt. 4:3). Jesus will also perform two unforgettable miracles in which he will feed needy masses with bread and fish (14:15–21; 15:32–39), both of which are important meals that evoke the Jewish hope for God's coming kingdom restoration. Both of these also anticipate the great event of the gospel story, the celebration of the Last Supper (26:17–30),[41] in which bread represents the body of Jesus broken with the effect of salvation and the inauguration of the new covenant (26:28). Additionally, two other important sections of the Sermon will return to this matter of God's provision for daily needs, particularly having bread to eat, both emphasizing that the disciple of Jesus has God as a Father who will always provide (6:25–34; 7:7–11). This is one of the ways that one can see how the Prayer is central to the Sermon and radiates its ideas. Jesus teaches his disciples to ask for daily bread and expounds on the idea in 6:25–34 with the encouragement to trust the (our) Father (6:9, 32), to seek first the kingdom (6:10, 33), and to worry about today and let tomorrow take care of itself (6:11, 34). Similarly, in 7:7–11 the disciples are encouraged to ask for their needs to be met because God is a good Father who knows our needs and "gives good gifts to those who ask him" (7:11).

The second element of the human-oriented part of the Prayer focuses on interpersonal sin and relational conflict. This connects to the second greatest commandment and the second half of the Decalogue. Disciples are instructed to pray that God would forgive their sins against other people, rendered metaphorically in the honor-shame culture of the ancient Mediterranean as debts owed to one another.[42] The centrality of this motif cannot be ignored because it will be reiterated in the conclusion to the Prayer (6:14–15) and

41. It has long been recognized that the evangelists intentionally link Jesus's wilderness feedings with both the Exodus (looking backward) and the Last Supper (looking forward). The latter is done not only conceptually but lexically as well, with the direct repetition of a sequence of verbs in the benediction at both the wilderness feeding and the Last Supper—Jesus *took, blessed, broke,* and *gave* the bread. See John Nolland, *The Gospel of Matthew: A Commentary on the Greek Text,* NIGTC (Grand Rapids: Eerdmans, 2005), 592–94; Donald Hagner, *Matthew 1–13,* WBC 33A (Nashville: Nelson, 1993), 418; France, *Gospel of Matthew,* 558–59.

42. Keener observes that while some have suggested the point here is an argument against debt-enslavement, "it is clear that 'debts' before God represent 'sins,' as they normally did both in Jewish teaching . . . and in the Aramaic term used for both concepts" (*Matthew,* 223). Supporting this understanding within Matthew, note the interchangeable use of "debts" and "forgiveness" in the parable of the unforgiving steward (18:21–35), and note also the change of terms, apparently used synonymously here, from *opheilēmata* (debts) to *paraptōmata* (trespasses)

because it is such a dominant theme throughout Matthew.[43] The unexpected and rather disturbing note in this otherwise understandable petition—for God to forgive us our sins—is the legal rider that is attached here and then unpacked explicitly in 6:14–15, that one must also forgive others who have wronged him or her (one's "debtors"). There is more to be said about this in the forthcoming discussion of 6:14–15, but we can note here that, consistent with the previous request and the whole Sermon, this is a matter of one's heart or inner disposition and way of being in the world. At no point, including in instruction on personal prayer, does Jesus allow his hearers to slip back into comfortable, externally focused religion; he wants them to experience a greater, deeper righteousness.

The third and final element of this portion of the Prayer is as fraught with difficulties as it is familiar. Followers are instructed to pray that they not be led into temptation but rather be delivered from the evil one.[44] The immediate question raised is why followers of Jesus would need to ask *God* not to lead them into temptation. This seems apparently contradictory to his fatherly nature. If the apparent tying of one's own forgiveness to one's forgiving of others is not disturbing enough, this is even more so.

Key to understanding this is to recognize the broadness and potential ambiguity/play in the Greek words involved, *peirasmos* (noun) and *peirazō* (verb). In English we have come to distinguish with two different words—"test" and "tempt"—what overlaps in the Greek terms. God "tests" his people to refine and discipline them, but always for their good (Deut. 8:2–3, 16; cf. Gen. 22:1); he does not "tempt" people, meaning that he does not seek the person's downfall through trials. That is the work of the evil one (Matt. 6:13b; cf. James 1:13–14).[45]

In light of the strong eschatological nature of the Sermon (and the entire New Testament), many in the history of the church have understood this as a reference to deliverance from "the Great Peirasmos" or the final testing of

---

in 6:12 and 6:14, respectively (France, *Gospel of Matthew*, 250). See note 16 above on my decision to translate both words as "trespasses."

43. In addition to the clear statement of love for others as the second greatest commandment (Matt. 22:39), an important and repeated theme in the First Gospel is showing mercy to others and forgiving others (esp. 18:15–35). In the exegeses, as we saw, this theme appeared both at the beginning and the end, in the prohibition against hating and the exhortation to love (5:21–26, 43–47).

44. See chap. 7, note 50 above on why this is best translated "evil one" rather than merely "evil."

45. James 1:1–17 provides a pointed discussion of the difference between the Father God "testing" (*dokimion* [1:3]; *dokimos* [1:12]) the character of his children for their good, to make them whole, versus their being "tempted" (*peirazō*), which he does not do but is rather a function of their own wrong desires (1:13–14).

the last days (Matt. 24:4–29). Thus, rather than being a request not to be led by God into temptation, one good reading is to see this as a prayer to be delivered from the Great Tribulation or time of testing. Closely related is the notion that the people of God should not test God, that is, they should not doubt and challenge his honor because of their trials and suffering. "Lead us not into temptation" in this sense can mean "Lead us not to test/tempt God" in the midst of our trials. We know from the Israelites' wilderness experience that this was one of the indictments leveled against them, that they "put YHWH to the test" by challenging him to prove he was with them (cf. Exod. 17:7). N. T. Wright points out that this idea is taken up and applied to the church in 1 Cor. 10, with Paul's exhortation not to be like the Israelites whom God slew in the wilderness because of their faithlessness. "What Paul, in effect, is saying is: You are the Exodus generation; therefore trust God to lead you out of your moment of testing without succumbing to it—that is, to deliver you from the evil one."[46]

All of this provides an important insight regarding this aspect of the Lord's Prayer. There is no promise or guarantee that Christians will be free from testing, trial, and suffering. Indeed, the opposite has already been predicted and is the strongest theme of the Beatitudes (5:10–12). Jesus is calling disciples and "a disciple is not greater than his or her master" (10:24). As Jesus was persecuted, so too will his disciples be (10:17–18, 25; Acts 4–5). As Jesus was tested and tempted in the wilderness (tested by God; tempted by the evil one) in the story that precedes his preaching ministry (Matt. 4:1–11), so too will his disciples be. The point of the petition in 6:13 is not for avoidance of all tests of faith and trials but for protection in trials so that the disciple is not tested "beyond what you can bear" (1 Cor. 10:13 NIV; cf. Matt. 10:32–33; James 1:2–17), lest he or she put God to the test.[47]

The highly structured Prayer begins with an introduction (6:7–8) and concludes with a commentary (6:14–15); together they frame the prayer proper (6:9–13). The introduction to the Prayer is an exhortation to focus on heart-driven, simplicity of prayer. The conclusion likewise focuses on the heart and inner disposition. The introduction emphasizes the heart disposition related to the first half of the Prayer—the divine—and the conclusion highlights the heart disposition of the second half of the Prayer—the human.

46. N. T. Wright, "The Lord's Prayer as a Paradigm of Christian Prayer," in *Into God's Presence: Prayer in the New Testament*, ed. R. L. Longenecker (Grand Rapids: Eerdmans, 2001), 146.
47. Keener's insightful discussion concludes similarly, and he points out that Matt. 26:41 is a very close parallel that helps make sense of 6:13. Jesus instructs Peter, James, and John to "watch and pray in order that you not be led into temptation/testing" (*Matthew*, 223–25).

As noted in the discussion of 6:12, this is an unexpected and rather disconcerting conclusion to the Prayer. It is a commentary on the Prayer that is meant to drive home the weightiness of interpersonal relationships among God's people, his church. As was mentioned earlier, mercy is a major theme in Matthew and the Sermon; it is supposed to be characteristic of the virtuous lives of Jesus's disciples. Here the matter is stated in stark terms for rhetorical effect—either you forgive others when they sin against you, or you cannot expect God to forgive you for your offenses against him. This theme will arise again in Matthew, especially in the fourth discourse that gives instructions for the church (*ekklēsia*) and life together as the people of God (18:15–35). Jesus puts great emphasis on this issue of love and mercy for others by telling the lengthy parable of the unforgiving servant (18:21–35). This parable depicts clearly how humanity's debt to God is many orders of magnitude greater than the sins others might do against one another, yet he forgives. With great emotional power the story stirs one's sense of the injustice of not forgiving debts owed. Most notably, the *nimshal*,[48] or the driving concluding teaching of the parable (Heb. *mashal*), in 18:35 evokes the language of 6:14–15 and makes the Sermon's point clear—"Thus, my heavenly Father will do the same to you [not forgive the unforgiving] if you do not forgive your brother from your heart." That final phrase is precisely the emphatic note sounded at the conclusion of the Lord's Prayer. This helps the reader make sense of 6:14–15 in the best way, recognizing that while this is not the only thing the Scriptures have to say about forgiveness and its basis, one cannot avoid the consistent theme: the people of God in Christ must have a righteousness that is greater than mere external obedience and outward appearance. As Adolf Schlatter observes, "There is no serious prayer for forgiveness except on the lips of a forgiver."[49] This does not contradict justification by faith but shows that a revenge-seeking heart is clearly not one that has believed in God's forgiveness of sins alone.

Matthew 6:16–18: Third Example—Fasting

[16]*And when you fast, do not be like the hypocrites who look gloomy, for they disfigure their faces so that they might be seen by others to be fasting. Assuredly I tell you that this is their only reward.* [17]*When you fast anoint your head with oil and wash your face* [18]*so that it doesn't*

---

48. For the important idea that wisdom sayings or parables usually have a *nimshal*, or "moral of the story," see Klyne R. Snodgrass, *Stories with Intent: A Comprehensive Guide to the Parables of Jesus* (Grand Rapids: Eerdmans, 2008), 17–22.

49. Quoted in Bruner, *Matthew 1–12*, 310.

look like you are fasting to others, but it is apparent to your Father who is in the secret place. And your Father who sees in the secret place will reward you.

Here we have the third and final example of true piety that meets the standards of Jesus's greater, heart-level righteousness, applied to fasting. It is clear by the structure and vocabulary that this example is part of the whole argument of 6:1–21, with a return to the same formulas that appeared in 6:2–4 (on almsgiving) and 6:5–6 (on prayer). In this additional illustration of the principle of 6:1, Matthew only slightly varies his wording for stylistic purposes, indicating that this is the third and final example to be given.[50]

Along with giving to the poor and prayer, intentionally abstaining from food (and sometimes drink) was a common practice among Jews in the ancient world and has continued in both the Jewish and Christian traditions. Jews engaged in a variety of fasts, both corporate and individual. It seems that in the first century many pious Jews fasted specifically for the giving of rain during the dry seasons, something absolutely essential for survival in an agrarian society. These men were often regarded with great respect for their fasting intercessions on behalf of the people, making the expectation for this kind of praise very real for many.[51]

As with giving to the poor and prayer, Jesus is not condemning or even diminishing the value of this practice of piety; his greater righteousness and kingdom-oriented living are never set against real-life practices and habits that inculcate humility, faith, and love. Rather, in accord with the vision of the Sermon, he is upholding and commending the importance of piety as done for God out of sincere devotion rather than for achieving honor from other humans.[52] In this Jesus is in continuity with many of the Old Testament prophets who also condemned hypocritical fasts (Isa. 58:1–12; Joel 2:12–17). The problem with fasting is that the desire to abstain from worldly pleasures and sustenance can get twisted and perverted into a badge

50. The twice repeated phrase *en tō kryptō* (in secret / in the secret place; 6:4, 6) is now rendered with a rare synonym of *kryptō*, *kryphaiō* (*en tō kryphaiō*; 6:18). This word, which also means "hidden, private" is found only four times in the LXX and only here in the NT. In addition to the stylistic reason for the variation there may also be a subtle allusion to one of the LXX uses, in Jer. 23:24—"'Can anyone hide themselves in secret places and I not see him? Do I not fill heaven and earth?' says the Lord."

51. Quarles, *Sermon on the Mount*, 224–25.

52. The tendency to focus on the externals is a perpetual and human problem. As Robert Grant points out, even in the very early reception of the Sermon in the *Didache* the interior emphasis is missed and the Didachist "tries too hard," arguing that because the Jews fast on Mondays and Thursdays Christians should fast on Wednesdays and Fridays (*Didache* 8:1) ("The Sermon on the Mount in Early Christianity," *Semeia* 12 [1978], 216).

of pride and honor that one's life is marked by such devotion. This is, Jesus says, hypocrisy.

The desire to have others reward one with praise for piety is a powerful drug. In the realms of almsgiving and prayer it is easy enough to perform outward actions to get the next "fix" of this praise-from-others drug. In the case of fasting it is not always apparent one is abstaining, so one way to drop this praise-fishing hint is to appear to others ragged and in need; this is the not-so-subtle hint that one is practicing great fasting piety and deserving of honor.

This perversion of the good of fasting deserves nothing less than the condemnation of hypocrisy. Instead, the follower of Jesus is to fast out of devotion to God and to do so secretly and thereby receive the true reward from God. As with almsgiving and prayer, it would be an overreading to interpret this to mean no one can ever know that another is fasting. The issue is not others' knowledge, but the motive at the level of the heart.

Matthew 6:19–21: Conclusion

> [19]*Do not lay up for yourselves treasures on the earth, where moth and rust disfigure and where thieves can break in and steal.* [20]*Rather, lay up treasures for yourselves in heaven where moth and rust cannot disfigure and where thieves cannot break in and steal.* [21]*For where your treasure is there also will be your heart.*

We now come to the conclusion to this lengthy exposition regarding greater righteousness. Unfortunately, very few commentators have seen the way in which these verses provide the fitting thematic conclusion to 6:1–21, resulting in a weakened understanding of the whole passage. Recognition of this structure enables us to see how the whole of this unit fits together with a common theme, with 6:19–21 as a reiteration of the *topos* already given in 6:1—pay attention to what you value or treasure the most because this will determine how you are rewarded.[53]

There are multiple notes sounded within these verses that show how they sum up the point of this lengthy, central unit of the Sermon. I discussed these more fully in chapter 5 on the structure of the Sermon, but we can reiterate them briefly here with some additional comments. The first indication that 6:19–21 is the conclusion to 6:1–18 is the repetition of the key word "disfigure"

---

53. One scholar who sees the way that 6:1–21 hangs together, utilizing my arguments from *Heaven and Earth*, is Nathan Eubank, referenced above. Eubank points out that my earlier arguments for the unity of 6:1–21 can be strengthened by recognizing that the language of "reward *with* your Father in heaven" in 6:1 is paralleled exactly by the idea of "treasures *in* heaven" in 6:20 ("Storing Up Treasure," 88–91).

(*aphanizō*) in 6:16 and then again in 6:19 and 20. This uncommon word[54] is used cleverly to refer both to the faces of the hypocrites when fasting ("disfigured") and to what happens to all earthly treasures eventually ("destroyed, caused to vanish"). This is not a mere coincidence but is meant to link these passages together with a satisfying wordplay, one that is unfortunately lost in translation.

Another hint that 6:1–21 is one unit comes from the fact that 6:19–21 is a perfect summary statement of the whole argument, namely, that this greater righteousness is a matter of the heart or inner person. The concluding aphorism of 6:21 sums up the whole point of 6:1–18: one's rewards can either be heavenly or earthly, the praise of others or the praise that comes from God. The choice between these two different orientations to the world is a matter of one's heart stance. The exhortation is clear and provides an appropriate and needed conclusion to this central section of the Sermon. Only a fool (cf. 5:13; 7:24–27) would choose to store treasures in a place that offers no security and promises destruction and loss. So too is performing one's righteousness for the praise of others. Once again, Jesus's instructions are in the form of a wisdom exhortation.

All of this confirms the consistent *kəlāl ûpərāṭ* pattern that marks the central section of the Sermon (5:17–7:12), namely, that each passage begins with a heading statement (*kəlāl*, 6:1), is expounded with particular examples (*pərāṭîm*, 6:2–18), and concluded with a restatement of the idea (6:19–21). In this instance, 6:19–21 is also a sectional overlap, serving simultaneously as the *kəlāl* for the following teaching (6:19–34).

There is one other note to make about the aphorism in 6:21. This saying about the heart being where one's treasure is in one sense simply reiterates the theme of the preceding section and really the whole Sermon, that true righteousness is a matter of the inner person. In another sense, this saying also makes a bolder statement, upping the stakes a bit. It does so because this statement is not merely a tautology, saying "what you value is what you love." Rather, because the Jewish conception of "heart" is more than emotions or affections but is the very nature or essence of a person, this statement is

---

54. In the LXX this verb occurs around ninety times with a variety of conceptually related meanings in its semantic range, including "put away, make unseen," "keep hidden," "cut off," and then eventually more metaphorically, "destroy." (This usage seems to become more dominant in later texts.) It only occurs five times in the NT, three of which are in Matt. 6:18–20, one in Acts 13:41 (which is coming from Hab. 1:5 LXX and perhaps Isa. 29:14 LXX), and one in James 4:14, whose reference to the goods of this life quickly vanishing is almost certainly an allusion to Matt. 6:19–21. The LXX uses that may be evoked most strongly for Matthew's Model Reader are Ps. 145:9; Prov. 10:25; 12:7; and 14:11, all of which are wisdom sayings about the way of the wicked being destroyed/vanishing in contrast to the righteous.

saying much more: what one values is who one really is as a person. Hence, the ones who value the praise of others rather than God are truly hypocrites, the opposite of what a disciple should be.

Matthew 6:1–21 and Human Flourishing

As with the other sections of the beautifully crafted Sermon, the language, concepts, and topics discussed all point to the fact that this message is about virtue and human flourishing. When read against the encyclopedic background of the Greco-Roman virtue tradition and the Second Temple Jewish wisdom tradition, Jesus's teachings here resonate and sing as invitations to human flourishing. There are several key words and concepts that reflect and evoke the virtue/wisdom tradition. These provide us with insight into what is being said and the vision that is being constructed.

The first flourishing concept employed here is *reward*. This is not the first time that the language or idea of reward has appeared in the Sermon. It is in fact the climactic, expanded promise in the ninth and final macarism (5:12); great "reward in heaven" is promised to Jesus's followers who are living the paradoxically flourishing life of persecution for being identified with him. It will also appear in other places throughout the First Gospel.[55]

Clearly reward is the repeated and dominant theme of 6:1–21. Reward from the heavenly Father appears in the thesis statement of this unit (6:1) and then is repeated formulaically throughout each of the three examples, both negatively ("they have their reward in full") and positively ("your Father who sees in secret will reward you"). The climactic conclusion to this highly structured unit slightly shifts the term from "reward" (*misthos*) to the closely related "treasure" (*thēsauros*) because it serves as the overlapping theme in this unit (6:1–21) and the next (6:19–34), but the theme continues unabated. This language is so prevalent in and governs over this section (6:1, 2, 4, 5, 6, 16, 18, 19, 20, 21) that it is often overlooked and not considered because of commonness, like silver in the presence of much gold. But there is no doubt from this tenfold repetition that this is the main impression one is to get from Jesus's teaching here—he is offering staggering and sure rewards that are treasures from God himself.

This much is clear from a close reading of the text. What may not be as clear to modern readers is that this notion of reward is trafficking in the virtue

---

55. The Greek word *misthos* (reward, recompense) is found ten times in Matthew (5:12, 46; 6:1, 2, 5, 16; 10:41–42 (3x); 20:8), and the related *thēsauros* (treasure) another seven times (6:19, 20, 21; 12:35; 13:44, 52; 19:21). Additionally, there are several instances of the idea of God paying or recompensing people accordingly (6:4, 6, 18; 16:27; 18:35; 20:8; 21:41). See chap. 4 above.

and wisdom traditions. In our post-Kantian understanding we not only have lost virtue and wisdom as the focal point and *telos* of ethics, we have also become skittish about the promise of reward, especially in the Protestant tradition. But all throughout the Scriptures there is the constant offer of reward, recompense even, for orienting oneself toward God. Reward is all ultimately a grace-gift from God, as the New Testament emphasizes, but it is still reward from God for wholehearted righteousness.[56] The Scriptures are not altruistic. "Well done" is a statement appropriate for a king to say to a servant or son (Matt. 25:21, 23).

So too in this central section of the Sermon. The rewards promised are definitively and decisively theistic and Christian—they are defined as coming from Jesus's Father in heaven—but it is still the language of "reward"/"recompense" for the righteousness of living virtuously toward God; righteousness understood as whole-person behavior that accords with God's nature, will, and coming kingdom. This is clearly what is in view here with these three practical wholehearted behaviors (almsgiving, prayer, and fasting) that are the kind of righteousness that is *teleios* (5:48) and surpasses that of the scribes and Pharisees (5:17–20).

All of this is another way of talking about the human flourishing promised now and in the future for the one who will pursue God-centered, whole-person virtue. All humans are motivated by the promise of future reward, even Jesus, who "for the joy set before him endured the cross, despising its shame" (Heb. 12:2). Like the pioneer and perfecter of the faith, surrounded by a great cloud of other reward-seeking witnesses (Heb. 11:1–40), Christians are being called to God-centered flourishing.

Desiring a reward is nothing to be ashamed of or any diminishing of virtue ("Get behind me, Kant!"). It is God's built-in motivation for the difficult life that wholehearted, God-centered virtue requires. This is true throughout the Greco-Roman virtue tradition as well as in the Jewish Scriptures. Aristotle motivates his followers to the often difficult way of virtue with the great reward/promise of *eudaimonia*, or flourishing. The Jewish Scriptures, especially the Wisdom literature, offer constant promise of life, flourishing, safety, and security through their many asherisms and hopes. This is not the opposite of grace or covenant, but is the universal God-human mechanism of motivation. It can be perverted, no doubt, like all loves and desires. One can come to view God mechanistically and pursue virtue from a disordered, non-*teleios* state of being. But God is not shy to reveal himself as a reward-offering Being,

---

56. See 1 Sam. 22:21; 1 Kings 8:32; Pss. 18:20–26; 58:1; Prov. 11:18; 22:4; Isa. 49:4; 62:11; 1 Cor. 4:5; Col. 3:23–24; Heb. 11:6; James 1:12.

appealing to his creatures to pursue the way of being that will offer them the only sure and true flourishing (cf. Matt. 16:27).

Closely related, the second concept in 6:1–21 that evokes the world of virtue and flourishing is the reception of glory or honor or praise (*doxa*) from others. Throughout the ancient world, including specifically within the virtue and wisdom traditions, a just and appropriate promised reward is the honor that comes from living virtuously, wisely, and uprightly. Such honor is the highest commodity in most ancient cultures.[57] This is a natural and expected fruit or consequence of a way of being in the world that accords with what is right. This is the external, community aspect of flourishing (*eudaimonia*) that matches the internal satisfaction of virtue. Indeed, the external honor is a helpful indicator and enhancer of the internal virtuous life.

In 6:1–21 this aspect of human flourishing is both assumed as natural and good, yet it can be explored further because of its great potential for disorder and perversion. The hypocrites' problem in these verses is not that they are wanting honor from virtuous living but that (1) they are not pursuing virtue out of a whole heart (= hypocrisy), and (2) they are pursuing this honor not from the heavenly Father but from earthly humans. Receiving glory/honor/praise from others is not inherently bad, nor is even "boasting" if the basis of one's confidence is sure.[58] But for any believer the greatest value must be receiving glory/honor/praise from God himself. Sinful humanity very easily distorts and perverts this and begins seeking honor from the wrong sources and for its own sake, not as the natural, motivating reward for God-centered virtue (cf. Jer. 2:13). This is where the problem lies and it is an inner-person problem.

This is precisely the issue Jesus addresses here repeatedly and at length. He is appealing to his hearers to avoid the foolish and disjointed hypocrisy of non-God-oriented virtue. It is not wholehearted and therefore will ultimately disappoint; "they already have their reward in full," the kind of reward that moth and rust will destroy and thieves will steal. Even as the wisdom and

---

57. Resources for the study of honor in the ancient world include David deSilva, *Honor, Patronage, Kinship, and Purity: Unlocking New Testament Culture* (Downers Grove, IL: IVP Academic, 2000); Jerome H. Neyrey, *Honor and Shame in the Gospel of Matthew* (Louisville: Westminster John Knox, 1998); Jackson Wu, *Saving God's Face: A Chinese Contextualization of Salvation through Honor and Shame*, EMSDS (Pasadena, CA: William Carey International University Press, 2012).

58. "Boast" is a common translation of the Greek *kauchaomai* but is probably too negative of a term in English now to gloss this concept, which means more generally "putting one's confidence in," rightly or wrongly. In the NT usage, human boasting is bad (e.g., Rom. 3:27; 4:2; Gal. 6:13), but boasting in one's work under God is appropriate (e.g., 2 Cor. 10:8–16; Gal. 6:4), and boasting in the Lord is true worship (e.g., 1 Cor. 1:31; 2 Cor. 10:17; Gal. 6:14; Phil. 3:3).

virtue teachers of old would appeal to children to live well by picturing for them the disasters of foolish living and the peace and flourishing of wisdom (cf. Prov. 1–9), so too Jesus as a virtue/wisdom teacher invites his hearers into the way of God-centered being in the world that will secure flourishing now and in God's coming kingdom.

A third and final way that 6:1–21 evokes the virtue/wisdom tradition is also related to the first two: it is the description and condemnation of hypocrisy. For most English speakers today, the word "hypocrisy" communicates a wrong way of life wherein someone is inconsistent in behavior and especially inconsistent regarding what they say is right and what they actually do in their own (private) behavior. This is certainly a kind of hypocrisy and deserves condemnation. But the kind of hypocrisy that Jesus is addressing here is, like the issue of seeking honor and praise, much more nuanced. The reason Jesus calls these practitioners of piety "hypocrites" is not because they really do not give alms, pray, and fast, but because they do so without a whole heart. Continuing with the same teaching in 5:17–48, Jesus again pushes the matter beyond mere externals to wholeness/integrity/virtue. The Pharisees' problem here is not a morality problem but a virtue one. Their hypocrisy does not consist of commending piety but then not doing it themselves. More subtly and more dangerously, they are actually practicing righteousness, but not from hearts that are in harmony with their actions, which is lack of wholeness. Jesus's followers need a "righteousness that surpasses that of the scribes and Pharisees." The point we are making here is that, again, this notion of wholeness evokes the wisdom and virtue tradition of human flourishing. This is the appeal Jesus makes.

9

Matthew 6:19–34

Overview

With 6:19–34 we have a new subsection within the central part of the Sermon (5:17–7:12). I have argued that the central section consists of three units: 5:17–48; 6:1–21; and 6:19–7:12. The third unit has a consistent theme of greater righteousness in relationship to the world, addressing first greater righteousness in relation to the goods of the world (6:19–34) and then in relation to the people of the world (7:1–6), followed by a conclusion in 7:7–11. I will comment on the two parts of this unit in two separate chapters on 6:19–34 and 7:1–12, respectively.

The preceding section of the Sermon (6:1–21) is the center of the center and climaxes with the very epicenter of the Sermon, the Lord's Prayer (6:7–15). With 6:19–34 we are going down the other side of the Sermon's mountain, having reached its apex with the Prayer.

The descent is tied closely together through the means of a link-word technique.[1] Throughout 6:19–7:12 there are several topics discussed and linked together, often by jumping from one topic to the next by some allusive sidestep. Also, as has been discussed, 6:19–21 serves a double-duty role as the climactic conclusion to 6:1–21 *and* as the introduction to the following unit, 6:19–34. The link centers on the overlapping ideas of treasure, reward, and money. For 6:1–21, the reference in 6:19–21 is to metaphorical treasure, meaning the

---

1. See Bruce Longenecker, *Rhetoric at the Boundaries: The Art and Theology of the New Testament Chain-Link Transitions* (Waco: Baylor University Press, 2005); and the discussion of this on pp. 130–31 in chap. 5 above.

reward of praise, honor, and glory that God the Father gives to those who seek
him with a whole heart. In 6:19–34 the treasure of 6:19–21 refers to actual
money, the main topic of greater righteousness in this portion.

This new unit explores how the goods of this world, the material possessions of life—and humans' natural anxiety about this—relate to being a
whole, virtuous person who experiences the greater righteousness. Human
flourishing at the physical level and the way of being in the world that accords
with this are the issues that Jesus addresses in this section.

Matthew 6:19–34: Greater Righteousness in Relation to the Goods of This World

Matthew 6:19–21

> [19]Do not lay up for yourselves treasures on the earth, where moth and
> rust disfigure and where thieves can break in and steal. [20]Rather, lay up
> treasures for yourselves in heaven where moth and rust cannot disfigure
> and where thieves cannot break in and steal. [21]For where your treasure
> is there also will be your heart.

Because these verses make up a sectional overlap, serving also as the conclusion to 6:1–21, we have already discussed many of the details in the previous
chapter of this commentary. In short, these verses give an appeal to human
flourishing based on the wisdom metaphor of two ways of being in the world,
one foolish and one wise. At the same time, the appeal ties into the greater
theme of whole-person/inner-person righteousness through the concluding
aphorism (6:21), which declares that whatever people value is who they truly
are. In the unit of 6:19–34, this point is explicated with regard to the issue of
physical accruements and the money that provides for living in this world.
The principle stated most clearly and practically is that one's relationship to
money is not a neutral matter but affects and reflects the inner person.

The logic of these verses is that there are two ways to relate to money. One
is to value it greatly because of the security and pleasure it brings. To lay up
treasures for oneself is inherently attractive and even has the appearance of
wisdom.[2] But Jesus subverts this apparent human wisdom by appealing not to
altruism (people *are* still encouraged to lay up treasures for themselves in v. 20)
but to true, spiritual, divine wisdom—that all human money is susceptible

---

2. Cf. the parable of the rich man and the bigger barns he plans in Luke 12:13–21. It would
miss the point of this teaching to prohibit savings accounts or budgeting, even as we saw in
Matt. 6:1–21 that the prohibitions cannot be understood universally.

to decay, loss, theft, destruction, and deterioration. It is not a matter of *if* human treasures will eventually be lost somehow but only a matter of *when*.

The other way of relating to money, then, is the wise way that will result in flourishing. The truly wise and righteous person will not store up treasures in an unsafe place. Even as only a fool would invest millions in a Ponzi scheme of overseas jewel mines, so too will the wise person avoid foolish treasure keeping. Instead, he or she will live in such a way with regard to money that their investment is not lost because it is based on the permanent reality of the kingdom of heaven.

Structurally, 6:19–21 continues the *kəlāl ûpərāṭ* pattern of the central section of the Sermon, here serving as the heading or thesis statement for the examples to follow. This section, 6:19–34, which concerns greater righteousness in relation to money, consists of two smaller topics/examples—on being singular versus whole (6:22–24) and on worry (6:25–34). Dale Allison also notes a pattern that spans 6:19–7:11, an exhortation followed by two short parables or metaphors (6:19–24 and 7:1–6). This is followed in both sections by words of encouragement about the heavenly Father's care (6:25–34 and 7:7–11) that are worded very similarly.[3] The result is a structure like this:

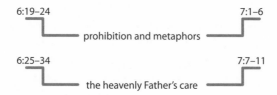

Matthew 6:22–24

> [22]*The eye is the lamp of the body. Therefore, if your eye is whole and generous then your whole body will be enlightened.* [23]*But if your eye is evil and greedy then your whole body will be darkened. Thus, if the light that is in you is darkness, what darkness that is!* [24]*No one is able to serve two lords, for the one he will hate and the other he will love, or he will be devoted to the one and think little of the other. You are not able to serve money and God.*

Typically in Bible translations and in many commentaries, 6:22–24 is broken into two distinct sections (6:22–23 and 6:24). The choice to treat this as one

3. Dale C. Allison Jr., *Studies in Matthew: Interpretation Past and Present* (Grand Rapids: Baker Academic, 2005), 187–93. See also W. D. Davies and Dale C. Allison Jr., *A Critical and Exegetical Commentary on the Gospel according to Saint Matthew*, vol. 1, *Introduction and Commentary on Matthew 1–7*, ICC (Edinburgh: T&T Clark, 2004), 626.

unit here reflects an understanding of the underlying unity of these verses and enables us to better perceive the consistent structure and flow of material in 6:19–34. While at first it may not appear to be a singular argument, 6:22–24 does indeed say one thing. These are not random sayings placed next to each other. It is part of the overall structure of 6:19–34, with the *kəlāl*/heading of 6:19–21 referencing money, followed by this first of two *pərāṭîm*/explanations in 6:22–24 and 6:25–34.

The reason 6:22–24 has often been broken up is twofold: (1) It is not immediately apparent to the modern reader how the image of the light and dark eye (6:22–23) and serving God and money (6:24) go together; and (2) there *is* somewhat of a transition between 6:22–23 and 6:24, though it is a natural shift from illustration to application, not a break into a new topic. We will return to these interrelations below after addressing 6:22–23.

Overall, these short, pithy verses are rich in metaphor and play on words, making it very difficult to translate them well into English. At the highest end of language usage—the poetic—translation is the most difficult because each word and phrase is thick with evocations from the original cultural encyclopedia. This is certainly the case with 6:22–24; the translation difficulties are legion. For example, how does the metaphor of the eye being a lamp work, and how does this relate to being full of light or darkness? How shall we translate *haplous* in verse 22—"whole," "sound," "healthy," "clear," "good," "generous," "single"? How are we to understand the word *mamōna* in verse 24? Is it best rendered with "money," or is there some reason to create a transliteration into English with "mammon," as many translations do?[4]

The metaphor of the eye as the lamp of the body has a number of different possible interpretations. Various scholars have debated how to understand this image based on what is called either the intromission or extramission view of sight in the ancient world. The difference between these views concerns whether ancient people thought about light/images going into the eye from outside (intromission, as modern people think of it today) or rather as the eye reflecting and projecting what is inside (extramission). There are good arguments to be made for the existence of both views in the ancient world as well as in Matthew's usage, and it is not entirely clear which is functioning here.[5]

---

4. For assorted reasons like these, Hans Dieter Betz describes 6:22–23 as "one of the most difficult and yet most interesting passages" of the Sermon (*Essays on the Sermon on the Mount* [1985; Minneapolis: Fortress, 2009], 438).

5. The strongest proponent of the extramission interpretation is Dale Allison. See Davies and Allison, *Matthew 1–7*, 635–41; Dale C. Allison Jr., "The Eye as a Lamp, Q 11:34–36: Finding the Sense," in *The Jesus Tradition in Q* (Harrisburg, PA: Trinity Press International, 1997), 133–67. Charles Quarles attempts to dismantle Allison's argument, though I am not convinced

For example, just within Matthew's usage one could argue that the strong internal/external person theme is at play here with the idea that the light or darkness inside of a person comes out in one's actions (being generous or greedy in relation to possessions); even as Jesus says elsewhere, it is what is inside a person, not what goes in, that defiles him or her because this is where the heart is (15:10–20). This would accord with the extramission view. On the other hand, one could argue that the way the metaphor in 6:22–23 works is that one's actions or way of being in the world (single and generous versus evil and stingy) create in us light or darkness, based on the "will be" in verses 22 and 23. This would be an intromission understanding.

While I am inclined to see the extramission view as the strongest understanding from the ancient world and the one that makes the most sense of Matthew overall, there is wisdom in not getting stuck on this debate, recognizing that either way the point is that the eye is a metaphorical window between the inside and the outside of a person.[6] This is clearly a major Matthean and Sermon theme—the organic connection between the inside and the outside of the person and the necessity of integration/wholeness for true righteousness.

This theme is crucial for understanding how to interpret the key word *haplous* in 6:22. In its most general and foundational sense, *haplous* refers to "singleness," seen in part by its contrast with *diplous*, "double, consisting of two."[7] *Haplous* does not mean "healthy" as many translations render it. It is the ancient idea of singularity or wholeness, the center of the idea of virtue that the whole Sermon has been promoting. It is connected to the Hebrew *tāmîm* and the Greek *teleios*, both of which have been explored above in chapter 3.

Wholeness as a root concept can take on many hues and connotations depending on the context. In the ancient Jewish context, when discussed in

he does so completely. See Quarles, *Sermon on the Mount: Restoring Christ's Message to the Modern Church* (Nashville: B&H, 2011), 244–47.

6. Ulrich Luz observes that although it appears initially that the point is the eye metaphor, continued reading reveals that this metaphor really serves rhetorically to get to a larger point in what is to follow (*Matthew 1–7: A Commentary*, rev. ed., trans. James E. Crouch, Hermeneia [Minneapolis: Fortress, 2007], 333). Considering Matthew's metaphor in light of rabbinic sources, Sinai Tamas Turan suggests that the combination of reference to "body" and "eye" may be connected to the Jewish teachings about the importance of examining the body of a bride-to-be when her eyes are apparently bad. These "physiognomic-ethical" teachings view the eye not as the mirror of the soul per se, but of the body, and then figuratively of the character of the person. See Turan, "A Neglected Rabbinic Parallel to the Sermon on the Mount (Matthew 6:22–23; Luke 11:34–36)," *JBL* 127.1 (2008), 90.

7. In yet another example of the way the Letter of James corresponds to the Sermon, one can note the overlap with *dipsychos* (double-minded, double-souled) in James 4:8 (cf. the Hebrew "divided" in Ps. 119:113). Also closely related is *-diplokardia* (double-heartedness) in *Did.* 5.1 and *Barn.* 20.1. See Quarles, *Sermon on the Mount*, 249.

conjunction with money and the goods of the world, *haplous* communicates the sense of "generosity" and "kindness"—singularity or wholeness that is free from envy and greed and malice, so whole-person generosity.[8] This is clearly the literary context here, with the heading of 6:19–21 introducing the theme of treasure, 6:24 emphasizing the choice between God and money, and 6:25–34 unpacking the soul-splitting danger of anxiety about the goods of this world.

Therefore, I have chosen to translate *haplous* with the phrase "whole and generous" to communicate the double meaning and play on words that *haplous* would easily communicate to Matthew's hearers. Matthew's word choice is a brilliant play that works well in the Sermon, tying in to the broader theme of wholeness and the more specific discussion of money. It does not map easily onto today's Western cultural encyclopedia, making it difficult to translate and certainly losing the pleasure of the poetic play.

Corroborative evidence that this is the best way to understand *haplous ophthalmos* (whole and generous eye) is found by noting the strong antithetical parallelism that 6:22–23 is built upon. The paired contrast to the whole and generous eye is the *ponēros ophthalmos*, "evil eye." The evil eye in the ancient world was especially associated with greediness, envy, and stinginess, especially when used in the context of material possessions. For example, Deut. 15:7–10 exhorts the people of God not to be stingy toward one another, in the Septuagint rendering: "Do not let your eye be evil [*ponēreusētai*] toward your brother" (Deut. 15:9). Proverbs 23:6 and 28:22 also describe a greedy or stingy person as having an evil eye.[9] Tobit 4:16 commands the giving of one's surplus as an alm, not letting the eye be envious/jealous (*phthonesatō*) when giving the gift. Even closer to home is an important text in Matthew in which he revisits this issue and refers to *ho ponēros ophthalmos* (the evil eye). This later occurrence is in the uniquely Matthean parable of the laborers in the vineyard in 20:1–16 (with "the evil eye" in 20:15). In this parable the climactic point, given in the words of the vineyard owner (who clearly represents God), is that disciples should not be envious or greedy—have an "evil eye"—toward the riches and blessings of others because it is God who is both just and sovereign.

Thus, in parallel with the translation of *haplous* in 6:22 as "whole and generous," I have rendered *ponēros* as another double-meaning phrase, "evil

---

8. See Luz, *Matthew 1–7*, 333–34. Quarles observes similar connections such as Prov. 22:9, which refers to the generous person as having a good eye (*Sermon on the Mount*, 248–49). We may note that the related adverb *haplōs* can mean "generously" (James 1:5) and the noun *haplotēs* can communicate "generosity" (Rom. 12:8; 2 Cor. 8:2; 9:11, 13). Cf. also *T. Iss.* 3:8.

9. Quarles, *Sermon on the Mount*, 248, mentions these texts in addition to several others in Second Temple Jewish literature.

and greedy." This maintains the dual-referencing parallelism that Matthew has intimated: the opposite of wholeness and generosity is being evil and greedy. The metaphor of light and darkness is entirely appropriate here then as well. Each person is aligned either with the light/good or the dark/evil, here manifested by how they approach the issue of money with respect to the heart or inner person. Their alignment results in a state of the soul as being either light or dark. In typical poetic wisdom form there is no in-between option envisioned.

Thus 6:22–23 flows naturally from 6:19–21 as a continuation of the same discussion of how disciples are to relate to money. Even as heaven and earth are a strong contrastive pair, so too are light and dark. The theme of treasure stays the same while the timbre changes from an appeal not to be foolish to a more direct warning against the soul darkness of greed.

Notice also the very significant point that for the Sermon "evil" is demarcated as the opposite of "single" or "whole." Even as righteousness is defined in the Sermon as virtuous wholeness, so too evil is typically depicted as the opposite of this—lack of integrity (hypocrisy) and doubleness, manifested in a wide variety of ways, here regarding money.

This understanding of 6:22–23 leads directly into the applied meaning that follows in 6:24. Because of this sharp light and dark contrast and its either-or reality, disciples are reminded that "no one can serve two masters . . . you cannot serve God and money." Again, continuing the flow from 6:19–21 into 6:22–23, there is a strong contrast placed before the hearer—heaven versus earth, light versus darkness, God versus money, all speaking to the issue of one's relationship to money. Thus, 6:24 is not a new idea or separate proverbial saying but the climactic point of 6:22–24—one must be singular in devotion to God.

One translation issue arises here that is worth noting—how to render *mamōna*. Many English translations have chosen to transliterate it with "mammon" rather than translate it, while others gloss this word as "money." The Greek word appears in the New Testament only here and in the Lukan parallel three times (Luke 16:9, 11, 13). In Greek this is actually a transliteration of the Aramaic word referring to property, possessions, or money.[10] Why Matthew chose to retain an Aramaic transliteration rather than translate it himself into a Greek word for either "money," "treasure," or "material possessions" is impossible to know for sure. Maybe it is simply the power of the well-known phrase from the Jesus Tradition in his own day. Or it may be that by keeping the foreign word as a transliteration it adds an element

10. See Quarles, *Sermon on the Mount*, 255.

of personification—God is pitted against Mammon, reminiscent of ancient Israelite showdowns between Yahweh and the false idols of the world.[11] The emphasis on oneness and singularity in this passage has already potentially evoked the Shema's emphasis on God's oneness and the necessity of whole-hearted, singular devotion to him (Deut. 6:4–5). All combined, this makes for a powerful rhetorical point. This evocation is difficult to discern in modern English readings, however, and I have chosen instead to render the word with a gloss of "money." This means more than "physical money" here, but the broader sense of "the goods of the world that money can buy."

We may make two final observations about 6:24 that unify the image-laden exhortation. First, note that, consistent with the rest of the Sermon's focus on the inner person, the language of this verse is not merely legal or cognitive but is heavily heart-focused, whole-person verbiage. Jesus says that one cannot serve both God and money because it is a matter of the heart—one will be hated and the other loved; one will be an object of devotion and the other despised. Choosing between God's kingdom and the goods of the world is not merely a matter of cool thinking; as in all ways of being in the world, it is ultimately a matter of the heart or inner person. As in Jesus's previous teachings in the Sermon, the ante has been upped; one cannot flirt with money as if it has nothing to do with one's inner person. As the proverbial wisdom has it, "the love of money is the root of all evil" (1 Tim. 6:10).

Flowing from this point and closely related is the second observation about Matt. 6:24: singularity/wholeness is the great emphasis. The image of the failure of serving *two* masters is appropriate and powerful in light of the consistent theme of singularity throughout the Sermon. The wholeness/virtue/inside-outside consistency that has been the theme of Jesus's teachings here finds in many ways its clearest expression in these short verses. Even as it is impossible to live for the praise of others and for the praise of God (6:1–21), so too it is impossible to live greedily focused on money and dedicated to God.[12] This is fundamentally impossible because disciples must be singular, whole creatures. The following section (6:25–34) will continue to unpack this idea, providing the ultimate solution in 6:33 with its exhortation to seek first God's kingdom and his righteousness.

11. See Martin Hengel, *Property and Riches in the Early Church: Aspects of a Social History of Early Christianity*, trans. John Bowden (Philadelphia: Fortress, 1974), 24.

12. H. Benedict Green points out that the integrity of the single, undivided heart of the macarism in 5:8 is contrasted with the one divided by the cravings of the *yēṣer hāra'* (evil inclination)—hunger and thirst, sexual desire, avarice. Avarice is especially important for Matthew and is the connecting theme of 6:19–24. See Green, *Matthew, Poet of the Beatitudes* (Edinburgh: T&T Clark, 2001), 240.

Matthew 6:25–34

[25]*On account of this I say to you: Do not be anxious about the things of your life, what you will eat or what you will drink,*[13] *nor about your body, how you will clothe yourselves, for is not life more than food and the body more than clothing?*

[26]*Consider the birds of the air, that they do not sow seeds, nor harvest crops, nor gather it into barns, and yet your Father in heaven feeds them. Are you not much more valuable than they?* [27]*Who among you is able to add even an hour to his life by being anxious?*

[28]*And why are you anxious about clothing? Consider the flowers of the field, how they grow; they do not work or spin thread for cloth.* [29]*Yet I tell you that not even Solomon in all his glory was clothed like one of these.* [30]*But if God in this way clothes the grass of the fields, which is here today but tomorrow will be thrown into the fire, how much more will he clothe you, people of little faith?*

[31]*Therefore, do not be anxious, saying—"What will we eat?" or "What will we drink?" or "What will we wear?"—*[32]*for the gentiles seek after all these things and your heavenly Father knows that you need all these things.* [33]*Instead, seek first the kingdom and the Father's righteousness, and all these things will be given to you.*

[34]*Therefore, do not be anxious about tomorrow for tomorrow will be anxious for itself. Each day has enough of its own trouble.*

Matthew 6:25–34 stands as a subunit with its own inherent logic and structure while also being the concluding portion of the broader section of 6:19–34. Internally, it is clear by the threefold repetition at the beginning, middle, and end that the main point of 6:25–34 is an exhortation for the follower of Jesus *not to be anxious* (6:25, 31, 34), with the solution given as a reorientation to the kingdom (6:33). In each case this counsel is introduced by a "therefore," indicating that it is the conclusion of a preceding argument and the "so what" application.

Following the *kəlāl ûpərāṭ* pattern throughout the central section of the Sermon, the command not to worry / be anxious is found in 6:25 and then is followed by two practical examples or illustrations of areas of potential worry. The first concerns daily sustenance, eating and drinking. The second concerns clothing. In both instances Jesus makes a typical "lesser to greater" argument

---

13. The manuscript witnesses for the phrase "or what you will drink" are mixed and difficult to decide upon with certainty. Several important early manuscripts do not have this phrase while others do. Sound arguments can be made for both its inclusion and exclusion. On balance I have decided that it is likely original. See the comments in Luz, *Matthew 1–7*, 338n1.

to persuade his hearers of the foolishness of worry.[14] In addition to this broader *kəlāl ûpərāṭ* pattern, we can also discern a more specific structure within:

General Heading (*kəlāl*): "Do not worry about your life, what you will eat or drink, nor about your body, what you will wear. Is not life more than eating and the body more than about being clothed?" (6:25)

First Topic: Sustenance
Positive Example—Birds of the air are fed by the heavenly Father (6:26a)
Lesser-to-Greater Argument—You are much more valuable (6:26b)
Reproof for Foolishness of Anxiety—No one can add to life by worry (6:27)

Second Topic: Clothing
Positive Example—The flowers of the fields grow and are glorious (6:28–29)
Lesser-to-Greater Argument—You are much more valuable (6:30)
Reproof for Foolishness of Anxiety—Those outside the community desperately seek after these things (6:31–32)

Concluding Exhortation and Rationale:
Seek first God's kingdom and righteousness and all will be added (6:33)
Do not worry, for each day has enough trouble (6:34)

The preceding unit (6:22–24) concluded with a choice between God and "mammon." Matthew 6:25–34 continues the idea with the things or goods of life that money can buy. I chose to gloss *mamōna* as simply "money" in 6:24, though we can see that its broader sense is unpacked in 6:25 with the two examples of sustenance and clothing. In this broad opening statement a pair of examples is given that plays on the words "soul" (*psychē*) and "body" (*sōma*), which often can be used to contrast the interior and exterior aspects of the person. Here, however, the word pair is functioning merismatically[15] to

14. This kind of argumentation is widespread in the ancient world. In the rabbinic tradition it is referred to as *qal wāḥômer* (light and heavy) and is tied to Rabbi Hillel, who was active in the time period just before Jesus. In Roman rhetoric it is called *a minori ad maius* (from the lesser to the greater). See David Turner, *Matthew*, BECNT (Grand Rapids: Baker Academic, 2008), 199.

15. A merism/merismus is a figure of speech that uses two opposite words to communicate a totality. The Greek *psychē* is difficult to translate into English because its breadth of possible meanings does not map clearly onto English concepts. "Things of life" is an attempt to communicate the function of *psychē* here.

encompass two illustrative examples of the basic concerns of life, sustenance and clothing.

Regarding the first illustration of sustenance—what one should eat or drink—the comparison is made to birds. Birds live a life of daily sustenance; they do not engage in the growing of crops or store up food they have harvested (6:26), yet God provides for them daily. If this is true of these lesser creatures, how much more will it be so for his highly valued humans? Jesus then adds what amounts to a mild rebuke—worrying about what one will eat and drink will add not one bit to the life being sought (6:27).[16] This is, like the rest of the Sermon, an appeal to wisdom and not foolishness. Hearers are invited to consider the foolishness of anxiety when anxiety can do absolutely nothing to improve one's security. This is reminiscent of the posture of dependence that Matthew has already extolled, both in the Beatitudes (5:3, 4, 5) and in the second half of the Lord's Prayer, with its petition for God to provide the food we need for daily sustenance (6:11); God-dependent prayer is the solution, not sustenance-focused anxiety.

Regarding clothing, Jesus makes a parallel argument. With equally memorable and poetic images, Jesus now directs his hearers to direct their mental gaze no longer to the skies ("the birds of heaven") but to the ground ("the flowers of the fields"). His listeners should consider the beauty and glory of the wildflowers growing ubiquitously.[17] Flowers are even more glorious than the famously garbed King Solomon. These beautiful flowers are merely temporal—as grass they are here today and tomorrow used as fuel.[18]

Beyond these agricultural resonances, one can also discern canonical evocations such as Isa. 40:6–8. This text was likely not far from the surface in the mind of the speaker (and hearers) with its strong poetic contrast between the permanent glory of God's words and the temporary glory of humanity, described as grass and flowers that wither and fade. Isaiah and some early form of Matt. 6:28–30 appear to be the inspiration for James 1:9–11, which

16. More strictly, the wording concerns adding to one's height or physical stature, but this appears to be functioning here as a hyperbolic metaphor referring to the impossibility of adding to one's length of life. English translations vary in how they gloss the expression. Either way, the point is that anxiety cannot bring about the desired good; only God controls one's physical height and length of life.

17. Luz points out that the Greek *krinon* does not necessarily mean "lilies" but can be a more generic term for "field flowers" (thus, "weeds"), not "garden flowers" (*Matthew 1–7*, 343). This makes better sense of the rest of the argument.

18. Grass being used for fuel, as well as how this correlates with flowers in the previous verse, seems odd to many in the modern West. The image works through an understanding that wildflowers, glorious in beauty as they grow in the grassy fields, would fade and become brittle, dried stems that together with the thick grasses would be cut and used as fuel in fires.

uses these same words and images of withering and perishing flowers and grasses to rebuke the person who arrogantly relies on his wealth, thus providing a profound rereading of the theme of Matt. 6:19–34.

Here again is the lesser-to-greater argument: If these short-lived flowers are clothed this beautifully, how much more will God provide for those whom he loves? And then at the end of 6:30, as in 6:27, Jesus adds a slight yet still pointed reproof. Using Matthean language that will appear as a description of the disciples elsewhere, Jesus calls his listeners "you of little faith."[19]

Matthew 6:31 sums up these illustration-laden arguments by repeating the exhortation against worrying. The disciple should not say to himself or herself, "What shall we eat or drink or wear?" This is followed by another reason for this in 6:32, again in the form of a mild reproof. When a disciple lives in anxiety, going around muttering these anxious questions, he or she is living just as a gentile or pagan does. This is reminiscent of the introductory words to the Lord's Prayer, which also emphasizes looking to the Father for daily provisions (6:11), with its identical reproof: "In your praying do not babble on like the gentiles, for they reason that with their many words they will be heard. Do not be like them, for your Father knows what you need before you ask him" (6:7–8).[20]

These references to gentiles are evocative statements, creating a new set of people-defining categories: the ones outside the kingdom (the "gentiles," to use the language of the Jewish Scriptures) are now the ones whose way of being is marked by anxiety because of their doubleness of living. By way of contrast, the followers of Christ are the ones who have God as their heavenly Father, the one who knows their needs and will provide for them. So once again Matthew's Jesus has redefined the people of God based not on ethnicity but on this new kind of righteousness, this new way of being in the world that Jesus is teaching (cf. the discussion of the theme of gentiles in chap. 4 above).

19. This neologism (*oligopistos*) appears but five times in the biblical corpus, four of which are in Matthew (6:30; 8:26; 14:31; 16:8). The fifth is in Luke 12:28 and a parallel to Matt. 6:30, indicating this was likely a Matthean word that Luke picked up on either directly from Matthew or from a shared tradition. The other instances in Matthew do not occur in Jesus's teaching but are his response to the disciples when they doubt his power and provision. The conceptual overlap between these occurrences is discernible. According to some Jewish traditions (e.g., *Mekilta* on Exod. 16:4; *Targum Pseudo-Jonathan* on Num. 11:32), one type of person described as having imperfect faith is the Israelite who wanted to gather manna and quail on the Sabbath (contrary to trusting in God's provision). This notion may be informing Matthew's usage here. See Luz, *Matthew 1–7*, 343n49.

20. Looking ahead in the Sermon, the theme of the Father's provision will appear again in 7:7–11. The contrast used there is the generosity of worldly, "evil" fathers versus that of God rather than the trust of gentiles versus that of believers, but both passages hinge on a comparison made regarding provision.

This passage reaches a climax with the important saying in 6:33—"But seek first the kingdom of God and his righteousness and all these things will be added to you." This verse is a thermographic hot spot in the Sermon with its reference to both the kingdom and righteousness, two key ideas throughout Matt. 5–7.[21] Leland White points out that "kingdom/rule" in this verse is put into close (Semitic) parallel with "righteousness."[22] This indicates that the rule of God and his righteousness are not two separate items to be sought but one. "Thus, the total execution of the divine demand is again the meaning of righteousness."[23] This recalls the macarism of 5:10, where those who are practicing righteousness (and receiving persecution as a result) are said to be possessors of the kingdom of heaven.[24]

The seeking "first" is also very important as a word that here speaks in chorus with the issue of singularity that marks the ethical view of the Sermon. "First" is to be understood logically more than chronologically; the first thing is that one's heart is the singular aim and goal. Taken together, then, the exhortation in 6:33 is a broad vision or marching orders for the Christian way of being in the world—being one who is dedicated to God's coming reign and the kind of Christ-centered righteous behavior that marks the kingdom.[25] In this sense, seeking first the kingdom of God and his righteousness is basically synonymous with the macarism of "hungering and thirsting for righteousness" (5:6).[26] By way of contrast, this seeking is the opposite of the gentiles' seeking after the meeting of their own needs in the previous verse.

Matthew 6:33 is also important as a testimony to the characteristic role that the Sermon plays in Jesus's ministry: it is simultaneously a piece of Second Temple Jewish wisdom literature *and* a manifestation of Jesus's emphasis on God's eschatological kingdom. As Hans Dieter Betz notes, the concept

21. On both of these topics, see chap. 4 above. Betz also sees this verse as an important part of the Sermon, emphasizing not only the themes of kingdom and righteousness, but also that of seeking, which he notes is a repeated, positive idea in the Sermon (7:7, 8; cf. 7:14) (*Essays*, 97).

22. Cf. Luke 12:31, which has only "kingdom" and no reference to the favorite Matthean theme of righteousness.

23. Leland J. White, "Grid and Group in Matthew's Community: The Righteousness/Honor Code in the Sermon on the Mount," *Semeia* 35 (1986): 79.

24. See R. T. France, *The Gospel of Matthew*, NICNT (Grand Rapids: Eerdmans, 2007), 271.

25. Note again that *dikaiosynē* in the Sermon does not refer to an imputed legal standing that one can gain from God through Christ; rather, in keeping with its more normal and widespread use, it refers to behavior that accords with God's nature, will, and coming kingdom. Thus, the typical Protestant reading of 6:33 as exhorting people to seek after Christ's imputed righteousness, as true and helpful as this is as a broader theological truth, has nothing to do with what this verse is saying. See chap. 4's discussion of righteousness in the Sermon.

26. This insight comes from Charles Lee Irons's work on the meaning of *dikaiosynē* in Matthew in his *The Righteousness of God: A Lexical Examination of the Covenant-Faithfulness Interpretation* (Tübingen: Mohr Siebeck, 2015), 265.

of seeking after the kingdom and the righteousness of God is foreign to the wisdom tradition, "and thus appears to be an aspect peculiar to the teaching of Jesus."[27] Jesus is more than another wisdom teacher or moral philosopher. At the same time, by adding the emphasis on seeking God's righteousness to his kingdom message, Jesus is indicating that the Christian life is not one of passivity, awaiting the coming eschaton. Rather, seeking first the kingdom is precisely the "concrete practice of righteousness as the Sermon on the Mount develops it";[28] it is the activity of the faithful disciple.

In the context of 6:19–34, this macro-level statement about seeking God's kingdom and righteousness serves as a concluding encouragement on the issue of one's goods and possessions regarding the matter of money. The final solution, then, to the anxiety-about-money problem is to set one's heart and mind to seeking God's way of being in the world and his coming reign, which promises to result in all of one's needs being truly met. Thus, the solution to anxiety is not a simplistic "Stop worrying," but a redirecting of the disciples' vision to the proper heart orientation, accompanied by a promise of provision.[29]

With the climactic sense of 6:33, we might wonder how 6:34 fits into this structure. Indeed, in some ways it does feel a bit like an afterthought or add-on; ending with 6:33 seems as if it would have been sufficient. However, 6:34 provides the rhetorically powerful *third* repeated exhortation against anxiety and thus provides a fitting reiterative conclusion to the entire unit of 6:19–34. This section began with the *kəlāl* idea that contrasted heavenly and earthly treasures, built on the treasure-heart principle (6:19–21). It ends with a memorable aphorism that serves as a life principle as the disciple looks to the present and the future. There is no need for anxiety because anxiety is living in worry about something that does not yet exist and will be dealt

27. Betz, *Essays*, 119. Coming from the angle of Jesus's audience, Luz states something comparable: These sayings are far from being "an expression of general theological wisdom" but are instead bound up with Jesus's message of the kingdom (*Matthew 1–7*, 345).

28. Luz, *Matthew 1–7*, 344.

29. The theodicy problem that the promise of 6:33 raises is the reality that God apparently does *not* always provide for all the physical needs of his children; plenty of faithful Christians have starved and lacked food, water, and clothing. This is, of course, not a NT problem alone but is a deep theological and personal concern throughout the Jewish Scriptures also (e.g., Pss. 73; 83; Job). Betz notes that Matt. 6:25–34 is in many ways an "apology for divine providence," stemming from a crisis that many ancient people experienced in wrestling with divine provision and suffering (*Essays*, 119). The Sermon is no different from the rest of Scripture in making true promises that reflect God's character and care but which all fly under the banner of God's mysterious providence and submission to his will in faith. Jesus himself provides the ultimate model of this posture in the garden of Gethsemane, where he seeks the Father's provision and deliverance but more deeply submits his prayer to the reality of "not my will but your will be done" (26:39).

with when it does—tomorrow's troubles. Each day's trouble, especially for the kingdom-seeking disciple, is enough. Or to follow the rhythmic, poetic play on words that Matthew provides—"Do not be anxious for tomorrow for tomorrow will be anxious for itself." Anxiety about the future reveals a focus too much on the things of this world and maintaining them, putting one into the foolish category of laying up earthly treasures (6:19).[30]

The big question that the argument of 6:25–34 raises is, why is this such a big issue? That is, why the rebukes in 6:27, 30, and 32? And especially, why does Jesus up the ante so high in 6:32 by making anxiety a matter of who is a true follower (those with the heavenly Father) and who is an outsider (gentile)?

The answer is that, consistent with the sustained argument throughout the Sermon, anxiety is an example of double-souledness; it is the opposite of the singleness that marks the whole-person virtue of the follower of Christ. As with the other kinds of examples Jesus gives throughout the Sermon, we do not have here the whole picture or a comprehensive catalog of every detail of the human life. These exhortations against anxiety about food and clothing are not arguing *against* the proverbial wisdom of preparedness or saving and planning for times of need; they are not saying that growing crops or owning more than one shirt (or a closet to hold them in) is wrong. Rather, these instructions are driving at the inner person or heart issue. The issues of food and clothing are treasure-heart matters (6:21). The person who lives in anxiety about providing for himself or herself reveals and perpetuates a double-heartedness, a splitting of the soul between the now (where the heavenly Father meets us) and an imagined (dreaded) future of need. This normal human experience is ultimately a lack of faith and therefore in need of instruction and reproof.

Matthew 6:19–34 and Human Flourishing

When we step back and examine 6:19–34 as a section, we can see that it flows logically as one unit. The *kalāl*, or heading, is laid out in 6:19–21, understood here to refer to real money and riches (as opposed to its more metaphorical use as "treasures in heaven" as part of 6:1–21). This leads naturally to the warning in 6:22–24 against double-souled greediness. Christian disciples must

30. Some interpreters have understood this passage to be speaking against planning and provision for the future, but as France points out, it is *worry* about tomorrow, not provision or planning for tomorrow that is condemned here (*Gospel of Matthew*, 267). The point of the passage overall is built on the contrast between trusting the Father and living in anxiety, not a contrast between planning or not.

be singular in devotion. If not, the result will be anxiety, which is the focus of the exhortation in 6:25–34. The alternative to doubleness, or put more positively, the way to serve God rather than money, is to seek first God's kingdom and his righteousness, which will result in gaining all that one needs (6:33), true human flourishing.[31]

Herein lies a deep irony of human existence. According to Jesus's teachings, when people seek to keep everything together and provide for themselves apart from God, the result is not the sought-after peace, but rather, anxiety. That is, there is an organic connection between the warning against greed in 6:22–24 and the exhortation against anxiety in 6:25–34. Greed *causes* anxiety. It is the non-God-directed heart that is laying up earthly treasures that ironically does *not* have peace. But the people who live like the flowers and birds, apparently foolish from the world's financial perspective, are the ones who are *free* from anxiety. They seek first God's kingdom and as a result get all their needs met without anxiety. This is not to say that *all* anxiety is caused by greed; there are many other sources of anxiety, real and perceived.[32] But it is to say that greed will inevitably result in the double-souled anxiety that is the opposite of the human flourishing to which Jesus is inviting his hearers.[33]

31. Later Matthew will use another agricultural image of flourishing (or lack thereof) in the paradigmatic parable of the sower (13:3–23), wherein what was sown among thorns is interpreted as one for whom the cares/anxieties (*merimna*, cognate of the verb used in 6:25–34) of the world and "the seductiveness of wealth" choke out the word and make the ground produce no fruit or abundance (13:22).

32. Turner sums up the issue well in saying that God does not promise an easy life for his children (cf. 5:10–12) and that his care "may entail poverty for some and wealth for others. Wealthy Christians are not necessarily greedy, and poor Christians are not necessarily free of anxiety about possessions" (*Matthew*, 202).

33. In Matthew's second major discourse, on being a witness in the world (10:1–42), the Father's provision versus anxiety and self-provision is also a core idea. The disciples are told not to seek to meet all their own supply needs (10:9–10), not to worry about how to answer when persecuted (10:19), and not to be afraid because they are much more valuable to the Father than sparrows (10:29–31).

10

Matthew 7:1–12

Overview

The final subsection of the central part of the Sermon to be discussed is
7:1–12. As noted above, 7:1–12 is actually part of the third and final portion
of the central part of the Sermon, which spans from 6:19 to 7:12. This unit
continues the theme of greater righteousness initiated in 5:17–20 and continued
throughout the Sermon. Here the notion of greater righteousness is applied
with regard to the disciples' relationship with the world, its goods (6:19–34),
and people (7:1–6).[1] The last portion of 7:1–12 is the concluding encouragement (7:7–11) and the overarching aphorism of 7:12, which concludes the
large unit of 5:17–7:12. We may represent the structure this way:

Greater Righteousness (GR) in Relation to the World (6:19–7:12)

    a. Introduction (6:19–21)

    b. GR in relation to the goods of this world (6:22–34)

---

1. Charles Quarles makes the intriguing suggestion that rather than a strong break at 7:1,
the broader context of 6:1 through much of chap. 7 is built around the issue of hypocrisy (the
word appears in 6:2, 5, 16; 7:5). He sees the two ills associated with hypocrisy that are addressed
in 6:1–34 (a focus on present reward rather than a heavenly one and a perverted set of priorities
that promotes materialism and anxiety). This is followed by a third symptom of hypocrisy:
hypocritical judgment. See Quarles, *Sermon on the Mount: Restoring Christ's Message to the
Modern Church* (Nashville: B&H, 2011), 283. While this argument has some merit and insight
(esp. seeing a consistent theme), overall the structure can be better explained with the theme
of greater righteousness, with hypocrisy as a subset of the opposite. Additionally, "hypocrite"
in 7:5 clearly functions differently than in 6:1–21 as a challenge to those *within* the faith community, not to the Pharisees.

c. GR in relation to the people of this world (7:1–6)

d. Conclusion (7:7–12)

Within 7:1–12 we encounter more of the pithy, applicable sayings that have made the Sermon so popular and memorable for two millennia. The command not to judge others, the image of having a plank of wood in one's eye, and the justly famous Golden Rule are all found in these short verses.

Yet at the same time, 7:1–12 presents a couple of difficulties for the interpreter seeking to understand the Sermon as a whole. The first is the vagueness of the meaning of 7:6, the most difficult verse to understand in the Sermon. The second is the question of how these verses hang together and make a coherent argument.

The latter question returns us to the perpetual issue of the structure of the Sermon. It is here at the end of the central part of the Sermon, just before the separate concluding section, that the structure becomes most unclear. Thus far it has not been overly difficult to trace the lines of Matthew's literary artistry. Here in 7:1–12 one is tempted to think that editorial fatigue and panic have set in for the evangelist. It may appear that Matthew has before him some real gems of Jesus-tradition sayings left in his memory chest, and here at the end in desperation he throws them together into a final hodgepodge. It is somewhat like the old contest in which the winner gets to run through a supermarket for two minutes, keeping for free everything she can throw into her basket. In the final seconds she ends up with some random items tossed in on an impulse just before entering the checkout line. Even particularly insightful scholars such as R. T. France despair of finding a satisfying way to see 7:1–11 as hanging together except in a very generic sense.[2] However, as has been argued already, there is in fact a consistent theme and structure to the whole, even if 7:1–12 initially seems more haphazard.

I will argue below that the theme or topos that ties this section together is that of evaluating or discerning correctly. This is an important wisdom instruction or paraenetic topic and thus is a fitting conclusion to the central teaching of the Sermon, even if the sayings collected here do not seem as intimately related to each other as we might desire.

Following the pattern observed previously, 7:1–12 is best understood in the *kəlāl ûpərāṭ* structure, thus:

• *kəlāl* = 7:1–2	On Evaluating Rightly
• *pərāṭ* = 7:3–11 (in two parts: 7:3–6, 7–11)	Regarding People and God
• Conclusion = 7:12	Concluding Aphorism

2. R. T. France, *The Gospel of Matthew*, NICNT (Grand Rapids: Eerdmans, 2007), 273.

Matthew 7:1–6: Greater Righteousness in Relation to the People of This World

Matthew 7:1–2

> [1]Do not judge unfairly, lest you be judged the same way. [2]For by the kind of judgment with which you judge others, you will be judged; and with whatever measure you measure to others, it will also be measured to you.[3]

In the structure suggested above, these opening verses (7:1–2) serve as the theme and main point of 7:1–12. They still flow naturally into the first example given in 7:3–6, but they also stand apart as the topos or heading. This *kəlāl* then finds its conclusion in the famous Golden Rule of 7:12, a generalized wisdom maxim to treat others as one would want to be treated, specifically here on the issue of how we evaluate or judge others. Taken together, this means that disciples should treat others how they would want to be treated, not judging or evaluating unfairly.

In a fundamental way the message of 7:1–2 is straightforward—in the God-ordained nature of the world and in his active justice, people reap what they sow (cf. Gal. 6:7–9). One's way of being in the world, whether it be judging people unfairly or not, determines one's experience of the world and ultimate *telos* or end. Anything else would be unjust and inconsistent with God's character and creation, which reflects his character. Thus, 7:1–2 heads this unit with a generalized, creation-based proverb about the wise way of being in the world: one must choose how to live in relation to others, and this will affect one's experience of others and even of God. If one has a condemning attitude toward others, this will be one's experience of the world; if one has a welcoming and accepting attitude, this will be one's experience. This is reminiscent of the fifth petition of the Lord's Prayer, concerning forgiving one another (6:12). The same logic is used in 6:14–15, the addendum to the Prayer that connects forgiving others with receiving forgiveness from God. The same proverbial wisdom is reiterated then in 7:12, the conclusion to this section.

Despite this basic point, there are two problems with how 7:1–2 is read and applied. The first problem is largely a result of a translation issue. The second problem is a function of a totalizing reading.

---

3. This translation is influenced especially by Donald Hagner, as seen in the addition of "unfairly" to clarify the sense of "judge" in 7:1, and the retention of the poetic repetition of "judgment . . . judge . . . judged" and "measure . . . measure . . . measured" in 7:2, which is typically lost in English translations. See Hagner, *Matthew 1–13*, WBC 33A (Nashville: Nelson, 1993), 167–70.

The translation issue concerns the key word in 7:1, often given in English as "judge." While this translation is familiar to English readers and is not completely wrong here, it narrows down the point being made to the issue of *condemnation* of others. This is because in English today "judge" (especially used as a verb) has come to mean almost exclusively "condemn." "Don't judge me" is a current cultural ethos, and it means on the modern English ear, "Don't condemn my actions."

The problem is that this use of "judge" as "condemn" is only a subset of the larger semantic range of the Greek word here, *krinō*, as well as the English word itself.[4] In the English of previous generations, "judge" still retained its more general sense of "evaluate, discern, separate, or decide." This is the role of a judge, one who listens, perceives, and decides what is *just* (notice the same root), and then dispensing *justice* (the same root again)—namely, favor, success, deliverance, safety, victory to the one who is in the right and condemnation and guilt to the one who is in the wrong. This discernment process is what it means to "judge" here.

It is an unfortunate turn in current English that the main, if not exclusive, evocation that "judge" creates in hearers is only the narrower, latter sense of the negative condemnation. This then distorts our sense of what justice is about—it is not just condemnation for the bad, but restoration of what is right, with its necessary good and bad consequences distributed accordingly.[5]

Thus, a better translation is "Do not judge unfairly." The point is not that all evaluations of others and situations must be avoided (see below) but rather that disciples must evaluate and discern properly and fairly. "One should not judge others more harshly or by a different standard than one judges oneself."[6] The focus of this teaching is on personal interrelationships. Scot McKnight describes the difference between judging and condemning as learning to distinguish moral discernment from personal condemnation.[7] France helpfully sums up the matter this way: This text deals with the "down-to-earth issue

4. France notes that *krinō* can be used for technical legal decisions but more generally for "forming judgments and reaching conclusions about both things and people" (*Gospel of Matthew*, 274).

5. This undue narrowing of our understanding of "judge" also affects one's reading of Holy Scripture in English. Many times translations will use the gloss "judge," insensitive to its broader meaning of "discern" or "evaluate," resulting in odd and even misleading translations. E.g., when the psalmist asks God to "judge" him or to "judge" the people of God, this does not mean "condemn," but "bring about justice" (cf. Pss. 7:8; 50:4; 72:2; 82:8; 98:9; and others).

6. Hagner, *Matthew 1–13*, 169. Hagner also points out the strong parallels to this idea in Jewish literature such as Sir. 18:20; *m. 'Abot* 1:6; *m. Soṭah* 1:7.

7. Scot McKnight, *The Sermon on the Mount*, The Story of God Bible Commentary (Grand Rapids: Zondervan, 2013), 227.

of unfairly critical attitudes to others, which, combined with a naïve lack of self-criticism, threaten to disrupt a close-knit community such as that of Jesus' first disciples."[8] Maybe the clearest (and earliest) exposition of this idea is found in James 2:12–13 and 4:11–12, which tie brothers and sisters judging each other to speaking evil against each other and judging the law itself and which emphasize that judgment without mercy will be measured to those who have not been merciful.

The same point can be seen in the poetic parallel in 7:2, shifting the language to a metaphor from the mercantile world: "measuring" properly. This idea is common in ancient Israelite literature as the idea of proper justice or even poetic justice: Samson's lustful eyes led him to sin, therefore the Philistines put his eyes out; Absalom gloried in his hair, therefore he was eventually hanged by his hair, and so on.[9] Again the exhortation concerns properly or fairly evaluating others, giving them a fair measure. This aligns with another crucial passage about forgiving others, the parable of the unforgiving servant in 18:21–35. The servant serves as a foil to proper measuring in that while he was forgiven a massive debt, he condemned his fellow servant for a very small debt.

This more nuanced understanding of how to translate and interpret *krinō* as "evaluate fairly" is related also to the second common problem in how these verses are read—the problem of totalization. Totalization here refers to the tendency to make one idea or verse the overriding principle by which everything else is evaluated and understood. The analog in politics would be a one-issue candidate, insensitive to how interrelated all the issues are and unaware of the nuance required to hold together a coherent worldview.

Matthew 7:1–2 has for some readers become *the* truth that Jesus is teaching, *the* principle by which all of the rest of Jesus's teachings and actions are supposed to be judged, namely, that nothing should be condemned or judged as wrong. This is a view that is found especially in those who are outside the Christian faith, looking to Jesus to be only a good moral teacher as exemplified in the Sermon. This view can also be found in those claiming Christian faith but who harbor some edgy disagreements with the tradition.

For such readers, "Don't judge me" becomes the mantra through which all of the Sermon and all of Jesus must be understood. Jesus is read here to be laying down a maxim that no one should ever "judge" or pronounce as wrong any other person's position or life. The problems with this view are that it lacks nuance and does not cohere with the rest of Jesus's teachings or

8. France, *Gospel of Matthew*, 273–74.
9. Quarles, *Sermon on the Mount*, 285.

actions. While it contains an important kernel of truth and does correspond to Jesus's great emphasis on extending love and mercy to others, it is too flat-footed of an articulation of a complex reality.

The fact that Matthew's Jesus does not offer a universal judgment against judgment in 7:1–2 can be seen already in 7:6, where the disciples are called upon to classify some people as pigs and dogs so as to avoid them. This is not ultimate condemnation, but it is a judging or discerning of right and wrong in people. The same is presupposed in 7:15–20, where disciples are warned to be discerning about who is a wolf and who is a sheep, despite initial appearances. Likewise, in 10:11–15 disciples need to render a judgment about who is "worthy" in every village and town they visit. Additionally, in Matt. 18:15–20 the church is likewise called upon to make discerning judgments about who is in the true kingdom-church and who is to be treated as an outsider, a gentile. The language of "binding" and "loosening" used in 18:18 (and 16:19) is very strong and pointed. The shocking thing about this pronouncement is not that God separates the good from the bad (or the sheep and the goats, in 25:31–46) but that he has given this authority and responsibility to the assembly of God's people, with the promise that in this gathering he is present and at work (18:20).[10] The point is that Christian disciples are instructed to distinguish the good from the bad, including good from bad people. Therefore, we must avoid reading 7:1–2 in a totalizing fashion that makes it incoherent with the rest of Jesus's teaching, including in Matthew itself.

McKnight summarizes the nuanced combination of 7:1–2 well: Christians can pronounce "that is good" and "that is wrong" but not "you are condemned by God." Jesus's divinely given ethics shape a society "for reconciliation instead of damnation."[11] Also particularly well stated are the comments of T. W. Manson:

> The whole business of judging persons is in God's hands, for He alone knows the secrets of men's hearts. This does not mean that we are not to use all the moral insight we possess in order to discover what is right and wrong; but that we are to confine ourselves to that field and refrain from passing judgment on persons. For our judgment is itself a factor in shaping their lives, and a harsh judgment may help a fellow-creature on the road to perdition.[12]

10. The Gospel of John provides the same content from the Jesus Traditions, but in different wording and at a more climactic point, as part of the final commission to the disciples. In John 20:21–23 the disciples are given the authority to pronounce the absolution of sins as a result of their being filled with the Spirit.
11. McKnight, *Sermon on the Mount*, 228.
12. T. W. Manson, *The Sayings of Jesus: As Recorded in the Gospels according to St. Matthew and St. Luke* (Grand Rapids: Eerdmans, 1979), 56, quoted in W. D. Davies and Dale C. Allison

Matthew 7:3–6

[3]*Why do you see the speck in your brother or sister's eye*[13] *but in regard to the plank of wood in your own eye you pay no attention?* [4]*How can you say to your brother or sister, "Let me remove that speck from your eye." Look! There is a plank of wood in your own eye!* [5]*You hypocrite! First remove the plank from your own eye and then you can see clearly to remove the speck from your brother or sister's eye.*

[6]*Do not give sacred things to dogs or throw pearls in front of pigs. If you do, the pigs will trample them with their feet and the dogs may turn and tear you apart.*[14]

As noted, 7:3–6 is the first of two examples that unpack the topic of proper evaluation of others that has been laid out in the heading of 7:1–2.[15] The theme of discerning right and wrong in others takes the form of a memorable and even humorous image—a person with a plank stuck in his or her eye attempting to remove a speck from another's eye. This image is evocative of an actual carpentry shop with two siblings working side by side (cf. Jesus as the "carpenter's son" in 13:55), but with an obvious broader application to the Christian community.

The problem with this speck-plank practice is not, as we have discussed regarding 7:2, that Christians can never discern right or wrong in another but that disciples often do so without awareness of their own blindness and inability to judge rightly. Indeed, 7:5 envisions a potential situation in which the speck in another is observed and help is given in removing it, though the extreme example of the plank-eyed person puts the emphasis not on speck removal but on self-awareness in evaluating others. As Donald Hagner observes, "the obvious implication [is] that an awareness of one's own faults . . .

Jr., *A Critical and Exegetical Commentary on the Gospel according to Saint Matthew*, vol. 1, *Introduction and Commentary on Matthew 1–7*, ICC (Edinburgh: T&T Clark, 2004), 669.

13. "Brother or sister" is a better rendering of Greek *adelphos* because not only males are in view here. At the same time, this is also better than the generic "someone else's eye" because the focus is on the Christian community, defined as the family of God (cf. 12:46–50).

14. Along with other commentators, I have repeated the references to pigs and dogs in the latter half of 7:6, recognizing that there is a chiastic structure in this poetic aphorism: dogs (A)—pigs (B)—pigs trampling (B')—dogs tearing (A'). The dogs are the ones that tear to pieces and the pigs do the trampling, not the other way around. It is therefore best to clarify this in the translation. See Davies and Allison, *Matthew 1–7*, 677; McKnight, *Sermon on the Mount*, 237; Grant R. Osborne, *Matthew*, ZECNT 1 (Grand Rapids: Zondervan, 2012), 260.

15. There is a shift from plural forms of the second-person pronoun ("you") in 7:1–2 to singular forms in 7:3–5. This indicates either a redactional seam (Hagner, *Matthew 1–13*, 168) and/or simply the envisioning of an individual situation beyond the general principle (France, *Gospel of Matthew*, 273). This confirms the *kəlāl ûpərāṭ* structure.

will make more charitable one's judgment of others," tying back into 7:1–2.[16] There is a call inherent in these verses to examine oneself with humility, become aware of one's faults, and repent. Only then can one be in a place to hope to see things clearly.

Jesus condemns the way of being in the world that focuses on specks without awareness of one's own faults with the strong Sermonic word "hypocrite" (7:5). This is the only time in the Sermon (or Matthew as a whole) where "hypocrite" is used in reference to a disciple rather than those outside.[17] In Matt. 6 it was the anchor term to describe the ones whose piety lacked wholeness and completeness (6:1–21). These same people are identified more explicitly in chapter 23 as the scribes and Pharisees who live for the praise of others (23:5–7) and who are hypocrites because of an inconsistency between external keeping of the law and the intent of the heart (23:13–36).[18] It is appropriate to warn disciples with this same strong term here because of the seriousness of the inconsistency of evaluating others (and condemning them) while being unaware of one's own faults (cf. James 1:26; 3:9–12). This hypocrisy is yet another example of the Sermon's theme of wholeness. Righteousness requires consistency between one's inner person and one's outer actions. Discerning the state of another without first examining one's own heart is a dangerous and deadly business precisely because it is a kind of doubleness.

There is one more saying in this subsection, and it is not without its difficulties in interpretation. At a fundamental level, Matt. 7:6 is unclear because of the many possibilities of each of the metaphorical nouns that are used—dogs, that which is holy, pearls, and pigs. It is the nature of such a highly abstract aphorism to use terms poetically; it makes for a pithy saying but not always clarity of intention. Or to understand this phenomenon more positively, this

---

16. Hagner, *Matthew 1–13*, 170.

17. The change to the vocative, "you hypocrite," raises the possibility that the addressees here are the overhearing Pharisees more than the disciples. (Cf. the discussion on Matt. 5:1–2 on who the audience of the Sermon is.) We should not press this difference too far, however, because as a whole and in its final Matthean form and setting the Sermon is given for all readers, and especially Christian ones. Nevertheless, if the Pharisees are included in the audience here, then in the first instance the point of the exhortation in 7:1–5 is for the Pharisees not to wrongly judge Jesus himself or his followers. Again, however, we must always remember that regardless of the original historical setting, what we have in the Sermon in Matthew is his stylized, appropriated, and applied message to his own Christian readers. There is no need to slice things too thinly here since the general message of being self-aware when discerning the truth in others applies fully to both Pharisees in Jesus's day and any Christian reader thereafter.

18. Each of the images of the woes of Matt. 23 (which intentionally match the macarisms of Matt. 5; see chap. 5 above) hang together on this external vs. internal lack of wholeness. The pair of metaphors that show this most explicitly are the cup and dish (23:25–26) and the whitewashed tombs (23:27–28).

is the beautiful nature of poetic and proverbial sayings: they invite many applications. This is certainly the case here.

For this particular teaching of Jesus we have a very early interpretation that applies this saying to the "fencing of the table" of the eucharistic meal from outsiders. *Didache 9.5* states that those who have not been baptized into the name of the Lord should not receive the Eucharist since this would be giving that which is holy to dogs. This applicational reading of Matt. 7:6 is certainly appropriate while also not limiting the other possible readings of this memorable saying.

In Matthew's day, "dog" (Gk. *kyōn*),[19] was certainly a term of contempt, as was "pigs" or "swine" (Gk. *choiros*). These epithets are clearly parallel in usage here and are used as descriptions of those who are despised, both in Jewish and non-Jewish usage. For Jewish people, with their strong traditional sense of clean and unclean animals, these terms are the most derogatory descriptors in their vocabulary.[20] Likewise, "that which is holy" and "pearls" are put in parallel and thus mutually color each other's sense. "Pearl" in early Judaism often refers to a valuable saying or excellent thought,[21] which inclines one to interpret "that which is holy" as teachings or truths.[22] Regardless, "pearls" and "that which is holy" are unmistakably seen as valuable, in contrast to the despised "dogs" and "pigs."

The question remains, what is this saying primarily communicating as a piece of proverbial Jesus wisdom? McKnight, following N. T. Wright, suggests that, with "dogs" and "pigs" referring to gentiles, this text fits with 10:5–6 as "a simple prohibition of taking the gospel and the kingdom vision to the Gentile world until after the resurrection, the Great Commission, the ascension, and Pentecost, which unleashed the Gentile mission."[23] I suggest instead that this means that the disciples should not waste their time wrangling with those Jews

19. Readers of Matthew as a whole will note the interesting, potentially parallel story of the Canaanite woman in 15:21–28, where this normally despised outsider is referred to in a sideways manner as a "dog." It should be noted that a different term for "dog" is used in these two passages, so the connection is not as immediate. Nevertheless, both terms still communicate something lesser and subhuman, and the conceptual parallels between the sayings make some connection seem likely. In 7:6 the word generally refers to a "dog of the street or farm" as opposed to a "house dog or lapdog" (Gk. *kynarion*), as in 15:26 (BDAG, s.v. *kynarion*).

20. Ulrich Luz, *Matthew 1–7: A Commentary*, rev. ed., trans. James E. Crouch, Hermeneia (Minneapolis: Fortress, 2007), 419.

21. *TDNT* 4:472–73.

22. Another interesting intra-Matthean parallel is the reuse of "pearl" in 13:45–46, describing the kingdom of heaven as having such value that one sells all else to get this great pearl.

23. McKnight, *Sermon on the Mount*, 238. With Luz, Quarles, and others, I think this reading does not accord with the emphasis on gentile inclusion that is already under way in Matthew's narrative. See Luz, *Matthew 1–7*, 355; Quarles, *Sermon on the Mount*, 292.

who refuse to believe the wisdom of the kingdom message.[24] Matthew 10:14, in which the disciples are instructed to shake the dust off of their feet as they depart from those who do not receive them, is more appropriate here. This reading is informed by other passages in Matthew that center on the theme of revelation and separation: Jesus reveals God's wisdom, and this results in the separation of all peoples—regardless of ethnicity—into those who believe and follow and those who do not. Elsewhere Matthew ironically and pointedly uses "gentiles" to refer to Jewish people (especially the Pharisees) who do not believe (e.g., 18:17). So too, here, the normal terms of derision for gentiles ("dogs" and "swine") are used to refer to unbelieving Jews (or anyone else) opposed to Jesus and his disciples. We may thus paraphrase this verse: "Do not toss your teaching to outsiders, lest they scornfully reject it and you."

We may rightly discern behind 7:6 some more direct reference to Matthew's own historical setting. That is, it is certainly possible that this saying is a direct and needed word to early Jewish Christians who are still connected religiously and culturally to the synagogue and temple. While all sayings have a broader, perpetual application to Christian readers, it is not difficult to discern that in its writing and first hearing this verse would prove very relevant and practical to such believers.

The final matter to address concerning 7:6 is how it fits into the literary structure. The connection between 7:3–5 and 7:6 is not immediately discernible. Many translations and commentators see no connection and isolate the verse as its own idea. We have already noted, however, that at the thematic level 7:6 is entirely appropriate in this section (7:1–12) that focuses on evaluating properly; disciples need to discern/judge fairly whether they are dealing with "dogs" and "pigs."

Nonetheless, 7:6 does not appear to flow smoothly from the very different speck-plank-eye metaphor of 7:3–5. There is, however, a connection. Namely, 7:6 provides the balancing wisdom to the instruction of 7:3–5. If 7:3–5 emphasizes hesitancy and extra care in discerning the faults of others, 7:6 supplies the counterweight or ballast lest we become foolish and undiscerning. Dale Allison calls this a *gemara* (commentary or analysis), given to counteract an extreme application of 7:1–5, providing a "moral symmetry." While disciples must always be careful in evaluating others, they should not become too lax or lose all critical faculties when it comes to sacred concerns. "One should

24. This reading has many adherents in the history of interpretation, including Luther. A related alternative reading, with roots in certain Jewish texts and also with a long Christian heritage, is that certain esoteric teachings and practices of Christianity should be kept hidden from those outside. The reading in *Did.* 9.5 aligns with this. See the discussion in Davies and Allison, *Matthew 1–7*, 676.

not always throw the cloak over a brother's faults. One must not be meekly charitable against all reason."[25]

Matthew 7:7–12: Greater Righteousness in Relation to the World (Conclusion)

Matthew 7:7–11

> [7]*Ask and it will be given to you. Seek and you will find. Knock and the door will be opened to you.* [8]*For everyone who asks receives, and everyone who seeks finds, and to everyone[26] who knocks the door is opened.* [9]*There is not a person among you, is there, who when his son asks him for bread, will give him a stone?* [10]*Or if he asks for a fish, he won't give him a serpent, will he?[27]* [11]*If you, therefore, who are evil know to give good gifts to your children, how much more will your Father who is in heaven give good gifts to those who ask him?*

As always with the Sermon, these verses exist within a series of structural concentric circles, functioning slightly differently depending on which level they are being discussed. In the innermost circle, these verses make up the second of two explanations or applications of the general rule in 7:1–2 about proper, wise discernment. At a broader level they are part of the third and final part (6:19–7:12) of the central section of the Sermon (5:17–7:12). At this level we can see consistent elements throughout this unit that apply the theme of greater righteousness to disciples' relationship to the world (its goods and its people). Notice, for example, that throughout 6:19–7:11 the "lesser to greater" argumentation is used to make the point. Additionally, 7:7–11 makes the same basic argument as 6:25–34, namely, that the heavenly Father will provide for all the needs of his children (including the invitation to "seek").

Returning to the more local structure of 7:1–12, as noted above, the assorted sayings collected within it do not appear to have the same degree of

25. Davies and Allison, *Matthew 1–7*, 674. So too in France, *Gospel of Matthew*, 273. Cf. 2 Cor. 6:14–18.

26. The Greek *pas*, "everyone," governs all three of the participles used here—the one who asks, who seeks, and who knocks. Therefore, I have repeated "everyone" each time to make this clear, unlike most English translations.

27. My translation of 7:9–10 varies somewhat from most English translations because I understand the Greek construction used in the latter half of both verses to expect a negative answer to the query (with the use of the Gk. *mē*), and I think it is important to bring this out in the translation more clearly. It is not easy to do so without some paraphrasing because the subject of both verses—"one among you"—is itself an interrogative phrase. This works easily in Greek but requires reordering to render in English.

coherence and consistency of argument as in the preceding sections of the Sermon. Scholarly opinions vary widely on whether there is any connection at all between the sayings in 7:1–12 and if so, what that connection is.[28] As mentioned when discussing 6:19–34, Allison suggests a pattern that spans across 6:19–7:11 of a prohibition followed by two short parables or metaphors (6:19–24 and 7:1–6). This is followed in both sections by words of encouragement about the heavenly Father's care (6:25–34 and 7:7–11) that are worded very similarly.[29] Allison sees the point of this being that in the midst of such high demands upon the disciples, the Sermon intersperses these highly encouraging sections to balance out the commands with the succor of grace.[30]

This suggestion has much merit. I would only add that the connection is not merely that of parallel passages being interspersed but also that the theme or topos of "judging/evaluating correctly" does seem to tie 7:1–12 together. Moreover, as modern readers who are far removed from ancient literary and rhetorical practices, we should not too quickly trust our own sensibilities. We may face a problem of cultural distance; what may not appear coherent to us may likely be something that the original writer and readers may not have stumbled over.

By itself, 7:7–11 is one of the most encouraging and hope-giving sections of the Sermon and even of the whole New Testament. In it disciples are given a straightforward invitation to seek God to meet their needs with confidence, based on the invitation to relate to God not as a mere omnipotent deity but as a good and caring Father.

The logic of the argument is by now familiar to readers of the Sermon: a general aphorism is given (7:7), followed by reasoning or grounding by example (7:8–11). Disciples are invited to ask God for their needs to be met, to seek after them, and to knock in need (7:7). This poetic triptych is at once memorable and heartening. Jesus follows up this invitation with confidence-inspiring

28. Allison surveys several options, including (1) that the asking and seeking is for wisdom to properly follow 7:1–6, (2) a comparison of how disciples are to act toward others (7:1–6) with how God deals with people (7:7–11), and (3) that it is a separate section designed to introduce the Golden Rule (7:12). Other options are also mentioned in Davies and Allison, *Matthew 1–7*, 678.

29. Dale C. Allison Jr., *Studies in Matthew: Interpretation Past and Present* (Grand Rapids: Baker Academic, 2005), 187–93. See also Davies and Allison, *Matthew 1–7*, 626. On p. 690 Allison refers to these two passages as fraternal twins.

30. Allison writes, "our sensitive author, anticipating the reader's perplexity [at his or her inadequacy to fulfill the commands], is moved to make manifest the goodness of the Father in heaven and to write reassuringly about seeking, asking, and knocking" (Davies and Allison, *Matthew 1–7*, 690).

reasoning. Why should disciples confidently ask God to meet their needs? Because everyone who asks, seeks, and knocks receives what they need. This language is reminiscent of the wisdom tradition,[31] which should not be surprising in light of the genre of the Sermon, and also recalls the exhortation in 6:33 to "seek first his kingdom and his righteousness."[32]

The emphasis is not, however, on the skill or even persistence of the seeker in prayer (cf. Luke 11:5–8; 18:1–8) but on the character of kindness of the heavenly Father. Even as the centrally important Lord's Prayer depicts the heavenly Father as knowing needs before people ask (6:8) and the seeking of God in childlike dependence (6:9–11), so too in 7:7–11.[33] Using the familiar "lesser to greater" argument, human fathers are compared with the heavenly Father. Since it is apparent that inconsistent and flawed fathers (here described hyperbolically as "evil") naturally give good gifts to their children, why would disciples expect anything less from their good heavenly Father? The comparison with Luke's version (11:11–13) of this same pithy pericope also highlights that for Matthew the issue is not a generalized abstraction to goodness or even the Holy Spirit (Luke 11:13), but is on topic here with God's provision for the disciples' daily needs, their relationship to the goods of the world. Note also, as was discussed at Matt. 6:25–34, as wisdom literature this saying is not making an absolute and universal promise that no child of God will ever suffer but is instead casting a hopeful vision that forms our understanding of God's character and way of being in the world.[34]

As a stand-alone wisdom saying, 7:7–11 is a powerful and effective piece. Considering it in the overall structure of the Sermon, we can see that it is tied to the theme of judging/evaluating correctly in that disciples are being called to reconsider and evaluate God's nature correctly as fatherly and giving. He is trustworthy and should be judged as such.

31. Cf. the idea of seeking wisdom in Prov. 8:17 (cf. 1:28) and Wis. 6:12. Cf. also the language of Jer. 29:12–13 (36:12–13 LXX) in the context of prayer, where God's people are promised that they will find him when they seek him "with a whole heart."

32. In his typically thorough and thoughtful way, Quarles makes a lengthy argument that 7:7–11 is not primarily about Christians seeking God in prayer to have their physical needs met but is instead, like 6:33, "an appeal to a gracious God for entrance into the kingdom." While there are many insights in his arguments, I am not fully convinced nor do I find it necessary to read this text as talking about the eschatological kingdom *or* the Father's provision of physical needs. Both readings are beneficial. See Quarles, *Sermon on the Mount*, 296–308 (the quote is from p. 299).

33. This is one of the reasons some scholars have seen the Lord's Prayer as the emanating center and 7:7–11 as the conclusion to the section that began in the Prayer.

34. See Luz, *Matthew 1–7*, 359–61, for a brief discussion of the history of interpretation on this issue.

Matthew 7:12

¹²Therefore, in everything, whatever you would want others to do to you or for you, in this same way treat them,³⁵ for this is the Law and the Prophets.

The famous Golden Rule[36] aphorism of 7:12 is climactic and significant for many reasons. It is one of the many memorable phrases from the Sermon that have simultaneously impacted Christian self-understanding and spread its teachings beyond the walls of Christianity into the broader culture. Both within and without Christianity the notion of treating others in love, which is the simplest and most comprehensive paraphrase, is recognized as the posture of Jesus. It has long served as a summary of Jesus's teaching on interpersonal relationships, therefore, for both Christians and non-Christians. Its applications even reach across time and space to appear as part of the State of Kentucky Department of Motor Vehicles' final word for those who must take their safe driving course—"Treat other drivers as you would want to be treated."

Matthew 7:12 is also climactic and significant for the structure, flow, and vision of the Sermon. It serves multiple structural roles, summing up the exhortation to evaluate each other fairly (7:1–11), concluding the theme of greater righteousness in relation to the world (6:19–7:11), and even more broadly, providing the right-hand bookend to the whole central section of the Sermon (5:17–7:12). The connective (*panta oun*) here is not intended to communicate a link only to 7:10 but also to these broader nested structures. I have rendered it "Therefore, in everything, whatever you would . . ." to try to communicate this summative sense. The connection with the broader section of the Sermon is not only thematic but also at the level of linking words: the "Law and the Prophets" of 7:12 is connected to the "Law or the Prophets" phrase in the summary statement of 5:17, thus concluding the central section of the Sermon.[37]

35. There are two main translation decisions to note here. First, "to you or for you" renders with ease the loaded and ambiguous *hymin* with the two possible notions that the Greek communicates. There is no singular English expression that contains the potential double meaning of the Greek term, applying both to things done negatively ("to you") and to things done positively ("for you"), hence the fuller expression in my translation. Second, the "want others to do to you or for you . . . treat them" pairing unfortunately covers up a parallelism of verbs in Greek but makes the English translation much smoother than a clunky repetition of the longer phrase.

36. There are differences of opinion as to the origin of this expression. France retells the traditional story of its coming from the third-century Roman emperor Alexander Severus, who was so impressed with this Christian aphorism as a way of life that, despite not being a Christian himself, he had it inscribed in gold on the wall of his chamber (*Gospel of Matthew*, 284). Quarles, siding with Betz and Keener, rejects this and instead sees the moniker as having unclear origins sometime in the Middle Ages (*Sermon on the Mount*, 306).

37. See chap. 5 on the structure of the Sermon. While these two phrases are easily striking enough to be seen as an *inclusio*, one may query whether there is a difference between "Law *or*

Regarding its meaning in the teaching of the Sermon, there are two observations to make. First, from a tradition-history perspective, Jesus's summative saying is in great continuity with the Jewish Scriptures and tradition. In particular, the Golden Rule can easily be understood as an aphoristic wisdom version of the second greatest commandment to love one's neighbor as oneself. This second part of the great summary of the law ("Love God and love neighbor"), which is itself a traditional summary of the two tablets of the Decalogue, was recognized as a valid way to express the highest goals of the law of God and is reiterated as such by Jesus in other places (Matt. 22:34–40).[38] "Do to others what you would want them to do to you" is a helpful, memorable adage in a proverbial form. Additionally, we know that in the Jewish traditions there was a similar aphorism, stated by Hillel in a comparable negative form: "What is hateful to you, do not do to your neighbor. That is the whole Torah, while the rest is commentary."[39]

This understanding likely best explains what Matthew means by saying that the Golden Rule "*is* the Law and the Prophets." That is, this wisdom aphorism is a proper summary of what it means to fulfill the teachings of Scripture, at least regarding interpersonal relations. Confirmation of this way of thinking is found in two statements by Paul, statements that are reminiscent of this saying in Matthew and are likely Paul's reflections on the Jesus Traditions he received. In Gal. 5:14 Paul writes with a similarly sweeping statement, "For the whole Law is fulfilled in one statement: 'You shall love your neighbor as yourself.'" And similarly, in Rom. 13:8 Paul exhorts his hearers to owe nothing to anyone except the debt of love because "the one who loves another fulfills the Law." These refractions of the Jesus Traditions in Paul help us see what is there implicitly in Matthew—that the language of "fulfilling the Law and the Prophets" in Matt. 5:17 is given in shorthand form in 7:12, with the idea being the same.[40] Further confirmation can be found in the expression used to describe the first and second greatest commandments in 22:34–40, where

---

Prophets" (5:17) and "Law *and* Prophets" (7:12). There is no difference in denotative meaning; both phrases envision these two aspects of the Jewish Scriptures in conjunction with each other. The disjunction in 5:17 is required by the syntax of the negative statement, "Do not think I came to abolish the Law *or* the Prophets."

38. Also note that like Matt. 22:34–40, one could see 6:1–21 as fulfilling the first tablet of the Decalogue (relationship to God) and 6:19–7:11 as fulfilling the second (relationships with others). See Osborne, *Matthew*, 263.

39. See *b. Šabbat* 31a, which contains the story of a gentile who approaches Hillel, saying he will become a convert if the whole Torah can be taught to him while he is standing on one foot, resulting in the response of Hillel given above. There are other parallels in Jewish literature that can be adduced. See Davies and Allison, *Matthew 1–7*, 687.

40. Allison describes 7:12 as "the most basic or important demand of the law, a demand that in no way replaces Torah but instead states its true end" (*Studies in Matthew*, 194n44).

"the Law and the Prophets" appears again: "On these two commandments the whole Law and the Prophets hang/depend" (22:40).[41]

The second observation concerns the broader issue of ethics and virtue being discussed in this book. That is, the Golden Rule is a prime example of a virtue-ethics vision over against a rules-based ethic, which also explains why sayings remarkably similar to this one are found in moral philosophy even far beyond the Jewish traditions.[42] Matthew 7:12 beautifully summarizes the way of being in the world that no amount of rules or regulations could ever encompass or hope to promote. The Golden Rule is not so much a rule but a vision (maybe better then, the "Golden Vision"). It is an invitation to virtue by giving a vision of how to relate to other people. In this sense it is properly considered both a "greater righteousness" and the fulfillment of the whole Law (5:17–20), as well as being another way to describe how to be *teleios* (5:48).[43]

Matthew 7:1–12 and Human Flourishing

If the argument of this book concerning the sapiential nature and human-flourishing focus of the Sermon is correct, then we should not be surprised to find the same theme here at the end of the main part of the teaching. This whole passage is describing a way of being in the world that is based on exhortations toward the good life, choices that will result either in judgment (7:2), being torn to bits and trampled (7:6), or receiving good things (7:11) and being treated as we would want to be (7:12). All of this, like the rest of the Sermon, is casting a vision and inviting disciples into a wide space of living well. It is an invitation to practical wisdom (*phronēsis*) that affects daily living, based on an appeal to our natural and good instincts for what humans all want, true happiness and flourishing. This collection of memorable, universally applicable aphorisms is very much at home in the shared context of the Greco-Roman virtue tradition and Second Temple Jewish wisdom literature, offering Jesus's answer to the great question of human flourishing.

41. We might even call this a prophetic reading of the Law, that is, a way of rightly interpreting Torah as the prophets do, focusing on the inner person and love, not just external obedience. Cf. Isa. 29:13; Jer. 31:31–34; Ezek. 11:19; 36:26; Hosea 6:6.

42. Parallel ideas can be found widely, including in Herodotus, Isocrates, Confucius, and others. See Craig S. Keener, *The Gospel of Matthew: A Socio-Rhetorical Commentary* (Grand Rapids: Eerdmans, 2009), 248.

43. We may note that in the same way that Matt. 5:48 summarizes not only the immediately preceding pericope (5:43–47) but also 5:17–47, so too does 7:12 function. And at the same time, it is not merely a coincidence that the final and climactic exegesis of Torah that is found in 5:21–47 concerns loving others, thus providing a parallel and another connection between 5:48 and 7:12.

11

Matthew 7:13–8:1

Overview

We have now reached the conclusion to the Sermon, with its fitting tripartite ending consisting of three metaphors. Together these drive home the exhortational thrust of the whole discourse. These three metaphors (7:13–14, 15–23, 24–27) provide three distinct images, yet they are tied together. Their bond occurs in three ways. First, consistent in all the metaphors is the difference between external appearance and internal reality, a theme at the heart of the Sermon. Second, there is a thematic thread of "two ways" that weaves its way through all three metaphors, including the idea that Jesus's hearers must be careful in their hearing and consider their response to this teaching. Closely related to the second, the third way this passage hangs together is the consistent theme of "doing the will of God" as essential to entering the kingdom.

In the first instance, we note that each of these images build on the theme of virtuous wholeness versus doubleness woven throughout the Sermon. This is communicated by portraying three examples of an unexpected reality—one cannot always initially tell by external appearances whether something is truly good, whether wholeness (external and internal) is present. The wide and broad and comfortable road is appealing enough to attract most travelers, but unexpectedly it leads to destruction (7:13–14); the false prophets cast out demons and do mighty works in the name of Jesus, but they are actually wolves in sheep costumes (7:15–23); an apparently fine house that is built on a sandy foundation looks no different from one built upon a rock until storms and floods come (7:24–27). Thus, the conclusion to the Sermon continues the

269

main theme of *makarios*-ness through *teleios*-ity that has marked the whole, with an added note of urgency in light of potential missteps and mishearing.[1]

This urgency connects to the other thematic bond in 7:13–27, the idea of "two ways." This theme is common in proverbial and exhortatory literature preceding and contemporary with the Sermon. In the Old Testament we have many examples, such as Deut. 30:15–20, where Moses sets before God's people the choice between life and death, good and evil, exhorting them to walk in God's ways. This idea is alluded to and reiterated in prophetic utterances like Jer. 21:8. Particularly important in light of the Sermon overall is the image of Ps. 1, which contrasts the wicked and the righteous based on two different paths taken or ways lived. Noteworthy is the observation, then, that this wisdom psalm shares the understanding of *makarios*-ness at the beginning of the Sermon (Matt. 5:3–12) and the contrast of the way of the righteous and the wicked at the end (7:13–27).[2] This theme of two ways continues in the Jewish tradition and into early Christian writings, most notably the *Didache* (1–6) and the *Epistle of Barnabas* (18:1–21:9).

This rhetorical contrast between two ways of being in the world is the universal appeal to wisdom that all sages, prophets, and preachers give. "Choose this day whom you will serve" (Josh. 24:15) in some ways stands as the subtext to every moral exhortation, religious or not. It is appropriate that, in light of the vision for true human flourishing that Jesus has just unpacked, he exhorts his hearers to consider carefully what he has said. But it is also necessary that he do so because while Jesus *is* offering human wisdom, the content is more than that: it is a claim to divine authority. Additionally, the content of the wisdom that Jesus teaches is topsy-turvy and dissonance creating, not merely natural, human wisdom. From the upside-down macarisms through the re-definitions of piety to the pointed commands regarding money and judging, Jesus's wisdom and way for human flourishing are not portrayed as the natural

1. R. T. France describes 7:13–27 as "a coda calling for decisive response rather than adding further instructions on the requirements of discipleship" (*The Gospel of Matthew*, NICNT [Grand Rapids: Eerdmans, 2007], 282).

2. The connections between Ps. 1 and the conclusion to the Sermon are manifold. There is a real sense in which the Sermon is an eschatological, Jesus-given expansion on Ps. 1. Both Ps. 1 and Matt. 7:13–27 invite hearers onto the path of wisdom (Ps. 1:1; Matt. 7:24); contrast two paths or ways of being in the world (Ps. 1:1, 6; Matt. 7:13–14); use fruit-bearing trees as a key metaphor (Ps. 1:3–4; Matt. 7:16–20); speak of final judgment and separation of the righteous from the wicked (Ps. 1:5–6; Matt. 7:13, 21–23, 26–27); contrast those whom the Lord "knows" and those he does not know (Ps. 1:6; Matt. 7:23); and emphasize hearing and heeding God's revelation (Ps. 1:2; Matt. 7:24). This connection between Ps. 1 and Matt. 7:13–27 seems much stronger to me than the proposal made by Dale Allison of the Deuteronomic background, though, of course, we are not forced to choose between an either/or of textual background. See Allison, *The New Moses: A Matthean Typology* (Minneapolis: Fortress, 1993; repr., Eugene, OR: Wipf & Stock, 2013), 190–91.

outflow of human thinking and reflection. It is an irruption into this world. This calls for a sharp contrast between two ways of possibly responding.

It is appropriate that Jesus gives these warnings at the end of the Sermon— because all of the discourse is framed in the context of eschatological urgency. The Beatitudes set this eschatological tone with their theme of kingdom-coming reversal, and an eschatological focus finds its anchor most clearly in the epicenter of the Sermon with the Lord's Prayer. Therefore, unlike the merely proverbial wisdom appeal such as Solomon might give, based on inviting his son to reflect on the human outworking of one's choices, the One greater than Solomon who is both Sage and eschatological Prophet must appeal to *more* than human wisdom, to an eschatological, kingdom irruption. This is why the closing to the Sermon is peppered throughout with the sense of urgency and the high-stakes language of life versus destruction.

The third and final way that 7:13–27 is bound together is with the strong Matthean and Sermonic theme of doing the will of God. As was discussed in chapter 4 above, righteousness from a whole heart (versus its foil, hypocrisy) is woven throughout the Sermon. It is intimately connected with Jesus's teaching that it is not those who merely obey externally or appear to be righteous who are in God's kingdom but rather those who actually *do* have a righteousness that surpasses that of the scribes and Pharisees (5:20). Another way to describe this is "those who do the will of God."[3] In addition to other places in Matthew where this language occurs (12:50; 21:31; cf. also James 2:14–26), this conclusion to the Sermon manifests this idea at its core. This idea is most explicit in the second of the three images (Matt. 7:15–23), where the good and bad are defined by whether they produce true fruit. This metaphor concludes with the explicit comment in 7:21 that it is not mere speech or even the production of (false) fruit that enables one to enter the kingdom, but it is only for "the one who does the will of my Father who is in heaven." It is also explicit in the final, climactic image of 7:24–27, where the wise and foolish are defined according to whether they hear and *do* Jesus's words (7:24) or hear and *not do* them (7:26).[4] This helps us see that the same emphasis on doing the will of God is also implicit in the first illustration (7:13–14), where the contrast is between living one way or

---

3. Charles Quarles helpfully summarizes this expression as "God's moral will as expressed through the commandments of the OT and the teaching of Jesus, especially the teachings of the SM [Sermon on the Mount]" (*Sermon on the Mount: Restoring Christ's Message to the Modern Church* [Nashville: B&H, 2011], 333).

4. It is easy to discern the resonances of these verses with James 2:14–26, which emphasizes that merely "having faith" is not sufficient if this faith does not have feet and hands in good works. One can also think of the parable of two sons (Matt. 21:28–32), where the good son is defined by the one who *does* the father's will.

another, using the metaphor of walking along a road. Thus, the same idea is at work—righteousness and entering into the kingdom are defined not in terms of a set of cognitive beliefs per se (as important as those still are) but as a way of being in the world or activity.

Matthew 7:13–27: Conclusion: Three Warnings Regarding the Prospect of Eschatological Judgment

Matthew 7:13–14: Two Kinds of Paths

¹³*Enter through the narrow⁵ gate, for the gate is wide and the road that leads to destruction is easy, and the ones entering through that gate are many.* ¹⁴*But how narrow⁶ the gate is and how difficult the road is that leads to life, and the ones who find it are few!*

The shift to the conclusion of the Sermon is marked by the stark contrast presented between two ways of being in the world, one described as a narrow gate and the other as a wide gate and broad path. These two contrasting ways lead to two opposite places—one to life (7:14) and the other to destruction (7:13). There is some debate among interpreters about how exactly the images of gate and road are meant to be understood, whether the idea is of two different gates that lead to different roads or rather whether gates and roads are used as closely comparable images both making the same point. While it seems the latter is more accurate, regardless, the larger point is clear: two ways of being are contrasted, one that appears to be better because of its ease and breadth but turns out to lead to destruction, and the other that is difficult and compressed and uncomfortable but actually leads to life. The comment that many people enter by the broad and easy way, while few find the narrow and difficult way, is hyperbolic and not focused on the quantitative difference. Rather, while it is true that the majority of people do not seem to respond to Jesus's message (cf. the parable of the sower in 13:3–23), the contrast in 7:13–14 concentrates on ease versus difficulty and on the varied outcomes of life versus death.⁷

5. The Greek adjective *stenos*, rendered in English here as "narrow" can have a spatial sense, but its metaphorical connotations of cramped, confined, distressed, or troubled are far more dominant. It is cognate with several other words whose meaning centers around trouble and even groaning. I have used "narrow" here because of the paired contrast with "wide," but the more metaphorical connotations with the Greek word are largely lost with this English gloss. See also note 9 below concerning the similar meaning of "difficult."

6. The interrogative gloss "But how narrow!" interprets the best rendering of the Greek text, which has a couple of different possible readings, hence the variety in English translations. See France, *Gospel of Matthew*, 284n3.

7. There may also be some significance in the contrast between the verbs used with the two ways. The many simply *enter into* (*eiserchomai*) the broad way while the few *find* (*heuriskō*)

These verses, with their opening imperative, are not merely a description but an exhortation to *enter* the way of life. This is a Second Temple Jewish way of talking about entering into the reign or kingdom of God in the age to come.[8] We can see this parallel language in the following pericope, where many will not "enter the kingdom of heaven" (7:21) but will be sent away (7:23), like the wood of a bad tree being thrown into the fire (7:19). Elsewhere Matthew will also talk about entering eternal life as entering the kingdom of heaven (18:3–4) and as the opposite of entering into eternal fire or the eternal fiery hell (18:8–9). Likewise, in the story of the rich young man who comes to Jesus (19:16–30) there is an enlightening interchange of expressions used concerning the kingdom and eternal life: "Having eternal life" (19:16), "entering into life" (19:17), "having treasure in heaven" (19:21), "entering the kingdom of heaven/God" (19:23, 24), and "being saved" (19:25) are all interchangeable metaphors used to describe the same thing. Most notable in connection with the Sermon, what prevents the rich young man from entering life/the kingdom is precisely his lack of *teleios* righteousness (19:21). Thus we see that at the conclusion of the Sermon we have returned to the theme that framed the Beatitudes (5:3, 10) and that is the most generalized statement of the content of Jesus's preaching, the kingdom of heaven (4:17).

Even though the theme of the kingdom is apparent and consistent, this closing exhortation to enter according to the narrow way may seem an abrupt shift toward merely external behaviors, unlike the emphasis on the internal wholeness that Jesus has been picturing throughout the Sermon. That is, "wide" and "easy" and "broad" sound like the life of loose morals, while "narrow" and "hard" conjure images of piety and self-sacrifice and duty. Historically this text has been read and pictorially represented with images that show the broad way as impious behaviors and the narrow way as acts of service and Christian duty. Has Jesus suddenly shifted gears from wholeness/ virtue to fiery-preacher behaviorism?

Quite the opposite. Despite a long Christian pietistic tradition of understanding the difference between the narrow gate and broad way as a contrast between immoral behaviors and pious practices, the distinction made here depends on the same internal versus external righteousness that has marked the entirety of the Sermon. The wide and easy way that leads to destruction is precisely what Jesus has been describing all along as living with merely

---

the narrow way. This recalls the exhortation and promise of 7:7 to "seek and you will find [*heurēsete*]."

8. See Craig S. Keener, *The Gospel of Matthew: A Socio-Rhetorical Commentary* (Grand Rapids: Eerdmans, 2009), 250.

external righteousness, while the narrow and "difficult"[9] way is the vision he has cast for righteousness that is *more and deeper* than behavior. The broad[10] and easy way is the way of the Pharisees, whose righteousness is easily definable and can be gritted out solely at the external level—not committing adultery, not murdering, and so on. The narrow and difficult way is Jesus's vision, a righteousness that requires deep roots and the exposure of one's whole person to God, true virtue. The imagery used here, then, is not a shift away from the theme of "virtue/wholeness as greater righteousness" that Jesus has been emphasizing. Rather, it is an appropriate exhortation based on the same idea and making the eschatological urgency apparent. This pointed reminder of the insufficiency of relating to God only at the level of external behavior has abiding significance for every generation of God's people, not only the Pharisees in Jesus's and Matthew's day.

Matthew 7:15–23: Two Kinds of Prophets

[15]*Watch out for false prophets, who will come[11] to you clothed like sheep but on the inside are ravenous wolves.* [16]*You will recognize them by their fruit. Grapes are not harvested from thornbushes, nor are figs from thistles, are they?* [17]*In the same way, every healthy[12] tree produces*

9. One of the clues that this saying is casting the same vision as the rest of the Sermon is the evocative connotation of the word translated as "difficult" in 7:14. The Greek lexeme here (*tethlimmenē*) is typically used in biblical Greek in both its noun and verb forms to describe oppression, affliction, and persecution. This brings to mind the climactic theme and emphasis on suffering in the Beatitudes (5:10–12). Read together, it seems that Matthew is saying that the narrow way is the difficult way, which results in persecution, even as the Beatitudes show. This is strengthened by understanding the metaphorical sense of "narrow" (*stenos*) as troubled and distressed. See note 5 above. Scot McKnight, *The Sermon on the Mount*, The Story of God Bible Commentary (Grand Rapids: Zondervan, 2013), 258n8; and W. D. Davies and Dale C. Allison Jr., *A Critical and Exegetical Commentary on the Gospel according to Saint Matthew*, vol. 1, *Introduction and Commentary on Matthew 1–7*, ICC (Edinburgh: T&T Clark, 2004), 700, both note this connection. Allison also notes the collocation of words related to tribulation, broad and narrow ways, and perishing in Isa. 26:1–19 and 30:18–26.

10. Another clue supporting this interpretation is the opposite play being made with the connotations of the word "broad" or "wide" (*plateia*). This is the same word used in 6:5 to describe that place where the hypocrites love to stand and pray to be seen by others. Additionally, the verbal form (*platynō*) is employed in the parallel passage (23:5) to describe what the Pharisees do with their phylacteries: they *broaden* them to be seen as pious by others. These kinds of poetic wordplay are typical of Matthew's artistry.

11. Though the tense-form for "come" is present (or better, imperfective in aspect), the surrounding discourse indicates a future exhortation beyond the current moment, hence my translation.

12. Glosses for *kalos, ponēros, agathos,* and *sapros* in Matt. 7:17–18 understandably vary by translation. In this arboreal context, "healthy" and "decayed" seem to describe the semantic notions for the state of the trees, as do "good" and "bad" for the fruit produced. It is interesting

good fruit, but every decayed tree produces bad fruit. [18]A healthy tree is not able to produce bad fruit, nor is a decayed tree able to produce good fruit. [19]Every tree that does not produce good fruit is cut down and thrown into the fire. [20]Thus, you will recognize them by their fruit.

[21]Not everyone who says to me, "Lord, Lord," will enter into the kingdom of heaven, but only the one who does the will of my Father who is in heaven. [22]Many people will say to me on that day, "Lord, Lord, in your name we prophesied, and in your name we cast out demons, and in your name[13] we produced many miracles, didn't we?" [23]And then I will pronounce to them, "I have never known you! Depart from me, you who work lawlessness."

The second of the three concluding images is described in the longest and most complicated way. Like the other two images, it traffics in the three ideas of internal/external righteousness, two ways, and doing the will of the Father. Structurally, 7:15–23 is different from its counterparts in that 7:13–14 and 7:24–27 both provide simple metaphorical images. Matthew 7:15–23, however, is more like the kəlāl ûpərāṭ structure that was used throughout the central section. There is a heading in 7:15—beware of false prophets—and an unpacking of this exhortation with two images (7:16–20, 21–23). The variation of metaphor from wolves to trees could lead one to see this as two separate sections (7:15–20, 21–23), as many English Bibles indicate. However, the return to the theme of false prophets in the latter half shows that this is to be taken as one complex unit. Additionally, the two illustrations (7:16–20, 21–23) under the heading (7:15) are each structured with inclusios—verses 16 and 20 are connected by the idea of recognizing (epiginōskō), while verses 21 and 23 both refer to speaking/declaring (legō and homologeō, respectively; also erō [fut. of legō] in v. 22). The two subunits are also connected by the repetition of the key word poieō, which is a very versatile word meaning generally "to produce"—for fruit in 7:16–20 and for miracles in 7:21–23.

Being aware of false prophets is the consistent message throughout 7:15–23 (cf. 7:6). In one sense we can connect this theme with the broad and narrow ways of 7:13–14, as the false prophets are ones who, among other things, would mislead people to practice piety along the lines of the broad way (external only) rather than the narrow way (wholehearted).[14] However, there is also an integrity and larger point to 7:15–23 that are not just flowing from that preceding image.

---

to note that for Matthew agathos is contrasted with sapros, not ponēros (which is paired with kalos), which is the word one might expect.

13. The thrice-repeated "in your name" of v. 23 is prominent and should be indicated in our translation, which I have attempted to do by fronting it in each phrase.

14. See Grant R. Osborne, Matthew, ZECNT 1 (Grand Rapids: Zondervan, 2012), 271.

The reality of false teachers and prophets and the warnings against them are not uncommon in the Old Testament (Deut. 18:20–22; Jer. 6:13–14; 14:14–18; 23:11; Lam. 2:14; Ezek. 13:1–23). Additionally, the New Testament teaches in multiple places that there will be many false teachers and prophets (even false apostles), especially arising in strong numbers of deception in the last days (Matt. 24:11, 24; 2 Cor. 11:13–15; 2 Tim. 4:3; 2 Pet. 2:1; 1 John 4:1–6; Rev. 20:10). In the context of the Sermon, false prophets and teachers are defined not so much as ones not speaking the truth (though that is implied) but as those who appear pious but do not do the true whole-person righteousness. Thus, the scribes and Pharisees are the first examples that come to mind (Matt. 5:20; cf. the pointed warnings and woes in 23:1–39).

This explains the somewhat unexpected and shocking final words of this pericope—"Depart from me, you who work lawlessness" (7:23). The wording here does not just generally mean "those who do evil," as some translations render it.[15] Rather, Matthew is directly quoting the Septuagint reading of Ps. 6:9 (6:8 in English translations) because it ties into the ironic assertions of the Sermon that true law keeping is not simply Torah observance, but obedience to Jesus, that there is a righteousness that is not merely external law keeping.[16] Thus, the evocative connotations of describing the false prophets in 7:15–23 (who are in the first instance mostly the Pharisees) as "you who work lawlessness" ties back to 5:17–48, where Jesus redefines law keeping as his own prophetic, eschatological, and christological authoritative reading of the law over against the scribes and Pharisees of his day. This connection is also made in 23:28, where the Pharisees are condemned for having an external appearance of righteousness but inwardly being full of "hypocrisy and lawlessness." It is also looking forward to the immediately subsequent and final image of the Sermon, where the wise and foolish are separated by whether they do Jesus's words (7:24, 26). Finally, "lawlessness" is one of the descriptors for those who are condemned in the eschatological future (13:41; 24:12) for not following Jesus.

15. France (*Gospel of Matthew*, 295) rightly notes that Ps. 6:9 LXX ("you who work lawlessness"), which Matthew is borrowing, is a translation of the more general expression in the Hebrew text of "you who do evil." The implication in France's commentary seems to be that there is no difference between "those who work lawlessness" and "those who do evil." Indeed, 1 John 3:4 notes that "everyone who does sin does lawlessness, and sin is lawlessness." However, while at the denotative level these ideas are the same, in Matthew's context the connotative difference between "those who work lawlessness" and "those who do evil" is significant. See further comments above.

16. The noun "lawlessness" (Gk. *anomia*) and its related adjective "lawless" (Gk. *anomos*) prove to be frequent and important Septuagintal words, occurring some 228 and 106 times, respectively. Many of these come from the Psalter, which proves to be a major stream of tradition that is flowing into the Sermon.

The other thing that Jesus will say to these false prophets on the day of judgment[17] is that he never *knew* (*ginōskō*) them. In addition to the little play on words of being able to "recognize/know" (*epiginōskō*) the false prophets, this language of being "known" by God is very weighty. "Knowing" in the biblical tradition communicates having a relationship, even sexually at times, but also serves as a way to speak of "God's special relationship with his people as in Amos 3:2."[18] Thus, once again, the stakes are very high in this teaching.

Looking back to the tree and fruit imagery that is used in Matt. 7:16–20, we can note that this powerful wisdom metaphor has already been utilized in John the Baptist's message about the necessity of "producing fruit worthy of repentance" (3:8). It will also reappear in 12:22–37 when Jesus is in sharp conflict with the Pharisees. He uses this same universal point about trees and fruit to refute their desperate argument against him that he is casting out demons by the power of the demonic world, by Beelzebub. Jesus's logic in 12:33–37 is that his opponents must either "declare the tree healthy and its fruit good or declare the tree diseased and its fruit bad" because (using a closely worded aphorism) "by the fruit the tree is known" (12:33). While the use of the verb *poieō* (make, do) is slightly different here (rendered here as "declare" because of the speaking context of verses 34–37), the deep logic is the same: growing things produce according to their nature, either good or bad. "Either my works are truly good," Jesus is saying, "and therefore I am good, or my works are truly bad and therefore I am bad." The ability to discern good and bad by fruit is consistent across all these examples.

The theme of the potential difference between external and internal righteousness in both illustrations in this section raises a potential dilemma. It is possible that what looks like a sheep externally is actually a wolf internally (7:15). It is possible that what looks like a powerful prophet externally is actually a false prophet internally, one who does not truly know God and will not enter his kingdom (7:21–23).[19] This serves as a reminder to Jesus's hearers that looks may be deceiving. Even as the magicians of Egypt performed several miracles parallel to Moses's (Exod. 7:12, 22), so too Jesus wants his hearers

17. The reference to "on that day" in 7:22 seems to come out of the blue unless one notes the thoroughly eschatological nature of 7:13–27 and the fact that "entering into the kingdom" in 7:21 would have evoked for Jewish hearers reference to God's eschatological return to establish his reign and peace upon the earth.

18. France, *Gospel of Matthew*, 295.

19. *Second Clement* 4.2 reads, "For he says, 'Not everyone who says to me, 'Lord, Lord' will be saved, but only the one who does righteousness.'" This is a very early reception of Matt. 7:21–22 that seems to reflect a sophisticated understanding of the Sermon's way of speaking about righteousness as doing the will of God. Bart D. Ehrman, trans., *Apostolic Fathers*, vol. 1, *I Clement, II Clement, Ignatius, Polycarp, Didache*, LCL (Cambridge, MA: Harvard University Press, 2003), 170.

to know that good works of piety (recall Matt. 6:1–21) and even miraculous prophecies, demon removals, and other mighty acts do not necessarily mean one is righteous and godly. It is possible to have an appearance of godliness without its true power and relationship to God (2 Tim. 3:5).[20] It is not difficult to think of the Pharisees as the prime example of this as Matthew portrays them, whose morality and piety were often merely external, hence Jesus's teachings in Matt. 5:17–48 and 6:1–21.

The complication or wrinkle in this otherwise straightforward teaching comes from the sudden shift in metaphor in 7:16 and the implication of the tree/fruit imagery that appears to communicate the *opposite* of the teaching on false prophets. That is, 7:16 teaches that one *will* be able to recognize false prophets by their actions, even as one can discern the health or diseased state of a tree by its fruit. John the Baptist and Jesus both use this clear image of the tree and fruit to make the same point elsewhere (3:10; 12:33–37). This is summed up explicitly again in 7:20—"you will recognize [the false prophets] by their fruits." The difficulty here is that this image seems to break down precisely in its application to false prophets. That is, it is the doing of false works that appear to be good that makes a false prophet false; wolves are precisely most dangerous when and because they appear to be sheep. Therefore, one *cannot* actually tell a false prophet by his or her actions—prophesying, casting out demons, performing mighty works; this is precisely what makes him or her successful as a false prophet. This is confusing and threatens to break down the whole metaphor.

How does this teaching fit into this context? The solution is that while both images function with the wholeness (*teleios*) idea—internal and external together are necessary—they both also recognize that there is an *eventualness* to the ability to discern the inner truth. As with a tree, the fruit does not appear immediately but eventually, revealing then the true nature of the tree. So with these false prophets—sooner or later, and definitely in the eschatological judgment,[21] the false prophet and the wolf will be shown for what they truly are. Jesus exhorts his hearers not to judge too quickly (7:1–2) yet to exercise discernment about the real danger of false prophets who always look good on the outside. We know this was an issue in the earliest days of the church (e.g., Gal. 1:7–8; Ananias and Sapphira in Acts 5:1–11), even as it has continued to be down through the centuries.

20. Paul's arguments in 1 Cor. 12–14 also reveal that the possession and use of *charismata* or "spiritual gifts" is not necessarily evidence of maturity or even true faith. There are also examples in Acts of exorcisms (or attempted ones) by those outside the Christian faith (Acts 16:16–18; 19:11–17). Josephus, rabbinic literature, and other Second Temple Jewish texts witness to assorted miracle workers in the ancient world. See the discussion in Quarles, *Sermon on the Mount*, 338–40.
21. The language of "entering the kingdom of heaven" and "being cut down and thrown into the fire" makes it clear that the images are being used eschatologically.

This teaching, especially in Matt. 7:21–23, can be very troubling to the Christian reader. The shocking turn to see people who by all appearances were godly miracle workers be rejected as false is not easy to handle when applied to oneself. "Could I be such a person?" the sensitive soul asks. The same question arises in the famous parable of the sheep and goats that concludes the fifth major discourse (25:31–46). However, like the strong exhortations in 1 John,[22] Matt. 7:21–23 is not given to cause morbid introspection or undue self-doubt for the believer but rather to exhort one not to be enamored with external gifts and powers and behaviors without paying attention to the soul and heart. Jesus is warning his followers to beware of such people precisely because they have the appearance of godliness and therefore may lead the little ones to stumble (18:6; 24:4–11). Moreover, there is no reason to assume that these false prophets were genuinely surprised that they were rejected. Rather, their remonstrance in 7:22 (and 25:44) is not one of genuine surprise but self-justification.

Matthew 7:24–27: Two Kinds of Builders

[24]*Therefore, anyone who listens to my words[23] and practices[24] them can be compared to a wise person who built his house on rock.[25] [25]The rain fell, and the rivers rose, and the winds blew and beat against that house. And yet it did not collapse because it had been founded upon rock. [26]But anyone who listens to my words and does not practice them can*

22. The First Epistle of John contains some of the starkest and potentially most troubling statements of the NT (e.g., 3:6–10), yet a careful reading of the letter shows that these are meant primarily to describe to those inside the church what is true of those outside rather than to cause fear and self-doubt. E.g., John writes, "They went out from us, but they did not really belong to us. For if they had belonged to us, they would have remained with us; but their going showed that none of them belonged to us. *But you have an anointing from the Holy One, and all of you know the truth*" (1 John 2:19–20 NIV [emphasis mine]; see also 2:12–14, 27).
23. Typically, English translations render the rather rough Greek construction of "my these words" as "these words of mine." I have chosen instead to render it simply as "my words" because this more clearly matches the emphasis on "my" that the Greek is communicating, which otherwise gets lost in the more traditional English rendering. That it is "these" words of the Sermon can be assumed. Moreover, it is the words of not only this particular discourse but also all of Matthew that must be in view in light of Jesus's broad statement.
24. The word translated "practice" here is the same verb (*poieō*) that appears in 7:17, 18, 19, 21, and 22 and is there translated "produce." Unfortunately, there appears to be no good way to sustain the concordance between those verses and the usage here in 7:24, despite the consistency in Greek. For more on this theme of "doing" in the Sermon, see below.
25. The translation choices here and in the following verse are between "rock" and "the rock," both of which can be argued as representative of the notion in the Greek articular construction. The sophisticated reader of Matthew may make a connection between this language and the reference to Peter and/or his confession as the "rock" in 16:18, and this is not entirely inappropriate. However, the articular form, "the rock," in 7:24 and 25 is more easily understood in English translated as simply "rock" (vs. "sand" in 7:26).

> be compared to a foolish person who built his house on sand. ²⁷The
> rain fell, and the rivers rose, and the winds blew and beat against that
> house, and it did collapse, and it was a massive crash.

At the broadest level the Sermon is an invitation to wisdom—practiced, Christ-centered, kingdom-shaped, eschatologically oriented wise living—and so it is both appropriate and revealing that the climactic words of Jesus's first discourse explicitly make up a *wisdom* exhortation.

This appeal to lived-out, practical wisdom (*phronēsis* in the Aristotelian tradition) is not only embedded in the image of two ways throughout the conclusion (7:13–27) but is also made explicit by the contrast of the two main types or characters who represent the two ways in the final image (7:24–27): the *phronimos* one and the *mōros* one. The "moron" or foolish one is the one who does not follow the way of Jesus's wisdom, while the wise one does.

Phronimos is an important word for the Greek virtue tradition and for Matthew. In the virtue tradition this term refers to one who has learned through practice to live prudently, with discernment, and "who not only knows the truth but acts upon it."²⁶ It is a well-known and common word for the model virtuous person, and it is the adjectival form of the important noun *phronēsis*, which is the descriptor for the everyday practical wisdom that comes from an intentional life of virtue.²⁷ This commonness makes its infrequent use in the New Testament overall (only seven times outside of Matthew) stand out in relief, and especially because it proves to be a Matthean favorite, used seven times in the First Gospel alone.²⁸ Moreover, in Matthew it is always a positive reference, while in the rest of the New Testament it is neutral at best but usually negative and used somewhat ironically and sarcastically.²⁹ As here in 7:24–27, the *phronimos* one is again contrasted with its opposite, the *mōros* one, in the conclusion to the fifth and final discourse. There we learn of a group of ten virgins awaiting their bridegroom, five of whom are practical and prepared, described as *phronimoi*, and five who are not, described as *mōrai* (25:1–13).³⁰

26. Donald Hagner, *Matthew 1–13*, WBC 33A (Nashville: Nelson, 1993), 190.

27. For an exploration of how the idea of *phronēsis* and "sapiential theology" work out in biblical hermeneutics, see Daniel J. Treier, *Virtue and the Voice of God: Toward Theology as Wisdom* (Grand Rapids: Eerdmans, 2006), 129–206.

28. The occurrences are Matt. 7:24; 10:16; 24:45; 25:2, 4, 8, 9.

29. This usage is typical of Paul who, in his own Greco-Roman context, often needs to contrast the gospel message with the supposed wisdom of the philosophers of his day. See Rom. 11:25; 12:16; 2 Cor. 11:19. The only other occurrences of the word in the Gospels are in Luke 12:42 and 16:8, the latter of which is similar to Paul's usage.

30. Additionally, we can connect the *mōros* one here with the non-salty person (*mōranthē*) who can anticipate being thrown out and trampled (5:13).

In the three-image conclusion to the Sermon, the first two sections are headed by commands—"Enter!" (7:13) and "Beware!" (7:15). Both of these are appropriate wisdom exhortations from a sage. The third and concluding piece pulls up to the highest altitude with a metaphor or parable whose exhortation is implicit rather than direct. This parable describes two ways to live in the world with their consequential outcomes, either flourishing or destruction. There are several important observations to make about this image.

First, the consistent theme of inner versus outer righteousness or better, the necessity of wholeness, remains at the core of this final teaching, confirming its existence throughout the preceding material. Specifically, the use of the image of the foundation of the house is significant here. The contrast between the wisely and foolishly built houses is not based on their appearance or outward construction; indeed, one can imagine the foolish one's house being possibly much more attractive and embellished, even as the Pharisees' fasting, almsgiving, and praying practices were, complete with long tassels and lengthy, open pontifications (Matt. 6:1–21). Rather, the difference between the house/person that withstands the storm and the one that does not is at the hidden level of the foundation, the unseen but essential starting point. Thus, in yet another powerful way the contrast of 5:17–20 is highlighted—to be a follower of Jesus means a whole-person, inward-oriented righteousness (cf. 23:25–28).

Second, we may notice that the call is to *put into practice* Jesus's teachings, not merely to believe in them or in him. This is wisdom literature. This is discipleship, according to Matthew. Disciples are called to a level deeper than cognition by *practicing* his teachings. This is precisely what James is arguing in 1:22–25 and 2:14–26 when he exhorts his readers to be not merely hearers and cognitive believers (like the demons), but *doers* of the word (certainly understood here as *Jesus's* word) who have both faith and works.[31]

In the Greek text of the Sermon this is communicated through the recurrent lexeme *poieō*, though this is difficult to discern in English translations. The wide variety of ways that this verb must be rendered in English—"do, make, bear (fruit), produce, declare, practice"—covers up the thread that weaves its way through the Sermon; *poieō* appears some twenty-two times in Matt. 5–7 alone.[32] Particularly important are 5:19; 6:1; and 7:12. In 5:19 (which is part of

---

31. Robert M. Grant, in comparing the Sermon with James, notes that they share the same "social and ethical attitudes" and that if James did know the Sermon he would have likely taken it literally, insisting on this faith expressing itself in works ("The Sermon on the Mount in Early Christianity," *Semeia* 12 [1978], 215).

32. *Poieō* occurs a total of eighty-six times in Matthew, often in a general sense, but also very frequently as part of weightier statements such as 12:48–50: "Who is my mother, and who are my brothers? . . . Whoever *does the will* of my Father in heaven is my brother and sister and mother" (ESV; emphasis mine).

the thesis statement of the entire Sermon) those in and out of the kingdom of heaven are defined by whether they set aside/break one of the commands or rather "do [poieō] and teach them." In 6:1, which is the kəlāl or heading for the whole-person piety commands, disciples are told to "practice/do [poieō] their righteousness" carefully. And in 7:12 the important Golden Rule/Vision is yet again based on doing—"Whatever you would want others to do [poieō] to you or for you, in this same way treat [poieō] them." All of this sets up the reader for the conclusion to the Sermon, where poieō proves to be a recurrent theme, appearing eight times in 7:15–27. The point is that the two ways are determined not in the hearing but in the doing, which is made most explicit in the final image (7:24, 26). It is difficult to improve upon the way Donald Hagner describes this text:

> Perhaps no passage in the NT expresses more concisely and more sharply that the essence of discipleship . . . is found not in words, nor in religiosity, nor even in the performance of spectacular deeds in the name of Jesus, but only in the manifestation of true righteousness—i.e., the doing of the will of the Father as now interpreted through the teaching of Jesus. [No words or random good deeds] can substitute for the full picture of righteousness the evangelist has given in the sermon.[33]

Third, it is important to note the radical Jesus-centeredness that undergirds this closing exhortation of the Sermon. Jesus does not say that the wise and foolish are distinguished according to how they obey God or practice Torah or follow the teachings of the elders. Rather, in words that foreshadow 24:35, where Jesus promises that heaven and earth will pass away before his words will, and 18:15–20, where what is done in Jesus's name is binding on earth and in heaven, Jesus emphasizes that the wise and the foolish are distinguished on the basis of how they respond to his words. While Jesus is certainly presented as both Prophet and Sage, he is also repeatedly offered as more than these roles—the true and final source of revelation itself. His hearers are invited to build the foundation of their whole lives upon his teaching and way of being in the world. He is presenting himself as the authoritative arbiter of God's revelation and the path to human flourishing. Each hearer and reader must decide whether to follow or not; as Matthew will say multiple times elsewhere, "He who has ears to hear, let him hear" (11:15; 13:43) and "Let the reader understand" (24:15).

Finally, we should also note that this closing metaphor of two ways of building one's life has the urgency of eschatological judgment built into its mini-narrative. While one can rightly interpret the rain and floods and winds as the "storms of

33. Hagner, Matthew 1–13, 188.

life" that every human faces (a tradition going back at least to Augustine), there is a further meaning evoked by these images, namely, that of the final judgment. These words in a Jewish and biblical context definitely conjure up the belief in the ultimate reckoning that all of humanity must face in the presence of their Creator. There are several biblical texts that use the image of a flood and rising waters to indicate divine wrath, including Gen. 6–7; Isa. 28:17–22; Jer. 23:19–20; 30:23–24; and Ezek. 13:10–16. Also relevant are several proverbs that paint the picture of the wise and/or righteous ones enduring storms and troubles (Prov. 10:25; 12:7; 14:11). Charles Quarles sums it up well: "Jesus' teaching merges OT depictions of eschatological judgment as a storm with the theme in wisdom literature that the righteous endure catastrophes that destroy the wicked."[34]

This final-judgment sense adds an urgency and weight to the teachings of the Sermon and the need to follow its Teacher that go beyond mere philosophical reflections and debates that mark the Greco-Roman tradition. People should be concerned not merely with human experience now and human memory after one has died but also with a reckoning and evaluation by the divine being who is giving the instructions. The later Christian reader cannot help but hear hints in Jesus's words of both the coming destruction of Jerusalem and the Pharisaical way of being in the world.

Matthew 7:28–8:1: Descending and Action

> [28]And when Jesus had finished saying these words the crowd was astonished at his teaching, [29]for he was teaching them with such authority, not as their scribes taught. [8:1]And when he came down from the mountain great crowds followed him.

These brief verses serve as a sort of epilogue to the Sermon. In them the narrator's/evangelist's voice-over appears again, providing both a marker that the discourse has come to an end and a historical-theological comment that frames the whole teaching. The marker is found in the phrase "And it happened when Jesus had finished saying [these words] . . ."[35] This phrase occurs five times in Matthew precisely because it is the aural and literary marker used to indicate the close of each of the five major discourses that the First Gospel systematically and artistically provides.

This repeated phrase invites the hearer or reader to consider how these five discourses relate and fit together. Though it goes beyond the purview of our

---

34. Quarles, *Sermon on the Mount*, 349.
35. This discourse marker appears in 7:28; 11:1; 13:53; 19:1; and 26:1.

discussion here, we may note briefly that consistent across all five discourses is the dual theme of revelation and separation. Each of the discourses presents Jesus as revealing truth and wisdom, resulting in the separation of hearers into two groups: those who receive the revelation and those who do not.[36] This Matthean theme can be described as a kind of theological epistemology or a theological explanation of how understanding occurs. This theological epistemology is highlighted in the tripartite conclusion to the content of the Sermon in 7:13–27 (discussed above), where the hearers are divided into two types, narrow-way versus broad-way goers, wolves versus sheep, and finally, wise versus foolish builders.

Here at the closing of the Sermon the crowds (who also appeared in 5:1 and who are the recipients of the message) are those who *do* apparently receive Jesus's teaching, at least on the level of amazement at its clarity and authority. Looking farther ahead in Matthew, with the third discourse of parables in chapter 13 we see that there is in fact a variety of responses to Jesus's teachings, including some who are initially amazed but then fall away (13:5–7, 20–22). Additionally, it is remarkable that after Jesus's parabolic discourse (13:1–53), wherein his teaching style has changed radically from the clarity of the Sermon to the opacity of the parables (13:10–17), the crowds similarly respond with amazement (*ekplēssesthai*, 13:54), but this time it is wedded to a skepticism that results not in reception but stumbling; they are *scandalized* (*eskandalizonto*, 13:57) by him and dishonor him.

The comment in 7:28–29 also serves Matthew's larger Gospel-wide purpose, going beyond the mere presentation of the Sermon's important material. Matthew uses this opportunity to contrast Jesus's teaching and its effect with his contemporaries, the "scribes." Who these scribes were exactly is not possible to say with absolute definitiveness, but it is likely they were experts in the law who were largely drawn from that conservative sect of the Pharisees. In contrast to the crowds' normal teachers, Jesus comes across as one with great authority. This is not a surprising or unexpected response in light of the boldness of the claims Jesus makes throughout the Sermon, whether it

---

36. In the four other discourses, the theme of revelation and separation can be seen in instructions to the missionary representatives (10:5–42), in the separation of seeds, fruit, wheat and tares, good and bad fish in the parabolic discourse (13:1–53), in the determination of who is in and out of the church in the ecclesiological discourse (18:1–35), and finally in the judgment discourse with its separation of true and false leaders, wise and foolish virgins, and sheep and goats (23:1–25:46). For a fuller discussion of the ways the five major discourses are connected and manifest the theme of revelation and separation, see my "Theological Epistemology in the Gospel according to Matthew: A Watsonian 'Canonical Perspective,'" in Joel Willits and Catherine Sider Hamilton, eds., *Gospel Writing and the Fourfold Gospel: An Examination of the Possibilities and Problems in Francis Watson's Recent Contribution to Gospel Studies* (London: T&T Clark, forthcoming).

be his famous "you have heard it said, but I say to you . . ." statements, his pontifications about the state of true *makarios*-ness, or the exhortation to build one's life on *his* words. One can hardly imagine any first-century Jewish scribe making such bold claims unless he were seeking ostracism at best or a crucifixion at worst—that is, unless a person did think of himself as having just such an authority. Matthew obviously believes Jesus is such a person and elsewhere emphasizes Jesus's authority both in word and in deed (chaps. 8–9 being an immediate example), including the climactic commissioning scene wherein Jesus's disciples are given this same comprehensive, heaven-and-earth authority to continue the work of the ascended Jesus in the world (28:18–20).

Here in 7:29 Matthew's comment also serves as a foreshadowing of the opposition that Jesus engenders in the religious authorities of his day, particularly those of the conservative, Pharisaical group. It is precisely these scribes who will eventually instigate enough opposition to have this authoritative teacher (and pretender, in their opinion) imprisoned, beaten, and put to death (12:14; 21:45–46; 26:3–4).

Matthew 7:28–8:1 formally ends the Sermon with a bookend that matches 5:1–2. This descent from the mountain, which corresponds to the ascent in 5:1–2, resituates the reader into the narrative flow of Matthew's Gospel, which is more than just a concatenation of Jesus's teachings but also a biographical narrative. The reference to the great crowds following Jesus leads directly into the next part of Matthew's narrative, chapters 8–9. Matthew provides coordinated summary statements in 4:23–25 and 9:35–38 that explain the content of the "gospel of the kingdom" as including teaching, acts of compassionate healing, and the calling of people to follow. Matthew 8:1 serves as the proper transition from the teaching portion to that of the healings and callings (chaps. 8–9). The descent from the mountain in 8:1 also reminds the reader of a foundational evocation that frames the whole Sermon, Jesus's role as the new and greater Moses, prophet, teacher, and arbiter of truth. See the discussion on 5:1–2 above in chapter 6.

Matthew 7:13–8:1 and Human Flourishing

Scholars have debated to what degree Jesus is presented in the Gospels as a sage.[37] It would be overreaching to make "sage" the controlling image of

37. Jesus as a sage or wisdom teacher has been employed in an overstated way by some associated with the Jesus Seminar and a certain brand of historical Jesus studies, such as author John Dominic Crossan. See Crossan, *The Historical Jesus: The Life of a Mediterranean Jewish Peasant* (New York: HarperCollins, 1991). A more balanced approach can be found in Ben Witherington III, *Jesus the Sage: The Pilgrimage of Wisdom* (1994; repr., Minneapolis: Fortress, 2000). See the critiques and more solid reconstruction of the Second Temple Jewish context

who Jesus is throughout the Gospels, but the Sermon from beginning to end does present Jesus's divinely wise way of being in the world, with him as its authoritative teacher.[38] Jesus may be more than a sage, but he is not less than one, especially in Matthew and the Sermon. However, in light of the arguments made above that sage or philosopher is deeply interwoven with ancient notions of kingship, Jesus as sage is not truly in competition with Jesus as king, thus making both of these descriptions of Jesus mutually informing and predominant.

As has been noted earlier, this explanation of Jesus as sage squares much more closely with the data than the oft-repeated notion that the Sermon corresponds—especially in its opening Beatitudes and closing warnings—to Deuteronomic covenant curses and blessings. While a covenantal concept is not entirely absent from the Sermon, and the connections with Moses are duly noted, from beginning to end the Sermon shows itself to be eschatological *wisdom* literature—with its macarisms at the beginning, through the assorted issues of practical morality, piety, and interpersonal relations in the middle, to the explicit, proverbial appeal to live wisely here at the end. Jesus as the greater Solomon is calling his sons and daughters of the kingdom to a way of being in the world that honors God and promises flourishing to his followers.

If a reader or hearer of the Sermon has not yet discerned that the whole point of the Sermon is to offer a well-crafted précis of Jesus as the Jewish messianic, eschatological prophet-sage in the Greek language and context, Matt. 7:13–8:1 should make that patently obvious. The themes of the two ways, the necessary wholeness of the internal and external, and the contrast of the wise and the foolish combine to communicate strongly what I have suggested throughout this commentary—that the Sermon is best read within its encyclopedic context of Second Temple Jewish wisdom literature intersecting with the Greco-Roman virtue tradition, all of which provides a thoroughly Christian invitation to true human flourishing.

---

in Grant Macaskill, *Revealed Wisdom and Inaugurated Eschatology in Ancient Judaism and Early Christianity*, JSJSup 115 (Leiden: Brill, 2007).

38. See John Yueh-Han Yeih, *One Teacher: Jesus' Teaching Role in Matthew's Gospel Report* (Berlin: de Gruyter, 2004), who uses a literary-critical approach to argue for Matthew's presentation of Jesus as a teacher, and who compares this depiction with the Teacher of Righteousness (from Qumran) and Epictetus.

Theological
Reflection

12

The Sermon
on the Mount and the Theology
of Human Flourishing

A Sketch

Overview

The goal of this book has been to provide a historically conscious theological commentary on the masterful text that is Matthew's Sermon on the Mount. I have argued and sought to demonstrate that the best reading of the Sermon occurs when it is understood as a work of wisdom literature that is born of two intersecting worlds, Second Temple Judaism and the Greco-Roman virtue tradition. Early Christianity, which comes into being in the time and place of Hellenistic Judaism, manifests the hallmarks of a theological understanding that is thoroughly rooted in the Jewish Scriptures, recontextualized and described in a language and culture that are Greek. The Gospel of Matthew and the Sermon are no exceptions to this. In the Sermon, therefore, we should not be surprised to find an eschatological, Christ-centered, kingdom-oriented piece of wisdom literature with roots in the Jewish Scriptures that invites hearers into human flourishing through faith-based virtue, expressed in language that overlaps with other first-century moral philosophies.

To argue this thesis I have explored the encyclopedic context of the origins of the Sermon, seeking to understand the evocations that assorted expressions and themes communicate in light of this context. At the deepest and broadest level I have argued that the combined themes of *makarios*-ness, *teleios*-ity, wholeness, singularity, righteousness, and others together create a vision (a "moral imagination")[1] for a way of being in the world that promises true human flourishing, now partially and eschatologically fully, through believing in and aligning oneself with Jesus Christ, God's authoritative Son. Jesus is the embodiment—even incarnation—of the ideal Philosopher-King, inviting people into flourishing in God's coming kingdom.

In this concluding chapter I will offer some theological assertions that seek to pull together several threads and themes to construct a theology of human flourishing rooted in the Sermon. This must only be a sketch, however. Due to time and space constraints, I am offering here a sketch in the form of six theses. These theses seek to summarize the arguments I have already made and to press them into areas that touch on larger theological categories. These six theses build on each other and overlap in content.

Thesis 1: The Bible Is about Human Flourishing

In chapters 1–3 above I made several arguments about how the encyclopedic context of Matthew's Gospel and early Christianity helps the reader discern that the Sermon is working with concepts of human flourishing. From a broader biblical, theological, and historical perspective many other scholars have argued for a human-flourishing understanding of the Bible and its message.[2] Rather than rearguing the lexical and conceptual arguments I have made earlier or attempting to rehash the work of these other scholars, I will simply assert here my understanding, based on preceding work.

In short, the proclamation of both the Jewish and Christian Scriptures is that the God of Abraham, Isaac, Jacob, and (Father of) Jesus offers the

---

1. This comes from the descriptive subtitle of Dale C. Allison Jr.'s little commentary on the Sermon, *The Sermon on the Mount: Inspiring the Moral Imagination* (New York: Crossroad, 1999).

2. Entry points into this understanding include: Brent Strawn, ed., *The Bible and the Pursuit of Happiness: What the Old and New Testaments Teach Us about the Good Life* (Oxford: Oxford University Press, 2012); Ellen Charry, *God and the Art of Happiness* (Grand Rapids: Eerdmans, 2010); Miroslav Volf and Justin E. Crisp, eds., *Joy and Human Flourishing: Essays on Theology, Culture, and the Good Life* (Minneapolis: Fortress, 2015); Miroslav Volf, *Flourishing: Why We Need Religion in a Globalized World* (New Haven: Yale University Press, 2016). N. T. Wright's *After You Believe: Why Christian Character Matters* (New York: HarperCollins, 2010) provides a creative and robust biblical argument for an eschatological, virtue-ethics understanding. The Yale Center for Faith and Culture also provides a rich trove of resources on theology and human flourishing: http://faith.yale.edu/god-human-flourishing/god-human-flourishing.

only true, full, and enduring human flourishing available in the world. This is because God is the creator and sustainer of all that is, was, and will be. It is no accident that both the opening and closing chapters of the Bible are images of flourishing—beautiful, nourishing, verdant places. As Miroslav Volf notes, these images "are part of a grand narrative arc starting with the world's creation and ending with new heavens and the new earth," visions of flourishing that are "rooted in convictions about the reality of the One who dwells in inapproachable light."[3]

Holy Scripture is making claims that are more than henotheistic (one should worship only one god), but radically monotheistic (there is only one true God), claims that are not only liturgical but also ontological. Consequently, humanity can only find the *telos* or end for which it has been created through relationship to its sole Creator (and by extension to the rest of this Creator's creation).

Entailed in this is the assumption—one that every philosophy and religion, including the Judeo-Christian writings and tradition, shares—that the end goal and universal desire of humanity is indeed to experience fullness of life, happiness, flourishing. Holy Scripture is asking and answering the same question that all religions and philosophies have always asked: How can one experience true and lasting happiness?

This thesis must be asserted anew within Christianity now because the history of the church manifests a loss of this eudaimonistic understanding of the nature of the faith and its ethics.[4] The loss of focus on human flourishing—indeed, the latent *fear* of speaking this way that plagues many faithful Christians, including many within the assorted Reformed, Lutheran, and evangelical traditions—often comes from a rightful and biblical desire to highlight a "God-centeredness" that keeps God and his creatures in a proper relationship of hierarchy and in proper focus; too much talk of the importance of

---

3. Volf, *Flourishing*, x.

4. Charry, *God and the Art of Happiness*, gives an overview of how she understands this devolution occurred, especially within the Western church and particularly Protestantism. The Roman Catholic tradition is certainly not monolithic, but the loss of the doctrine of happiness/ human flourishing is not as profound or pervasive there. Many within Roman Catholicism, especially its moral theologians (or ethicists), continue the Augustinian tradition of framing ethics and theology in terms of happiness. See, e.g., Servais Pinckaers, *Morality: The Catholic View*, trans. Michael Sherwin (South Bend, IN: St. Augustine's Press, 2003), an abridgment of his weighty *The Sources of Christian Ethics*, 3rd ed., trans. Mary Thomas Noble (Washington, DC: Catholic University of America Press, 1995), in which he argues that the Christian tradition has wrongly shifted toward thinking of morality in terms of obligations and prohibitions rather than, with Augustine, as the freedom-giving capacity for happiness experienced through Christian virtue.

humanity sounds to many like a slippery slope to the loss of the Bible's focus first on God.

I think this fear of theological human flourishing is also motivated by an awareness that Jesus calls his followers to self-sacrifice (Mark 8:34–35; Luke 9:23–24), to cross carrying (Matt. 10:38; Luke 14:27), to considering others as more important than themselves (Phil. 2:3–8). However, as I have argued above, this cannot be construed as a flat-footed denial of one's own reward, recompense, satisfaction, or ultimate flourishing. Indeed, every time Jesus calls people to sacrifice it is based on promises of future reward and recompense, even as we saw in the Sermon (e.g., 6:1–21). This is described as the motivation even for Jesus's own sacrifice, not some Kantian altruism—look to Jesus, "the founder and perfecter of our faith, *who for the joy that was set before him endured the cross*, despising the shame, and is seated at the right hand of the throne of God" (Heb. 12:2 ESV, emphasis added; cf. Phil. 2:8–10). As Charles Taylor points out, Christianity's call to serve and worship God cannot be construed as mere renunciation, a kind of Stoic view of flourishing. The call to sacrifice now and to love others and to renounce some goods "doesn't negate the value of flourishing; it is rather a call to centre everything on God."[5]

Related, at the core of the Protestant tradition, especially its Lutheran and Reformed versions, is an emphasis on the sinfulness of humanity in distinction from God. The pervasiveness of this emphasis can be seen in an experiment I have done in class among my (mostly Reformed) evangelical students: I ask them to offer the first word that comes to mind when I say the word "humanity." Nearly always the answer is "sinful." From a biblical and Protestant perspective it is certainly accurate and true that humanity is sinful and separated from God as a result. This foundational reality is at the core of the gospel message: humanity needs to be rescued and reconciled to God because of sin.[6] Yet it is fair to inquire whether this sinfulness is the first or properly primary descriptor of humanity from God's perspective. At least we can observe descriptively that this common answer reveals like a Rorschach test what lies at the core of much of evangelical anthropology. There is an enculturation or training of sensibilities and habits such that the primary evocation or association that is made with "humanity" is "sinful."[7] I would

---

5. Charles Taylor, *A Secular Age* (Cambridge, MA: Harvard University Press, 2007), 18.

6. In an insightful blog post, Michael Kruger notes that while the people of God are called many things throughout the NT, "sinners" is not one of them, but rather, typically it is "saints." Kruger points out that this affects the Christian's identity and should create a cognitive dissonance between what we have been made into in Christ and our sinful lives (http://michaeljkruger.com /saint-or-sinner-rethinking-the-language-of-our-christian-identity/).

7. Stemming from and reinforcing this idea is the frequent quoting of Isa. 64:6—"all our righteous acts are like filthy rags" (NIV)—as evidence for the foolishness and inaccuracy of

recommend instead that "sinful" is an appropriate *second* word to say about humanity. The first reaction/word according to the Bible's vision should be instead "loved" or even "beautiful."[8]

The point of this brief excursus into theological anthropology is this: one effect of this difference of enculturated approaches is that for many in the Protestant tradition the idea that the Bible's message and God's goal for humanity is human flourishing may seem misplaced. The focus on human flourishing could be wrongly perceived as somehow unrelated to or the opposite of being saved from sin. Or for some, any talk of radically bad humans experiencing flourishing and happiness may be perceived as opposed to God and *God's* glory being the end goal of the world.

These are false and unfortunate dichotomies, however. The Bible's *telos* is simultaneously God centered and human focused. To put it in the words of John Piper's now-famous retooling of the Westminster Confession, "The chief end of man is to glorify God *by* enjoying him forever."[9] Or more profoundly, we can hear the voice of Jonathan Edwards (the source of Piper's perspective) who reflects on the connection with humanity's happiness and union with the Triune God:

> God's respect to the creature's good, and his respect to himself, is not a divided respect; but both are united in one, as the happiness of the creature aimed at is happiness in union with himself. The creature is no further happy with his happiness which God makes his ultimate end, than he becomes one with God. The more happiness the greater union: when the happiness is perfect, the union is perfect. And as the happiness will be increasing to eternity, the union will become more and more strict and perfect; nearer and more like to that between God the Father and the Son; who are so united, that their interest is perfectly one.[10]

----

humanity's attempts at earning God's favor through deeds. While this is true, it is important to note that this hyperbolic and poetic statement is not *all* that Scripture says about righteousness, good deeds, and humans doing beautiful things that bring honor to God, including in the Sermon on the Mount (e.g., Matt. 5:16, where people see the "good works" of believers and glorify God as a result).

8. That God *loves* the creatures uniquely made in his image must certainly be the primary and ultimate message of the Bible, explaining why, despite our rebellion and sinfulness, there is a gospel message at all and why the incarnation occurred. My point here is slightly different from Kruger's noted above, which is specifically about the primary identity of Christians as "saints" rather than "sinners," but it is analogous to consider the primary identity of creatures made in God's image as loved before sinful.

9. The Westminster Shorter Catechism begins: "What is the chief end of man? Man's chief end is to glorify God, and to enjoy him forever."

10. Jonathan Edwards, "The End for Which God Created the World," in *The Works of Jonathan Edwards*, ed. Paul Ramsey (New Haven: Yale University Press, 1992), 8:533–34.

I have sought in this book to make a small contribution toward remedying this false dichotomy between God-centeredness and human flourishing by offering a reading of the Sermon that I hope is both coherent and plausible, showing that the Sermon is offering an invitation to human flourishing through Jesus the Christ while maintaining a radically God-centered perspective. Jesus is more than a moral philosopher and purveyor of human-flourishing wisdom, but he is not less than these things. One clear and strong manifestation of this is the Sermon, which is an epitome that invites all people to his revealed way of being in the world, which alone will result in their flourishing.[11]

Thesis 2: The Bible's Vision of Human Flourishing Is God Centered and Eschatological

The Jewish and Christian Scriptures share with other contemporary religions and cultural contexts an emphasis on human flourishing. The answer that the Old and New Testaments give to the question of what constitutes human flourishing and how to obtain it differ from the Bible's contemporaries, however. There was no monolithic answer in the ancient Near East or in the Greco-Roman world as to what the flourishing life comprises, and especially not on the philosophical questions of what role Fortune and specific virtues play in obtaining the state of *šālôm* or *eudaimonia*.[12] Thus, evaluating the content of the Bible's theology of human flourishing can never be a simple comparison to some consistent ancient standard. Nonetheless, there are insights that can be gained by noting some aspects of biblical human flourishing that are shared with other contemporary approaches and ways in which they differ.

As was noted in chapter 1 above, the Sermon shares with the Jewish Scriptures, Second Temple Judaism, and the Greek tradition an emphasis on virtue as necessary to achieve human flourishing (*makarios*-ness, *'ašrê*-ness,

---

11. Robert S. Kinney summarizes that the Sermon "is not only successful in presenting Jesus as an authoritative mediator of both law and heavenly reward for those who follow his exhortations to righteousness; it is also successful in presenting Jesus as a Socratic figure—one who gathers disciples, teaches disciples, and so mediates their development for *the good*" (*Hellenistic Dimensions of the Gospel of Matthew* [Tübingen: Mohr Siebeck, 2016], 215 [emphasis original]).

12. The different Greek philosophical schools engaged in a long debate about what the nature of *eudaimonia* was and what role Fortune and emotions played in obtaining it. See Darrin McMahon, "The Pursuit of Happiness in History," in *The Oxford Handbook of Happiness*, ed. Susan A. David, Ilona Boniwell, and Amanda Conley Ayers (Oxford: Oxford University Press, 2013), 254. See also McMahon's fuller treatment, *Happiness: A History* (New York: Grove, 2006). Another recent and helpful collection of essays can be found in Øvyind Rabbås, Eyjólfur K. Emilsson, Hallvard Fossheim, and Miira Tuominen, eds., *The Quest for the Good Life: Ancient Philosophers on Happiness* (Oxford: Oxford University Press, 2015).

eudaimonia). This virtue has at its core the necessity of whole-person functioning, pursuing the goal of becoming complete and unified (*teleios*-ity). This much is the same.

The Christian understanding of human flourishing (found in both the Old and New Testaments), however, has a distinct shape and tone that are rooted in its radically monotheistic (and finally, christological and trinitarian) understanding of the world.[13] This foundation in and orientation to the revelation of God in Christ means that for a Christian theology of human flourishing, (1) full flourishing can only be experienced when one is in relationship to and communion with God, (2) full flourishing will only be experienced in the eschaton when God establishes completely his rule and reign (the kingdom of God), and (3) flourishing is missional, priestly, and outward focused, spreading God's glory throughout the earth. I explore each of these points below.

(1) Other religions of the ancient world clearly had a relationship to the divine as part of their depiction of how to obtain flourishing, and even in the Greek philosophical tradition there is an acknowledgment (even if it is relegated to a minor role) of the true happiness (*makaria*) of the gods and the role of Fortune in obtaining it. However, the Christian understanding, rooted as it is in the Jewish revelation, is that apart from a covenantal relationship with the one true God any flourishing humans experience is derivative and temporary. Wisdom literature such as the Psalms and Proverbs often depicts the foolishness, shortsightedness, and ultimately short-lived and destructive nature of ungodly pleasures that promise no lasting happiness.[14] The prophetic literature likewise often appeals to God's people to avoid the allure of idol worship because while it promises flourishing, its end is destruction.[15]

The Sermon shares this same understanding and emphasis. For example, the central section of the instructions on piety (6:1–21) notes with a pointed irony that the non-God-centered Pharisees "have their reward in full," a reward that will prove to be eaten by moths and destroyed by rust (6:19–21). And in the climactic close to the Sermon we see three exhortative images that are built on the idea that what appears good and beneficial now will prove to be

---

13. Christopher A. Beeley explores the pervasive theme of human flourishing throughout the church fathers and shows how radically christocentric their understanding was. Jesus doesn't just promote human flourishing through his saving work, but more fundamentally, through his very identity. "Christ is himself the archetype and first instance of human flourishing, and other human beings flourish by participating in Christ's divine-human life" ("Christ and Human Flourishing in Patristic Theology," paper presented at the Yale Center for Faith and Culture, available at http://faith.yale.edu/sites/default/files/beeley_christ_and_human_flourishing_in_patristic_theology_-_final.pdf).

14. E.g., Ps. 73; Prov. 1:8–19.

15. E.g., Isa. 44:9–20.

destructive and ultimately destroyed—broad roads and gates, wolves in sheep's clothing, and a foolishly built beachside house upon the sand (7:13–27). The Christian theology of human flourishing is an appeal to wisdom, but one that is rooted in an explicitly theistic and christological understanding and covenantal relationship.

(2) Another key difference between the early Christian understanding of flourishing and that of its contemporaries is the emphasis that is put on the ultimately eschatological nature of flourishing. God's work in the world, according to Scripture, has a linear trajectory and a final goal, the restoration of creation itself and the establishment of a redeemed and re-formed humanity in a paradisiacal state of flourishing.[16] The New Testament frames this message in terms of the Triune God bringing his kingdom from heaven to earth, vanquishing his enemies, and establishing justice and peace between people and all of creation. The entirety of the New Testament is leaning forward toward this eschaton. This is not yet the situation, however. The Christian experience is one of waiting, longing, and preparing for God's return to the earth in Christ's second coming. Therefore, human flourishing cannot be experienced fully because the end for which God created the world and humanity has not yet been consummated. Indeed—and this is the most paradoxical element of the Christian understanding—human flourishing is experienced now in the midst of suffering and the brokenness of the world. In fact, the reality of the already-not yet, eschatological goal of the world necessitates this. Because the end has not yet come, human flourishing will only be experienced in a paradoxical way that combines loss, longing, suffering, and persecution with true happiness, joy, satisfaction, and peace. The Beatitudes establish and explicate this experiential enigma by emphasizing that *makarios*-ness is experienced now through moments of need, loss, brokenness, poverty, and even outright persecution, and ultimately when God reestablishes his kingdom.

(3) Flowing out of the eschatological nature of the Bible's theology of flourishing is the third and crucial difference between a Christian understanding and that of its closest cousin, the Greek eudaimonistic tradition. Namely, the *telos* of the Bible's eschatology is a "restor(y)ing of the world,"[17] a restoration

16. This is the greatest strength of N. T. Wright's exploration of a biblical virtue ethics—his insight that the NT's understanding of *eudaimonia* and the *telos* of humanity is to *enter into full humanity*, to fully and genuinely reflect the image of God as part of Christ's new-creation redemption. See esp. Wright, *After You Believe*, chap. 5, "Transformed by the Renewal of the Mind."

17. This language comes from the final chapter of James K. A. Smith, *Imagining the Kingdom* (Grand Rapids: Baker Academic, 2013), which itself is indebted to insights along these lines by N. T. Wright.

of *šālôm* to the entire creation. It is not just about the individual's personal experience of happiness; it is also missional, priestly, and outward focused, spreading God's glory and love throughout the earth. Indeed, the communal aspect of human flourishing is essential to the Christian understanding of *makarios*.[18] N.T. Wright says it this way: The early Christians did not abandon the framework of shaping one's life based on the *telos* or goal, but they did replace the Aristotelian goal with a different one. The goal is, according to Gen. 1–2, what humans were made for in the first place, and according to Exodus, what Israel is called to—"It is the task of being the 'royal priesthood,' worship and stewardship, generating justice and beauty."[19]

Nicholas Wolterstorff deserves credit for seeing and articulating this difference most clearly.[20] He observes that for all the good of the Aristotelian eudaimonistic tradition, ultimately that tradition centers on the individual and his or her personal experience, and it lacks a necessary component of the good life: compassionate relationships.[21] The biblical and Christian understanding of flourishing, however, is not just a means for the individual to experience the good but is a universe-sized mission to spread God's *šālôm* (flourishing) or peace throughout his creation. Wolterstorff terms this "eireneism" rather than "eudaimonism," based on the Greek translation of *šālôm*. This eireneism entails seeing an inherent good in others and a necessary focus on the recipient dimension of morality. That is, while eudaimonism does include the notion of friendship and community, "it lacks the self-denying characteristic of the recipient-dimension of morality. . . . *Eireneism* is exemplified by acts of 'true'

18. Debra Dean Murphy observes that in the Christian tradition happiness was understood as a *political* reality—"the flourishing we experience as we seek to practice the goodness of God together." Jesus's Beatitudes are "an invitation to particular forms of behavior that bind us in love and responsibility to one another" (*Happiness, Health, and Beauty: The Christian Life in Everyday Terms* [Eugene, OR: Cascade, 2015], 6–7).

19. Wright, *After You Believe*, 82–83.

20. In addition to his collection of essays related to Christian education, *Educating for Shalom: Essays on Christian Higher Education*, ed. Clarence W. Joldersma and Gloria Goris Stronks (Grand Rapids: Eerdmans, 2004), Wolterstorff develops his distinction between eudaimonism and eireneism (based on the Greek word for "peace" [*eirēnē*]) in his *Justice: Rights and Wrongs* (Princeton: Princeton University Press, 2008), esp. chaps. 7–8. He continues this thinking and creates the term "agapism" (based on the Greek word for "love" [*agapē*]) in his *Justice in Love* (Grand Rapids: Eerdmans, 2011).

21. Apart from Wolterstorff, there is criticism of the eudaimonistic tradition as being egotistical, and there are debates about how to understand this. Julia Annas provides a balanced perspective in *The Morality of Happiness* (Oxford: Oxford University Press, 1993). For a discussion of some later Greek philosophers who consider the role of others in the pursuit of *eudaimonia*, see Miira Tuominen, "Why Do We Need Other People to Be Happy? Happiness and Concern for Others in Aspasius and Porphyry," in Rabbås, Emilsson, Fossheim, and Tuominen, *Quest for the Good Life*, 241–64.

compassion (suffering with and for others)."[22] The answer to the question of what human flourishing is cannot be just "How shall I live?" but "How can I bring good to others as well?" Indeed, we might observe that similar to the paradox that flourishing is experienced in the midst of suffering, so too individual flourishing can only be fully known when one is engaged in the greater, outward-focused work of bringing God's peace and love to the world. Christian virtue points away from itself, outward to God in worship and to the world in mission.[23] Happiness is found when one is not pursuing it directly for oneself.[24]

It is not difficult to see that the Gospel of Matthew frames the wisdom/ flourishing exhortation that is the Sermon on the Mount in the same way. From beginning to end Jesus in Matthew is outward focused, on a mission to come and "rescue his people from their sins" (1:21). The book then ends with the Great Commission, which establishes for any disciple-reader the ongoing orientation of one's life—being an active agent in the world, proclaiming and teaching what Jesus has said and done, bringing the revealed way of being in the world to the world. The flourishing that the Sermon envisions and promises can only be found through being an outward-focused disciple of Jesus as pictured throughout the entirety of Matthew.

Thesis 3: The Moral View of the Bible Is a Revelatory Virtue Ethic

As noted, the Bible shares with many of its contemporary philosophies and religions the understanding that ethics or morality is agentic and aretegenic. That is, ethics is about who people are and a certain way of being in the world, about becoming more virtuous as the means to flourishing. As also noted above, the Bible's goal in this ethics of virtue is particular, however, in being

22. This way of phrasing it is based on Wolterstorff's work but comes from Court Lewis's insightful essay applying this idea to children's literature, "*The Cricket in Times Square*: Crickets, Compassion, and the Good Life," in *Philosophy in Children's Literature*, ed. Peter R. Costello (Lanham, MD: Lexington Books, 2012), 220. From a Wesleyan perspective, Murphy describes it this way: "the Church is a social body (*polis*) whose end (*telos*) is the flourishing of all creation in the goodness of God. . . . The Sermon on the Mount is not a list of impossible demands intended for the individual Christian's personal faith but a description and summons to a communal way of life" (*Happiness, Health, and Beauty*, 8).

23. Wright, *After You Believe*, 243.

24. This paradoxical human experience has been observed by many. C. S. Lewis describes his experience of the elusiveness of joy in his autobiographical *Surprised by Joy: The Shape of My Early Life* (London: Bles; New York: Harcourt, Brace & World, 1955). This truth is also one of the takeaways from the profound and well-produced 2014 film, *Hector and the Search for Happiness*.

eschatological and universally missional; it is not just about the individual's human flourishing but also God's ultimate restoration of *šālôm* to the world.

Related to this and shaping it is another key element of Scripture's ethical stance: it is revelatory. That is, while the Bible's mode of moral exhortation is sapiential, and crucial texts like the Sermon are wisdom/virtue literature (paraenesis), it is an exhortational wisdom that is *based in and shaped by divine revelation.* God is a speaking God who reveals himself through nature and through humans reflecting on creation and the articulation of this wisdom. "Consider the ant . . ." Prov. 6:6 exhorts us.

But God also reveals himself through speaking, inscripturated in the Bible and ultimately in the Son, the Word of God. Therefore, any articulation of a virtue-ethics understanding of Holy Scripture must include an emphasis on the foundational revelatory nature of the wisdom being offered; virtue is found by reflecting not merely on culture and human experience but ultimately on God's words.[25] N. T. Wright notes that even though ultimately what matters is that the heart be renewed and that we be people of character, moral rules still matter—"one cannot play off virtue against rules and hope still to be making sense."[26] Wolterstorff likewise notes the problem of a pure virtue-ethics approach without an external standard of rightness in that the ethical agent has no way of determining which are the right dispositions and affections to have.[27]

In chapter 1 above I cited Scot McKnight's helpful analysis of three different approaches to ethics in the Sermon—ethics from above, ethics from beyond, and ethics from below. These correspond to morality based on commands (such as in the Law), based on the future eschaton (as in the Prophets), and on wisdom (as in the Wisdom literature).[28] McKnight rightly argues that Jesus teaches in all three ways (as does the whole Bible), yet unfortunately we often treat ethics and the Sermon from only one of these perspectives. I suggested in chapter 1 that we must not flatten these out into simply three

---

25. Oliver O'Donovan notes that we need more than a list of all the moral instructions and principles in the Bible to be wise; we need a moral vision. "We will read the bible seriously only when we use it to guide our thought towards a *comprehensive* moral view point, and not merely to articulate disconnected moral claims. We must look within it not only for moral bricks, but for indications of the order in which the bricks belong together" (*Resurrection and the Moral Order: An Outline for Evangelical Ethics*, 2nd ed. [Grand Rapids: Eerdmans, 1994], 200 [emphasis original]).

26. Wright, *After You Believe*, 132.

27. Wolterstorff, *Justice: Rights and Wrongs*, 165. This is part of Wolterstorff's argument as to why eudaimonism is not sufficient in itself to establish a just society with rights for all.

28. Scot McKnight, *The Sermon on the Mount*, The Story of God Bible Commentary (Grand Rapids: Zondervan, 2013), 1–17.

different ways of approaching ethics, but instead we should understand that the goal and focus of biblical ethics is people learning virtue rooted in God's commands. Regardless, McKnight is correct in arguing that the ethics of the Bible is simultaneously revelatory, eschatological, and wisdom based.

To use more traditional ethical categories, for the last 150 years or so the debate has been about whether the nature of ethics is deontological, utilitarian, or agentic/virtue based.[29] The point of my third thesis is to assert, based on what we have seen in the reading of the Sermon given above and fitted into the context of the whole Bible, that biblical ethics is a virtue ethic—focusing primarily on humanity learning and growing to be a certain way in the world, emphasizing the importance of the agent/person, not just the action—*but a virtue ethic that is rooted in, shaped by, and encircled by divine revelation.* We might describe this as a revelatory virtue ethic. Jesus invites hearers into a way of being in the world that needs *teleios*-ity (5:48; 6:1–21) and promises *makarios*-ness (5:3–12) *based on* his unique claims to authority as the final arbiter of God's covenantal instructions (5:17–48; 7:28–29).

In this I am suggesting once again that much can be learned from the premodern Christian tradition, especially as found in Augustine. Augustine's understanding of morality is clearly focused on the pursuit of happiness, which can only be found in God himself and properly ordered loves. Yet despite this eudaimonistic focus, or better, *because* of its divine orientation, Augustinian morality is based on obligation to divine revelation.[30] "Sin is an action, word, or desire that contravenes the eternal law. The eternal law is divine reason or the will of God who commands us to maintain the natural order and forbids us to violate it."[31] Sin has at its root the disordering of love, failing to love God and his law properly.[32] The opposite of sin, then, is virtue pursued in and through love for God and others. Thus, Augustine holds together both the focus on a eudaimonistic virtue ethic and God's revelation.

Jonathan Wilson's succinct book *Gospel Virtues* provides a contemporary evangelical appropriation of virtue ethics that keeps the centrality of God

29. The literature on this topic, of course, is massive. Over the last forty years the field of ethics has experienced a renaissance of the virtue-ethics approach, rooted in a robust recovery of the Aristotelian and Thomistic traditions, much of which can be attributed to the seminal work of Alisdair MacIntyre, *After Virtue: A Study in Moral Theory*, 3rd ed. (Notre Dame, IN: University of Notre Dame Press, 2007).

30. Helpful here is the discussion in Albert Plé, *Duty or Pleasure? A New Appraisal of Christian Ethics*, trans. Matthew J. O'Connell (New York: Paragon House, 1987), 17–22.

31. Augustine, *Contra Faustum Manichaeum* 22.22, translated in Plé, *Duty or Pleasure?*, 21.

32. For an introductory and practical discussion of this idea, see David K. Naugle, *Reordered Love, Reordered Lives: Learning the Deep Meaning of Happiness* (Grand Rapids: Eerdmans, 2008).

and his revelation as the foundation.[33] Wilson explores the rediscovery and revitalization of a virtue-ethics approach from a distinctly evangelical perspective, raising theological concerns that must be taken into account. One of these concerns is how divine commands fit into virtue ethics. He concludes that God's moral instructions must be included—"any ethic that is grounded in Scripture must attend to God's commands"—while also noting the superiority of virtue ethics over merely divine-command ethics. A virtue ethics rooted in Scripture is superior because it directs our attention to the kind of person that God wants for his creatures and because it directs our attention toward the biblical emphasis on *growth* and growth through habituation in the Christian life (Gal. 5:22–23; Eph. 4:22–24; Phil. 4:8; 2 Pet. 1:5).[34]

Thesis 4: The Sermon Teaches That Salvation Is Inextricably Entailed with Discipleship/Virtuous Transformation

In many ways this thesis seems obvious and uneventful, but because of perpetual confusion and assorted pear-shaped theologies, it needs to be stated clearly from the perspective of the Sermon.[35] As we have seen, a major Matthean theme, including in the Sermon, is the necessity of having a greater righteousness (5:20) and doing the will of God (7:21–23; 12:50; 21:28–32; 26:39; see chap. 4 above). To enter God's kingdom one must have faith in Christ, but this faith must never be construed as mere mental assent or hope apart from a life of discipleship and faithfulness. James addresses this head-on in his famous reflections on the necessity of both faith and works that originate from faith (James 2:14–26), and the Sermon does as well with its focus on what the necessary greater righteousness looks like—a whole-person, wholehearted devotion to God. We might simply call this discipleship.

The theological elephant in the room for this discussion is the Protestant emphasis on Paul's doctrine of justification and how the Sermon's focus

33. Jonathan R. Wilson, *Gospel Virtues: Practicing Faith, Hope, and Love in Uncertain Times* (Downers Grove, IL: InterVarsity, 1998).

34. Ibid., 38.

35. As is well known, Dietrich Bonhoeffer's classic book *The Cost of Discipleship*, trans. R. H. Fuller and Irmgard Booth (New York: Macmillan, 1959; repr., New York: Touchstone, 1995) is based on the Sermon on the Mount and lays out the Christian faith in terms of "following Jesus" (cf. *Nachfolge*, the title in the original German). A succinct narrative of Bonhoeffer's life and the role the Sermon played in his conversion and life can be found in Glen Stassen and David Gushee, *Kingdom Ethics: Following Jesus in Contemporary Context* (Downers Grove, IL: IVP Academic, 2003), 125–27. See also the thoughtful reflections of Bonhoeffer's wrestling with application of the Sermon in Glen Stassen, *A Thicker Jesus: Incarnational Discipleship in a Secular Age* (Louisville: Westminster/John Knox, 2012), 175–95.

on the necessity of virtuous discipleship squares with this (or not, as some would have it).[36] In short, I suggest that it is a misunderstanding of Paul if one reads him as being in conflict with Jesus's emphasis on discipleship and the necessary and effectual work of God's grace given to believers through the Holy Spirit.[37] Paul and Matthew are in fundamental agreement and share the same ethical and eschatological worldview, even though at times they are addressing different questions and speak in somewhat different terms (as do James and Paul).[38] Even though Matthew and Paul talk about righteousness differently (for Paul in his polemical Jewish setting this is a category dealing with imputation and God setting the world to right, while for Matthew it is always connected to ethical behavior), that does not mean they have different views of discipleship and salvation. Indeed, Paul is as radical about the need for a transformation of the heart as Matthew is (Rom. 12:1–2; 2 Cor. 3:18; Eph. 4:22–24), and Matthew is as radical about the need for faith in Christ as Paul is (Matt. 8:10; 9:2, 22, 29; 15:28; 21:21; cf. 6:30; 13:58).[39]

36. For all the erudition and insight that Hans Dieter Betz provides on the Sermon and its Greco-Roman background, he missteps in understanding both Paul *and* the Sermon when he pits them against each other, even going so far as to suggest that when Matthew declares that the one who "sets aside the least of the commandments and teaches others accordingly will be called least in the kingdom of heaven," he has in mind Paul! See Betz, *Essays on the Sermon on the Mount* (1985; Minneapolis: Fortress, 2009), 19–21. Orthodox Christianity has long seen many other ways to explain the unity within the diversity of teachings of the NT without needing to resort to such a strong antithetical interpretation of the various texts of earliest Christianity.

37. One of the most surprising and enjoyable books I have read on this topic is Joel D. Biermann, *A Case for Character: Towards a Lutheran Virtue Ethics* (Minneapolis: Fortress, 2014). Biermann, a Missouri Synod Lutheran, makes a strong and irenic case both historically and theologically that Luther, Melanchthon, and the Lutheran tradition both did and should have a place for a virtue-ethics understanding within the Lutheran theological system. He also offers a constructive paradigm for how to understand three kinds of righteousness from a Lutheran perspective. On the Reformed side of the aisle, also worth reading is Kirk J. Nolan, *Reformed Virtue after Barth: Developing Moral Virtue Ethics in the Reformed Tradition* (Louisville: Westminster John Knox, 2014), which argues that a Barthian Reformed tradition can be squared with the virtue tradition as well.

38. It would be a misunderstanding of Paul to think he conceives of *dikaiosynē* as separate from moral transformation. Protestantism's interpretation of the term in Romans has often obscured what it is seeking to clarify. As Oliver O'Donovan notes, "The correlate of a 'justification' which has nothing to do with 'righteousness' is a righteousness that has nothing to do with justification, and this soon presented itslf to Protestant thought under the heading of 'sanctification.' The improper divorce of sanctification from justification bequeathed to Protestant churches their characteristic tension between a gospel with no concern for life in the world and a concern for life in the world which has lost touch with the gospel" (*Resurrection and the Moral Order*, 254).

39. David A. deSilva has provided a well-written exploration of Paul's thinking about the gospel as transformation in his *Transformation: The Heart of Paul's Gospel* (Bellingham, WA:

One helpful book that addresses this question directly is Roger Mohrlang's *Matthew and Paul: A Comparison of Ethical Perspectives*.[40] Mohrlang offers a careful analysis of the ethical teachings of both Paul and Matthew and notes that while there are obvious differences in perspective, the contrast between them is not as simple as it first appears. Mohrlang sees Paul and Matthew as representing "somewhat different views of the essential nature of the Christian life," but not in contradiction to each other, and with elements of both law and grace in both of them.[41] Matthew stresses the life of discipleship, based on doing God's will, while Paul emphasizes "living in committed and grateful response to God's grace in Christ."[42] Both see Jesus as a model to emulate, but for Matthew Jesus is a model of righteousness while for Paul he is a model of self-giving love and service. There are, according to Mohrlang, several factors that underlie these differences of perspective and emphasis between Paul and Matthew, including social, polemical, and genre differences.[43] Mohrlang's work provides many helpful insights, though I think he sees more contrast between Paul and Matthew than is there. It is true that they are writing from different situations and that they do put things differently at points (the meaning of "righteousness" is an important example), but what Mohrlang does not see is that both Matthew and Paul are operating from within the Jewish, Greco-Roman concept of virtue ethics. When one understands that both apostles consider the goal of the Christian life to be Christ-centered, true human flourishing in God's coming kingdom, then the differences in ways of speaking and emphasis can be seen as more complementary.

Approaching the question from a different angle is the more recent and very important work of John Barclay in his highly regarded volume, *Paul and*

Lexham, 2014). He discusses the gospel's transformation in terms of the freedoms it gives—freedom to become a new person in Christ, freedom to relate to one another in new ways, and freedom from the world's rules so as to witness to God's rule.

40. Roger Mohrlang, *Matthew and Paul: A Comparison of Ethical Perspectives* (Cambridge: Cambridge University Press, 1984). Dan Via also reflects on the relationship between Matthew's and Paul's thought from a more existential perspective, using the concepts of self-deception and wholeness, in *Self-Deception and Wholeness in Paul and Matthew* (Minneapolis: Fortress, 1990; repr., Eugene, OR: Wipf & Stock, 2005).

41. Mohrlang, *Matthew and Paul*, 127.

42. Ibid.

43. He lists seven factors—social (living in different communities), polemical (different *Sitze im Leben*), motivational (how ethics are motivated), psychological (different conceptions of human nature), christological (Jesus as teacher vs. Jesus as supreme example of grace), literary genre, and interpretive (Matthew simultaneously part of both Jewish and gentile communities) (ibid., 128–31).

the Gift.[44] This detailed study cannot be done justice in this brief sketch. But suffice it to say that Barclay convincingly shows that the ancient and biblical idea of gift or grace (*charis*) necessarily entails a kind of reciprocity on the part of the recipient. Throughout ancient cultures and throughout much of the world still today, apart from the modern West where the notion of a "purely free" gift develops, gift giving or grace was understood in *relational* terms. Benefactors and recipients are often not equal in status, gifts are often lavished in an incongruous way, and reciprocity is not seen as a mere paying back or as equal to the gift. Nonetheless, the relational (we might even say from a biblical perspective, "covenantal") nature of grace or gift giving entails a response of gratitude, loyalty, and faithfulness.[45]

For Paul and the rest of Holy Scripture, to use Barclay's words, grace is "unconditioned" but not "unconditional."[46] Simple reflection on biblical texts such as Rom. 6:1–23, 2 Cor. 5:9–10, Gal. 5:13–26, Eph. 2:8–10, and Phil. 2:12–13 shows that this "unconditioned but not unconditional" model of God's radical, Christ-centered, initiating grace/gift makes much sense of these passages.

I suggest that this helps us understand the close correspondence between Paul and Matthew as well. Matthew's strong emphasis on salvation as responding to God's grace with wholehearted discipleship in no way contradicts Paul's similar but differently framed understanding of God's grace calling people to faithful following and the offering of one's life as a living sacrifice, which results in being conformed to the *teleios* image of Christ (Rom. 12:1–2). Therefore, although the Sermon itself does not explicitly emphasize grace, this in no way requires any kind of strained relationship between its vision of virtuous discipleship and Paul's emphasis on God's grace in Christ. This is even more clear when one considers the whole Gospel context of the Sermon, in which the virtue teacher is also shown to be the sin-bearing Savior, coming "to rescue his people from their sin" (Matt. 1:21), who pours out his own blood "for the forgiveness of sins" (26:8).

As I discussed in chapter 2, commentators on the Sermon often divide as to whether they see the Beatitudes as statements about God's favor (often as entrance requirements) or proclamations of eschatological reversal. There

44. John M. G. Barclay, *Paul and the Gift* (Grand Rapids: Eerdmans, 2015).

45. Although not as thorough and approached from a somewhat different angle, social-scientific studies of honor-shame cultures have similarly shown that in patron-client, honor-shame cultures (such as those of both the OT and NT), gift giving was the glue of society socially and economically, and this included reciprocity of loyalty and gratitude on the part of the recipient. See, e.g., the helpful discussion in David deSilva, "Honor and Shame," *DNTB*, 518–22.

46. Barclay, *Paul and the Gift*, 492.

is also often great emphasis put on the fact that God's grace precedes any commands that the Sermon levies.[47] This is good and true. But in some ways it is unnecessary because the call to virtuous discipleship does not actually conflict with the idea of grace for either Paul or Matthew.[48]

Thesis 5: Virtue and Grace Are Compatible, Not Opposites

Intimately related to the preceding thesis, I must again state what should be obvious but needs brief and clear articulation nonetheless. The Christian faith, based on the writings of the New Testament, entails both the indicative and the imperative, both grace and virtue, both divine gift and human habituation, and these are compatible, not opposites. God's grace through Christ makes sinful and spiritually dead people come alive and into a new covenantal relationship with the Triune God, worked out through the abiding presence of the Spirit. This indicative is the ontological and chronological foundation for salvation. Even though there is great overlap between the New Testament teachings and Aristotle in terms of the focus on character, unlike the Greek virtue tradition, God's grace undergirds and overarches the whole message. In discussing Paul's emphasis on transformation, Wright rightly observes: "Never for one moment does Paul imagine, as one might from reading Aristotle, that morality is simply a matter of a human being deciding to adopt a particular set of characteristics and discovering in herself or himself the capability and energy to get on and reform one's life in that way."[49]

This grace/indicative reality is the starting point, but it is neither the whole story nor the whole of the gospel. The indicative exists in a dialectical and mutually informing relationship with the imperative. Rooted in God's initiating

47. One clear example of this approach is Dale C. Allison Jr., who states, "Succor comes before command" (*Studies in Matthew: Interpretation Past and Present* [Grand Rapids: Baker Academic, 2005], 198). Ulrich Luz provides an excellent summary of the history of interpretation of command and grace in the Beatitudes and similarly concludes: "For Matthew the narrative framework of the entire Gospel is an expression of the priority of grace that makes of his beatitudes 'dona virtutum.' Jesus' demands are demands of the 'Immanuel' who accompanies and helps his community" (*Matthew 1–7: A Commentary*, rev. ed., trans. James E. Crouch, Hermeneia [Minneapolis: Fortress, 2007], 201).

48. Donald Hagner reflects on the strong commands of Jesus in addition to the gracious emphasis on the dawning of the kingdom and concludes that "the teaching of Jesus is to be taken in all seriousness, as even Paul would have insisted. And the Sermon on the Mount stands within the canon of the Church as a proper antidote to a Paulinism that (unlike Paul himself) champions a gospel of cheap grace. The gospel of the NT has room for the stern ethic of Jesus, without ceasing to be gospel" (*Matthew 1–13*, WBC 33A [Nashville: Nelson, 1993], 191–92).

49. Wright, *After You Believe*, 137.

work, his creatures who are being redeemed (and appropriately called a "new creation" in 2 Cor. 5:17) are called to respond with faithfulness and obedience, to be true to the transference of servitude (Rom. 6:1–23) and kingdom allegiance (Col. 1:13) that they have experienced. Believers have been given the Spirit and the gifts that come with this, and now they are called upon to "walk by the Spirit" and bear fruit (Gal. 5:22–24).[50] This is all grace.

I am speaking here primarily with Pauline concepts and terms. This is also entirely compatible with how the Gospels depict the Christian faith, described primarily as being disciples. The Gospels, including the important constituent part we call the Sermon on the Mount, understand the Christian faith as following after, learning from, and becoming like the Master, Jesus, who is teaching the wisest and truest way of being in the world. This is why the opening step and the dominant amount of space in the New Testament consist of biographies, lives of Jesus, and our four canonical Gospels. Christianity is a religion centered not first on a *book* or on theological *ideas* but on a person, the God-man Jesus the Christ. One writes biographies to invite would-be disciples into a life of learning and becoming, and thus it is appropriate that Christianity's foundational documents are of this genre.[51] Jesus is clearly presented as an ethical model, a model for emulation. This does not make him less than divine or diminish the Gospels' christological claims, nor does it contradict grace.

Jonathan Wilson addresses the theological objection that some have raised against a virtue-ethics approach, namely, that we should speak of graces, not virtues, because the latter seem to indicate a human ability and achievement apart from God's grace.[52] Wilson sagaciously acknowledges that the human propensity toward self-justification and the denial of a need for God's grace mean that a Christian virtue ethic must be very circumspect and hear these admonitions. Nonetheless, Wilson rightly notes that, while recognizing God's sovereign grace, Christian virtue ethics can give an account of the *work* of grace and *how* that grace takes shape in human lives. Built on the foundation of God's grace, aware of human sinfulness and the need for the Spirit's work, Christian virtue ethics "directs us toward the habitual patterns of the Christian life—enabled by God's grace through the Holy Spirit, to be sure—that

50. Wright sums it up well—"Christian virtue, including the nine-fold fruit of the Spirit, is *both* the gift of God *and* the result of the person of faith making conscious decisions to cultivate this way of life and these habits of heart and mind" (ibid., 197).

51. On this, see Jonathan T. Pennington, *Reading the Gospels Wisely: A Narrative and Theological Introduction* (Grand Rapids: Baker Academic, 2012); and Allison, *Studies in Matthew*, chap. 7.

52. Wilson, *Gospel Virtues*, 34–35.

witness to the gospel."[53] And virtue ethics is important not just for the individual but also for the church because it "directs the church toward the kind of community that embodies and forms these virtues."[54]

Charles Talbert also provides helpful insights into the relationship of indicatives and imperatives, specifically in Matthew and how being a disciple relates to this. He notes that scholars have tried to fit the indicatives and imperatives together in a variety of ways, some pitting them against each other, others seeing them as having either an implicitly or explicitly hierarchical relationship in one direction or the other.[55] He concludes that Matthew's understanding "is neither soteriological legalism nor legalistic covenantal nomism. Like Paul, his soteriology is by grace from start to finish."[56]

Talbert also notes that this "divine indicative" that runs throughout is accompanied by "divine enablement," and this is how the two fit together. Disciples of Jesus are not just called to imitate but are *enabled* to do so through God's initiating and sustaining work. This enablement comes through being in the presence of Jesus. God is with us in Jesus (Matt. 1:21), and being with Jesus brings about transformation.[57] Talbert observes that this notion of transformative discipleship through divine presence "is a philosophic variation on the general Mediterranean belief that being in the presence of a deity causes transformation of the self. . . . All such cases involved human transformation by vision."[58]

53. Ibid., 35.
54. Ibid.
55. In his Paideia commentary on Matthew, Charles Talbert deftly surveys the views of Willi Marxsen, Petri Luoamen, Roger Mohrlang, Ulrich Luz, David Seeley, Hubert Frankmölle, and David Kupp (*Matthew* [Grand Rapids: Baker Academic, 2010], 9–12). A fuller discussion can be found in Talbert, *Reading the Sermon on the Mount: Character Formation and Decision Making in Matthew 5–7* (Grand Rapids: Baker Academic, 2006), chap. 4, "Is Matthew a Legalist? Enablement of Obedience in Response to the Sermon."
56. Talbert, *Matthew*, 27. Kari Syreeni similarly ties the Sermon's commands to other aspects of Matthew's teaching on grace: "While urging that solely the doing of Jesus' words mattered, he asserted that this was an easy yoke (11:28–30). And while stressing that the disciples must seek and pursue righteousness, he also asserted that one who seeks will find (6:33; 7:7–11)" (*The Making of the Sermon on the Mount: A Procedural Analysis of Matthew's Redactoral Activity* [Helsinki: Suomalainen Tiedeakatemia, 1987], 219). Law and grace together form a healthy reality.
57. Talbert argues that, given the strong OT background to the idea of God being with his people, "one would have to conclude that when Matthew uses the formula 'with you' or 'in your midst,' he is speaking of God's prior enabling activity (the indicative), activity that empowers individuals to do the tasks set before them. It also may explain why Matthew's discussion of the Spirit is so underdeveloped. This formula (with you/in your midst) was an alternative, but less explicit, way of speaking of God's activity among his people" (*Matthew*, 16).
58. Ibid., 21. In his commentary on the Sermon on the Mount, Talbert provides several examples of statements from Greek philosophers to this effect. See, e.g., Achilles Tatius,

On this point and indeed on the others preceding, what I am suggesting was long ago articulated well by Augustine.[59] Augustine was clearly versed in the Greek traditions of *eudaimonia* and agreed that the goal of ethics was human flourishing/happiness and that this is only obtainable through the stable possession of the supreme good (*summum bonum*). His thoroughly Christian understanding of this eudaimonism means more specifically that happiness can only be achieved if one has God, who alone is the supreme and unchanging good. Moreover, Augustine deviates from classical eudaimonism in understanding that ultimately happiness can only be experienced in the life of the blessed after the resurrection. Additionally, and relevant to the particular point at hand, Augustine emphasized that human flourishing, which requires the pursuit of godly virtue, is itself a gift of grace. It is not possible for humans to achieve happiness through their own power, nor is one saved through one's merits, otherwise grace would cease to be grace. Thus, we have in Augustine a robust understanding of the mutual entailment of necessary Christian virtue for flourishing, but all of which is a *dei donum*, gift of God.[60]

The point of all of this is that a proper understanding of Matthew's vision enables us to see that faithful discipleship, what Matthew calls being "righteous" and what we can call "virtue," is entirely compatible with God's initiating and sustaining grace.[61] These two come together in the vision of what it means to be a follower/imitator of Jesus, which is the ultimate perlocutionary purpose of the Sermon.

Clitophon and Leucippe 5.13 ("The pleasure which comes from vision enters by the eyes and makes its home in the breast; bearing with it ever the image . . . it impresses it upon the mirror of the soul and leaves there its image") and Philo, *On Rewards and Punishments* 114 ("to gaze continuously upon noble models imprints their likeness in souls which are not entirely hardened and stony") (Talbert, *Reading the Sermon on the Mount*, 43). Further evidence of this idea can be found in Julia Annas's discussion of Plato's notion of virtue as becoming like the gods. In Platonic thought, virtue does not just result in happiness (as with Aristotle and the whole Greek tradition) but "virtue turns a human life into something different in kind," becoming like the gods (Annas, *Platonic Ethics: Old and New* [Ithaca, NY: Cornell University Press, 2000], 53).

59. The following comments are based on the succinct discussion in Christian Tornau, "Happiness in This Life? Augustine on the Principle That Virtue Is Self-Sufficient for Happiness," in Rabbås, Emilsson, Fossheim, and Tuominen, *Quest for the Good Life*, 265–66.

60. The Reformers consciously modeled much of their understanding on Augustine, and I would suggest a rediscovery of this Augustinian balance, especially because later evangelicalism has sometimes produced a reduced form that has lost the tensive nuance present at the Reformation.

61. Via puts it this way: "In the most direct way Matthew makes ethics depend on the gospel's transformation of the heart. Grace as power enables both inner being and ethical acts (13:14–17, 23; 19:25–26; 20:28–34). Thus it is not human beings as such but human beings transformed by grace who are assumed to be able to fulfill the demand of God for obedience from the heart" (*Self-Deception and Wholeness*, 134).

Thesis 6: Biblical Human Flourishing Provides Crucial Insight into the Meaning and Shape of God's Saving Work

Finally and most briefly, I suggest that a main contribution of the reading of the Sermon I offer here is that it highlights the major biblical theme of human flourishing and invites reflection on how this squares with the biblical emphasis on God's salvation of his people.

There is a rich treasure trove of metaphors in the Bible to describe God's redeeming/salvific work: salvation, redemption, adoption, transformation, from glory to glory, union with Christ, new creature, new creation, (being) in Christ, entering into the kingdom, built into the temple of God, built into the house of God, new humanity, and so forth. There is no single metaphor that encapsulates comprehensively the multifaceted, loving work of God on behalf of his creatures. A weakness and common problem in many theological systems is the totalizing effect, where one conceptualization or set of metaphors becomes the exclusive one(s) by which God's work on our behalf is framed and received. But the complexity of human nature, human experience, and of God himself necessitates the use of many true and mutually compatible metaphors.

I suggest that while "human flourishing" is certainly not *the only* metaphor to describe the message of the Bible, it is a way of describing God's work that needs to be restored to a place of stature and that provides insights into the whole message of the Bible. Specifically, I mean that the concept of human flourishing is quite comprehensive in tying together several other themes and images of the Bible, providing a framework for understanding what God's work in creation and redemption is ultimately about. This is seen even more when we understand the overlapping categories in the ancient world of philosopher and king, showing that Jesus's teaching on human flourishing is simultaneously teaching about the kingdom of God. Additionally, human flourishing as a theological concept helps us hold together many antinomies of the biblical witness, particularly how grace and virtue, as well as faith and discipleship, exist together in tensive, dialectical relationships.

The truth is a knife-edge from which one can easily fall by imbalance and overemphasis of either part of the dialectic. Such is the case with the Christian theology of human flourishing. The church, as noted above, has largely lost a clear understanding of biblical human flourishing, primarily due to an otherwise good emphasis on the eschaton, the final state of God's kingdom, the new creation, while also losing connection with this emphasis in ancient philosophy and religion. My contention is that a close and careful reading of the Sermon will help the church recover the profound and pervasive theme of

310   Theological Reflection

human flourishing in God's redeeming work in the world. We must not be, in the language of Stephen Pope, only "verticalist" or "horizonalist" Christians. Verticalist Christians rightly root their understanding in God's saving work in Christ but understand human flourishing as only eternal salvation. Horizontalist Christians see flourishing as encompassed in liberation from human oppression. Instead, Pope argues, we need a third way that integrates the primacy of the spiritual reality with real-life engagement in the world. Christ's incarnation is the foundation of all of this. "Human flourishing is social and material as well as moral and spiritual, temporal as well as eternal."[62]

As the church awaits the return of the risen Savior, the disciples of Jesus are invited into a way of being in the world that leads them into an experience of present-but-not-yet-full human flourishing, aligning them with the reason God created the world as the place of life and peace for his beloved creatures, and empowering them to be engaged in bringing flourishing to the world. Jesus is the sage and king who is inviting hearers into his coming kingdom of flourishing and life. The Sermon is at the center of this message. As one scholar observed, even as the law of Moses shaped the history of the Jewish people, so too and even more "the Sermon on the Mount contains within itself the potential to create, direct, and transform history: the history of the People of God, our personal history, and even the history of all humanity."[63]

62. Stephen J. Pope, "Jesus Christ and Human Flourishing: An Incarnational Perspective," paper presented at the Yale Center for Faith and Culture, available at http://faith.yale.edu/sites/default/files/pope_christ_and_flourishing.pdf.
63. Servais Pinckaers, *The Pursuit of Happiness—God's Way: Living the Beatitudes*, trans. Mary Thomas Noble (Eugene, OR: Wipf & Stock, 1998), 12.

Author Index

Scripture and Ancient Writings Index